Soli Deo Gloria Publications
P.O. Box 451, Morgan, PA 15064
(412) 221-1901/FAX 221-1902

*

This edition of *The Young Man's Friend and Guide through Life to Immortality* and *The Young Man from Home* is taken from the 1860 edition published by Hamilton Adams and Co., London. This Soli Deo Gloria reprint is 1995.

*

ISBN 1-877611-97-2

CONTENTS.

THE YOUNG MAN FROM HOME.

THE YOUNG MAN'S FRIEND AND GUIDE THROUGH LIFE TO IMMORTALITY.

———

Thou shalt guide me with thy counsel, and afterwards receive me
to glory.

PREFACE.

I INSCRIBE this volume to every young man, who, by the prompting of his own mind, or by the persuasion of others, shall be induced to peruse it. To every such youth, I say, with all seriousness and earnestness, ponder well its title "The Young Man's Friend and Guide through Life to Immortality." Do you desire a friend? I offer myself: and I believe you will find me to be such in these pages. Do you need a guide through life, with all its duties, temptations, and perplexities? I am willing to perform this service for you: and I dare pledge the truth power and love of God, that if, by his grace, sought by faith in Christ and fervent prayer, you follow the directions here laid down, you will rise to respectability usefulness and comfort in this world, and everlasting happiness in the next.

Eternal and Almighty God! thou Source of light love and purity, who didst send thy seraph with a coal from off thine altar to purify thy prophet's lips; and didst cause thine Holy Spirit to descend, like cloven

tongues of flame, upon the heads of thine apostles; and
who art still willing to grant wisdom to all who seek it
through the mediation of our Lord Jesus Christ; send
down thy blessing upon the youth of our age and
nation; and grant, in thy great mercy, that many
of them may by this volume be guided in safety through
the dangers of this sinful world, and led, by patient
continuance in well-doing, to glory honour and immortality in the world to come.   Amen.

CHAPTER I.

*Let thine eyes look right on, and let thine eye-lids look
straight before thee. Ponder the path of thy feet, and
let all thy ways be established.* PROVERBS iv, 25, 26.

I THINK you cannot be ignorant, Young Men, that I
have felt a great solicitude for your moral and spiritual
welfare, and have taken some pains to promote it. I
say, your moral and spiritual welfare; for in an age like
the present, when education is so much improved, and
so widely extended, when the discoveries of science and
the inventions of art have been so rapidly multiplied,
and the means of knowing them have been placed to
such an extent within the reach of the multitude, there
is danger lest that which is moral and spiritual should
be neglected amidst the attention to that which is
merely intellectual; lest talents should be appreciated
more highly than virtues, and secular, be more eagerly
sought than religious, knowledge. Yet it must be
obvious to you upon reflection, that happiness, even for
this world, to say nothing of the next, depends much
more upon the state of the heart and the practice of the
life, than upon the culture of the understanding. Not
that these are antagonistic to one another. None but
infidels, or weak-minded Christians, will ever attempt

to set piety and science at variance.   They are neither
enemies nor aliens, but friends, and reciprocally helpful
to each other.   Under the influence of this anxiety to
promote your moral and spiritual well-being, I have, in
the course of my ministry, addressed to you several
courses of plain and practical discourses; and have
also published a treatise to those of your class who have
left the parental roof to embark on the stormy and
dangerous ocean of human life.   I have been rewarded
for this "labour of love," by the attention with which
my efforts have been received, and the benefit which I
believe they have imparted, and am thus induced to
continue them, and now invite your serious and medi-
tative attention to the following course of subjects.

I.   Preparation for life.
II.   Entrance upon life.
III.   Indecision as to religion.
IV.   Amiability without religion.
V.   Perplexity occasioned by Religious contro-
versies.
VI.   The character of Joseph.
VII.   The study of the book of Proverbs.
VIII.   Failure or success in business.
IX.   Emigration.
X.   Disappointment or fulfilment of the hopes of
parents.
XI.   The importance of the present age.
XII.   Death in youth or the review of life in old age.

You will perceive at once that these subjects are all
of an entirely practical character.   Speculation and controversy are, with one exception, both excluded: and
even doctrinal matter is but sparingly introduced.   Not

that these things are unimportant or unnecessary in
their proper place, but they do not come within my
design. I am a practical man, and am most at home
on practical subjects: and at the same time that I
believe that holiness is founded upon truth, and that
christian duties are drawn from christian doctrines, and
are to be enforced by them, I am still of opinion that
what is practical will be more for your edification,
than what is theoretical or controversial. Speculation,
novelty, dry criticism, or thorny controversy, will have
a less beneficial influence upon your future character
and happiness, than the subjects contained in this course.

My first chapter is on preparation for life. We often
speak of preparation for death; and most momentous,
most necessary that is, but we too much neglect to
speak of preparation for life. And yet how fit is such a
subject for our discourses, and your serious consideration.

The passage of Scripture placed at the head of this
chapter is much in point. It is selected from a portion
of Scripture which is of incalculable value, and which
proves that the Bible is a book, not only to make men
wise unto salvation, through faith in Jesus Christ, but
to serve as a guide to them in their passage through
this life, and in reference to their temporal condition: a
book to form not only the saint and the devout man,
but the tradesman, the parent, and the member of domestic and social life in general.

In the passage quoted above, you will at once perceive
that a habit of consideration and forethought is incul-
cated. We must not only consider the past by looking
back, or the present by looking round, but the future
by looking on. All these are important; we must look
back to consider what we have done that we should not

have done; what we have not done that we should have done; and what we have done well, that we might have done better; that thus from the past we may draw lessons for the future. It is true that in your case so short a space of life has yet elapsed, as to afford comparatively few materials for reflection, and little aid for your future guidance. But even youth has something to look back upon, and the practice of retrospection cannot be adopted too early. It is well to begin life with the formation of a habit of self-scrutiny and self-accountability.

We must also consider well the present, because there is always some duty now to be done, the doing of which is our immediate business, which no reflection on the past and no anticipation of the future, should lead us to neglect. Still, however, we must let our "eyes look right on, and our eyelids look straight before us." We have not only memory, but a certain measure of prescience. True, we cannot look into futurity, so as to ascertain particular events, but we can anticipate general conditions; and it is a mark of a well-governed mind to anticipate the future as far as possible. We should consider what in all probability is to happen to us, and prepare for it. Young people are not unapt to look forward, but rather in a sentimental and romantic, than in a practical, manner, and as an exercise of the imagination rather than of the judgment. Be thoughtful, then, and let your thoughtfulness have respect to the future. Let your eyelids look straight on; and ponder the ways of your feet.

There is a world of practical wisdom in some single terms: among them is that momentous term, prepare. How many evils, in some cases, would have been avoided, had men prepared to meet them ! How many benefits would have been secured, had men prepared to appropriate them ! How much that they have done would have been better done, if they had prepared to do it. How often, already, have you had regretfully to say, " I wish I had prepared for this !" Well then, let this impress you, and guide you for the future. Let your own limited experience in the little things which have yet happened, be a warning to prepare you for the greater ones which will happen. I know very well that the opposite evil of always preparing and never acting, which is the case with some, is also to be avoided. There are many who are ever getting ready to act, but when the moment for acting arrives, are so irresolute, so timid, so procrastinating, that they let the time for acting go by. But this is by much the rarer case of the two. This chapter, then, meets you about to enter on life, and it gives out to you the momentous note of preparation.

Preparation is often half the doing ; and the easier part too. Preparation for life ! How impressive an idea ! Not for one particular act, or scene, or engagement, but for the whole of future existence. Life ! How much is included in that weighty term. A love of life is an instinct of our nature, wisely implanted in us for important purposes by the Great Author of our existence. It was the language of truth, though uttered by the father of lies, " Skin for skin, yea, all that a man hath, will he give for his life." Surely, then, if it be incumbent upon us to prepare for everything else, it must be of incalculable moment to prepare for life, since it is the most valuable thing we can covet or possess.

But it will be asked, perhaps, what is meant by

preparing for life? I intend then by it, preparing to act well our part upon earth, so as to secure to ourselves the greatest measure of happiness and usefulness in this world, and eternal happiness in the world to come: preparing to live successfully, religiously, usefully, and happily, so as to secure to ourselves the promise of God to Abraham, " I will bless thee, and thou shalt be a blessing."

The injunction to prepare for life implies that whatever constitutes the felicity and usefulness of life must be matter of choice, pursuit, and labour; that it will not come spontaneously. This is very true. The continuance of even existence itself, is not independent of man's own volition, action, and preparation. We do not live in spite of ourselves, or without ourselves, the vital spark at first communicated to us without our own acting, is still fed and sustained by our own action. We take food and medicine, and wear clothes, and dwell in habitations, to preserve life; and we must manifest no less solicitude, and put forth no less effort, to secure the blessings of life. It depends very much upon every man's own choice and labour, how life turns out.

To spend life in happiness and usefulness, we must prepare in the early stages of it, for what is future. There is no truth in the Platonic notion of the pre-existence of human souls. We cannot in another and antecedent state anticipate our existence on earth, and go through a training in some previous world, and thus learn how to act our part here. Such an advantage, if indeed it would be an advantage, is denied us. We must come into life and learn as we go on. We must by thoughtfulness, observation, and experience, pick up knowledge by the way. This wonderfully increases the peril of our situation, and the necessity for our cultivating and exercising a reflective and cautious habit. Still though we cannot in a previous state of existence anticipate our dwelling and conduct upon earth, we may be trained for the subsequent stages of our being by the conduct we pursue in the earlier ones. We cannot first live to know how to live, but we can be educated for the future in the first part of life. Boyhood and youth are life, physically considered, as well as manhood and old age; but intellectually, morally, and socially considered, they are rather introductory to life, than life itself. I am, therefore, in this view of the subject, to consider the processes preparatory for future life.

I. First of all, is Education. I am aware that most of those who will read this work, will have passed through their school-days already. Yet this will not be the case with all, and the subject is so important that I must say a few things upon it. Education includes on the part of those by whom it is conducted, not only instruction, but the right application of knowledge to practical purposes; in other words, the formation of character. This is beautifully expressed in the proverb, "Train up a child in the way he should go." Not merely in what he should know, but in the way he should go. And this should ever be remembered by the pupil as well as the teacher. His mind is, of course, to be stored with knowledge, but his judgment, heart, will, and conscience, must also be trained to act rightly. The term of school education is of immense consequence to future life, and should, and does, lead all considerate parents most anxiously to look out for suitable persons to entrust with the education of their children, when they are no longer able them-

selves to educate them at home. But however judicious
the selection of a teacher may be, all young persons
should recollect that every one must, to a certain extent,
be self-educated, and that it remains with themselves
to determine whether the pains bestowed upon them
shall be successful or fruitless. It is not in the power
of man or woman, or of all men and women combined,
to educate a young person, if he will not be educated, or
if he does not determine to be well trained. The
intellect is not a cup or a bottle into which knowledge
can be poured, whether the mind will receive it or not;
nor is the heart a piece of passive clay which may be
shaped at will by the teacher, irrespective of the will
of the pupil. No. It depends on yourselves whether you
will be educated. And all your future life, for time and
eternity, depends upon your education. "The child is
father of the man," and education forms the child.
What you are when you leave school, that you may be
expected to be through all future existence. Would
that I could impress this upon all young persons: would
that I could lead them, especially the older pupils, to
look forward and to reflect that they have to pass
through life, and that they are just entering upon it;
and to consider with what measure of knowledge, and
with what form of character, they wish to fill up their
place in the great community.

II.   Self-education must not stop, but be considered
as having only just begun when you leave school. You
must still carry on your improvement by a thirst after
knowledge, a studious habit, and a love of reading,
thinking, and observing. Books must be your companions, and if they are good and useful ones, they will
be your most profitable associates. In this wonderful

age, when knowledge is so rapidly and extensively widening its boundaries; when science and the arts are ever astonishing us with new discoveries, inventions, triumphs and wonders; when they are incorporating themselves with all the practical business of life; when to be ignorant is not only disgraceful to a man's intellectual reputation, but injurious to his temporal interests; when to have any weight in society he must know ten times as much as his grandfather knew before him; and when such facilities are afforded for mental improvement; no young man can be considered as preparing well for life who neglects the cultivation of his intellect. It is a love of knowledge, young men, not a love of pleasure, that will prepare you to act well your part in life. Understand and remember this.

III. The acquisition of a knowledge of some secular calling is another most important part of the preparatory processes of life. Most of you are intended for business, either in the way of manufacture, trade, or one of the professions, and are already for that purpose apprenticed or articled, to some one who is to teach you your business; to some one who ought to feel himself bound by every principle of honour, justice, and religion, to instruct you in all you are sent to him to learn. And if the child be the father of the man, so it is equally true that the apprentice is the father of the tradesman. What you are as to industry, application, and ability, now in your term of service and secular education, that you will be in all probability as the future tradesman. Subordination is essentially necessary. We learn to command by first learning to obey. It is of immense consequence to remember this: a refractory, turbulent, disobedient apprentice or servant,

will most probably make a capricious, tyrannical, and
ill-judging master. The apprentice whom his master
cannot govern, will be the master who cannot govern
his apprentice. This is not simply one of the retribu-
tions of Providence, but one of the natural results of the
course of things. The great principle which gave to the
Jesuits such prodigious power in past ages, was unhesi-
tating and unlimited obedience to their Superior. Heroes
have usually been trained in the school of obedience and
discipline. So our most thriving tradesmen, especially
the men that have risen to a high situation, have first
served well in a low one. But when I recommend
submission and obedience, I mean that which springs
from principle, and not merely from compulsion and
fear. In this, as well as in every thing else, you should
do that which is right to be done, because it is right.
Call in your judgment, your conscience, your sense
of propriety. It is just and good to obey the authority
of a master. The principle of fear, the mere sense of
compulsion, will train you badly. The slaves of tyrants,
who obey only from dread of punishment, upon their
emancipation make the greatest tyrants. A character cast
in the mould of fear must be a mis-shapen one. As to
capability of application, dispatch, sagacity, quickness,
perseverance, in the situation of a master, you must get
all these while learning your business as an apprentice.
If not learned then, you never will be. An idle apprentice will make an idle tradesman; a pleasure-loving
youth a pleasure-loving man. On the other hand, a
quick, sharp, clever boy, will make a quick, sharp, clever
man. Tell me what the apprentice is, and I will tell
you what the tradesman will be. Be diligent, be submissive, be honest, be attentive to business. Determine,

by God's blessing, to excel. Aim to be eminent. Do not be contented with dull mediocrity. Have ambition to stand well and to rise high. A clever, industrious, successful, religious tradesman, is an ornament to his town and his country. Future life is before you, prepare for it thus.

IV. But the chief preparation for life, without which no reliance can be placed on any other preparation, is the formation of a moral and religious character. Having already reminded you how much the happiness and usefulness of life depend, even in this world, upon the formation of character generally viewed, I now refer to religious character. Genuine religion, the parent of sound morality (and no religion is genuine that does not produce morality) is the surest guide to success in this world; other things being equal, he will be almost certain to be the most successful tradesman, who is the most consistent Christian. And as religion is the best guide to happiness in this world, it is the only way to happiness in the world to come. It has been a thousand times told you, on the authority of Holy Writ, that " Godliness is profitable for all things, having the promise of the life that now is," mark that, " as well as of that which is to come." Who will contradict it? Religion will preserve you from all the habits that tend to poverty and misery, and aid the formation of all that tend to wealth and happiness. Have you ever studied, for I would not so reflect upon you as to suppose you have never read, Solomon's exquisite allegory, in which he so beautifully describes the nature and consequence of true religion? " Happy is the man that findeth wisdom, and the man that getteth understanding. For the merchandise of it is better than the merchandise of silver, and the gain thereof than fine gold. She is more precious than rubies; and all the things thou canst desire are not to be compared unto her. Length of days is in her right hand; and in her left hand, riches and honour. Her ways are ways of pleasantness, and all her paths are peace. She is a tree of life to them that lay hold upon her; and happy is every one that retaineth her." Now the wisdom here so exquisitely described, and so forcibly recommended, is true religion. Who will rise up to say that religion ruined them? And how many millions could rise up, some on earth, and some from hell, to say they were ruined for want of it?

If the formation of character is one of the preparatory processes of life, then you should not have your character to establish, your principles of action to choose, when you want them to use. Your rule should be laid down, your standard adjusted, your purpose formed, when you begin to act. You are about to set sail on the perilous ocean of life, not as a passenger merely, but as both captain and owner of a vessel; and should you not have learned navigation, and have prepared a chart, and a compass, and a sextant, and acquired practical skill to use them? There are rocks and shoals to be avoided, and storms and contrary winds to be encountered, at your going out of port. Without fixed religious principles, and established moral character, you may be wrecked before clearing the harbour. It is of infinite consequence that you should possess the fear of God, a hatred of sin, and dread of judgment to come, before you embark. Remember, therefore, your Creator in the days of your youth. Set the Lord always before you. Be rooted and grounded in the love of Christ.

Be a young disciple, and then you are ready for everything. Religion will be your guide in perplexity, your shield in danger; your companion in solitude; your comfort in sorrow; your defence against temptation: and (if it be genuine, earnest, and consistent) it will not fail to make you holy, happy, and useful.

V. There is another thing I would most earnestly enforce upon you as a preparation for life, and that is, a deep sense of the importance of habit, and the necessity of forming good habits while young. Among the words of our vocabulary which you should select, as having greater importance than others, and as deserving to be more intently pondered upon, is habit. Dwell upon it; it is a golden term of incalculable value. It means the facility of doing a thing well, acquired by having done it frequently, together with a certain impulse or inclination to do it. It differs from instinct, not so much in exercise as in origin; habit being acquired, and instinct natural. I shall not trouble you with a discussion upon the philosophical theory of habit, but only advert to its importance. Consider, then, of what moment it is to do by habit what is right, and thus to have everything which is good and proper to be done made easy; not to have disinclination, difficulty, and awkwardness to encounter every time a right thing is to be done, but to go to it with the impulse and ease of habit; to be good, not only from principle, but from habit. On the other hand, how dreadful is it to be carried forward in the way of evil, by the double force of inclination and habit. Now childhood and youth are the time for forming habits. We see this in the mechanical arts, and it is so in all the mental and moral processes. Industry and self denial, forethought

and caution, religion and virtue, will all be comparatively
easy to the man who has acquired the habit in early
life. Through God's grace, the most difficult duty, the
most rare virtue may thus become easy.

And now let me enforce this preparation for future
life upon you. Recollect what it is I am urging upon
you. Ponder it well. Weigh it in the balance of
reason. It is preparation for life. What a sentence!
How pregnant with meaning! Suppose you were going
upon a voyage to a strange land, never to return to
your own country. Would you not prepare both for
the safety and comfort of the voyage, and also for your
well-being in the country where you were going to
dwell for the remainder of your existence; and would
not everybody be astounded at you, if you were busy
about a variety of things, and yet gave no care at all to
the work of preparation for your voyage and your
foreign residence? And what is your life but a voyage
to eternity, a state requiring preparation both for itself
and what lies beyond it? Now if in the former case
you would be anxious to get a safe vessel; to select a
skilful and agreeable captain; to choose a comfortable
berth; to sail with pleasant companions; to lay in a
good stock of necessary articles; and if you would
commence the preparation in due time, that when the
hour of embarkation arrives you might have nothing to
do but to go on board, how much more necessary is it
that now in youth, you should be diligently preparing
by and by to embark on the ocean of human life. And
if in the case I have supposed, you would be still more
anxious about the foreign land in which you were going
to dwell than even about the comfort of the voyage
itself, how much more important is it that you should

be more careful about that eternity to which this life leads, than the comfort of life itself?

Not only does life require preparation, like everything else, but more than everything else. If every situation in life demands previous consideration, provision, and training, if every new scene or pursuit demands an adaptation, a meetness, a bracing up of the mind to it, how much more the whole of life. Who can do well any thing that is novel, difficult, and important, without forethought, plan, and purpose? Who then should think of entering upon life without preparation, and stepping upon the stage of existence without learning to act well a part in the great drama? A life altogether unprepared for, must be a life of perpetual mistakes, faults, and miseries. A man cannot live happily, righteously, usefully, or successfully, who does not prepare to do so : that is, he cannot at all expect to do so, and ordinarily he does not do so.

You are to recollect, young men, that while the brute creation are prepared by instinct for their life, and without any previous education perform all the functions which are necessary to their well-being and to answer the ends of their creation, you can be prepared only by an education in which you must take a part. The bird constructs her nest, the spider her web, the bee her cell, and the beaver his house, by instinct, and they do their work as well and as perfectly the first time as the tenth. They are taught in no school, are apprenticed to no master; there is no preparation necessary for their life. He that gave it, gave all necessary preparation with it. But it is not so in your case. Instinct teaches you to eat, drink, and sleep, and perform other functions of the animal economy; but in all that pertains to art, science, literature, business, and religion; in short, in all that pertains to you as social, rational, moral and immortal creatures, you must use your reason, under the guidance, in some things of revelation, and in all, in dependence upon the help and blessing of God. One of the purposes for which this reason is given you, and for which it ought to be exercised, is to prepare for life. It is to assist you of course in life, but it is also to prepare you for it. You must think, compare, choose, weigh evidence, and determine. You must prepare to live, by taking up and fixing in your mind in early youth, certain great principles which unquestionably will not grow and establish themselves there spontaneously. Such for instance as these, That in all things and in all events God is to be obeyed. That there is an essential distinction between sin and holiness, in all actions, thoughts, determinations, and feelings; and that sin, whatever temporal advantages or pleasures it may yield, is absolutely the most dreadful evil, and ought to be avoided. That nothing ought to be done which must be afterwards repented of. That judgment and conscience should always prevail over inclination. That no good is to be expected from anything without effort and labour. That you should never put off to futurity what can and ought to be done immediately. That what ought not to be done twice, should not be done once. That what should be done at all, should be always well done. And that the future should predominate over the present. Now reason dictates that all these should be written in the soul as the preparation for life. And it is equally clear that reason dictates great caution in drawing practical conclusions, and forming determinations from mere impressions of fancy or feeling, or from some casual situation into which you may be thrown. In other words, you must judge of principles, whether theoretical or practical, good or bad, not by adventitious matters, such as the persons by whom they are held, or the fascinating or repulsive manner with which they are set forth, but by themselves, apart from all circumstances.

Remember, that if God determines to continue you on the earth for any considerable length of time, (as in all reasonable probability he does,) life, with all its situations, duties, trials, cares, difficulties, and responsibilities, will come, whether you are prepared for them or not. You are in life, and must go on in it. Childhood and youth must of necessity leave you in manhood. The time of your entering upon all the unknown solicitudes of man's condition on earth approaches. You must soon leave school, if you have not already; and come out of your apprenticeship, if you have not yet done so. You must soon be as that young tradesman who has entered upon the race of competition for a livelihood or wealth. You must soon plunge into the vortex of care and labour which is whirling him round and round on the rapid stream of human life, and its manifold business. All the perplexities which harass his mind, must soon harass yours; all the temptations which assail his integrity, must soon assail yours; and prepared or unprepared, you must meet them. What! enter into that conflict unprepared by forethought, by knowledge, by principle, by habit! Alas! poor thoughtless youth, I pity you, and without a prophet's gift, can foretell what terrible work you will make of life. Poor, defenceless, untaught lamb, the wolves are before you, and what is to become of you!

That for which you are required to prepare, I repeat, is your whole life, not a particular situation; not a term of years, however long; not some contingent circumstance; but your whole existence upon earth. You may die in youth, it is true, and therefore I admonish you with all the persuasiveness in my power, to prepare by true piety for death; and nothing else will prepare you for it. Should you die young, I remind you that preparation for life is also preparation for death. Religion, which meetens you to perform well your part on earth, is your education, your training for heaven. True, your education, your knowledge of business, may seem, in the event of your early death, to be useless. But it is not so; the habits of submission, self-denial, and proper application of your mental powers, which, even in those secular things, were called forth under the influence of principle, all go to the training of your soul for the higher state of your existence. But in all probability most of you will live, some forty, others fifty, others sixty, and some few of you will linger on to seventy or eighty years; and it is preparation for all this term that is now urged upon you. What a comprehension of scene, circumstance, and situation, does that term include! Imagine what may happen, must happen, in sixty or seventy years. Through what a variety of situations, temptations, difficulties, trials, changes, even if there be nothing at all extraordinary or out of the common course of man's history, you will be called to pass! And should not they all be prepared for? It is impossible for you to foresee the designs

of Providence in respect to you. I would not excite
and influence your imagination to anything merely
romantic; or set you upon building castles in the air;
or lead you to leave off plodding, and to seek in the
exercise of unauthorised ambition, by a leap or bound
to reach an exalted situation, or by a stroke to grasp a
large fortune. Still it is impossible to conjecture what
opportunity you may have given you, by patient and
successful industry, to rise in life. In this happy country
there is no chain of caste which binds a man down to
the situation and circumstances of his birth. The very
heights of social and commercial life are accessible to
all, from whatever low level they commence the ascent.
The grandfather of the late Sir Robert Peel was at one
time a journeyman cotton-spinner. He that laid the
foundation of the greatness and wealth of the Arkwright
family was a barber. Carey, one of the greatest linguists
and missionaries of modern times, was a cobbler.
Stephenson, the great engineer and the first constructor
of railways, was a working collier. No one knows
what openings God may set before him in life, and
should he not be prepared to take advantage of them?
This very preparation, in many cases makes the opening.
Ignorance, idleness, and vice can never rise. They will
ever sink by their own weight, and effectually close any
door which Providence might set open. What a painful
reflection it is for any man to make in future life, when
some rare and golden opportunity presents itself for
bettering his condition, "Alas! I cannot avail myself
of it. I am disqualified. I made no preparation. With
tolerable diligence at school, and during my apprenticeship, I could have fitted myself for it; but my indolence

then, and my folly and sin subsequently, have put it
quite out of my power to seize the advantage thus
offered me."

Consider, again, if any great mistake, as to the end
and purpose of life, and the manner of spending it,
should be made for want of due preparation, there is
ordinarily no such thing as rectifying it. There is no
going back, and beginning again; no living life over
again; no profiting by experience; no repetition of the
opportunity for preparation. "The wheels of time are
not constructed to roll backwards;" nor can the shadow
retrograde on any man's dial. There is but one life and
one death appointed to any man, and therefore only one
opportunity to prepare for death, and only one to prepare
for life. All depends on one cast of the die. How
momentous that is! How does such an idea deserve to
be pondered by every young man! What, only one life
in this world, and only one in the next, to be prepared
for, and that one neglected! Vain are the regrets and the
wishes of the man, who, amidst broken fortunes, poverty,
misery, and disconcerted schemes, has thus to reflect,
and thus to reproach himself.—"It is my own fault; I
have no one to blame but myself. I was forewarned
and admonished that life's duties, trials, and happiness,
required preparation. Even from childhood I heard it.
At school I was inattentive and idle. During my
apprenticeship I loved pleasure rather than business. In
youth I sought bad companions rather than good books.
I neglected all mental culture, and I feared not God.
I entered life without any preparation. I have succeeded
in nothing, for I was fit for nothing. My only chance
is gone. I am prepared for neither world, and now

I am miserable here, and must expect to be miserable hereafter."

How many whose history has verified all this painful self-reproach, have we, who are older than you are, known! You are young, and have not yet seen much of life. Take our testimony, who have. We will not deceive you. We speak that which we know, and declare to you that which we have seen. We have watched the docile scholar, the diligent, industrious apprentice, and the pious youth, as he rose and ripened into the successful, holy, and happy tradesman, and Christian; and thus became the joy of his parents, the ornament of his family, and the blessing of society. While, on the other hand, we have seen with grief those who in their boyhood and their youth manifested an idleness and a waywardness which no culture could instruct, and no discipline correct; who hated knowledge and despised reproof; who, in the spring time of life, sowed the seeds neither of piety nor of social excellence; who made no preparation for life, except it were for an unholy, unfortunate, and unhappy one; we have, I say, seen many such become their mother's shame, their father's grief, the disgrace of their friends, the curse of society, and their own torment and dishonour. Both are common scenes; and you will exemplify one or other of them in your history.

Your own happiness, then, it is apparent, is deeply involved in this preparation. You are created to be happy. God wills your happiness, and has provided for it. You ought not to be indifferent to it. Your happiness is in your own hands. All the world cannot, and God will not, make you happy, irrespective of your own conduct. Understand at the outset of life this great principle, that happiness arises more from disposition, character, and conduct than from possessions; from what we are, more than from what we have. Its springs, to a considerable extent, lie in your own nature. It is a beautiful saying of Holy Scripture, "A good man shall be satisfied from himself." This deserves your attention, your study, your practical recollection. The happiness of life depends in a great measure upon youth. A bad boy seldom makes a happy man; though God sometimes changes him, and calls him in manhood to an entire renovation. Suppose, for instance, young men, there were two kinds of seeds, one of which you must, by some necessity of nature, or compulsion, sow every spring, and on the fruit of which you must, by the same necessity, live every winter; one fruit bitter and nauseous, and inflicting severe pain; the other, pleasant to the taste and beneficial to the constitution; would you not be very careful which you selected and sowed in your garden, knowing, as you would, what must be the inevitable result? Why, this is your condition of existence and your employment. You are always sowing in youth what you must always reap in manhood. But apart from its results, the very act of preparing for life is itself a part of the happiness of life. Diligence at school, attention to business, mental cultivation, true religion, and good habits, independently of the consequences they bring after them, are themselves the elements of enjoyment. An idle man is the most miserable of God's creatures, except him, who, as is generally the case, adds vice to indolence. Woe to the man who brings upon himself the pains and penalties of laziness.

It is not, however, your own happiness and well-being alone, that will be affected by your conduct and character, but the well-being of others. Your own individuality is something, yea, much to you, and you are not to be indifferent to it. God, by his own authority, protects you against yourself. He says, "Do thyself no harm." He will not allow you to be reckless of your own happiness. He has given you a capacity for bliss, and made provision for it, and accounts it an opposition to his beneficent designs, if you do not endeavour, in His way, aud according to His purpose, to be happy. But then you are a social creature, born in society, intended for society, and bound to promote the well-being of society. Most of you will be husbands, fathers, masters, neighbours, citizens; and you ought to prepare to act well your part in all those relations. You will contribute something to the well or ill-being of the community. You will be the nettles, briars, and brambles of the land, or its oaks, myrtles, or fir trees; its strength or its weakness; its beauty or its deformity. Your country has claims upon you. You are therefore to prepare to serve it, and to serve it well. You should by an intelligent and moral patriotism, implanted early in your heart, seek to bless the land of your birth. Piety and sound morality are a nation's strength, more than its armies and its navies; its wealth, more than its commerce; and its glory, more than its literature, science, and victories. Young men, you belong to the greatest nation upon earth; be worthy of your distinction. Cherish more than a Roman's patriotism, without a Roman's pride. Let Britain's present welfare, and her future destiny, be near your hearts. Let your youthful bosom swell with the noble ambition to do something for the land of your ancestors and your posterity. Add by your prayers a stone to her bulwarks, and by your personal excellence a ray to the glory that beams around her head.

But this is perhaps too large a scale on which to view your influence: too wide a circle for you to see yourself diffusing happiness or misery. Consider, then, the family relationships you will sustain. Look on and anticipate what kind of a husband, father, master, and tradesman, you are likely to make; and how you shall preside over the domestic economy. Some woman's destiny for life will hang upon you, and the happiness of a family, perhaps a numerous one; and then upon their conduct will depend, by an onward succession, the destiny of others to descend from them. You will thus commence a dark or a bright line of human existence, which will run onward through all future generations, and be still going forward when the last trump shall sound. Misery or bliss, at the distance of centuries, or at the very antipodes, may be traced back to you. It is not, therefore, permitted you to be perfectly isolated and neutral. You are not to dwell in a hermitage or a monastery; nor in a cave of the wilderness; nor on some solitary mountain, where no eye will observe you, no ear will hear you; but amidst the busy and crowded haunts of men, where influence to a greater or a smaller extent will go out from you, and you must be the salt or the poison of the earth. You must, you do, mingle with others, whose lot is to a considerable extent mixed up with yours. Ought you not to think of this, and prepare for it? You are destined to light up the countenance of your fellow-creatures with smiles, or to suffuse their eyes with tears; to inflict wounds or to heal them;

to "break the bruised reed," or to "bind up the broken heart." With what emphasis, therefore, may I now say to you, Prepare to live; society, futurity, your country, and the world demand it of you.

But there is another reason, the last, the highest, and most momentous of all, why you should prepare to live; and that is, the life you lead in this world is the preparation for the life you are to live in the next. What the term and purpose of school pursuits, and an apprenticeship, are to the present life, that the whole of the present life is to the one beyond the grave. You are now, and ever will be on earth, in a state of pupilage for heaven and eternity. Upon your fugitive existence in this world hangs your everlasting existence in another. You are constructing a character, the form of which, whatever it be, is to last for ever. How momentous an idea! Yes, there is another world, an eternal world, a world of everlasting and ineffable happiness or woe. Yes, you are immortal beings. Immortality, the highest attribute of God, is yours also. In this, as in other things, God made man in his own likeness. Before you lies the shoreless ocean of eternity. Look over the vast expanse. Every step you take in this world is to heaven or to hell. This little span, this inch of time, our life, is all we have to prepare for all that lies beyond. Human life is the brief, the uncertain, the only preparation time, for those ever-rolling ages. Take this view of it, I beseech you. Meditate on the wondrous theme. Learn at the outset of life, and ever remember through all its future stages, that it is given to you as a discipline and probation for eternity. You have entered upon the trial; the awful probation is going on. Do not let the thoughtlessness of youth hide it from you. Do not let pleasure lead you to forget it. Do not permit companions to divert your attention from it. There it stands before you, the dread, the glorious, and grand reality of man's existence, Immortality. Look at it, ponder it, I beseech you. Let it possess you, literally possess you. Feel as if you could not cast it out from your mind, as if you would not be dispossessed of the wondrous conception. Repel with indignation the attempt to lead you into an oblivion of this your noblest distinction, your richest birth-right. Treat the man who would despoil you of the right consideration of this your highest dignity, as you would the thief that would rob you of your purse, or the assassin that would destroy your life. Prepare, then, by true religion, for that life which is, in its turn, to prepare you for immortality.

To sum up all I have said, there you are, a rational, sinful, immortal, accountable creature, just about to start in the career of active life, with time and eternity before you, heaven above you, hell beneath you, dangers all round you, and many corruptions and imperfections within you. Does it become such a creature, in such a position, to make no preparation? Whether you think of it or not, two worlds, this and the next, are to be inhabited by you. What your lot may be in the present one, none but He who is omniscient can even conjecture. An impenetrable veil hides the future from your view, and not the smallest rent or opening suffers a single ray of light to reveal what is before you. Whether you shall die young or live to old age; whether you shall fail or succeed in business; whether you shall rise or sink in society; whether you shall wear out existence in sorrow or in joy; no one but God can tell, and he will not. Much will depend upon Him; but let me remind you, much also will depend upon yourself. Abandon the heathen notion of fate. I believe in Providence, but not in fate, and I admonish you to believe in it also, and by constant prayer to seek its blessing; but do not forget that Providence never blesses idleness, thoughtlessness, negligence, and extravagance. Providence helps those that help themselves. Everything, therefore, cries to you, " Prepare for life." Your teachers, your parents, your masters, your ministers, say to you, " Prepare to live." Your reason, your conscience, your weakness, your ignorance of the world, say to you, " Prepare to live." The prosperity of those who have succeeded, and the poverty of those who have failed, say, " Prepare to live." The duties, trials, difficulties, and dangers of earth, the joys of heaven, and the torments of the bottomless pit, say, " Prepare to live;" and above all, the great God who has given you existence, who is willing to help you to live holily, usefully, and happily, and who will call you into judgment for the manner in which life has been spent, says to you, " Prepare to live." Can you, dare you, will you, turn a deaf ear to voices so numerous, so solemn, so consentaneous?

CHAPTER II.

In all thy ways acknowledge Him, and He shall direct thy paths. PROVERBS III, 6.

THIS passage of the Bible may be called the pole-star of human life, placed by the hand of God in the firmament of Scripture, for the eye of man to observe upon earth : and he that fixes his attention upon it, and steers his course by it across this troubled and dangerous ocean, shall enter at length the haven of everlasting peace. It is applicable to all persons and to all situations : but especially to those who are just entering upon the duties, dangers, and perplexities of man's terrestrial course. As a rule of conduct it is brief, simple, intelligible, and unmistakeable, easily remembered, and delightful in its observance. If it does not assert, it implies, the existence and operations of an all-comprehensive, all-wise, all-gracious Providence, which appoints, directs, and controls the affairs of men; a Providence which is not only general, as guiding the destinies of nations and worlds, but is particular and minute, as shaping the history of individuals. Some, who profess to believe in Providential interposition in the great events of history, deny it in regard to the minute affairs of individuals. But who can tell what, in fact, is great, and what is little, or how far great events are influenced by lesser ones? The destinies of nations have sometimes hung upon a thought. But we need not reason upon this, since Christ has asserted that "a sparrow falleth not to the ground without the knowledge of our Heavenly Father." Without this view, the doctrine of Providence might be grand as an object of contemplation, but it could yield little consolation as a subject of faith. Individual trust, prayer, hope, and praise, all rest upon the ground of individual Providence. It is not what God is to the universe at large, but what he is to me as an individual, that is the chief source of my comfort, and the strongest motive to my duty. Now the text proposes him to us as an oracle to which we may individually repair: and the injunction means, that, really believing God by His Providence directs all things, we should consult him by reading His Holy Word, where He has revealed His will; and that by sincere and earnest prayer we should seek His leave for everything, His direction in everything, His blessing upon everything, and His glory by everything, we do. In short, it means a devout and practical remembrance of God, as the Disposer of all things, in all the varying circumstances and all the changeful situations of life; and it promises us His wise and gracious direction in all our affairs. How easy, how safe, how tranquil, how dignified a course of action! How vast the privilege of this access to an omnipotent, omnipresent, omniscient, all-sufficient Friend, for advice, direction, and consolation! A wise and benevolent human counsellor ever at hand is a blessing, how much more one that is Divine!

So much for the introduction of this chapter : I now come to its subject, entrance upon life : by which I mean that period of a young man's existence which follows his education and apprenticeship, when he usually leaves his father's house, and becomes a shopman, clerk, or journeyman ; the intermediate stage between the youth and the man of business. Yet it may be remarked that the periods and situations intended to be described and distinguished as separate, in the last chapter and this, run much into one another, and extend onward to settlement in life and the commencement of business.

This, young men, is the situation of the greater part of those whom I address ; you are most of you not in business for yourselves, but looking forward to it ; you are away from your parents, and support yourselves by your industry, and therefore are just stepping upon the stage of active life, and commencing your part in the great drama, with the scenes already shifting before and around you.

Let me, then, remind you, a little more at large,

I. Of your actual situation. It is one of deep and pressing solicitude to your parents and other friends. They have parted from you, and sent you forth, almost with the feeling and the fear that you were going as lambs among wolves. They know, for they have passed through them, the dangers of youth, and especially of youth away from home. If your good conduct and well-formed character at home, have inspired them with confidence, their solicitude is somewhat abated ; but even then an anxious father will exclaim, " What if this fair blossom of parental hope, which grew so beautifully and looked so lovely, when sheltered under the parental roof, should now be blighted when removed to the ungenial blasts of the world's temptations; the very possibility makes my heart bleed. Oh, my son, my son!" How intensely aggravated is this painful solicitude, if unhappily his child is going forth undecided in religion, unconverted to God, with no "armour of righteousness on the right hand and on the left," to defend him from the assaults of temptation; and if even at home portents of future misconduct have showed themselves. "Oh," says the distressed father, "if the wholesome laws, the firm yet mild restraint of parental authority and domestic order, could not repress the outbreaks of youthful irregularity, what is to become of him, when these are withdrawn, and he is left to the unchecked strength of his own corruptions, and the force of surrounding temptations? Oh, my son, my son!" Young men, you cannot know all a father's and a mother's agonizing solicitude for you, on your going out into the world; but you can conceive of it in part, by the scenes of that sorrowful hour when amidst so many tears your mother parted from you, and, with a voice half choked, your father grasped your hand, and sobbed out, "Farewell, my boy. Behave yourself well, and comfort our hearts by your good conduct." How anxious are they to hear from you and of you, to have their fears dissipated and their hopes confirmed. How eagerly, joyfully, and yet how tremblingly, they open every letter to judge from its contents whether there are any signs of incipient moral mischief in your character. Respect their feelings, reward their affection, relieve their solicitude. Call it not suspicion, jealousy, distrust. No, no, it is love trembling over its object, affection agonizing for its loved one. Many an

hour is that mother kept waking at midnight, thinking
and praying for her son who has recently left her to
enter upon the world's business; and often amidst other
cares, does that father feel it to be one of the mightiest
of them all, to consider how his boy conducts himself
in his new situation.   Let me plead, then, for the peace
of those two hearts which throb so anxiously for you,
and for the peace of which, so far as it is in your keeping, your own ought to throb most responsively.

But I now turn from your parents, and remind you
of the momentous and infinite importance of this period
of your life to yourselves.   It is, in all probability, the
crisis of your history, the hinge of your destiny, the
casting of your lot for both worlds, the formation
of your character for time and for eternity.   Through
every hour, almost every minute, of this term, and in
every scene, your character is passing from that state
of fusion in which it was left by boyhood and youth,
into the cold, hard solidity and fixedness of manhood.
It depends chiefly upon the time that is now passing
over you, what you are to be, and to do, through all
time and eternity.   The next two years will very likely
determine the great question, concerning the character
of your whole existence.   The observable tendencies
of boyhood and youth, the significant prognostication
from the pupil and the apprentice, the declaratory signs
of earlier years, will now receive their full and perhaps
final confirmation.   Your character, which has been
growing, like your body, through the previous stages
of existence, now, like that, arrives at that full shape
and maturity, which it will hereafter retain and exhibit.
Can you be thoughtlessly and carelessly indifferent at
such a crisis?   Is it possible?   Can you help saying,

"Is it so, then; am I really now, just at this period, becoming my permanent future self? Am I determining for all time, and for all eternity, what kind of moral, social, and intellectual being I am to be? Am I now casting my lot, forming my destiny, choosing my character? What thoughtfulness, seriousness, devotedness, and prayer for God's Holy Spirit to assist me, ought I to manifest! What do I wish to habitually be in and through all future life, and through all eternity? What I am now, that, in all probability, I shall be. I am entering upon life, and as I begin, so am I likely to continue." Yes, dwell upon that consideration. It is of immense importance to start well. He that at the beginning of his journey takes the wrong road, diverges at every step farther and farther from the right path; and though return is not impossible, yet at what an expense of time and comfort is it made! Take care, then, to begin well. Solomon says, "Better is the end of a thing than the beginning;" especially if it be a good end of a bad beginning. But how rarely does a thing end well that begins ill! The fruit is better than the blossom; the reaping than the sowing; the victory than the battle; home than the journey to it; the reward than the service. But then all these better endings depend on good beginnings. There can be no rich fruit in autumn, without a good blossom in spring; no plentiful reaping without plentiful sowing; no victory without a well-fought battle; no returning home without a journey along the right road. So there can be no rational expectation of a good end of life, without a good beginning.

II. I will now remind you of the dangers that attend your entering into life. Yes, dangers; and I really

wish to excite your fears by the word. I am anxious
to awaken your apprehension by thus ringing an alarm
bell. Not indeed by raising spectres which have no real
existence; not by calling up spirits from the vasty deep
of a gloomy imagination. No, there is no need in
order to excite your fears, of passing before you the
dark shadows and the ghosts of romance. The sober
and dread realities of daylight and of every-day existence,
are sufficiently numerous and appalling to justify the
use of the most solemn, impressive, and earnest warnings
we can give. Young men, it is a truth, and a dread and
anxious one for you, that the moral dangers of life stand
thickest around its entrance. The most perilous rocks
and shoals in the voyage of life, are at the mouth of the
river where it enters the ocean; and notwithstanding
the lighthouse which in the Holy Scriptures and the
faithful labours of authors and preachers, ever holds out
its friendly warning over these dangerous places, more
shipwrecks are made there than anywhere else.

These dangers are so numerous, that they must be
classed. There are some which may have been thrown
in your way perhaps, by the injudicious conduct of your
parents. They may have altogether neglected your
moral training and left you to go forth into the world
without any fixed principles, any good habits, or any
rightly formed character. By a system of false and
weak indulgence, they may have partially unfitted you
for the trials, the difficulties, the roughness, and self-
denial of life. We will not dwell upon their conduct
with the severity it deserves; but be you aware of their
mistake, and call up your own wisdom to correct it.
They have left you something to undo, as well as to do.
Supply, by your own resolute will, the deficiency of

hardihood with which they have left you. Abandon the
soft and effeminate habits in which they have trained
you, and determine to be men, and to acquire a manly
character. You can, if you will, make up their deficiencies; but it will require much effort and more
perseverance.

There are, next, the dangers that are inherent in
yourselves, and these are the greatest of all. You not
only go to meet perils, you carry them forth with you.
Now at the head of all this class, I must place the
corruption of your own hearts. " Know thyself," was
supposed by the ancients to be a maxim so replete with
wisdom, as to have descended from heaven. No man
can properly exercise self-government without self-
knowledge. False notions on this subject must, of
necessity, lead to practical errors of a most momentous
kind. I cannot, I dare not, I will not flatter you by
speaking highly of the native goodness, the moral
dignity, of human nature. Scripture, observation, and
experience, must combine to prove, to any impartial
mind, that man is in a lapsed condition, alien from
God, and estranged from righteousness. This is a first
principle, not only in all true religion, but in all sound
philosophy. Leaving out this, it is impossible satisfac-
torily to account for the present condition and general
history of the human race. Forgetting or denying this,
your whole system of religion and morals will be wrong,
and your whole course of action defective and erroneous ;
you will not, cannot know, the chief source of your
danger, and that which alone can account for the
existence and power of other dangers: nor will you
know how to begin or proceed in watching and guarding
against them. There is, you know it, you feel it, and

perhaps some of you lament it, a fatal propensity to evil, which, though inclining to what is wrong, yet, as by divine grace it may be resisted and removed, is, neither an irresistible tendency nor an invincible necessity, but a voluntary choice, and is therefore no excuse for actual sin, though it may account for it. It is not danger from without only you have to fear, but also from within; not from others merely, but from yourself. You carry your tempter in your own heart; you are your own tempter. You will be surrounded by external seductions, and you will expose to them a nature too willing to be seduced. There is in you " an evil heart of unbelief in departing from the living God." You have more need to be afraid of yourself than even of Satan or of the world. They cannot tempt you but through your own corruptions. Hence the imperative need of your seeking first of all the entire renovation of your own hearts, and keeping evermore a constant watch over yourselves. You will be most inadequately prepared to grapple with temptation, unless you know what it is that gives it force.

But the corruption of the heart assumes a different form in different persons, and shows itself in manners appropriate to their age, circumstances, and temptations. In your case there are those " youthful lusts," from which by apostolic injunction you are exhorted to flee. In addition to an inflammable and prurient imagination, the rashness and impetuosity of temper, the thoughtlessness and recklessness of disposition, the pride of independence, and the headstrong waywardness which are all too common in youth, there are the animal appetites and propensities exhibiting themselves in all their force: those promptings of licentiousness and impulses of sensuality, to which there are so many incentives, and which require so strong a restraint from reason and religion; I mean, young men, the vices which form the drunkard and the debauchee: those illicit gratifications which degrade the man into the brute. The danger here exceeds all the alarm I can possibly give. No warning can be too loud, no intreaties too importunate, in regard to this peril. Voices from the pulpit, from the hospital, from the hulks, from the workhouse, from the lunatic asylum, from the grave, and from the bottomless pit, all unite in saying, " Young men, beware of sensuality." Flee from this as from a serpent or a lion. Read what Solomon says, who could speak on such a subject from his own unhappy and dishonourable experience : " The lips of a strange woman drop as an honey-comb, and her mouth is smoother than oil : but her end is bitter as wormwood ; sharp as a two-edged sword. Her feet go down to death, her steps take hold on hell: let not thine heart decline to her ways, go not astray in her paths. For she has cast down many wounded : yea, many strong men have been slain by her. Her house is the way to hell, going down to the chambers of death." Prov. v., vii. Read these chapters, and, in connection with them, Job xx., 11-14. 1 Cor. vi., 15-20. 1 Thess. iv., 2-5. Heb. xiii., 4. Rev. xxi., 8.

There is also another form which the corruption of our nature assumes, and which the apostle calls " the deceitfulness of sin." " Exhort one another daily, lest any of you be hardened through the deceitfulness of sin." Deceitfulness is not only one of the characteristics of sin, but is its most dangerous one ; and none are so much in danger of being imposed upon by it as

the young; nor are they at any period of youth so
much so as when just entering upon it. You have
never, perhaps, looked upon it sufficiently in this view
of it. You may have dwelt upon its exceeding sinfulness, but its deceitfulness has escaped you. Yet this is
what you have chiefly to guard against. Sin is a most
cunning and artful foe. Observe what pains it takes to
disguise itself, and conceal its hideous nature. It does
not appear in its own proper and genuine dress, nor call
itself by its own proper name. It puts the mask of
virtue upon its face, and wraps itself in the cloak
of dissimulation, by calling vices virtues, and virtues
vices: thus excess and intemperance are called a social
disposition and good fellowship; prodigality is liberality;
pride and resentment are honour, spirit, and dignity;
licentious levity is innocent liberty and cheerfulness;
lying artifice is skill in business; sordid avarice is
frugality. Virtue meets with the opposite treatment,
and is always called by some disgusting or contemptible
name. True religion is sour puritanism, or hypocritical
cant; tenderness of conscience is narrowness of mind;
zeal for truth is bigotry. Now, my young friends, do
not be imposed upon by such shallow artifices as these:
recognise in such attempts, a wicked and daring attempt
to confound all moral distinctions, which must bring
down the woe denounced against those " who call evil
good, and good evil." Disdain this cajolery, this
attempt to impose upon your understanding, by merely
changing the names of things, while the things themselves remain the same. Consider that not only your
moral, but your intellectual nature, is insulted by such
a feeble effort to mislead it. Take it with you as a
maxim of great importance to remember, that the

generality of men are more governed by words and names than by things, and never more so than in questions of virtue or vice. Do you endeavour to be governed by things, and not by names.

And then, in tracing the deceitfulness of sin, mark the excuses it makes for itself; the insensible degrees by which it leads the sinner on in his course: at first tempting to little sins, thus preparing him for greater ones; at first urging only to single sins, afterwards soliciting a repetition; at first asking for secret sins, soon emboldening him to open ones; at first allowing him to sin in decent company, at length drawing him into the society of the notoriously wicked; at first allowing him to blush, then making him glory in his shame; at first leaving him content to sin himself, then prompting him on to tempt others; at first telling him that if he does not choose to go on, he can soon and easily retrace his steps, then cutting off his retreat by involving him in such a complexity of transgression, that he feels it almost necessary to go forward, adding sin to sin; at first telling him repentance is too soon, because his sins have hitherto been so trivial; then suggesting it is too late, because they have been so great; at first assuring him God is too lenient to notice his beginnings of sin, then declaring that he is too just to forgive his crimes; thus by perpetual, though ever-varying delusions, leading him into, and keeping him, in the path of transgression. Such is the horrid nature of sin: a horrid, practical lie; a deadly deceit; the greatest imposture in the universe; the most destructive fraud ever perpetrated in the world's history. And you, young men, are the selected victims of its wiles. The arch-deceiver is more intent on you

than on any others. There the siren sits on the rocks
of the sea which you are just entering, sending forth
her dulcet but deadly strains, enrapturing you for your
destruction; making you willing to be wrecked, and to
die in her fatal arms.

Your inexperience endangers you. Life is an un-
trodden path. You are only just beginning to live; its
difficulties, dangers, temptations, are all new to you.
You are ignorant to a considerable extent of the machinations of Satan, the wiles of the world, and the devices
of your own heart. You are ignorant of your own
ignorance; and know not your own weakness and instability. You have hitherto been in some measure sheltered in private; now you are to be exposed in public.
Forms of iniquity, of which hitherto you were happily
ignorant, will rise up with fascinating appearances in
your path. Scenes never anticipated by you, and for
which therefore you can make no special preparation,
will open before you, and ere you are aware draw you
by their specious attractions into temptation. Assaults,
sudden and altogether new, will be made upon your
principles, almost before you can have time to buckle
on your armour. And what will greatly increase the
danger is your own self-confidence, rashness, and impetuosity. You give yourselves credit for a degree
of sagacity to detect, resolution to vanquish, and power
to overcome, evil, which you do not really possess. You
rush in where others, possessing more knowledge,
caution, and experience, would fear to tread; you
advance boldy to a contest from which it would be your
wisdom to retire; and you are ready to resent a suspicion of your being in danger, as a disparagement of
your strength of mind, purity of heart, and resoluteness

of purpose. You are therefore likely to afford another proof and example that "he who leaneth to his own understanding, and trusteth to his own heart, is a fool." Show me a young man setting out in life with high notions of his own sagacity, virtue, resoluteness of will, and inflexibility of purpose, and there, without a prophet's inspiration, I can foretell, will be a sad illustration of the Scripture which declares that "pride goeth before destruction, and a haughty spirit before a fall."

Then there are dangers from the corrupt state of society. With such hearts as yours, there is, in the best state of public morals, wickedness enough to constitute just ground for alarm and for watchfulness. It may not be that your country is worse than all others, or your times more profligate, I think they are not; but it is enough to know that the aboundings of iniquity, and the overflowings of ungodliness, are such as to make all who have any regard for youthful purity afraid. The undoubted fact of the growing prevalence of infidelity in its most seductive forms; the multiplication, as by a fresh inspiration of the wisdom from beneath, of all kinds of sinful indulgence; the increasing desecration of the Sabbath; the endless new stimulants to worldly pleasure, the demoralised state of the public press, the new and ostentatious zeal and spread of Popery: all combine to load the moral atmosphere with the pestilence that walks in darkness, and to send forth the destruction that wastes at noonday. Never were there so many malign influences combining and conspiring against the religion and virtue of our young men as now; and never was it more necessary for them to be aroused to a sense of their danger, and to be put upon their guard.

Young men, the world is full of temptations; and its inhabitants are divided between the tempters and the tempted. Buckle on your armour, for you will need it; the helmet, the breastplate, the greaves, the shield. The enemies are lurking around, the ambush is laid, the aim is taken, the arrow is fitted to the string, the bow is bent. Beware: there are evil companions to be avoided. What says the Scripture, The companion of fools shall be destroyed. I repeat what I have said, the workhouse, the lunatic asylum, the prison, the hulks, the convict ship, the gallows, the bottomless pit, all, all, attest the truth of this, by the millions they have swallowed up in their jaws of destruction. Evil companionship has ruined more characters, more fortunes, more bodies, and more souls, than almost anything else that could be named. This is one of your first and most pressing dangers. It will meet you the very next day after you have entered into life. Man is a gregarious animal; he is made for society, and will have it, and the social instinct is strongest in youth. Beware, then, I implore you, to whom you give your company, and whose company you accept in return. You must take your character, to a certain extent, from your companions. Your companions will seek to stamp their image upon you, and that at a time of life when your mind is in a state to receive the impression; and if they did not, you would insensibly, perhaps designedly, copy it. As waters, however pure when they issue from the spring, take the colour of the soil through which they flow; as animals, transported from one region to another, lose something of their former habits, and degenerate by little and little; so character assimilates to that which surrounds it. You may be forced to have bad connexions, bad acquaintances, for perhaps you cannot avoid them; but you need not, and for your soul's sake, and for the sake of everything dear to you, do not, have bad companions. Men who scoff at religion, ridicule the godly, who make light of sin and laugh at conscience, who are lewd in their actions, or obscene in their conversation, who are Sabbath-breakers, who are lovers of pleasure more than lovers of God, who are extravagant in their habits and loose in their moral principles, these are the fools of whom Solomon speaks, who will bring their own destruction upon you, if you do not avoid them.

With much the same emphasis do I warn you against bad books, the infidel and immoral publications of which such a turbid deluge is now flowing from the press, and depositing on the land a soil in which the seeds of all evil grow with rank luxuriance. Infidelity and immorality have seized upon fiction and poetry, and are endeavouring to press into their service even science and the arts. But besides these, books that inflame the imagination and corrupt the taste, that by their excitement unfit the mind for the sober realities of life, or that indispose it by everlasting laughter for what is grave serious and dignified, are all to be avoided. In some respects bad books are more mischievous than bad companions, since they are still more accessible, and more constantly with us; can be more secretly consulted, and lodge their poison more abidingly in the imagination, the intellect, and the heart. A bad book is a bad companion of the worst kind, and prepares for bad companions of all other kinds.

There are bad places, also, which endanger you, as

well as bad companions and bad books; where, if you have not already formed bad. companionships, you are sure to find them. All these are the avenues to ruin; the wide gates that open into the way of destruction. Many who have been kept out of the way of these places at home, on entering life have indulged, in the first instance, rather a prurient curiosity than an inclination to sin, and have thought they would go once to them, just to see what they are, and whether there is all the harm that has been represented. Fatal curiosity! Oh that once, that first wrong step, that slip off from the summit down the incline plane! The door of evil was opened, never again to be closed. Never trust yourself even once in a place where you would not feel justified in going habitually. Never go even once, where you are sure you would not be followed with the approbation of your father, your conscience, and your God, and from which you would not be willing to go immediately to the judgment-seat of Christ. In illustration of the danger of a single visit to an anti-Christian scene of amusement, I may here repeat the fact which I have given in another publication, of one of the primitive Christians, who for a long time resisted the importuni-ties of a friend that invited him to witness the gladiatorial fights in the amphitheatre. At length he was subdued, but determined that he would sit with his eyes closed, and thus quiet his own conscience, while he yielded to the solicitations of his friend. An unusual shout of applause which followed some display of skill or courage, excited his curiosity. He opened his eyes, he was interested, could not close them again, went again voluntarily, became a constant and eager attend-ant, abandoned Christianity, and died a pagan. How many more have been victims to one visit to forbidden places.

I mention also bad habits, habits of extravagance in the way of apparel, ornaments, and pleasure-taking. A love of gay personal appearance, and sensual gratification, leads to expense; and as extravagance must have resources, if honesty and industry cannot supply them, dishonesty will create them. Be frugal, economical, prudent. Begin life with a determination to live within your income. Have no needless artificial want. Dispense with the cigar. Young men have often involved themselves in debt and consequent disgrace by this indulgence; besides it is costly in itself, excites an appetite for liquor, leads to evil company and evil places, and introduces other expenses and other habits.

Next I notice the love of pleasure. Here again is danger, imminent danger. Do you remember the words of Solomon on this subject? "He that loveth pleasure shall be a poor man." Never was there more occasion for sounding this in the ears of the public, than now. Men were never more bent upon pleasure, and never had opportunities for enjoyment so much at command. It is a proof of human depravity that science and the arts never confer a benefit on society, but man's wickedness turns it into a means of sinning against God. What an incentive to Sabbath-breaking has the railway system proved! The sanctity of the Lord's day is in danger of being trampled down by the unholy foot of pleasure. Sunday excursion trains have become not only a snare and temptation to multitudes, but a source of annoyance to the quiet and godly inhabitants of several places on the lines of our railways. But it is not this only; invention is racked by those who cater

for the public taste to find new pleasures, and fresh
gratifications of sense and appetite. High and low, rich
and poor, young and old, are all hungering and thirsting after pleasure, as if this world was given to us for
no other purpose than to be a play-ground for its inhabitants : the multitudes are rushing after it with the
atheistic language which the apostle puts into the lips
of those who deny the resurrection of the dead : "Let
us eat and drink, for to-morrow we die." Young men,
I do not wish to deny you pleasure, but only say, let it
be intellectual and spiritual, rather than sensual; individual and private, rather than social and public ;
economical, rather than expensive ; an occasional recreation, and not an habitual pursuit; and such as shall
rather fit than disqualify you for the business of life.
No man will less enjoy pleasure than he who lives for
and upon it ; and paradoxical as it may appear, it is true,
the way to enjoy pleasure is not to indulge in it to
excess, but ever to partake of it in moderation. Honey,
and other luscious sweets, will do to taste, but not to
live or feast upon. Cyprian beautifully remarks, that
" the greatest pleasure is to have conquered pleasure." I
repeat the impressive proverb, " He that loveth pleasure
shall be a poor man ;" for it is an expensive taste, which
grows, like every other, by indulgence. It will make
you poor in youth, poor in manhood, poor in old age ;
and this is a poverty which no one will pity, or be forward to relieve.

III. I will now lay before you the state of mind
which befits you in this critical juncture of your history.
I deliberately select this phrase, critical juncture. It is,
whether you think so or not, most critical; and
something will be gained by this chapter, if it only bring

you in sober seriousness to respond to the expression,
and say, "Yes, I am now in the crisis of my temporal
and eternal destiny, and I own it, feel it, and will reflect
upon it." Indeed, this, I will confess, is my main object
and my chief hope in this volume. I have not touched
upon controversy, as I have already intimated, nor is it
my aim to suggest or supply topics of abstract thought
or speculative inquiry; neither is it my purpose, if it
were in my power, to gratify your curiosity by novelty,
your imagination by taste, nor your love of controversy
by logic. Time is too short, life too important, to be
all spent upon such things. I have other purposes and
aims: I want to make you seriously reflect upon your
life and condition, your character and conduct, your
present and future means and plans of action, usefulness,
and happiness. I am ambitious to check the levity and
thoughtlessness with which so many are entering upon
the most momentous period of their existence: and
without producing an unnatural gravity or gloom, and
without extinguishing the joyousness, happiness, and
buoyancy of youth, still to make you deeply feel how
solemn and eventful is the period of entering life. Remember, that as the power of reflection increases with
your years, so the habit should strengthen also; and
that if it should have awakened solemn thoughtfulness
to consider that you were about to enter life, it should
excite no less apprehensiveness to consider that you have
actually started in the eventful race. And this thoughtfulness should embrace some specific subjects, take some
practical form and direction, and induce some active
habits. Nothing can be less likely to be serviceable to
you than a dreamy pensiveness, a moody and morbid
fancy, and a disposition to speculate upon possibilities,

and spend in imagining situations in life that time which should be employed in meeting your real condition. The thoughtfulness that I inculcate is not that which supplants action, but prepares it, incites to it, and guides in safety through it.

I will now take up, and place before you, the only special direction which the apostle Paul lays down for the guidance of your conduct, "Young men, exhort to be sober-minded." The very injunction supposes that this is a state of mind, not only peculiarly necessary for young men, but in which they are usually deficient. Now, do not be alarmed at the expression, and "recoil from it as from something which could come only from, and is suitable only to, old time-worn people, whose feelings are dried up into a kind of cold and stiffened prudence, which they wish to have reputed as wisdom; persons who, having suffered the extinction of all vivacity in themselves, envy the young for possessing what they have lost. A dull, heavy, spiritless, formal, and calculating thing; almost mechanical in all pursuits and interests; the type of a person narrow in his notions, plodding in his operations, gloomy in his aspect, and placed wholly out of sympathy with every thing partaking of ardour, sensibility, adventure, and enthusiasm, and at the same time taking great credit to himself for all this. No, we may be quite sure that Paul's 'sober-minded young men,' were not to be examples of a sapient formality, of a creeping prudence, of extinguished passion, of a cold aversion to animated interests, in short, not examples of the negation of every thing that is really graceful and excellent in youth."* What then did he mean? What is sobriety of mind? The pre-

* Foster's Lecture upon Sober-Mindedness.

dominance of true religion and sound reason over vice and folly, temper and fancy, imagination and passion, absurdity and extravagance. It is, in short, the mastery of the imagination by the judgment. Imagination, in the minority of reason, is the regent of the soul. Almost everything is looked at, judged of, and ruled by, this miscalculating faculty, and is rendered much more dangerous by the ardour of passion. Things thus seen through a wrong medium are distorted and discoloured. Evils and dangers which are seen by other eyes in all their magnitude of mischief, appear to the young (if, indeed they appear at all) reduced to almost invisible spots; while little matters of real or supposed good, are swelled out of all proportion, and adorned with the brightest hues with which fancy can invest them. Hope, untutored and unchecked by knowledge of the world and experience, is ever building castles in the air, and treating as certainties what all others perceive to be improbabilities. Sobriety of mind is reason arrived at its majority and sanctified by religion, ascending the throne of the soul to take the sceptre out of the hand of imagination. It means the capacity of forming a right estimate of things as they really are. This, young men, is what you need, but of which persons of your age are often lamentably destitute. But I will select one or two subjects which sobriety of mind will especially bring under consideration, and of which it will lead you to form correct ideas.

It will, above all things, lead you to a serious and devout consideration of the supreme end of life. I say the supreme, the chief end of human existence; since there are many subordinate ones arising out of our numerous and complex relations. Pause and ponder this question

then, " What is the supreme end of existence ? " Mark
well the subject; it is not what are all the ends of existence, but what is the supreme one, life's great business,
the one thing needful, which being accomplished, whatever else we have missed, we still have not lived in vain;
but which not having secured, we have lived in vain, gain
whatever else we may. What, I say, is your errand, your
object? Surely, surely, if anything be worthy the attention of a living, rational creature, it must be the object
of life : and if at any time, at the beginning of life. Proceed not another hour, take up no plan, no purpose, no
pursuit, till you have settled the question, " What is the
supreme end of life ? " Whatever it be, it must combine
all the following characteristics; it must be something
lawful, which God and your conscience approve; something appropriate to your character and circumstances,
and to all the changing scenes of life ; something attainable; something worthy your existence; something
adapted to satisfy the desires of an immortal mind and
make you contented and happy; something which shall aid
rather than hinder you in accomplishing all the subordinate ends of existence; something which shall combine
your present with your everlasting destiny ; something,
in short, which God himself has fixed upon and proposed
to you, as His supreme end in your creation. Is not
this true ? Must not the great end possess all these
characteristics ? Answer me. Must it not ? And
what, I ask, can do this but true religion ? And it does.
Here, then, is the great end of life, that religion which
leads to the salvation of the immortal soul, to glory,
honour, immortality, and eternal life. " Compared
with this, the objects of earthly ambition, which engage
the attention and engross the affections of many in

public life, are all vain, empty and unprofitable. The
eager strifes and ephemeral victories of political leaders ;
the feverish dreams of the wealthy capitalist and the
commercial adventurer, seem little better than toys and
baubles. The sportive swarms of insects floating in the
sunbeams of a summer evening appear to be a fit
emblem of our vast cities and their busy crowds." " Believe, then, that the only supreme end worth living for,
is an end which shall endure, an end which can never
perish. Do not squander so precious a boon as life
upon secondary objects. Throw not away upon the
perishing objects of an earthly ambition, your immortal
soul, a jewel, compared with which " the Mountain
of Light," the richest trophy of our Oriental conquests,
or any nobler product of the diamond mines, is a thing
of nought.

Sobriety of mind will lead you also to consider the
shortness and uncertainty of life, and the necessity
of being always prepared to surrender the precious gift ;
and always so prepared by having secured that which
is of the highest importance. The man who has achieved
the chief end, is prepared, at any moment, to give up
in death all subordinate ends ; while he who has sought
only subordinate objects, is never ready to give them
up. He who has true piety, however young he may die,
has effectually accomplished the chief purpose of his
creation ; while he who neglects religion, whatever
of rank, wealth, honour, or even earthly usefulness, he
may have acquired, and however long he may live to enjoy
them, has missed the chief end of his being ; and will
very soon look on his life as a lost adventure. Equally
true is it, that such a state of mind cannot be obtained
otherwise than by the adoption of the principles neces-

sary to secure the end of life; in other words, true religion, a strong habitual faith in the Bible, in God, in Christ, in Providence, in judgment, in heaven, and hell. Faith expresses itself not only in worship, in religious emotions, in zeal, in almsdeeds, but in an enlightened and tender conscientiousness both towards God and man, and in a systematic and strong restraint upon the passions, fancy, temper, and appetites.

In entering, then, upon life, take religion with you. This will ensure you the protection of omnipotence; the guidance of omniscience; the companionship of omnipresence; the supplies of all-sufficiency. It will fill your intellect with the thoughts of God's own mind, and your soul with the joy of God's own heart, and thus furnish you at once with the supreme truth, and the chief good. It will set before you the most perfect examples, and the strongest motives to the practice of holiness and virtue. It will add the sanctity of the Christian to the virtue of the moral man, and mingle its own heavenly pleasures with the pure delights of earth. It will prepare you either for success or failure in business, and preserve you equally from the snares of prosperity and the withering blasts of adversity. It will be your nurse in sickness, your companion in solitude, and your preserver amidst the corruptions of society. It will be your shield against temptations to sin, and the insidious attacks of infidelity and false philosophy. It will go with you across the sea, and dwell with you in a foreign land, if called by Providence to leave your native country, or make you honourable and useful members of the community, if you remain at home. It will be the guide of your youth, the protector of your matured life, and the prop of your old age. It will prepare you for early death, or for a multitude of years. It will smooth the pillow of death, by giving you immortal hopes amidst the dissolution of nature, will rise with you from the grave in that day when death shall be swallowed up in victory, and having put you in possession of glory, honour, immortality, and eternal life, will dwell in your soul for ever, as the chief element of your heavenly and everlasting felicity.

But still I would not forget that there are things on earth to be attended to as well as things in heaven : and religion, as I have already said, neither detaches you from them, nor unfits you for them; and next to this due regard to the claims of God, and as a part of it, industry and diligence in business are indispensable. Honesty to your employers requires this. You have contracted with them, for so much stipend, to give them your time, the faculties of your mind, and the members and powers of your body. That man who does not serve his employer to the best of his ability is, to all intents and purposes, a thief, not by stealing his master's goods, but his time; and I would give nothing for his moral principle who can defraud his employer even of this. It is not, however, merely in this light that I speak now of industry, but as your own safeguard : "For Satan finds some mischief still for idle hands to do." Our idle days are his busy ones. An indolent young man invites temptation, and will soon become a prey to it. The diligent man is the protected man. Temptation comes and addresses him, but he is pre-occupied; he says, "I am too busy to attend to you." Indolence unmans the faculties, impairs and debilitates the whole intellectual system. One way or other, be always employed. An idle man is the most miserable of all God's creatures; a contradiction in nature, where nothing is at rest. Among all other habits which you can form, next to religion, the most valuable is a habit of activity. This must be acquired in youth, or never. Keep the ethereal fire of your soul alive and glowing by action. Not only have occupation, but love it. Let your mind take a pleasure and a pride in its own action. Nature, it is said, abhors a vacuum, and if nature does not, you should.

IV. Let me now lay before you a few opposite extremes, which, in passing through life, it is necessary you should avoid; and with which, when just entering upon it, you should be intimately acquainted. Avoid, then, on the one hand, a depressing solicitude, and on the other, an utter carelessness and lethargic indifference, about the future; a disposition to distress the mind by the question, " How am I to get on?" or the opposite extreme, of a total destitution of all forethought or care about the matter. The former is not only a distrust of Providence, but it defeats its own ends by wasting those energies of mind in useless care which should be employed in preparatory action; while the latter casts away that partial prescience which is given to us for wise and gracious purposes. Be hopeful, but not sanguine; moderate, but not indifferent. Let your expectations be sufficiently high to encourage exertion, but not so extravagant as to bewilder you.

Equally to be avoided, as connected with this, is inordinate ambition to rise in life, and the opposite extreme of that low and creeping satisfaction with things as they are, which is rather the result of an indolent and abject mind, than of a contented one. The determination by any and by all means to get on, and the lazy disposition to make no effort, are equi-distant from moral excellence. Determine to do for your just advancement all that skill, industry, frugality, and honourable principle can accomplish, but nothing more. Set out in life thoroughly convinced of the truth of the apostolic declaration, " They that will be rich fall into temptation and a snare, and into many foolish and hurtful lusts, which drown men in destruction and perdition. For the love of money is the root of all evil, which, while some covet after, they have pierced themselves through with many sorrows." Young men, guard against this low, sordid, mischievous avarice, this coveting of wealth for its own sake : this determination to get it, if by fair means, well; if not, by foul means. Begin your career of honest and honourable industry, with the poet's impressive, sarcastic aphorism before your eyes, " That loudest laugh of hell, the pride of dying rich." Guard against the self-diffidence, distrust, and despondency, which would lead you to form too low an opinion of your own capability and resources, on the one hand ; and on the other, against the complacent self-reliance, confidence, and conceit, which would lead you to think you can do everything. While you do not lean altogether upon your own understanding, and trust implicitly to your own heart, remember they can both do something for you, and are both to be employed. Start upon the journey of life with the conviction that you can, by God's help and blessing, do something, yea, much, for yourself. Have faith in God first of all, and next to this, have faith in yourselves as God-sustained. Enter into the apostle's words, catch their spirit, and imitate their union of personal activity and confidence, with dependence on divine help,

"Through Christ strengthening me, I can do all things."

Take heed against flexibility of principle, purpose, and character, in reference to what is right, and obstinate perseverance in what is wrong. Be master of yourself. Have a will of your own, but be governed by your own convictions. Knowing what is right, do it, though you stand alone, and though the world laugh in a chorus. Possess that due degree of moral courage which, while it leaves you in possession of true shame when doing what is wrong, shall extinguish all false shame in doing what is right. It is a noble sight to behold a young man stand, with his back against the wall of truth, and, with the shield of faith, repel the arrows of a multitude of assailants. Be an oak, not an osier. Let it be seen that you can resist the force of persuasion, the influence of oratory, the ridicule of the witty, the sarcasms of the scornful, the contagion of sympathy with the multitude. It is a great, good, and glorious thing, to be able in some circumstances to say, " No ;" and to stand by it. On the other hand, it is no less great, good, and glorious, to say, " I am wrong," when charged with an error, and convinced that you have committed it. An obstinate perseverance in a bad course, to avoid the shame and humiliation of confessing that you are wrong, is neither dignity nor greatness of mind, but stubborn imbecility ; the obstinacy of a brute.

Avoid equally a total indifference to the good opinion of others, and a craving after admiration and applause. Seek to be approved rather than to be admired. Covet the esteem of the wise and the good ; but do not hunger after the indiscriminate praise of any and everybody.

Rather seek to be excellent, than desire to be thought so. To wish to stand well with those whose praise is virtuous, is lawful; but to be always anxious for the admiration of others, is contemptible. The former is itself an exercise of virtue, the other is mere vanity. Guard against this vanity; it will make you far more solicitous about praise than principle, and willing to sacrifice the one for the other.

Avoid the extremes of credulity and suspicion in reference to mankind; of trusting everybody, as if all were worthy of your confidence; and of trusting nobody, as if all were knaves. Be cautious whom you trust, but do not suppose that everyone will betray you. It is well to be reserved, but not to be suspicious; to be prudent, but not misanthropic. On the other hand, as the danger of the young lies rather in being too frank, open, and ingenuous, than too retiring and exclusive, study well the character of every one, before you give him your confidence.

V. Perhaps I cannot do better than add to all I have said a few maxims, which may be considered as condensing some parts of the substance of this chapter, and which, as most easily remembered, may be of some service to you in your progress through life.

Your future history and character will be in a great measure of your own making, therefore pause and consider what you will make yourself.

What you would be in future, that begin to be at once; for the future is not at a great distance, but close at hand: the moment next to the present is the future, and the next action helps to make the future character.

While you consult your friends on every important step, (and this is at once your duty and your privilege,) rely less upon them than upon yourself; and ever combine self-reliance with dependence upon God, whose assistance and blessing come to the help of a man's own industry.

If setting out in life in the possession of property, let your dependence for success, after all, be less upon this, than upon industry. Industry creates capital, but beginning with capital has in many cases made a man careless and improvident, and destroyed his industry.

Consider the importance of the first wrong step. That first one leads to many others, and may be more easily avoided than any that follows it.

True religion (which means the habitual fear of God and sin), is your best friend for both worlds; multitudes owe their all to it; and multitudes more who have been ruined by vice, folly, and extravagance, would have been saved from them all had they lived in the fear of God.

They who would live without religion would not die without it; but to enjoy its comforts in death, you must submit to its influence in life; and those who would have it in life, should seek it in youth.

The perfection of human character consists of piety, prudence, and knowledge. Make that noble trio your own.

Whatever specious arguments infidelity may put forth in defence of itself, and whatever objections it may bring against Christianity, hold fast the Bible till the infidel can furnish you a more abundant evidence of truth, a better rule of life, a more copious source of consolation, a surer ground of hope, and a more certain and glorious prospect of immortality. And remember that spiritual religion is a better defence against the seductions of infidelity and false philosophy than the most powerful or subtle logic.

Enter upon life as you would wish to retire from it, and spend time on earth as you would wish to spend eternity in heaven.

I now leave the subject for your most devout and serious reflection. Entering upon life! How weighty the phrase, how momentous the consideration, how solemn the anticipation! A hundred millions perhaps of your fellow-creatures are at this moment like you entering upon life. What an infinity of weal and woe is bound up in the history of that vast aggregate of human beings. But this, all this, is of less consequence to you than that one life on which you are entering. For in the history of our world, in the convulsions of nations, in the revolutions of empires, in the stream of universal history, yea, in the chronicles of all other worlds than your own, there is less to affect your happiness, than in that one life which is before you. You are in life; you cannot go back; you must go on. Whether you shall exist or not, is not left to your option; it is a question settled; you are in being, never, never, to go out of it. What you have to determine is, (and oh! what is involved in the determination!) how existence shall be spent by you, and whether it shall be to you an infinite and eternal blessing, or an infinite and eternal curse. In view of such a career, let me with an importunity which words are far too feeble to express, beseech you to take up the language of the passage at the head of this chapter, as the rule of your conduct: " In all thy ways acknowledge him, and he shall direct thy paths."

CHAPTER III.

And Elijah came unto all the people, and said, How long halt ye between two opinions? If the Lord be God, follow him : but if Baal, then follow him. 1 Kings xix, 21.

THE scene to which this passage of the Jewish narrative refers, is one of the most sublime and important to be found in the whole range of history, being no less than the great trial between true and false religion in answer to the challenge of Elijah, which terminated so gloriously in the complete triumph of the former. A strange and almost incurable propensity to idolatry had ever been evinced by the Israelitish race, obviously springing from that depravity of their nature which made them long for deities congenial to their own corrupted taste. The spirituality and purity of the true God offended them. They could not be content with a religion of which faith was the great principle of action ; but coveted objects of worship which could be presented to the senses, and which would be tolerant of their vices. Among the idol gods of antiquity, Baal sustained a distinguished place. Such is the power of example, especially when it falls in with our corrupt inclinations, that the Jews, notwithstanding the revelation they had received from God, and the care he took to preserve them from the abominations of the surrounding nations, often forsook the worship of Jehovah for idols, or attempted to incorporate idolatry with Judaism. The kingdom of the ten tribes was in this respect the most guilty. Ahab, one of the wickedest of their monarchs, had married Jezebel, the daughter of the king of the Zidonians, by whom Baal was worshipped. Through the influence of this wicked woman, the worship of Baal was diffused to an enormous extent in the kingdom of Israel. Against this abomination the prophet Elijah, with the dauntless courage of a reformer, set himself in determined opposition. After reproving the monarch, and rousing against him the malignity of Jezebel, who sought his destruction, he sent a challenge to Ahab, to put the claims of Baal and Jehovah to a fair and decisive test. In an evil hour for the credit of Baal the challenge was accepted : the decision was to be sought by each party preparing a sacrifice, and calling upon their God to answer by fire ; and the scene of contest was Mount Carmel. It was an august and awful spectacle ; the question to be determined being to whom rightly belonged the throne of Deity. There on one side were Baal's priests arranged in troops, to the number of one hundred and fifty, patronised by the monarch and his wife, full of confidence, and flushed with hopes of victory. On the other appeared one man, to the eye of sense solitary, unbefriended, unpatronised, unprotected. But that solitary man was Elijah, the prophet of the Lord of Hosts. Strong in the Lord and in the

power of his might; assured of the triumph that awaited
him, he surveyed calm and undismayed the array
of priests, the frown of Ahab, and the malignant eye
of Jezebel flashing fury and revenge. What dignity
was in his looks, and what majesty in his deportment!
The congregated thousands of Jewish spectators witnessed, in awful silence, the preparations. Heaven,
with serene confidence, and hell, with dread and dismay,
watched a scene, which not only for that occasion, but
for all time, was to decide whether Jehovah or Baal was
the true God. How much was at stake; what interests
were involved; what a question was to be decided! One
can imagine all nature was hushed in dread suspense;
that the waves of the Mediterranean ceased to roll;
that the winds of heaven were still; that the forests
of Carmel were listening. The prophet towards the
close of the day put an end to the suspense. Advancing to the assembled multitude of Israelites, he
said, " How long halt ye between two opinions? If the
Lord be God, follow him; if Baal, then follow him.
Ye are not yet in conviction quite alienated from the
Lord God of your fathers, the God of Abraham, and
Isaac, and Jacob; yet your allegiance is shaken, and
you are divided in opinion and practice between Jehovah
and Baal. Your irresolution is as guilty as your suspense must be painful; and your indecision is as uncomfortable as it is dishonourable and wicked. Ye worship
Baal. I worship God. I am here to prove which has
the rightful claim to your fealty and obedience. Upon
that which I now propose I will rest the issue of the
present contest. Let each party prepare a sacrifice,
and call upon his God; and the God who answers by
fire, let him be considered as the true God." You

know the sequel;* and I drop the narrative, only turning back for one moment to dwell upon the indecision of the people: they halted between two opinions. You wonder at their indecision, and condemn them with language of severest reprobation; and very justly so. But do you not in this also condemn yourself? Are not you undecided in a case which, if not so palpable to the senses, is no less plain to the judgment.

But before I describe the nature, and pronounce the character of your indecision, let me set before you the opposing parties in reference to which it is maintained. On the one hand there is the Lord God of hosts, the Jehovah of the Jews, under the fuller and clearer manifestation of himself as the God and Father of our Lord Jesus Christ, there are his ministers demanding the acknowledgment of his claims, and there is presented his service, the faith, hope, and love of the gospel. On the other side are the Baalim of this age, in all the various forms under which they are the objects of human idolatry. It is true you are not called, invited or disposed, to bow the knee to idols of wood, stone, or metal, either graven or molten, either in the rude images of barbarous worship, or the grotesque and monstrous creations of Hindoo polytheism, or the fascinating forms of classic mythology. These, however, are not the only way in which idolatry may be practised. What,

---

* Infidel wits have flippantly asked, "Where did the people get the water to fill the trenches at the command of the prophet, since the drought had caused all the water of the land to fail?" They forget, as they generally do, when they offer sceptical observations, the one main fact of the case, that the scene of the contest was not very far from the sea shore. [There has also been discovered on the spot assigned as the scene of the miracle a well which never fails. See Professor Stanley's Palestine.]

in fact, have ever been the objects of false worship but the evil qualities and passions of man's fallen nature, visible embodiments of his own lusts and pleasures exalted to the skies, to be there seen invested, as on Olympus of old, with all charms and splendours ; or sent down to the infernals, to receive the stamp of their authority and malignity, so to come from either place with a sanction and a power to make men wicked. Every one has a God, and if man does not love and worship Jehovah, he will make a deity of his own image, and this deity cannot surpass himself. Survey, young men, the idols which you are called upon from many quarters to worship, and between which and the only living and true God, (O unutterable folly and sin !) you are hesitating. Among them, sustaining a high place, is the idol of sensuality, "That reeling goddess with a zoneless waist," decked out with all that can pollute the imagination, inflame the passions, or excite the propensities of a youthful heart. Before this image multitudes of devotees of both sexes bow the knee and offer the most costly sacrifices of property, health, principle, and reputation. Near her is the bewitching and smiling image of worldly pleasure, with the sound of music, the song, and the dance, alluring the giddy and thoughtless to its orgies, and throwing the spell of its fascinations over the imagination of multitudes who go merrily to their ruin. Mammon, the sordid deity of wealth, is there, glittering with gold, and offering riches to his eager followers as the reward of their diligent and faithful adherence. His liturgy is the cry of "money, money, money ;" his sacrifices, notwithstanding his large promises of happiness, are the time, the bodies, the souls, the principles, and the comfort of his worshippers; and his officials are the greedy speculators and commercial adventurers of our country and our age. There is also the Baal of infidel speculation, with false philosophy as his high priest to conduct the ceremonial; by his promises to free the intellect from the shackles of superstition inviting the youthful aspirants after mental liberty to come into his service. Near this is the shrine of human knowledge: evil only when raised into the place of faith, piety, and virtue, but when thus exalted above revelation, a deceiving, corrupting idol; the false Minerva of a Pantheon of Vices. Nor must we leave out the idols of false religion, the chief of which is Popery, the anti-Christ of the Apocalypse, "the Man of Sin," described by the apostle, as "sitting in the temple of God, exalting itself above all that is called God." This idol, taking the name of Christ as its designation, assuming the cross as its symbol, and boasting of an apostle as its first minister; enriched by wealth, venerable for antiquity; dignified by learning; decorated by sculpture, architecture, and painting; and adding the profoundest policy, and most serpentine craft, to all these other dangerous qualities, has fascinated countless millions; and, notwithstanding the monstrous absurdity of its doctrines, the blood-stained page of its history, and its hostility to the liberties of mankind, is now putting forth the most arrogant claims, and making the most audacious attempts for the conquest of our country. Such are the principal idols which oppose themselves to the King, eternal, immortal, invisible, as the claimants of your heart. Such are the objects which have induced an indetermination in your minds whether you shall serve them or your Creator, Preserver, and Benefactor.

By the undecided in religion I do not intend the confirmed infidel, profligate, scoffer; or those who live in total and absolute rejection of religion. These are not undecided; they are in the fullest sense decided; they have made up their minds, though unhappily on the wrong side. They have chosen their god, and are the determined and devoted worshippers of Baal; they have decided against God. They have hardened their hearts, seared their consciences, and perhaps outlived all misgivings upon the subject, except it be an occasional qualm in the season of death or sickness. They congratulate themselves upon their having thrown off all the weaknesses and fears of superstition, and upon their being now enabled to pursue their downward course unchecked by the restraint of conscience, unterrified by the spectres of imagination. Unhappy men, blind, and glorying in their blindness; benumbed in all their moral faculties, and exulting in the dreadful paralysis; with every tie cut that held them to piety and feeling, and accounting it a privilege that they are drifting unobstructed to destruction, determined to be lost, and rejoicing that nothing bars their path to perdition! The undecided man, generally, is the irresolute man, the man thinking of two things, but absolutely choosing, with full and practical purpose, neither, the double-minded man, or, as the word is in the original, the two-souled man, the man who is like a light substance ever floating between two objects, now carried by force of the tide towards one, and then towards the other. This indecision is manifested in many towards religion.

Perhaps the subject of indecision will be better understood if we consider its opposite, and show what is
meant by decision. By decision in religion I do not
mean merely the choice of a creed, or a decision
between conflicting theories of religious opinions.
This is all very well and proper, and to a certain extent
involved in the state of mind which I am recommending. A man ought not to be undecided either in regard
to religious doctrine or ecclesiastical polity. It is
incumbent upon him to make up his mind on the
question at issue between the advocates and opponents
of secular establishments of religion; or between
Unitarian and Trinitarian views of the Scripture; and
so with other theological matters. These things are
important, and his opinions should be formed and fixed
upon the ground of satisfactory evidence; and his
mind being once made up, he should hold fast what
he believes to be truth, and not allow his convictions
to be shaken by any sophistries, and plausibilities
brought against the views he has espoused. Religion,
however, is something more than opinion, than
ecclesiastical relationship, than ceremony; it is not only
light, but life; its seat is not only in the head,
but in the heart; it is a thing of the will, affections, and conscience as well as of the intellect and
memory. It is a deep conviction of guilt in the sight
of God; an humbling sense of the corruption of our
nature; true faith in Christ as the great atonement;
peace through belief in the gospel; supreme gratitude
and love to God; a spiritual and heavenly mind;
and a holy life. It is the mind of Christ; the
image of God; His word laid up in the heart as
the rule of the inward and outward life; a God-

wrought, heaven-descended, eternally-living thing. To be decided, then, is the intelligent, deliberate, voluntary, entire, and habitual, yielding-up of ourselves, through faith in Christ, and by the aid of the Holy Spirit, to God; to enjoy his favour as the chief good, to make his will our fixed supreme rule, and his glory the chief end of our existence. It is making God the supreme object; salvation the supreme business; eternity the supreme aim. .Not talking about it, wishing it, intending it, but conscientiously doing it. Such a man says, "I have made up my mind, I am resolved, I am for God, for Christ, for eternity, my heart is fixed." To be undecided is to be in a state of hesitancy, irresolution, unfixedness. An undecided man is occasionally impressed; at other times in a state of total indifference. His judgment inclines to religion, and sometimes nearly draws round his heart. He goes out half-way to meet it; then turns back again. Now he looks towards true Christians as the happiest people, then he hankers after the company and amusements of the people of the world. He cannot quite give up religion, nor can he fully embrace it. He has occasional impressions and wishes; but no fixed, deliberate choice.

In this hesitating, undecided, irresolute state of mind, very many are to be found. Yes, indecision is fearfully common; perhaps, among those whom I now address, the most common state of mind. Comparatively few are decidedly pious; still fewer, I hope and believe, decidedly infidel or immoral; the bulk are midway between the two, hesitating, halting, turning away from the one, but not turning to the other. How shall we account for this? It is not for the want of adequate information on the nature of the two claimants and the justice of their respective claims. Of this you have all possible and necessary particulars in the Scriptures. You are not left to the dim twilight of nature and the deductions of your own weak and fallible reason. The sun of revelation has risen upon you in full-orbed splendour, and, walking amidst his noon-tide glory, you see on every hand the character and the claims of God. You know not only there is a God, but who and what he is. You are not destitute of natural ability, you are not hindered by Divine sovereignty, there is no invincible power of natural depravity, you cannot plead a want of time, means, and opportunity, you do not justify and perpetuate it on the ground of Scriptural difficulties, nor on the inconsistencies of professors. Sometimes you may feel inclined to plead these things, but the plea is soon given up. No, the causes subsidiary to the power of inward corruption are the following:

Many do not properly consider the necessity of decision, and the sin of hesitation. The subject has never seriously engaged their attention. Then it is high time it should. Begin now; God demands it, reason demands it, the importance of the matter demands it. On what is decision so necessary as on religion? This is the business of the soul, of salvation, of eternity.

Not a few are wanting in moral courage, they know what they ought to be and to do; but they have friends whose frown they dread, or companions from whose laugh they shrink. This is very common: and thus multitudes flee from the frown of man to take shelter under the frown of God, propitiate their friends by the sacrifice of their souls, throw away religion and salvation to escape from a jest, and make themselves the laughing stock of devils, to avoid the ridicule of fools. Young

men, will you be jeered out of heaven and salvation ?
What, be turned from your eagle flight to immortality,
by the ridicule of owls and bats!

In many cases, some one besetting sin keeps from
decision. That one sin exerts an influence over the
whole soul and all its purposes, benumbing its energies,
beclouding its moral vision, bewildering its steps, and
enfeebling its efforts. Such persons could give up all
but that one sin : but that they cannot part from. How
melancholy, how dreadful, to be willing to perish for
that one sin ! Rather than pluck out that right eye, or
cut off that right hand, to suffer the loss of the whole
body! How infinitely better and more noble would it
be, by one mighty struggle, aided by Divine grace, to
burst that chain, and decide for God ! Consider well,
if this is not the cause of indecision in your case, and
if it be, perceive the necessity of your resolutely and
immediately directing your most vigorous efforts to
remove that hindrance. When you have mastered that
mightiest of your spiritual foes, you may then hope that
the greatest obstacle is surmounted : and that the subjugation of your other enemies will be a comparatively
easy conquest. But till that is done, nothing will be
done to purpose; and he that has been halting between
two opinions, and wavering in his practice, will be halting and wavering still.

There are some who, like Felix, have trembled, and
dismissed the subject till a more convenient season.
They give neither a direct negative, nor a direct affirm-
ative, to the solicitations of judgment and conscience ;
but put them aside by saying, " I will think of it when
I have opportunity, I am busy now." Here and there
one and another goes farther still ; they intend, actually

intend, to be decided at some time or other. They forget the uncertainty of life; the frailty of human resolutions: the thousand incidents that are continually rising up to occupy and divert attention; the ever-increasing improbability of coming to a decision if the subject be postponed from the present moment; and above all, the demand of God for immediate decision. Now, is the accepted time: now, is the day of salvation. There is a world of importance in that seemingly insignificant word, Now. Millions have been ruined for both worlds by overlooking the momentous significance of the all-eventful, Now. Rhetoric might be employed; sermons might be preached; volumes might be written; to enforce the import of that monosyllable, Now. Remember, "he that is now good will in all probability be better, he that is now bad will become worse, for there are three things that never stand still, vice, virtue, and time."

Perhaps as a hindrance to decision might be mentioned, mistaken views of what is requisite to come to this state of mind. Two opposite errors are indulged: some persons throwing out of consideration the free agency of man, and others the sovereign grace of God. The former supposing that man can do nothing, attempt nothing, but wait passively for the Spirit of God: the latter, on the contrary, believing that man is and does everything in religion without God, never seek by prayer, nor expect by faith, the aid of the Divine Spirit. Both are wrong, and therefore both fail. In all things, both in nature and in grace, God's doings and man's doings go together. Man works and God works. Man's efforts are not superseded by Divine grace, nor Divine grace superseded by man's efforts. This dualism which

pervades all things, is especially conspicuous in the
Bible, and has its culminating point in the conversion
and sanctification of the human soul, as set forth in
that wonderful passage : " Work out your salvation with
fear and trembling, for it is God that worketh in you to
will and to do of his good pleasure."

Having stated the causes of indecision, I now go on
to consider its characteristics.   Is it not irrational ?
What is reason given us for but to examine all things
that concern us, to weigh evidence, to discriminate
between things that differ, to prove all things, and hold
fast that which is good.   When man uses his faculties
thus, he does what he was designed to do, and answers
the end of his being.   When he does not, but suffers
himself to be swayed and bent different ways, and to
float upon uncertainty, he forfeits the great prerogative
and most distinguished advantage of his reasonable
nature.   The perfection of man is to be like God in his
attributes, and, among others, in some measure in this
glorious one of immutability in that which is good : but
to be irresolute and undecided in this, is to live as much
at random, and without hold, as if the breath of the
Almighty were not in us.   " Indeed, unless reason gives
us a fixedness and constancy of action, it is so far from
being the glory and privilege of our nature, that it is
really its reproach, and makes us lower than the horse
or the mule, which have no understanding : for they,
without that, act always regularly and constantly themselves, under the guidance of instinct, a blind but sure
principle."   There are two things equi-distant from
sound reason : to decide without evidence, and to remain
undecided amidst abundant evidence.   To be undecided

in religion comes under the latter condemnation. The irrationality of indecision is also in proportion to the importance of the matter to be determined. Young men, I appeal to your understanding against this extreme folly. What? Is religion the only matter on which you will not make up your mind? Religion, which all nations have confessed by their rites, ceremonies, and creeds, to be man's supreme interest? Religion, which comes to you in God's name and asserting his claims? Religion, which affects your own well-being for both worlds? Religion, which relates to the soul and her salvation, eternity and its unalterable states? Religion, the highest end of your existence, and the noblest effort of your reason? What, this the matter to be left in a state of unsettledness and hesitancy, when such means and opportunities are furnished for coming to a conclusion? When the Bible, with all its evidences, doctrines, promises, and precepts, is ever in your hand and appealing to your intellect and heart, your will and conscience, and even your imagination? When the pulpit and the press are ever calling your attention to the subject, and aiding your inquiries? Undecided whether you shall be saved or lost for eternity? Whether you will answer or defeat the end of your existence? Whether you will run counter to God's design in bringing you into being, or fall in with his merciful purposes concerning you? Call you this reason? Talk not to me of your rationality; boast not to me of your high intellectuality in pursuing literature, science, or the arts: I say, the man who remains undecided in religion, who has not settled this question (of God, the soul, salvation, and eternity) is, whatever stores of knowledge he may have acquired, or whatever opinion he may have formed of himself, a learned maniac, a philosophical lunatic, a scientific idiot.

I go further, and say that indecision in religion is contemptible. Whatever may constitute the beauty of character, decision is its power. There is something noble and attractive in the spectacle of an individual selecting some one worthy object of pursuit, concentrating upon it the resources and energies of his whole soul; holding it fast with a tenacity of grasp, and following it with a steadiness of pursuit, which the ridicule of some, the frowns of others, and the ignorant surmises of all, cannot relax; clinging the closer to it for opposition, gaining courage from defeat, and patience from delay. Where such decision is displayed in a bad cause, there is something terrifically grand about it. Hence some have fancied that in this way Milton has thrown too much majesty over the character of Satan. In opposition to this, how despicable is indecision. Foster, in his inimitable Essay on " Decision of Character," has set forth this in a very striking manner. " A man without decision of character can never be said to belong to himself; if he dared to say that he did, the puny force of some cause, about as powerful, you would have supposed, as a spider, may make a capture of the hapless boaster the next moment, and triumphantly exhibit the futility of the determinations by which he was to have proved the independence of his understanding and his will. He belongs to whatever can seize him; and innumerable things do actually verify their claims on him, and arrest him as he tries to go along; as twigs and chips floating near the edge of a river are intercepted by every weed, and whirled in every little eddy. Having concluded on a design, he may pledge himself to accomplish it, if the hundred diversities of feeling which may come within the week will let him. As his character precludes all forethought of his conduct, he may sit and wonder what form and direction his views and actions are destined to take to-morrow; as a farmer has often to acknowledge that the next day's proceedings are at the disposal of winds and clouds." True as this is in reference to every thing, it is most true in reference to religion. Never, is indecision so contemptible as in reference to it. In such a career and in reference to such an object, to be the slave of accidents; the poor tame victim of every little incident that can arise; the prey of every insignificant yelping cur that can drive you hither and thither with his biteless bark! O shame, shame upon your understanding, to say nothing of your heart and conscience, when with such a subject as religion to consider and settle, you can allow not merely the most magnificent objects which the world can present, but innumerable contemptible and sinful littlenesses, to shake your resolution, to invalidate your purpose, and to keep you halting between two opinions! It is the last and lowest degree of despicableness for a man thinking about glory, honour, immortality, and eternal life, to allow himself to be brought to a stand, and made to hesitate and halt, by matters of insignificance. What would have been said of the man who in ancient times hesitated whether he should become a competitor for the Olympic crown, or for some paltry office in a Grecian village? Or what judgment should we have formed of Columbus, if, when meditating the discovery of a new world, he hesitated whether to embark on the

Atlantic, or to engage in picking up shells on its shores? But what are these instances of folly and littleness, compared with that of the man who halts between the infinite and eternal blessings of religion, and the pleasures, acquisitions, and possessions of this world?

Indecision in religion is uncomfortable. If reason is given us to decide upon modes of action, and if in the matter of religion, revelation furnishes us with rules of action, it is most natural we should decide, and altogether unnatural we should remain for another hour in a state of wavering and unsettledness. What is natural is easy, graceful, and pleasant; and what is unnatural is always awkward and painful. The natural state for the mind to be in, is first inquiry, and then decision. No mind can be serene and peaceful in a state of suspense and incertitude. May I not appeal to universal experience for proof, that a man who is going alternately backwards and forwards; ever divided in opinion; now determining one way and now another; now fixed in purpose, then unsettled and altering his plan; now resolute, now hesitating; and who has thus found no ground to rest upon, cannot be happy. This is true in reference to everything. A mind thus at odds with itself, even in little things, cannot but be very uneasy; and he therefore who would consult his own comfort, should by much self-discipline endeavour to rid himself of this instability of action, this infirmity of purpose. I would not, young men, inculcate the opposite evil of inconsiderate and reckless conduct; a headlong course of action, begun without examination, and continued without reflection; and which, even when discovered to be wrong, is persevered in without alteration, merely for the sake of perseverance, and of un-

willingness to confess a mistake. This is not rational
decision, but blind impulse and unreflecting obstinacy.
The decision I recommend is a habit of patient investi-
gation, united with a capability of weighing evidence,
and followed by a prompt and resolute determination
to do, and to do immediately and perseveringly, the
thing which ought to be done. Acquire an ability to
say in matters of right, I must, I can, I will. "There
is a wonderful potency in these three monosyllables.
Adopt them as the rule of your conduct. But I am
considering the unhappiness of indecision in regard to
religion. I repeat the assertion made in reference to
other characteristics, the more important the subject is
about which this indecision is maintained, the greater
must of course be the uneasiness which it produces;
and as religion is the most momentous of all subjects,
so the uneasiness resulting from it must be the greatest.
But even here the uneasiness also varies with circumstances. An amiable youth who has not fallen into
vice, and has kept within the boundaries of virtue, but
who yet has not given his heart to God and made
religion his supreme business, cannot have poignant
remorse, as if he had been guilty of profligacy; but
even he is uncomfortable; he knows he is not a christian, in the spiritual sense of the term. His conscience
disturbs him; letters from home make him uneasy;
awakening sermons alarm him; in the company of the
pious he is not at home; his neglected Bible, given him
perhaps by a mother's hand, silently reproaches him.
He is not happy. How can he be in such circumstances? He resolves, breaks his resolution, and adds
to his uneasiness the guilt of broken vows.

This indecision is sometimes attended with serious

aberrations from the path of sanctity and regularity, though not perhaps of morality. In such cases, the mind of a youth whose heart is not hardened, is often in a state of still more painful disquietude and perturbation. It is an impressive truth, that ease of mind, quietness, or rather insensibility of conscience, belongs often rather to the decidedly wicked, than to the undecidedly good; for the former may have hardened and stupified his conscience so far that it lets him alone; but he who sins and repents, and then sins again, in a continued circle, is sure to be followed in his miserable round with the reproaches of his memory and the lashes of his conscience. " His good fits are but the short intervals of his madness, which serve to let the madman into a knowledge of his own disease; whereas it would in some kinds of lunacy be much more for his satisfaction and content if he were mad always." O the misery of that man whose life is spent between sinning and repenting; between the promptings of conviction and the impulses of inclination; between the difficulty of forming resolutions, and the guilty consciousness of breaking them; between hopes ever frustrated by disappointment, and fears ever realised by experience. Indecision is its own punishment.

This indecision is in the highest degree sinful. You can see this clearly and impressively, with regard to the Israelites whom the prophet addressed on Mount Carmel. What a crime to hesitate for a moment between Baal and Jehovah, to be undetermined whether to serve that dumb idol, or the living and true God. You wonder at their stupidity; you are incensed at their impiety. You take sides instantly with the prophet against the people. His zeal is not too burning; his indignation is not too

severe; his irony is not too cutting for the occasion.
How horror-struck you would be to witness such sense-
less impiety. But how much less wicked is your conduct, though of course far less gross and revolting, in
hesitating whether you shall serve God or any of those
idols of the mind, worldly pleasure, infidelity, covetousness, or sensuality? The idols of the heathen are, as I
have said, but the vices of the human heart personified,
embodied, and made perceptible to the senses. Human
lusts and passions are the archetypes of them all; the
one is the abstract, the other the concrete, form of the
idol; and how much less guilty is it to·bend the knee to
an idol, than to bow the heart to a vice? Dwell upon
God's divine glory, his infinite majesty, his ineffable
excellence, his boundless, inconceivable beauty, and
every attribute of his glorious nature. " To Him all
angels cry aloud : the heavens and all the powers therein.
To Him cherubim and seraphim continually do cry,
Holy, Holy, Holy, Lord God Almighty ! The glorious
company of the apostles praise Him. The goodly fellowship of the prophets praise Him. The noble army
of martyrs praise Him. The holy church throughout
the world doth acknowledge Him," and there are you,
a poor frail child of man, halting between two opinions,
and hesitating whether you shall serve Him or Baal. O
what an ineffable insult to God! Every Christian on earth
cries out Shame ! Every angel in glory cries Shame !
Every page of scripture cries Shame ! While God himself, indignantly and awfully, completes the cry of reprobation, and says, "Be astonished, O heavens, at this
and be ye horribly afraid." Consider then, the crime
against God which you are guilty of while undecided.
He desires and demands immediate surrender to his

claims. Yield yourselves unto God, at once, is his imperative injunction. To hesitate whether you shall serve him, is to be undetermined whether you shall be the friend or foe of God, the loyal subject of his government, or a traitor to his throne : whether you shall love or hate him, reverence or despise him, dishonour or glorify him. Every attribute of his nature makes indecision sinful, every gift of his hand aggravates the sin, every injunction of his word increases the aggravation.

Indecision is dangerous. The Israelites found it so : after hesitating and halting between two opinions, whatever slight transient impression was produced by the scenes of Mount Carmel, they went over to the wrong side, bowed the knee to Baal, and, as the punishment for their sin, were carried into captivity. Indecision on religion is a state of mind fraught with most imminent peril; for when long persisted in, it generally ends in decision upon the wrong side. It gives time for the wicked and deceitful heart to collect and concentrate all its forces of evil, emboldens evil companions to ply with redoubled energy their temptations, encourages Satan to multiply his machinations, and to complete all, provokes God to say, " My spirit shall not always strive with man. He is tied to his idols, let him alone. Woe be unto him when I depart from him." Every hour's delay increases the peril, and exposes you to the danger of being left by God. But there is danger in another view of the case : you are entering life, and are exposed to all the hazards enumerated in the last chapter ; and is indecision, I would ask, a state of mind in which to encounter the dread array? Is it in this halting and unsettled condition that you would meet the perils of your path? Why, it is like a soldier going into battle without having settled which army he shall side with, and which general he shall fight for. Even the decided youth, who has fully made up his mind on the great subject; who has put on the whole armour of God, and is defended at all points with right principles, good resolutions, pious habits, and well-formed character, even he finds it difficult sometimes to stand his ground against the mighty foes of truth, piety, and virtue. Even he who, grasping the sword of the Spirit, and opposing the shield of faith to the darts of his enemies, exclaims, with heroic voice, "I am for God and religion," and who by his very decision and firmness drives back the assailants of his steadfastness, even he is often sorely tried. How then can the irresolute, the halting, the vacillating, stand? What a mark is he for every foe! What a butt for every arrow! His indecision invites assault, and prepares him to become an easy prey to whomsoever will aim to capture him.

But this is not all. There is a danger of dying in this undecided state. Life is uncertain. Your breath is in your nostrils. A fever, an inflammation, an accident, may come upon you any day, and leave no time for reflection, no opportunity for decision. Death often springs upon his prey like a tiger from the jungle upon the unwary traveller. Millions are surprised by the last enemy, in an undecided state. They are shot through the heart, with the question upon their lips, "Shall I serve God or Baal?" and are hurried into the presence of the Eternal Judge himself to have it answered there. Dreadful, most dreadful! To meet God, and in and by his presence to have a full exposure

of the guilt and folly of hesitating between his service
and that of sin! What a question to come from the
God of Glory to the poor, naked, trembling, and con-
founded soul, "Are God and Baal so nearly alike, that
you should have halted between two opinions, which
you would serve?" Mark this, in God's view there is
no such thing in reality as indecision, this word is used
not to express things as they are, but as they appear.
In fact there are, in point of religion, but two classes
of men, the converted and unconverted. The undecided
man belongs to the latter class no less than the infidel
and the profligate; only he may not have gone to such
an extent of actual sin, and may feel more the unhappiness of his situation, and the desirableness of changing
it. But the choice of God's service has not been made,
and he will be dealt with as belonging to the class
of those who are against him. Indecision is utterly
inconsistent with the character of the godly, the terms
of salvation, and the hope of eternal happiness! God
will not allow of neutrality, and considers every man
who is not decided for him as decided against him, and
will treat him as such. No matter that such a man
feels the weight of sin's fetters, and the galling burden
of its yoke: no matter that he sometimes feels a desire to
escape from its bondage, and makes some feeble and
occasional efforts to effect his emancipation, nothing
will be of avail to his salvation, but an entire surrender
of the heart to God, and a complete and voluntary
yielding-up himself to his service, as the supreme
business of life. There is no promise in all God's word
to the unstable and wavering, no hope held out of his
safety, no salvo provided for his conscience, no middle

condition in which he can take his lot between the decidedly good and the decidedly bad.

And now what remains but that I call upon you to renounce your indecision, and in the language of intelligent, deliberate, and settled purpose, to say with Joshua: "Let others do what they will, as for me I will serve the Lord." Reject Baal, and surrender to God, without compromise and without delay. You cannot have two masters. You cannot have two Gods. You cannot harmonise sin and righteousness, nor reconcile a life of piety and a life of worldliness. You must be one thing or the other. Religion, if not the first and great thing with you, is nothing. To be undecided in such a business is the most irrational state of mind in the whole range of mental conditions. Look inward upon your own immaterial, immortal, wonderful spirit, craving after appropriate and adequate sources and means of happiness: the question is, whether you shall satisfy or mock its insatiable cravings. Look up at the eternal God, your Creator, Preserver, and Benefactor, and the everlasting Paradise of ineffable delights he has prepared for them that love him: the question is, whether you will submit to his claims, enjoy his favour, bear his image, inhabit his high and holy place; or wither away for ever under banishment from his presence, and the effect of his curse. Look down into that abyss of woe which divine justice has made ready for those who serve not God: the question is, whether you will escape that awful retribution upon sin and unbelief, or endure its intolerable burden for ever and ever. Look onward to the ever-rolling ages of eternity; that interminable existence whose perspective no eye but

the Omniscient One can reach : the question is whether
that endless being shall to you be an ocean of bliss or a
gulf of torment and despair.   Undecided on such questions?   If such conduct is known in heaven, how must
angels wonder at the folly of mortals hesitating whether
they will inherit their bliss : if it be known in the abode
of apostate spirits, how must those once dignified but
now degraded beings marvel with uttermost astonishment, that sinful men in danger of their misery should
hesitate about escaping from it.   Infidels, scoffers, and
men of profane minds, may scoff at these appeals to the
awful realities of eternity : just as many a felon, who
has expired at the drop, once made himself merry and
seasoned his mirth with vulgar jokes about the gallows.
Miserable wretch, he found at last that execution was a
dreadful reality, with which the most hardened ruffian
could no longer trifle.   I believe, and therefore speak,
and by arguments no less weighty than these drawn
from eternal realities, I conjure you to remain no longer
undecided.   But clearly understand and bear in recollection what it is I require.   It is not, as I have said,
merely the adoption of any particular set of religious
opinions ; nor merely joining any particular body
of professing Christians ; but repentance towards God,
faith in our Lord Jesus Christ, and a character formed,
and a life regulated, by the Word of God.   Every
known sin must be abandoned, and every Christian
virtue practised.   Evil companions must be forsaken,
and your associates be chosen from the godly and
virtuous.

If there be loftiness and nobleness in decision of
character, it is most lofty, most noble, when shown

with regard to religion. You need not go for instances of this, and for the admiration which they are calculated to afford, to such examples as Foster brings before you in his inimitable essay, to examples selected from history, to Marius sitting amidst the ruins of Carthage, to Pizarro, to Richard III, to Cromwell: nor even to those drawn from the records of Scripture, to Daniel, and to Shadrach, Meshach, and Abednego: or to those supplied by Christian martyrology, to John Huss and Jerome of Prague: nor to those borrowed from the annals of philanthropy, to Howard, to Wilberforce, and Mrs Fry; these are all grand, impressive, beautiful, but they are not the only ones that may be cited; nor with whatever radiance (whether lurid or serene) they may be surrounded or emblazoned, are they those which are the most appropriate for you to contemplate, or which perhaps will have the greatest weight with you. Look at that manly, pious young man, who has left the shelter and protecting wing of his father's house and home, and is now placed in a Manchester warehouse, and surrounded by fifty or a hundred fellow-shopmen, among whom he finds not one to countenance him in the maintenance of his religious profession, and the greater part of whom select him, on account of his religion, as the object of their pity, their scorn, their hatred, or their contempt. Among them are infidels, who ply him with flippant and specious cavils against the Bible; pleasure-takers, who use every effort to engage him in their Sunday parties, and their polluting amusements; men of light morality, who assail his integrity; a few lovers of science and general knowledge, who endeavour to allure him from

religion to philosophy. How fearful is his situation,
and how perilous! Usually it would be better to leave
it, for how few can hold fast their integrity in such a
situation! But there he, this decided, this inflexible,
this noble-minded youth, stands firm, unyielding,
decided. He is neither ashamed nor afraid: he neither
denies nor conceals his principles. At proper times,
before some of these laughers, he bends his knees and
prays; in presence of that jeering set, he opens his
Bible and reads; from that pleasure-taking company
he breaks off, amidst their scoffs, to go to the house
of God. He bears the peltings of their pitiless storm
of ridicule or rage, unruffled in temper, unmoved in
principle, and only casts upon his persecutors a look
of gentle pity, or utters a mild word of expostulation,
or silently presents the prayer, "Father, forgive them,
for they know not what they do." He keeps, by his
firmness, the whole pack at bay. A secret admiration
is bestowed upon him by others, while even they who
hate him most are often astonished at his inflexible
resolution, and it may be that one and another at
length say to him, "We must go with you, for we see
God is with you." Talk of decision of character!
There it is in all its force, beauty, and utility. I know
of no case in God's world in which it is exemplified
with more power than in that. It is a rich manifestation of divine grace, by which alone it is maintained.
It is a sight on which angels might look down with
delight, and in respect to which God is ever saying,
"Well done, good and faithful servant." It is not
martyrdom literally, but it is so in spirit; and such a
youth ranks with confessors, who bear witness for Christ

amidst "cruel mockings." In persecuting times that noble youth would have died for religion upon the scaffold or at the stake. Young men, behold your pattern. This is the decision for which I call upon you: and I call upon you to copy it without procrastination. You ought not to dare to delay any more than to deny. Every moment's hesitation is a moment of rebellion. You have no more right to halt than you have to refuse. God's claim is upon you now, and your next business after reading this chapter, is to rise and yield yourselves to God. When Pyrrhus attempted to procrastinate, the Roman ambassador with whom he was treating, drew a circle round him on the earth with his cane, and, in the name of the Senate, demanded an answer before he stepped across the line. I do the same: the place in which you read this chapter is a circle around you, and before you lay down the volume, I demand, in the name of God, an answer, whether you will serve him or Baal.

Put me not off with the excuse that it is an important matter and requires deliberation. It is important, most momentous, and on that account requires instant decision; and as to deliberation, how much do you require? A year? A month? A week? What! to determine whether you shall serve God or Baal? You have hesitated too long, and another moment's deliberation is too much. Excuse not procrastination by the allegation that it is God's work to change the heart. It is, but it is yours also. The Spirit of God is striving with you while you read this. All the influences necessary for salvation are this moment submitted to the appropriation of your faith. Turn not away with the purpose and the promise of coming to a decision at some future time. Future time! Alas! there may be no future for you. Upon the present hour may be suspended your eternal destiny. The instant of your reading this may be the determining point, for to-morrow you may die, or be given up by God to hardness of heart. I press you, therefore, for immediate decision.

Oh! what a scene is now before you! How solemn and how momentous! In what transactions, amidst what spectators, with what results and consequences have you been engaged while perusing this chapter! Three worlds, heaven, earth, and hell, are at this moment feeling an interest in you, as if your eternal destiny hung upon the appeal now made to you. Amidst the prayers of anxious parents; amidst the labours of earnest ministers; amidst the sympathies and solicitudes of the Church of Christ; and rising still higher, amidst the eager hopes of angels, waiting to minister to your salvation, and the jealous fears and dread of demons no less eager for your destruction; and, above all, under the watchful notice of the glorious Redeemer waiting to receive you among his disciples; you have been urged to decide for God and religion, against any and every thing that can be put in opposition. What shall be your decision? It is recorded of an American preacher that while he was once urging similar claims on his audience, and demanding who would be decided, he paused; a solemn silence ensued, which was at length broken by an individual who had been inclined to infidelity, rising, and with strong emotion simply saying, I will. The point was that hour decided. From that moment he became a determined, consistent Christian.

Young men, who will imitate this example, and say in the hearing of Him to whom the audible voice is unnecessary, " I will ?" That monosyllable, uttered in sincerity, will go up to heaven and engage it in a chorus of praise over your decision, will go down to the bottomless pit and exasperate the host of darkness with the shame and the rage of a new defeat, and go through eternity with you as the source of infinite delight. Let this then be your resolution, " I will."

CHAPTER IV.

Then Jesus beholding him loved him. MARK x, 21.

THE narrative of which this forms a part, is thus given: "And when he was gone forth into the way, there came one running and kneeled to him, and asked him, Good Master, what shall I do that I may inherit eternal life? And Jesus said unto him, Why callest thou me good? There is none good but one, that is God. Thou knowest the commandments, Do not commit adultery, Do not kill, Do not steal, Do not bear false witness, Defraud not, Honour thy father and mother. And he answered and said unto him, Master, all these have I observed from my youth. Then Jesus beholding him loved him, and said unto him, One thing thou lackest; go thy way, sell whatsoever thou hast, and give to the poor, and thou shalt have treasure in heaven; and come, take up thy cross, and follow me. And he was sad at that saying, and went away grieved; for he had great possessions."

The character of Christ, as delineated by the pen of the evangelists, is one of the brightest glories of revelation, and one of the many internal evidences of its divine origin. Even the infidel Rousseau confessed, that if the gospel were a fable, he that invented the character of the Saviour, must himself be greater than the hero of his tale.   What a union, without confusion, of the human and the divine; what an exhibition of the awful and the amiable, of the stern and the tender; at one time denouncing with terrific vengeance the crimes of the Jews; at another, weeping over the approaching fulfilment of his own predictions; now casting out demons from the possessed, then taking little children in his arms; and just after, looking with deep and tender interest on a youth, amiable, but not decided to follow him.   All this, and infinitely more than this, is exhibited in the character of our Lord.   Young men, study this sublime, beautiful, and superhuman character, and say, if both this, and the book which contains it, must not be of God.   Could such a pattern of matchless truth, purity, and benevolence, be the offspring of delusion, falsehood, and depravity, which it must have been, if it be the production of imposture?   To what page of uninspired history can infidelity direct you for anything which even remotely resembles it in greatness, goodness, and unearthliness?

We now advert to a single incident in the life of Christ, one of great instructiveness and interest to you.   By consulting the chapter from which the fact is taken, you will find that a youth of rank, fortune, and office, came to Jesus with deep solicitude to know what he must do to obtain eternal life.   The whole narrative shows that he was a moral and amiable young man, and also concerned about religion, but depending upon the merits of his own good doings for acceptance with God; and at the same time loving his wealth far more than was consistent with his high pretensions of love to his

neighbour, and concern about eternity. Believing that
Christ was a teacher sent from God, he wished to know
from him whether there was anything more which he
could do to strengthen the basis of his hopes, and to
confirm his assurance of salvation. It is important to
remark, and recollect, that in replying to him our Lord
deals with him on his own grounds. Christ, in what
he said, neither disclaimed his own divinity, nor
preached to him the doctrine of justification by works;
but merely asked him how, with his views of the person
he then spoke to, he could address him, and flatter him
with a title which he knew in its absolute meaning
belonged only to God. So also in telling him that if he
kept the commandments with unsinning perfection from
the beginning to the end of life, he would on the ground
of his own obedience be justified, his divine Teacher
did not mean to say that such a thing as unsinning
obedience would be found in him or any one else; but
that if it really could be found, it would justify the man
who had it. Our Lord soon showed to him, by the test
he applied to his judgment and conscience, that he was
not so holy as he thought he was; for upon being commanded to go and sell his possessions and give to his
neighbours, which, as he regarded Christ as a divine
teacher sent from God, he ought to have done, he
"went away sorrowful, for he had great possessions."
Thus proving that with all his professions of having
kept the law, he loved his money more than he loved
God, or his neighbour, and that the world was even
then his idol. We are not to suppose from this injunction of our Lord, that no one can be a Christian who
does not dispose of the whole of his property in alms-

deeds. Christ laid down a general principle, that supreme love of the world and earnestness after salvation are incompatible with each other: and gave it such a special application and extent in this case as its peculiarity required.

Still, we are told that, " when Jesus looked upon him he loved him." Love is a word of wide and comprehensive meaning; in some places signifying approval of, and complacency in, character; in others, meaning nothing more than a general interest and good will. There are sometimes appearances in the character and conduct of those with whom we have to do, that deeply interest us; yet all the while, there is much in them that we condemn. This was the case before us. The humanity of Christ partook of the sinless instincts and properties of our own. His bosom was susceptible of the emotions of friendship, and of all that is honourable and graceful in our nature. On this occasion there was something in the circumstances, character, and manners of this young man, which attracted the heart of Jesus to him; his youthful appearance was prepossessing; his manners pleasing; his address courteous; his language respectful; his disposition so deferential .and docile, that Jesus beholding him, loved him. He noticed, recognised, and approved all the good qualities he possessed, he was interested in his youthful age, combined as it was with some concern for religion; he cherished benevolent wishes for his welfare, and a friendly willingness to do him good. This was all; his regard for what was holy and just and good, prevented him from going farther. His inward emotions all the while amounted to lamentation, that so much seeming excellence should be tainted with that which rendered it of no worth in the sight of God, and of no avail to the young man's salvation.

You see what was the defect in this man, he possessed not the faith which overcomes the world. He wished to unite two things utterly irreconcileable, the love of God and the love of the world. He wanted to serve two masters, God and Mammon. It was not vice and profligacy that kept him from true religion here, and from heaven hereafter; it was the more decent and reputable sin of supreme attachment to things seen and temporal. He could give up many sins, but he could not give up his besetting sin, supreme regard to wealth. He could do many things, but he could not give up all to follow Christ. He could give up vice, but he could not deny himself and take up his cross. He had many good qualities, but he lacked that one thing which alone could give holiness to them all. If vice has slain its thousands, worldliness has slain its tens of thousands. Of all the false gods mentioned in the last chapter, the shrine of Mammon is most resorted to: it is from that temple the broadest and most beaten path to perdition will be found. In the crowd which press along that path, are included, not only the knaves, the cheats, and men of dishonourable character of every kind, but men who follow whatsoever things are just, and honest, and true, and even lovely, and of good report; who yet withal rise to no higher grade of moral excellence, and no more exalted character, than to be just and honourable worshippers of this sordid deity. Yes, even Mammon can boast of devotees who, though they do not act from a principle of religion, yet scorn all that is mean, dishonourable and unjust. Consider the words of an inspired apostle, " If any man love the world, the love of the Father is not in him;" and begin life remembering that in the broad road that leadeth to destruction there is a path for the lovers of the world, as well as for the lovers of vice.

Before I go on to take up and consider the subject of this chapter, there are a few remarks which may with propriety be made upon the case of this young man viewed in connection with our Lord's feelings towards him. How much concern may in some cases be felt about religion without the subject of that solicitude being truly religious! Here was some anxiety, earnestness, and inquiry, yet not true, intelligent, and scriptural religion, a character which is by no means uncommon. We sometimes see a tree in spring one mass of blossom, beautiful to the eye, and full of promise to its owner; and yet we afterwards see all that blossom drop without setting, and the tree stand in autumn a collection of branches and leaves without a single fruit. Alas! alas! how many young persons resemble such trees, and excite the hopes of parents, ministers, and others, by incipient appearances of religion, only to disappoint them! Do not add to the number of these promising but deceptive appearances, and the bitter disappointments which they inflict.

How much good and evil may be mixed up in the same character; requiring the most careful discrimination and the most impartial exercise of judgment! Here were lovely traits, corrupted and spoiled by others of an opposite quality. In heaven and hell there are no mixed characters, the former being inhabited by the purely good, and the latter by the entirely bad. No speck is on the bright and burnished surface of the former; not a spot of brightness relieves the black ground of the latter. On earth, however, we frequently meet with a blending of apparently good and really bad qualities. The fall of Adam, though it struck out from the heart all that is holy towards God, did not extinguish all that is amiable towards man. Lapsed humanity is not, indeed, as angelical as its ignorant or false flatterers would represent; but neither is it always as unlovely, diabolical, or brutal, as its injudicious detractors assert. If no plant of paradise grows in man's heart till planted there by grace, there are wild flowers of some beauty and pleasant odour which relieve the dreariness of the wilderness " and waste their fragrance on the desert air." Where this mixture exists, let us recognise it, and neither allow the good to reconcile us to the evil, nor the evil to prejudice us against the good. It is very disingenuous to talk in superlatives, as though every man who is a sinner was a perfect villain.

The possession of some good qualities is no compensation for the want of others; nor any excuse whatever for the possession of bad ones. Nothing is more common than for men to try to set up a sort of compromise between religion and morality. Some imagine that attention to the duties of the latter will release them from obligations to the former, and the performance of their duty to man serve instead of what they owe to God; while others seem to think the performance of religious duties will exonerate them from their obligations to truth, justice, and purity. So also in these separate departments, attention to one branch of duty, especially if rather strict and rigid, is thought to be a compensation and atonement for the omission or violation of others. It will not do. It is a deceptive and destructive attempt. The word of God forbids this wicked compromise, and requires absolute perfection, in the highest degree in every particular, both in reference to religion and morality. It is one of the chief glories of the Bible, that it prescribes, requires, and aids the acquisition of a complete character; a character in which piety towards God and morality towards man, the elements of heavenly and earthly excellence, all that is true, and beautiful, and good, harmoniously combine. Our Lord would not accept this young man's morality in excuse for his want of true piety; nor his concern about the future world as an apology for his love to the present one.

We should not fail to own and even love general excellence wherever we find it, though it may not be in association with sanctifying grace. It is good in itself and useful to others, though it will not lead on its possessor to heaven. An amiable youth, who is his parents' comfort so far as general excellence is concerned, even though he may not be a partaker of true conversion to God, is not to be placed upon a level with a profligate prodigal. We must not say of any man, I hate him utterly, and abhor him in all respects, because he has not true holiness. Thus did not Christ act toward this young ruler. He knew he was not holy, yet, behold how he loved him.

Whatever general excellence we may see in those with whom we have to do, and however we may admire and commend it, we should still point out their defects, and endeavour to lead them on to seek the supply of them. This especially applies to a want of religion associated with the possession of many excellences. We are all too apt to be thrown off our guard here, and to allow ourselves to think there must be piety where there is so much besides that is lovely : or if not, that it could add but little to such excellence. It is to be recollected, however, that as long as these general good qualities are associated with an unrenewed and unsanc- tified nature, they are utterly destitute of that prin- ciple which only can make them truly virtuous, which alone can render them lovely in the sight of God, and which alone can connect them with salvation. No false tenderness to the feelings of such persons, no disposition to flatter them, no regard to the opinions of others, should lead us to conceal from them that we know they are destitute of what it is necessary they should possess in order to their salvation. How faithfully did our Lord say " One thing thou lackest yet." Our judg- ments in matters of morality and religion should be formed by, and follow, that of God. The Bible is the standard, and God the judge, of true excellence. The conventional opinions of men on these subjects are often very different from those of God. He looks at the heart, while man oftentimes looks no further than the outward bearing. He looks at the state of the heart towards himself: man too generally looks no further than the conduct towards society. In reference to many a lovely specimen of general excellence, man would ask the question, " What can be wanting here ?" God replies, " Religion." Man asks further, " What could religion add to this ?" God answers, " The first of all duties and excellences, love to Me." Man still questions, " Would any one consign this to destruc- tion ?" God replies, " Is this what I demand for salvation ; or is it that which constitutes meetness for heaven ?"

It is important to remark the interest our divine Lord takes in the welfare of the young, and especially of young men. Nothing like what is said of Christ's disposition towards this young man is said of any other unconverted person in all the Word of God. No other individual seems in the same way to have called forth the sensibilities of our Lord. That it was an exercise of his regard towards a particular individual is admitted; but it may well be imagined it was intended to be a type of his interest in a class, and that class is yours. Jesus looks from his throne of glory upon you, addresses himself to you, is waiting for you, will receive you, and that with special complacency. Go to the book of Proverbs, and see how conspicuous a place you sustain in the attention of the writer.

But I go on now to discuss more particularly the subject of amiability combined with defects of character. By amiability we mean what in common discourse we call good nature, a kindliness of disposition, a willingness to oblige, sometimes united with a gentleness of manner, and a lovely frankness of conduct: that, in fact, which constitutes general loveliness of character. Now this, so beautiful in itself, may be, and often is, found in a character which is very defective in reference to other important and necessary things.

I. There are several general views that may be taken of this defectiveness, which I will lay before you, before I come to that special case which is brought under review in the case of the young man in the gospel.

Many persons confound amiability with an easy nature. The two are very different : the former, as distinguished from the latter, means a kindliness of nature, and a disposition to accommodate and oblige, but under the regulation of a sound judgment. Real amiability is always watchful against the undue influence of others, and can resolutely refuse to comply with a request for any thing improper in itself, however importunately solicited. It may, and often does, most firmly and even sternly say, " No." But an easy nature rarely can, or does. It has not the power to resist entreaty, but allows itself to be persuaded by almost every body, and to almost every thing. Such a disposition resembles an osier, which any one that pleases can bend in any direction, and which in fact bends of itself before the gentlest breeze. True amiability has eyes to see and examine, as well as ears to hear; an easy nature is quick of hearing, but stone-blind: amiability is self-moved and self-governed; an easy nature is a mere automaton, which others move and guide without any resistance of its own: amiability is a kind heart in association with a clear head; an easy nature is all heart, but no head. Such an easy disposition is a very dangerous one, and has led multitudes to their ruin. Never surrender yourselves thus, even to your friends; for if you do, you may soon find yourselves in the hands of your enemies. He is not your friend who desires to be your master. Be a slave to no man. Never give away your judgment : and instantly dismiss from your society the individual whom you suspect of imposing on good nature, and who takes you for a poor dupe that has neither opinion nor will of his own, but can be led to do anything by entreaty and coaxing. Acquire strength as well as beauty of character. Learn to say, " No," as well as " Yes," and how to abide by it.

Sometimes we see much amiability associated with

much ignorance. There is much that is really very kind and obliging; much to conciliate affection, but very little to command respect. Hence the excellence that is in the character does not do the good it might, for want of talent or acquirement to give it weight. It is of such a person said with a sneer, " Very good, but very weak." I say, therefore, do not be an amiable fool, an obliging ignoramus, a mere kind simpleton; but cultivate your intellect, and let knowledge recommend virtue. In this respect, as well as in others, do not let "your good be evil spoken of."

It has not unfrequently occurred that amiability has unhappily been associated with infidelity and immorality. Perhaps more frequently with the latter than with the former. Speculative infidelity has a tendency to make men cold, hard, gloomy: it freezes the genial current of the soul, withers and starves benevolence, and petrifies the heart into selfishness. But dissipation and vice are often frank and vivacious; full of mirth and merriment. Modern refinement in demoralization has selected a term of some attraction to describe a profligate, and he is said to be "gay." Colonel Gardiner, before his conversion, was called "The Happy Rake." Of all the characters on earth that are dangerous to you, and should be shunned by you, the amiable profligate is the one most to be dreaded. The man of kind disposition, insinuating address, polished manners, sparkling wit, and keen humour, but of bad principles or bad conduct, is the most seductive agent of the Wicked One for the ruin of youth. He has the fascination of the eye of the basilisk; he has the glossy and beautifully variegated skin of the serpent, concealing the fang and the venom; he is the golden chalice

that contains the poisonous draught; or, to reach the
climax, he is Satan transformed, if not into an angel
of light, into a personification of polished and attractive
vice. Of such men beware.

II. I now more particularly refer to amiability
without religion. I remark, that young men may, and
often do, possess many qualities which are lovely and
interesting, while at the same time they are destitute
of true piety. There may be a delicate sensibility, the
heart may be susceptible, the imagination glowing, and
the feelings alive to whatever is tender, pathetic, or
heroic, and yet all the while there may be no sense
of sin, no gratitude to Christ, no love of God, no delight
in holiness, no aspirations after heaven. There may be
natural genius; acquired knowledge; large information;
their possessor may be able to argue logically, to discourse with ready conversational power, to the delight
of friends and the admiration of strangers, and yet one
thing may be lacking, for there may be no knowledge
of God or of eternal life; and over that mind which is
so bright and so brilliant as regards the present world,
may brood the darkness which involves it in the shadow
of death. You will sometimes see a young man so eager
in the pursuit of knowledge as to trim his lamp at
midnight, and anticipate the dawn by his studies, till
his eye waxes dim, his cheek grows pale, and the seeds
of disease begin to spring up in his constitution enfeebled
by mental application; and yet he cares nothing for the
mysteries of the kingdom of heaven: there is one book
he studies not, and that the best of books: and one
science he cares not to know, and that the science
of salvation. To such it was well said, "By what dexte-
rity of irreligious caution did you precisely avoid every

track where the idea of God would meet you, or elude
that idea when it came? What must sound reason
think of that mind which amidst millions of thoughts
has wandered to all things under the sun, to all the
permanent or vanishing appearances of creation, but
never fixed its thoughts on the supreme reality, and
never approached, like Moses, to see that great sight."
There may be docility and meekness, gentleness of disposition, and the utmost general loveliness of character,
and yet none of the humility of genuine religion, none
of the true poverty of spirit, none of the meekness and
gentleness of Christ, none of the mind that was in
Jesus. There may be great sobriety of mind; all the
passions may be under the restraints of reason; all the
propensities may be ruled by the most entire self-
government; yet there may not be that holy sober-
mindedness, which is the subject of the apostle's
exhortation, and which consists in keeping the great
end of life in view, and adopting such principles as are
connected with it. There may be in young people the
assiduities of an active benevolence, a willing co-opera-
tion in schemes of usefulness for the benefit of the
nation or the world, or of some particular class
of objects of human compassion; much labour may
be bestowed, much self-denial practised; and yet all
this while there may be no working out their own
salvation with fear and trembling. There may be
honesty and trustworthiness as a servant, exemplary
diligence and perseverance, and yet there may be no
giving diligence to the great work of pleasing God, and
no exercise of solicitude to serve the Lord Jesus Christ.
Yea, as in the case of the young man mentioned in
the text, there may be some concern about religion, a

regular attendance on the ordinances of the sanctuary; some occasional impressions and convictions; some transient concern about eternity; and yet there may be no entire giving up sin and the world; no complete surrender of the soul to Christ; no regeneration of heart; no faith in Christ; no holiness. The youth may know the truth and not love it: he may hear the gospel and not believe it: he may contemplate the scheme of redemption, and not avail himself of it; he may know something of the doctrine of the cross, and yet not appropriate it for the salvation of his soul: and he may speculate about the glory of the Saviour, and the suitableness of his character and work, and yet not embrace the Saviour and his righteousness as the ground of his everlasting hope. It is most impressive and affecting to consider to what a list of general excellences, to what an assemblage of virtues, in the same character, the sad declaration must be sometimes added, " Yet there is one thing lacking."   O ! to look successively upon the varied forms of unsanctified moral beauty, as they pass before the searching eye of christian scrutiny, and to have to say to each as it goes by, " Yet lackest thou the one thing needful !"

Any character, however otherwise excellent, if deficient of true religion, is, viewing its possessor as an immortal creature, essentially and ruinously defective. And in what other light than an immortal creature can he be viewed, if we really include his whole being and his highest relation ? I will suppose, then, the possession of many things, yea, I will carry the idea as far as it can be carried, and will suppose the possession of everything, except this one thing, true religion, and in the lack of that, there is a chasm which all the rest cannot fill up, a deficiency they cannot supply. To say of a human being, a rational, sinful, and immortal creature, he has everything but religion, is as if we should say of a citizen, he has everything but patriotism; of a child, he has everything but filial piety; of a husband, he has everything but conjugal affection. It is just that want for which no assemblage of acquirements and other excellences can be the smallest substitute or compensation. Collect a garland of beautiful flowers, and wreathe them round the brow of a corpse, lovely even in death, and ask, " What is wanting here ?" And the very silence answers, Life. This is a just representation of the unsanctified excellences of a young person without religion. Look at this defect in various relations.

In relation to God. Other qualities may have no direct reference to him, but this has. It is what he demands. Some of the other things he leaves to your taste; but this he imposes upon your conscience. He demands your faith; your love; your submission; your devotedness: and yet you are content with excellences that have no reference whatever to your Creator, Preserver, and Benefactor ! You can be content to smile upon your fellow-creatures, and be smiled upon by them, without ever asking, " Where is God, my Maker, that I may enjoy the light of his countenance, and reflect it back in gratitude and love?" Is God, then, just that one Being whom you may leave out of all consideration and regard, and treat as least worthy of being acknowledged and thought of? Is God just that one friend, whom it is quite a venial sin to banish from the mind, and who is to be no more regarded than if he were some idol in a temple in India? Is love to God just that one state of heart which can be best spared from the

virtuous affections, and the absence of which is no defect? Shall you by civility, courtesy, good nature, seek
to please and gratify everyone besides, and not seek to
please God by religion? Did it ever occur to you to
ask, " How must I appear in the sight of God himself,
with this one defect, a want of religion?" How hate-
ful, and desperately wicked, in his sight, must that one
defect make you appear. What must be his displeasure,
that while you are the delight of your friends, giving
and receiving pleasure, you neither maintain nor seek
communion with him; and that he sees in you no
sincere pouring out your soul in the way of fervent
desires for his illumination, his compassion, his forgiveness, his transforming operations: no earnest penitential
pleading in the name of Christ for his favour: no
solemn, affectionate dedication of your whole being to
his service, but instead of all this, mere general excellence, giving you a good standing among your fellow-
creatures, but having no more reference to him than if
he did not exist. Ah! what a defect that one want
must be in the sight of God!

View it now in reference to the Bible, the book
of God, and all the great subjects which it contains. It
was to implant this one thing in your heart, that the
Son of God became incarnate, and died upon the cross;
that the Holy Spirit was poured out; that the Scriptures
were written; that the law was given; that the Psalmist
was inspired to record his sorrows, confessions, aspirations, and devotions; that prophets uttered their predictions; that apostles penned their gospels and epistles.
Heaven has opened and poured forth its splendours and
its revelations; not to make you simply amiable, which
you might have been without this series of communica-

tions from the invisible world; not merely to bestow a few general ornaments upon your character, leaving its substance unchanged, defective and corrupt as it is: not merely to fit you to give pleasure in the circle of your earthly friends, while still alienated from God and holiness. Oh, no! The Bible, that wondrous book; that silent testimony for God and from him, was penned to bring you under the influence of vital, experimental religion. And yet you are content with amiabilities, of which you might have been possessed, if that volume had never been written! The Bible, God's Book, written by the inspiration of God's Spirit, containing God's thoughts, expressed in God's words, calls you then, not to mere general excellences, but to this one thing which you lack. Patriarchs, priests, prophets, apostles, martyrs, all say to you, " Yet lackest thou one thing." Every writer, every page of the holy book, repeats the admonition.

View this defect in reference to yourselves. All other things fall short of your faculties, your capacity, your wants, your desires. Amiability, intelligence, sprightliness, do not meet your case, you need something higher and better. You want religion, whether you desire it or not. You may, to a considerable extent, be ignorant of your necessity in this respect, but it exists. Religion is the one thing which you not only lack, but need. It is not to be viewed as a thing which your Creator imposes upon you by a mere arbitrary appointment, as if he would exact, simply in assertion of his supremacy, and in requirement of homage from his creature, something which in itself is foreign to the necessities of your nature. It is not a kind of tree of knowledge of good and evil, a simple test of obedience. No. By its intrinsic quality it so corresponds to your nature, that the possession of it is vital, and its rejection mortal, to your happiness. From the spiritual principle of your soul, there is an absolute necessity that it should be raised into complacent communication with its Divine Original. It is as much constituted to need this communication now and for ever, as the child is to receive the nourishment which Providence has provided in the breast of its mother; and it seems as rational to suppose the infant could be satisfied and fed, and made to grow, by the ornaments that might be lavished upon its robes, while its mother's milk is denied, as that a soul formed to enjoy God can be satisfied with any general excellences of character, while religion, which leads it to the fountain of true happiness, is neglected. If the soul be not so exalted as to be placed in communion with God, it is degraded and prostrated to objects which cannot, by their nature, adequately meet, and fill, and bless its faculties. No matter what you are, or what you have, if you have not religion; for if you have not religion, you have not God: you are without God. And what can make up for that privation? Consider only one single view of your situation, that of the loneliness of a human soul without God. " All other things," says Foster, " are necessarily extraneous to the soul: they may communicate with it, but they are still separate and without it; an intermediate vacancy keeps them for ever asunder; so that, till God, whose essence pervades all things, comes in and is apprehended and felt to be absolutely in the soul, the soul must be, in a sense, in an insuperable and eternal solitude." But when religion comes into the soul, then God comes to dwell in it, and thus "the interior, central loneliness, the solitude of the soul, is banished by a most perfectly intimate presence, which imparts the most affecting sense of society; a society, a communion, which imparts life and joy, and may continue in perpetuity." Happy is the man whose soul has this one thing which meets all its faculties, wants, and woes. What can other and lesser things do in time of sickness, of misfortunes, of bereavement, and of death? Will a sprightly disposition, a merry temper, a humorous fancy, or even a well-stored intellect, be of any service then? What will these things do in such circumstances? They may grow as flowers in the path of life, but will they bloom in the valley of the shadow of death? Infidelity, indeed, gives us one instance, and it has vaunted it as a proof that an unbeliever can die happy. I mean Hume, who, in prospect of eternity, (which, with his views, presented nothing but the shadows of eternal night,) could find no higher or better employment than playing at cards, reading novels, or cracking jokes upon Charon and his boat. Such levity ill comported with such anticipations; and was perhaps nothing better than the act of a timid boy going through a church-yard at night ' Whistling to keep his spirits up.' But view these endowments in reference to the day of judgment and the scenes that follow. There is a day ordained, in which God will judge the world in righteousness, by Jesus Christ. " Rejoice, O young man, in thy youth, and let thy heart cheer thee in the days of thy youth, and walk in the ways of thine heart, and in the sight of thine eyes; but know thou that for all these things God will bring thee into judgment." Imagine that day were come: that you heard the trumpet sound; that you saw the dead rising from their graves; the world in flames; the Judge descending; the great white throne in the air; the nations gathered round the dread tribunal waiting their doom. What an awful, ineffable, inconceivable scene will the last day present, the judgment of the world, the close of time, the commencement of eternity, the opening of heaven and hell to receive their ever-abiding inmates! Conceive, if it be possible to grasp, to hold, to endure the conception, of your going up to the tribunal, to have your character scrutinized, and your doom pronounced, and when listening for the result, to hear only that dreadful sentence, "Thou art weighed in the balances and found wanting. Thy amiabilities are of no avail here. Thy good nature, thy sprightly temper, thy varied intelligence, thy attractive amenity, have not the weight of a feather, are not the small dust of the balance in which thy character is determined. Thou hast lacked one thing, that one thing is everything here. Thou art weighed in the balances and found wanting." How, how will you endure that decision? It has been very strikingly observed, that "At the day of judgment, the attention excited by the surrounding scene, the strange aspect of nature, the dissolution of the elements, and the last trump, will have no other effect than to cause the reflections of the sinner to return with a more overwhelming tide upon his own character, his sentence, his unchanging destiny; and amidst the innumerable millions who surround him, he will mourn apart."

View this unsanctified amiability in relation to heaven. The loveliest of all dispositions, and the possession of the richest excellences, apart from faith in Christ, and the love of God, have no reference to that state, and constitute no meetness for it. Heaven is a holy place and state for a holy people, and "without holiness no man shall see the Lord," whatever else he may have. Will good temper, amenity of disposition, vivacity, wit, or humour, alone prepare the soul for converse with God? Are these the things that meeten for the communion of holy angels and holy men in the presence of a holy God? At best such attainments are the flowers of an earthly soil, and not plants of Paradise. How completely would the possessors of such qualities, without a holy heavenly taste and bias, find themselves out of their element in that region of which holiness is the pervading character, and which, while it attracts to itself all that is holy, rejects every thing else!

I now address myself to three classes of young persons.*

I. To those who have some things generally lovely and excellent in their character, but are destitute of true religion, to you that have sweet dispositions, or good talents, or acquired knowledge, or attractive wit and humour, or vivacious temper, or all these together, but have them unsanctified by piety, unconsecrated to God, unemployed for Christ, alas, alas, what a wilderness of blooming weeds of various forms and colours is here, but weeds still, only weeds, and as to any good influence upon your destiny in eternity, useless and vain; they would be no crown of amaranth for the glorified spirit in heaven and eternity; they form only a garland for the immortal soul on her way to perdition; they will not afford any,

---

* Some of the sentiments and expressions in this conclusion, are borrowed from Dr. Watts's Sermon on the same text, entitled " A hopeful Youth falling short of Heaven."

not even the smallest relief, under her miseries in that
world of hopeless despair to which her want of religion
must inevitably consign her. With a fidelity which my
regard to truth, to God, and yourselves, alike require,
I assure you that no combination of amiable and attractive qualities, can, in the absence of religion, by possibility
save you from the perdition that awaits ungodly men.
There is an infinite diversity both of kind and degree
in the sins to be found in the character and conduct
of unrenewed and unsanctified men, from those that
resemble the amiable youth in the text, to the blas-
pheming infidel and the vicious profligate; and all will
be dealt with by a rule of proportion, but all must be
swept away together, the most beautiful weeds and the
most noxious ones, with the besom of destruction; and
however dissimilar and discordant while living and growing upon earth, they will be blended in one common
mass of irrecoverable corruption. In merely human
excellence, not springing from love to God, and the
grace of the Holy Spirit, there is no imperishable principle; no germ of divine, heavenly, and immortal life;
it is, the very best of it, but of the earth, earthy, must
die in the soil from which it rises, and can never be
transplanted to the paradise of God. I pity the noble or
amiable natures, which neglecting to seek after divine
grace, are ruined for ever by the want of religion. I pity
the man of sweet temper, without sanctifying grace;
of solid judgment, without sound piety; of lively
imagination, without living faith; of attractive manners, but not himself attracted to the cross of Christ;
of courtesy towards man, but yet enmity towards God:
a polished gentleman, yet still an unconverted sinner;
the admiration of his companions, and yet an object

of displeasure to his Creator. So much general excellence infected by a deadly taint that corrupts it all! How at the last day will such persons be mortified, enraged, and tormented to see men preferred to themselves, whom when on earth they despised as undeserving of their notice, men of ignorant minds, clownish manners and rugged exterior! Yes, but under all that outward repulsiveness were concealed the principles of true religion, repentance towards God, faith in our Lord Jesus Christ, and a holy life. Much that was amiable was wanting in them, but they had religious principle. To see them owned by the Judge, exalted to his throne, and crowned with his glory; while unsanctified genius and irreligious amiability are rejected as base metal, how profoundly humiliating, how terribly exasperating to those who then will be thrown aside by God as rubbish and refuse! And following these rejected youths of unsanctified amiability onward to their eternal state, what miserable spectacles do they present! You that were the life of every company into which you came, and whose absence was mourned as that of the charmer of the circle, will your gay fancy brighten the gloom of those regions of sorrow, or give an air of gladness to those doleful shades to which you and they will then be banished? Will you, by any of your present acquirements be able to relieve yourselves or your companions from the torture produced by the recollection that it was these very arts of wit and humour, sometimes turned against religion, that helped you on to that place of punishment? Will sallies of wit, sportive jests, bursts of merriment, playful humour, beguile the dreadful round of the miseries of the lost soul, and make the wheels of eternity move faster and lighter, as they did those of time? How will you, of soft and gentle nature, of amiable disposition, bear the banishment from the regions of peace and concord, the paradise of love, the habitation of all holy friendship; and imprisonment with demons and demon-like men to which you will be condemned? " How will your souls endure the madness and contention, the envy and spite, of wicked angels; you that delighted on earth in works of peace, what will you do when your tender dispositions shall be hourly ruffled by the uproar and confusion of those dark regions; and instead of the society of God and blessed spirits, ye shall be eternally vexed with the perverse tempers of your fellow-sinners, the sons of darkness? O that I could speak in melting language, or in the language of effectual terror, that I might by any means awaken your souls to jealousy and timely fear! That so many natural excellences, as God hath distributed among you, might not be wasted in sin, abased to dishonour, and aggravate your everlasting misery."

I most earnestly exhort you to supply the defect to which this chapter has directed your attention, and admonish you to add to all that is amiable, that which is holy; to all that is lovely in the sight of man, that which is well-pleasing in the sight of God; to all that is earthly in the way of excellence, that which is heavenly, divine, and eternal. Bear in vivid recollection what it is you need; you have, or are supposed to have, attractive endowments of mind, heart, character; but no real, decided, spiritual religion. And will that religion, if you have it, interfere with any of your other excellences? Will it displace them to make room for itself? Will it pull up all those flowers and throw them away as inimical to its own nature and prejudicial to its growth? Nothing of the sort. Amiability is of like nature with religion: the former is loveliness in the sight of man, and the latter loveliness in the sight of God. When the grace of God enters the soul of man, what it finds beautiful it makes more beautiful. It comes not like the cold chills and dark shadows of evening or of winter to shut up the flowers, and hide their beauties, and nip their strength; but like the rising sun, to open their petals, to reveal their beauties, to brighten their colours, to exhale their fragrance, and to invigorate their strength. Religion is itself the chief amiability, and the cherisher of all other kinds. Hence it is that holiness is spoken of as beauty.

II. There is another class I would briefly address. I mean those who are as defective in amiability as they are in religion. Alas! how many are there of this character, who have neither gentleness nor graciousness; who are possessed neither of the beauties of holiness, nor the attractions of kindness, godliness, or courtesy; but who are as unlovely as they are ungodly; and have scarcely any to take delight in them either in heaven or upon earth. Morose, ungentle, unaccommodating in their disposition, they are incapable of enjoying happiness, and unwilling to impart it. They have not even external and tinsel ornaments to compensate for the want of internal and substantial excellences. They are like flowers which have no beauty of colour to divert attention from their offensive odour; like fruits which are as bitter to the taste as they are unsightly to the eye. Unhappy young men! See them at home; they are tyrannical, morose, selfish, domineering, the troublers of domestic peace, the constant cause of disquiet and disturbance. Even to their parents they are ungrateful,

disrespectful, and wayward: unmelted by a mother's
gentle influence, unsubdued by a father's mild authority,
and unsoftened by the gentle fascination of a sister's
love. And how often do they go still further in this
want of amiability, and by adding immorality and profligacy to unloveliness, do much to break a mother's
heart and bring down a father's grey hairs in sorrow to
the grave! Ah! how many parricides and matricides
walk our earth, whom no law but that of God can
arrest, and no justice but that of heaven can punish!
How many carry the heart of a savage under the name
of a son, and the poison of asps under their tongues
and in their tempers; and towards even their parents
transvenom all emotions of filial piety into the wormwood and gall of intense hatred of those to whom they
owe their existence! What an object of abhorrence
must such a youth be to that divine Saviour who evinced
towards the individual alluded to in this chapter his
sensibility not only to the beauties of holiness, but to
the loveliness of general excellence. Is there such a
youth reading these pages? Go, young man, from this
volume to your closet, your Bible, your knees, and your
God, and implore that grace which has said, "Instead
of the thorn shall come up the fir tree, and instead
of the briar shall come up the myrtle tree."

III. I address those who are in earnest after religion,
and who really possess its essential principles, but are
somewhat deficient in the more lovely and ornamental
beauties of the Christian character. This is not defective
amiability merely, but defective religion. Observation
convinces me that this is not a supposititious character.
It ought not to exist, but it does. Religion, in itself
the very type of all that is true, and good, and beauti-

ful, should draw after it everything else that is beautiful. The supreme should command the subordinate loveliness, but it does not always. It must be sorrowfully admitted that a mind enlightened by the Spirit of God, a heart renewed by divine grace, a life regulated by Christian principle, are not always associated, in a proportionate degree, with the ornament of a meek and quiet spirit, an amiable temper, and a courteous demeanour. We have sometimes seen a form of distinguished personal beauty disfigured by a want of cleanliness and by a slovenly attire. The exquisite symmetry could not be altogether concealed; but how much more attractive would it have appeared with other and more suitable accompaniments! So it is with character; there may be real beauty of holiness, but in sad and slovenly attire of temper. Changing the illustration, I may observe, the brilliancy of the most valuable diamond may be hidden by earthly incrustations; the lustre of gold may be dimmed for want of polish; and the most majestic portrait be half covered with dust or mildew. So religion, which is more precious than rubies, more valuable than gold, and the very image of God in the soul of man, may have its worth and its excellence depreciated by infirmities of temper and an amiable deportment. Religious young men, be amiable as well as pious: not only your happiness, but your usefulness requires it. You know that vice has not unfrequently its attractions in the amiability with which it is associated, and that some are reconciled to it on that ground. It is equally true that religion may be associated with repulsive qualities, and that some may be driven from it by these partial deformities. Be it then your desire, your endeavour, your prayer, to unite the holy and the amiable; let the diamond, with its flashing hues, be thus seen in the most tasteful setting, and the gold in its brightest polish. Win your companions to piety, by the attractive qualities with which it is combined in you. Make them feel that religion is not the frowning and spectral form they have been accustomed to consider it; a gloomy spirit that cannot smile; a vampire that sucks the life's blood of joy from the soul of youth. On the contrary, let them see that it is angelical and not demoniacal in its nature; that with a seraph's sacred fervour it combines his sweetness, gentleness, and ineffable loveliness. It is this which while it will prepare you to pass through life, blessing and being blest, happy in yourself and diffusing happiness around you, will also prepare you for the immortal felicities of the celestial world. " It is this which, transferred to heaven, will kindle with new and immortal lustre, and will be set in that constellated firmament of living and eternal splendours. Of that brilliant world, that region where all things live, and shine, and flourish, and triumph for ever and ever, the glory, the excellence, is eminently the union of all that is holy, and all that is lovely. There, all are brethren, and all love, and are loved, as brethren. All are divinely amiable, and excellent friends. Every one possesses in absolute perfection the moral beauty that is loved, and the virtue which loves it. Every one, conscious of unmingled purity within, approves and loves himself for that divine image, which in complete perfection, and with untainted resemblance, is enstamped upon his own character. Each in every view which he casts around him, beholds the same glory shining and brightening in the endless train of his companions; one in nature, but diversified without end in those forms and varieties of excellence by which the original and eternal Beauty delights to present itself to the virtuous universe.   There, everyone conscious of being entirely lovely and entirely loved, reciprocates the same love to that great multitude which no man can number, of all nations, kindreds, and tongues, which fills the immeasurable regions of heaven.   Out of this character grows a series, ever varying, ever improving, of all the possible communications of beneficence, fitted in every instance only to interchange and increase the happiness of all.   In the sunshine of infinite complacency, the light of the new Jerusalem, the original source of all their own beauty, life, and joy, all these happy nations walk for ever, and transported with the life-giving influence, unite in one harmonious and eternal hymn to the great Author of all their excellences and all their enjoyments, Blessing and honour, and glory, and wisdom, and thanksgiving be unto Him who sitteth on the throne, for ever and ever.   Amen."

CHAPTER V.

What is Truth? JOHN xviii, 38.

SUCH was the momentous question which Pilate proposed to the illustrious and holy Martyr who then stood as a prisoner at his bar. It has been said there are two things in the Scripture account of this circumstance which surprise us, the silence of Christ, and the indifference of his judge: that Christ should not answer such a question, and that Pilate should not press it until he obtained an answer. One of these wonders is the cause of the other, and if you consider them in connexion, your astonishment will cease. The levity of the querist was the cause of the silence of the oracle. Truth, in awful majesty, though veiled and insulted, stood before him, and indignantly refused to unfold its secrets and its glories to one who discovered frivolity on such a subject. On his lips it was the question of idle curiosity, not of deep solicitude; it came from the surface, and not from the lowest depths of the heart. If Christ gratified his curiosity, well; but he did not think truth of sufficient importance to inquire after it a second time.

The conduct of Pilate to Jesus and of Jesus to Pilate

is repeated every day. Multitudes, by a little attention to religion and their Bibles, ask, "What is truth?" but it is in such a careless and undevout manner, that Jesus Christ leaves them to wander in their own dark and miserable conjectures. Hence so many prejudices; hence so many erroneous opinions in religion; hence so many dangerous delusions, in what is called the Christian world. Still there have been very many who in sober and solemn inquisitiveness have asked the question, "What is truth?" Myriads of human intellects of the highest order have engaged in the pursuit of this great object; and, as regards scientific knowledge, have by demonstration and experiment echoed in unison, and with something of the rapture with which it was originally uttered, the Eureka of Archimedes. But in reference to moral and religious truth, how multitudinous and how contradictory are the voices which answer the inquiry. If we may judge from the present state and aspect of Christendom, the day is far distant when, in answer to the question, all tongues shall proclaim one doctrine, and triumphantly reply, "This is truth." Hence the perplexities of many young persons at the outset of their religious life.

Many things, young men, will perplex you at the outset of a religious life, and tend, in the early stages of your inquiry into this momentous subject, to embarrass you. The mysterious nature of the whole subject of religion, so far as it relates to divine, heavenly, and eternal truths; the general neglect of it, to all practical and serious purposes, by the multitude around you; and the lukewarmness and inconsistency of many of those who make a profession of it; will all be apt to produce an unfavourable impression upon your mind, to shake your resolutions, and render your steps hesitating and faltering. There is also another cause of perplexity, I mean the number of religious sects, the diversity of creeds, and the ceaseless and yet unsettled controversies which prevail throughout all Christendom. Bewildered by such diversity, and distracted by such contentions, you are ready to abandon the subject in hopeless despair of arriving at the truth. I sympathise with you, my young friends, in your difficulties, and this chapter is intended, by God's blessing, to extricate, relieve, and guide you, and if it do not remove the difficulty (for what can remove it?) may do something to lessen it.

I. I will state particularly what it is that perplexes you. I descend into the depths of your secret thoughts, and I find there some surprise that on such a subject as religion, especially after a revelation from God, there should be any controversy, or any room for controversy at all. You may be ready to suppose that all would be so plain as to preclude the possibility of diversity or mistake. But do men think alike on any other subject? Is there consentaneousness of opinion on any one topic that is sustained only by moral evidence? Was there ever a statute or law passed, (they are usually so framed as to exclude, if possible, all difference of opinion,) about which lawyers can not, as to some of its clauses, raise doubts and difficulties. Now, is not a written revelation from God, inasmuch as it relates to subjects foreign to ordinary matters, remote from our senses, and out of the usual track of our thoughts, just that one thing about which, beyond all others, diversity of opinion might be expected? Consider the thousands of propositions contained in the Bible; the imperfections of language; the mysteriousness of the subjects; the endlessly diversified temperament of human minds, and the various circumstances in which those minds are placed; and you will see at once that nothing short of an astounding and constant miracle could produce absolute uniformity of opinion. Nor is this all; for such is the corruption of man's heart, that his mind is not only on this ground likely to go wrong in its judgments, but it is actually opposed with very strong dislike to many of the truths revealed, and on that account it really wishes and attempts to pervert them, as being too humbling for his pride, too pure for his depravity, and too authoritative for his love of independence. Here again we see reason to abate our surprise at the diversity of opinion.

The young enquirer about religion is not unfrequently scandalised and disgusted by the bitterness of sectarianism, and the rancour with which controversy is conducted. He sees the evil passions of our corrupt nature, "malice, wrath, and all uncharitableness," as rife in the writings, and therefore in the hearts, of religious polemics, as they are in those of the fiercest political antagonists; and he says in thoughtful seriousness, "Was not Christianity sent to produce peace on earth, and good will to men? Is it not said that love is its cardinal excellence? Can these men, any of them, really believe in the Christian religion, which places charity at the top of the Christian virtues?" I admit to you without hesitation, all this bitterness is wrong, cannot be justified, and is condemned by the volume about which these men contend. To speak the truth in love is one of its own injunctions. But recollect that even the best of men are imperfect, and that nothing so strongly appeals to our imperfections, and brings them into such activity, as contradiction and controversy. It is not true to say there is more bitterness in theological controversy than in any other kind; but it is true that there ought to be less. One thing should not be forgotten, that the importance of the subject naturally renders men more earnest than any other does, and that earnestness, it must be admitted, too generally degenerates into unseemly violence and bitterness. There is in every human heart, however morally excellent and holy, some corruption lying underneath its excellences which by controversy is too often brought to the surface; just as sediment at the bottom of clear water is stirred up by agitating the vessel containing it.

The equal mental power with which opposing systems are maintained, is to a mind unskilled in dialectics, and unable to detect the fallacies which lurk, and the sophistry which abounds in erroneous argumentation, often very trying. It is admitted, it is impossible to question it, that great ability is possessed and displayed by all parties in the arena of religious strife, by the combatants for error as well as by those who support truth. And who can wonder at this, since the father of lies has perhaps the most wonderful intellect in the universe, next to the Deity. In contending armies upon the field of battle, equal courage, skill, and prowess, are often displayed for a long time by both sides, the wrong as well as the right; and a spectator of the awful conflict might be at a loss to determine which would gain the victory, and which deserved to gain it. There is no error so palpable even to common sense, but it may be defended by arguments so ingenious as to defy ordinary minds to detect their fallacies and expose the sophistry by which they are urged. Truth is often with the weaker party, I mean weaker in the use of dialectic weapons. A skilful polemic may often make error appear more plausible than truth.

The apparent equality of moral excellences in the advocates of opposing systems of opinions, is sometimes perplexing, and in some cases, even greater amiability may seem to be with those who advocate error, than with those who contend for truth. It must not be forgotten that religious truth is intended to produce two results, love to God and love to man : in other words morality and piety. Remember this, for it is of vast importance you should remember it. Penitence, faith, inward holiness, devoutness, heavenliness, are all parts of religion, without which the fairest morality, and most beautiful amiability, are, in the sight of God, nothing worth, and will be found totally unavailing to salvation. There may be much general amiability without an atom of genuine piety. The only true standard of moral excellence is the Bible, and that places God before us as the first object of regard. Systems, as well as men, are to be judged of by their fruits; but then we must always ask what kind of fruits they are designed to produce. Bible truths must produce Bible fruits, and these are something more than the moralities, amiabilities and courtesies of life, valuable, and necessary, and important, as these are.

The present unsettled state of controversy completes the perplexity. It would seem as if we were no nearer the adjustment of our differences than ever. Sects are as numerous, their creeds as various and as diverse, and their contests as eager as ever, after all the reasoning which has been employed, and the volumes which have been written through so many ages. But surely this should not add much to your difficulty, for if diversity of opinion exist at any time, it may be expected to exist at all times. Men's minds are constituted in one age as they are in another, and may be expected to differ in all ages. It may, however, be hoped that, under the prevalence of a more earnest piety and the establishment of sounder canons of criticism and interpretation, aided by the dispensations of Providence, and a more copious effusion of the Holy Spirit, a greater approximation of sects and opinions will take place; and for such a state of things all should devoutly pray and hope. In looking at this prevalence of diversified opinion, and seemingly endless controversy, let us enquire if, while admitting it to be an evil, we may not discover some good, which, by the ordering of Providence, will be eventually, and even now is, brought out from it. Does not this diversity of sects, and sharpness of controversy, effectually tend to preserve the purity of the sacred text of the Bible? Suppose there were in some large town one public reservoir, from which all the inhabitants drew their supplies of water; and suppose, further, there were some considerable diversity of opinion as to the real qualities and properties of the water, while all considered the water to be necessary; would they not all watch each other that no liberty whatever was taken with the common source, to corrupt it by infusing into it anything which would make it more agreeable to the purposes and tastes of any party, or any individual, or to diminish the supply, or any way to interfere with the general benefit? They might sometimes dispute, and very sharply too, about the quality of the water, and some bad feeling might be generated in the course of their disputes; but still their natural jealousies would make them all protectors of the reservoir, and guardians of its purity and preservation. Something like this occurs in the diversity of sects; they have the Bible common to them all, and they all profess to be founded upon it. They differ in opinion as to its contents, but this very difference makes them keep a sharp look-out upon each other, to see that none of them corrupt the text, either by way of interpolation, emendation, or excision. Such attempts were indeed made in earlier ages, but they were detected and exposed. And copies multiplied by millions, in various languages, and held in the hands of various churches and denominations, prevent this now. The existence of sects and controversies guarantees to us, therefore, a pure and uncorrupted Bible.

Then, does it not tend to make the Bible more examined and thoroughly searched? How little is this book explored in Popish countries, where differences of opinion are repressed and controversy forbidden! How much more gold is brought up in California, where any one may dig and explore for himself, than in those places where the mines are a royal monopoly, and none may dig but by authority! What additions are made to the stock of scriptural knowledge, where the stern voice of the church forbids the exercise and right of private judgment, the publication of individual opinion, and the existence and maintenance of controversy? Even if error by this means could be shut out, how much of truth is excluded with it! How little, as compared with Protestant writers, have Roman Catholics added to our stores of Biblical knowledge!

Has not God overruled the zeal of party for the

spread of his cause? Do not the sects quicken each other's zeal by the power of rivalry? Is not this the case both at home and abroad? I acknowledge that in this zeal there is an infusion of sectarianism, and so far it is a corruption; but there is nothing absolutely pure in our world, and this very infusion may stimulate the efforts of the zealot. A propagator of Methodism, Church of Englandism, Presbyterianism, or Congregationalism, may be stimulated by sectarianism in his efforts to spread his particular opinions, but still with these he carries something more and something better, for he carries with him the gospel of salvation. I have no doubt that sectarianism does add something to our zeal, even in our home and foreign missions, and so far may seem to corrupt it: but on the other hand, it prevents us from sinking into a state of inertness and stagnancy. The Roman Church tells us she can do this without the rivalry of sects. This is not quite true. It is this very rivalry which has in part enabled her to gain her wide extent and dominion. Witness the controversies as to doctrine between the Jesuits and the Dominicans, and between the Jesuits and the Jansenists, the conflict of the Gallican and Ultramontane opinions, and the disputes between her various missionary orders as to their respective proceedings in the East.

The existence of this diversity gives opportunity also (alas that so few should be forward to avail themselves of it!) for manifesting our forbearance towards each other, and bringing into exercise that " charity which is the bond of perfectness." It would be difficult to say which would be the most beautiful spectacle, a church uniform in opinion, or a church somewhat multiform in sentiment, yet maintaining a unity of spirit in the bond of peace. We thus see that some good may be brought out of the evil of controversy and the prevalence of sectarianism. The entrance of moral evil into God's wise, benevolent, and holy administration, seemed to be evil, and only evil; yet how has God overruled it for a brighter and completer manifestation of his character !

II. I shall now advert to the wrong methods which many adopt to relieve themselves of the perplexity occasioned by this diversity. In some cases it leads, or tends to lead, to general scepticism, and a total abandonment of all religion, under despair of ever finding out the truth. Men are apt to say, "We will give it all up, for who amidst such endless diversity can hope to find the truth?" But is this rational? Do men act thus in other matters about which much diversity prevails? Do they give up politics because of the numerous parties into which, on that controverted subject, men are divided? Do they abandon the subject of finance, political economy, or metaphysics, on this ground? And why should they do it in religion? How many have found out what they conceive to be the truth, and are reposing in peace upon their convictions! And why may not you? Abjure then the idea of abandoning religion on this ground. You will find this to be no excuse at the day of judgment. God has given you an intellect capable of investigating the subject, and will hold you responsible for the exercise of it in this particular. Men are divided in opinion upon food, medicine, and the best means of promoting health; and will you therefore give up all care about the best way to maintain your life, health, and comfort? Truth is to be found somewhere, and it is an indolent disposition which leads us to give up the pursuit, because we do not by a kind of intuition, or a hasty first view of the subject, know what it is, and where it is to be found. You must search after it. Your salvation depends upon your finding and embracing those truths with which it is connected. Multitudes have found it, and so may you.

Some few persons, unable to decide upon the truth as regards doctrines, have contented themselves with observing, as they suppose, the practical parts of religion, and have relinquished all care about what they call dogmas. They have attempted to construct a religion to be irrespective of the peculiarities of sect or creed, and to consist wholly of moral duties, with perhaps a few exercises of general devotion. This is deism. It is true they thus get rid of controversy, but at the same time they get rid of Christianity also. The Scriptures are set aside entirely, and all the great facts and truths of revelation are repudiated. The Bible is not merely a code of morals to be obeyed and practised, but a declaration of facts and truths to be believed. Scripture ethics rest on Scripture doctrines. Faith, as well' as practice, is the demand of revelation.

But the great and effectual relief from the perplexities of controversy, is supplied, say Papists, by Roman Catholicism. The Church of Rome professes that it is by its doctrines and discipline, as set forth in its councils, canons and creeds, a perpetual living tribunal, to decide all matters of religious faith and practice, and thus to prevent all controversy. All doctrines are settled and determined for its members by the church as the authoritative and infallible expounder of the truth. This is the lure it holds forth to those who are without its pale, who are perplexed with controversy and distracted by religious strifes, and the multitudes of religious sects, "Come with us, we are the true church, possessing authority and infallibility to decide upon doctrine, which is thus provided for you, without the labour of inquiry, the pain of suspense, the disquietude of doubt, or the peril of mistake. Receive the faith of the church, and believe as the church believes; it guarantees your safety in all that you receive with this implicit faith. You will thus be taken out of the divisions, distractions, and controversies of Protestantism, and find rest for your weary soul in the lap and on the bosom of your holy mother, the Church." This is somewhat attractive, it must be confessed, and if it were true would be quite satisfactory; but it is awfully deceptive. Where in the Scripture is any church invested with the authority to be a living umpire, and to decide all controversies? Where is there any allusion to such a tribunal? Is it not to the Scripture, and not to the church, we are everywhere directed for settling the question, "What is truth?" Even if the church were this living tribunal, we contend that the Papacy, so far from being the true church, is an awful apostacy, and repugnant to every part of the New Testament. Instead of being the judge of truth, it is a false witness, whose testimony is a compound of the most palpable falsehoods and soul-destroying errors; whose voice continually speaks lies and nonsense. The claim of the Church of Rome to infallibility, which is the basis of its living tribunal, is repugnant alike to reason, to Scripture, and to the facts of its own history. It acknowledges that infallibility is not the attribute of its individual members, but only of the Pope or of the collective body of the church, assembled in a General Council. But is it not an universal law of logic, that what is in the genus must be in the species? If, therefore, the collective body is infallible, so must be its individual members. How can a collection of fallibles, multiply them as you will, make up an infallible? Besides, it is not yet decided, and never has been, where this infallibility resides : whether in the Pope without a General Council, a General Council without a Pope, or a Pope and a General Council. Thus the claim is repugnant to reason. It is equally so to Scripture, which in a thousand places proclaims the liability of all men to err, except such as are under Divine inspiration. Nor is the claim less contradictory to the history of Romanism, which declares that Pope has been against Pope, the same Pope against himself, and Council against Council. There is scarcely a doctrine of Popery which has not been the subject of controversy within the bosom of the Papal community. The variations of Popery have been almost as numerous as those of Protestantism. Where, then, is its infallibility? The claim of the Church of Rome to be this living tribunal, which is to settle once for all and for every body what is truth, and to prevent all controversy by forbidding the exercise of private judgment, is in direct contradiction to the Word of God, which calls upon every man for himself to " search the Scriptures," " to prove all things," and " hold fast that which is good." To constitute the church the tribunal which is to decide for us what is truth, without our examination of the Scriptures for ourselves, is to make all its members believers in the church rather in the Word of God, and thus to put the church in the place of the Bible as the object of faith. This method of deciding controversies, and settling the question what is truth, renders the Scriptures all but useless for the people; and therefore is only consistent with the prohibition of the free use of the Scriptures by them. This scheme is an utter degradation of man's nature as a rational being, and is a plan never adopted in reference to anything else. Who would endure such a method of determining questions of literature, science, politics, law, or art? Why, therefore, should a man be debarred from engaging on the most momentous of all topics, and he be exposed to the consequences of eternal ruin by implicitly trusting to the judgment of others? How is any man to know whether he really believes what the church believes, and all it believes? Who can search the numberless folios which contain the faith of the church, and be satisfied that he has not omitted something which the church requires of him? And though creeds drawn up by Popes, and catechisms and manuals by learned doctors and eminent bishops, may be put into the hands of the people, yet as no individual man, however elevated, even the Pope himself, is infallible, how is any one to be satisfied that there is no error in these compositions? Besides, as no one can have access to the church except as it is represented to him by some individual priest, who is in the place of both God and the church to him; how can anyone be sure, since that individual priest is fallible, but that he may err in the views he may give of the church's doctrine? This living tribunal, by suppressing controversy, destroys liberty, and turns the whole subject of religion into a matter of slavish submission to human authority. And with liberty, piety also to a considerable extent expires.

The dull uniformity produced by the compulsion of authority, is no compensation for the loss of that activity and spirit which are kept alive by the neighbourhood and zeal of rival sects. "The Gallican Church no doubt looked upon it as a signal triumph when she prevailed upon Louis xiv. to repeal the Edict of Nantes, which repeal, by refusing toleration to the Huguenots, suppressed the voice of controversy and the existence of sects. But what was the consequence? Where shall we look, after this period, for her Fenelons and her Pascals? Where for the distinguished monuments of piety and learning, which were the glory of her better days? As for piety, she perceived she had no occasion for it, when there was no lustre of Christian holiness surrounding her: nor for learning, when she had no longer any enemies to confute, or any controversies to maintain. She felt herself at liberty to become as ignorant, as secular, as irreligious as she pleased; and amidst the silence and darkness she had created around her, she drew the curtains and retired to rest. The accession of numbers she gained by suppressing her opponents, was like the small extension of length a body acquires by death; the feeble remains of life were extinguished, and she lay a putrid corpse, a public nuisance, filling the air with pestilential exhalations."* Such then are the objections to a living and infallible tribunal for the decision of controversy, as claimed by the Church of Rome.

But perhaps it will be asked whether all denominations even of Nonconformists, do not put forth creeds, articles, and catechisms, which they not only teach, but require their members to believe? Certainly, as

* Robert Hall's "Zeal without Innovation."

acknowledged compendiums of their views of the Word of God; but they allow every man to test them by the Scriptures, and to reject them if he sees fit. They are held forth to guide, but not to compel. They are proposed, but not imposed. They are submitted for examination and instruction to the judgment, but they are not made to bind the conscience.

You see, then, young men, that the perplexities of controversy cannot be avoided by surrendering up your judgment into the hands of priests; but that you are to employ it diligently for yourselves in coming to a conclusion upon the various questions which divide and agitate the religious world.

III. The question, however, comes back: What is to be done? How is the mind to be relieved from its perplexity in listening to the contradictory views which reply to the question, 'What is truth?' Is an inquirer to set about to read and study the religious opinions of all the denominations in existence? That would be an endless and needless labour. It would be a useless consumption of time, and would only end in still deeper and more painful perplexity. Take the case of any other book than the Bible; a legal statute, or a history, or any other document about which a great diversity of interpretation existed, and which was in your own hands; would you, in order to know its true meaning, think it necessary to read all the conflicting opinions? No! You would say, "I will read and study the document itself. I have it in my possession in the vernacular tongue, and I will read and judge for myself." Act thus in reference to the Bible and religious differences.

Study the Scriptures. Search the Word of God for yourselves. Be intimately acquainted with your Bibles, especially the New Testament. But there is a right and a wrong way of doing this. The exhortation to search the Scriptures is expressive of a particular state of mind, as well as of an outward duty. Carry to the Bible no preconceived notions with which it is your previous determination to make everything square. Read the Word of God with a simple and sincere desire to know its real meaning. In reading the Scriptures there must be no attempt to try what, by the aid of ingenuity and a previous bias, they may be made to say; but a simple desire to know what they do say. Read with entire and absolute impartiality, just as you would the prescription of a physician who had given you directions for food and medicine, to restore and preserve your health. Let there be an humble and teachable disposition. " Receive with meekness the engrafted word." " The meek will he guide in judgment, the meek will he show his way." " Except ye be converted, and become as little children, ye shall in no case enter into the kingdom of God." And whatever exercise of our intellect may be carried on, and however convinced we may be that the intellect must be exercised, there should always be entertained an humble and wholesome distrust of our own understanding. In searching the Scriptures we must consider their design as well as their meaning; that they are intended not only to communicate knowledge, but faith and holiness. The Bible is a book to make us wise unto salvation. It contains a " doctrine according to godliness." " Sanctify them through thy truth," was the prayer of Christ for his disciples. Divine truth is intended to produce a divine life. To read in order to know, or to support and defend, a system, is a low and unworthy end. To search the Scriptures aright, you must give up and abstain from all sinful indulgences. "Laying aside all filthiness, and superfluity of naughtiness, receive with meekness the engrafted word," is the injunction of the apostle. The lusts of the mind, the pride of intellect, the love of wealth, thirst after human applause, as well as the lusts of the flesh, impair the mental vision, and smite the soul with spiritual blindness, insomuch that holy truth, however plain, remains undiscovered.

There is another disposition to be carried to the Scriptures in our perusal of them, and that, on account of its importance, I place by itself, that it may be very conspicuously seen, as seriously considered, and as vividly and practically remembered; I mean that suggested by our Lord, where he says, "If any man will do his (God's) will, he shall know of the doctrine which I speak, whether it be of God, or whether I speak of myself." A real obedience to the will of God, as far as we at present know it, united with a sincere and hearty determination to do it upon all further discoveries of it, to whatever risks, sacrifices, and inconveniences such obedience may expose us, is the best way of coming to a right knowledge of the truth. We must love truth, not only for its own sake, but for its holy tendency and effect: and he that is most anxious to obtain holiness by truth, is most likely to ascertain truth for the sake of holiness. Right dispositions are the way to obtain right opinions. Divine truth, unlike scientific knowledge, is intended, as well as adapted, to produce moral results; and if we are not anxious to obtain these, we are not likely to come to a knowledge of the truths themselves.

There must also be very earnest prayer for the

teaching of the Holy Spirit. There are undoubtedly some things in the Bible hard to be understood; but in what pertains to salvation, all is as clear as crystal. But if there be light in the Bible, there is darkness in us. " The natural man receiveth not the things of the Spirit of God, for they are foolishness unto him, neither can he know them, because they are spiritually discerned." The safe and proper, and only safe and proper manner of approaching the heavenly oracle, is that which David manifested, when he thus prayed, " Open thou mine eyes that I may behold wondrous things out of thy law." So also the Apostle entreated for the Colossians, " We do not cease to pray for you, and to desire that ye might be filled with the knowledge of his will in all wisdom and spiritual understanding." It may not strike some, that although we have the book, it is necessary, in addition, to have the teaching of the Author: and if it were not absolutely necessary, yet surely this would be considered a privilege, even as regards a human production. But it is in this case necessary. How powerful is the influence of our inward corruption in blinding and bewildering our judgments! How liable are we to err! How momentous a matter is it on which to mistake! How numerous and how fatal are the mistakes that are made! Unless, therefore, we not only pray, but give ourselves to prayer for divine illumination, we are likely, even with the Bible in our hands, to go wrong. That the meaning of the Bible may be mistaken, and is so, no one can doubt. The subject of this chapter proves it. How many errors are there in the world on the subjects of divine revelation!

As your safest guide amidst the diversities of religious

opinions which exist, and as the best mode of relieving your mind from the perplexity occasioned by controversy, acquire the elements of decided personal godliness. These lie within a very narrow compass, are common to most denominations of professing Christians, and, with whatever other sentiments they may be associated, will secure the possession of eternal life. Be sure to be right on great and fundamental points. Be upon the foundation, and then, though you are a little off the perpendicular, yet you will not fall. And what are these grand essentials, without which no man can be saved, and with which every man will be saved, whatever in other respects may be his creed or his church? Repentance towards God, faith in our Lord Jesus Christ, and evangelical holiness. I do not mean to say that these constitute all that God has revealed, and therefore all that we need concern ourselves about. By no means. There are innumerable other matters which are found in the Word of God, but these are the substance of it, the great essentials to salvation. Personal godliness is the great preservative from serious error. As there are instincts in irrational creatures which lead them to select good and wholesome food, and to refuse and reject such substances as are noxious; so there are certain sentiments and systems as to which it is scarcely necessary to prove to the spiritual mind that they are false, for the spiritual taste pronounces them to be bad. The holy life within refuses and rejects them at once as repugnant to its nature; and the stronger and healthier that life is, the greater is the force of this repugnance. Hence the necessity, not only of our being possessed of true personal godliness, but of high degrees of it. He who feels all the vitalising power of sound doctrine in making him holy, heavenly, and happy, will be in small danger of mischief from other doctrines, and feel little necessity to inquire into other sentiments.   The man who finds his strength firm, his health glowing, his spirits buoyant, upon good, plain, nutritious food, will have no need to study the various systems of medicine and dietetics.   He may let physicians wrangle on, without troubling himself about their conflicting opinions.   So the man strong in faith, lively in hope, and ardent in the love of God and man : he who has joy and peace in believing : he who is able to mortify his corruptions, and invigorate his graces, by the views of divine truth which he has gained, need not read through a book of religious denominations to find out what is truth, for he has the " witness in himself."

It would be of material service, and a great help to you in deciding for yourself in matters of controversy as to what is truth, to gather from the Scripture, by a devout and careful perusal, some broad comprehensive views of its general purport and design, in reference to doctrine, ceremonies, and government.   Broad and general views on any subject greatly assist us in understanding its minuter parts and details.   Survey the system of divine truth in the Bible as you would a vast and complicated piece of machinery, not by first of all examining each particular part, but by taking a view of it as a whole, in its general design and larger combinations.   Faith in the truths of revelation is not to be obtained by the separate examination at first of its various points, historical, doctrinal, or practical ; and no one would be likely to become an intelligent and firm believer in Christianity, if he endeavoured to make every fact, every doctrine, and every precept, clear, certain, and beyond dispute, before he adopted the whole as a divine revelation, and before he had become acquainted with its general design and more important and fundamental truths. Those are most likely to understand details who are best acquainted with generals, as from them light comes upon particulars. Lord Bacon compares the conduct of those students and defenders of Christianity, who act upon the principle of beginning with particulars, and going on to generals, to those persons who would light a large hall by placing a candle in each corner, instead of hanging in the middle of it a large chandelier, which would send its light into the darkest recesses. Or, to change the metaphor, he who seizes and keeps possession of the great whole of Christianity, in its general truths and designs, is like a confident and successful victor, who seizes and keeps possession of the metropolis and the citadel; while he who spends his chief time, or his first pains, in getting a knowledge of mere details, is like the soldier who wastes his strength on the frontier, without ever making any grand attempt to possess the whole country.

As regards what are usually called doctrines, the Scriptures everywhere assert the lapsed, corrupt, and condemned state of human nature : in other words, that man is a guilty and unholy creature, who has fallen from his original state of righteousness, and who, if recovered from this condition and restored to the favour of God, must be saved by some aid from without: that the design of the incarnation and death of our Lord Jesus Christ is to effect man's redemption from sin, guilt, and death, in a manner harmonious with the perfections of the divine character, and the principles of God's moral government: that the blessings consequent to man upon this system of mediation are pardon, peace, and holiness here, and eternal life hereafter: and that the conditions on which (as a sine qua non, but not as a meritorious cause,) these blessings are bestowed, are repentance towards God, and faith in our Lord Jesus Christ; in short, the salvation of sinners, and at the same time the manifestation of the glory of God's moral character. Now this, one would think, must be conceded by every one who has obtained the least acquaintance with the Word of God. What a guide would these views prove to the settlement of many controversies! Through what labyrinths of opinion would these first principles of the Christian scheme lead you in safety! How many details would they include, and how many connected doctrines would they unfold, and establish, and render evident! Let them, then, be deeply rooted in your minds as so many fundamental truths, and be made to bear on all the controversies of which you may hear or read. Bring all other senti- ments to the ordeal of this question, " Do they profess or deny the corruption of human nature, so clearly laid down in the Word of God, and its recovery from guilt and depravity, by a system of mediation through Christ, which unites the redemption of man and the manifesta- tion of God's glory?"

A similar general reference to the ceremonial of the New Testament will help you to settle many contro- versies on this subject. You cannot possibly read the Gospels and Epistles without observing the contrast in one striking point of view presented between Judaism and Christianity, the former exhibiting so much that was ceremonial, the latter so little: the one being eminently a ritual system, the other no less eminently

a spiritual one. When Christ suffered on Calvary, and
expired with that triumphant shout, "It is finished!"
he changed the whole aspect of revealed religion. On
one side of the cross you behold the Law, with its
priests, its sacrifices, and its rites, retiring from sight;
on the other, you behold the Gospel, with its simple and
spiritual institutions, coming forward into view. From
that hour the great design of Christianity was to form
a character, of which a new, divine, and inward life
should be the animating soul, and holiness in all its
branches and beauties, be the external manifestation.
Christianity was intended, if not to put an end to
ritualism, yet so to subordinate it to spirituality,
holiness, and love, that it should be but as the fillet round
the brow, or as the bracelet upon the arm, of piety.
Christianity has left us nothing, in the form of ceremony, but baptism and the Lord's supper, and has said
so little even about them, as to lead us to suppose it
considers them of very inferior importance to what is
moral and spiritual. Just ask the question again,
"What kind of religion does the New Testament
chiefly design to teach, a ritual or a spiritual one?"
Here again you will be furnished with a test of many
a system. Connected with ceremony is priesthood.
Observe what is said in the New Testament about this.
How very little is said about religious officials, or func-
tionaries of any kind, compared with what is said
of other things. Christ is our Great High Priest, and
all Christians are the priesthood. No other priest is
mentioned. And as to bishops, pastors, or elders, their
only functions mentioned are teaching and ruling. A
sacerdotal order and sacerdotal acts, are nowhere referred
to. It nowhere appears the design of the apostles to

make much of man, or to invest him with domination or spiritual authority in the church. Even they disclaimed being lords of God's heritage.

So again with regard to ecclesiastical polity; it will be well to take a general view of this question, as furnished by the New Testament. I say, the New Testament, for the Old was the code of law for Judaism, as this is for Christianity. It would be no more proper to look to the constitution of the Jewish theocracy for the model of the Christian church, than it would be to the temple, its priests, and sacrifices, and ceremonies, for the regulations of Christian worship. The same difference is observable in the ecclesiastical character of Judaism and Christianity as is evident in their ceremonial. The Divine Author of our religion has furnished, by his confession before Pilate, " My kingdom is not of this world," that which is the key to all social religion, and ecclesiastical organisation. The elaboration, complexity, and secularity of earthly kingdoms do not appertain to His church, of which the characteristics are simplicity and spirituality. The design of church government is not so much the conversion of men's souls, as the fellowship, edification, and comfort of those who are already converted. The church of Christ, consisting of the company of believers, must in all its institutes be adapted to spiritual men, and have respect to their order, harmony, and mutual helpfulness. It has nothing worldly in its nature or design. It is in the world, but not of it. The more spiritual and simple a scheme of ecclesiastical polity is, the more likely, upon the general principle now laid down, does it seem to be that it is an approximation to that which was set up by our Lord Jesus Christ. The

more clearly it exhibits the church as a separate community, like the Jews amidst surrounding nations,
dwelling apart by itself, governed by its own laws,
animated by its own spirit, and pursuing its own objects,
the more does it accord with all which the New Testament teaches us on this subject.

An attention to these general aspects of Divine
revelation will greatly assist us in coming to a conclusion
upon most points of religious controversy.

Having made up your minds, upon evidence, as to
what is truth, then have as little to do with religious
controversy as you can.　Seek a practical rather than a
polemical religion.　Treat it as a something rather to be
done, than to be talked about.　Be not fond of dispu-
tation.　Be no religious knight-errant, running a-tilt
against every one who differs from you.　A pugnacious
disposition, whether it be from natural combativeness,
or prevailing vanity, is a dangerous thing to piety,
which, like the dew, falls only in a still atmosphere, and
lies longest in the shade.　Be too much taken up with
adding " to your faith virtue, and to virtue knowledge,
and to knowledge temperance, and to temperance
patience, and to patience godliness, and to godliness
brotherly kindness, and to brotherly kindness charity,"
to have much time for strife and contention.

Let it be your great concern to eat of the Bread
of Life, pure and unadulterated, rather than mix up
with it the grit and chaff of controversy ; and to drink,
and not trouble and foul, the clear Water of Life.
Avoid a taste for curiosity in things unrevealed, a
speculative turn concerning things mysterious, and a
distempered zeal for what, if true, is comparatively
little.　" There is," says an old author, " a kind of in-

temperance in most of us, a wild and irregular desire to make things more or less than they are in themselves, and to remove them well-nigh out of sight by our additions and defalcations. Few there are who can be content with truth, and settle and rest in it as it appeareth in that nakedness and simplicity in which it was first brought forth; but men are ever drawing out conclusions of their own, spinning out and weaving speculations, thin, unsuitable, and unfit to be worn, which yet they glory in and defend with more heat and animosity than they do that truth which is necessary and by itself sufficient without this art. For these are creatures of our own, shaped out in our phantasy, and so drest up by us with all accurateness and curiosity of diligence, that we fall at last in love with them, and apply ourselves to them with that closeness and adherency which dulleth and taketh off the edge of our affection to that which is most necessary, and so leaveth that neglected and last in our thoughts, which is main. As we read of the painter, who, having stretched his fancy and spent the force of his imagination in drawing Neptune to the life, could not raise his after thoughts to the setting forth the majesty of Jupiter."

Love the closet of devotion more than the arena of contention; study the Bible more than the volume of angry discussion; and seek the company of the sons of peace, rather than association with those who say, " We are for war." It is well, of course, to make yourselves acquainted generally with the subjects of controversy, especially those of the leading controversies of the day. No young man, for instance, should be ignorant of the evidences of Christianity, or of the great principles of Evangelical truth as opposed to

Rationalism or Unitarianism; or of Protestantism as against Popery, in all their range and bearing. These are the questions of the day. And in order to contend earnestly for the "faith once delivered to the saints," we must know what the faith is, and both how it is assailed, and how it can be defended. Every man should know what he believes, and why he believes it; and thus "be able to give a reason, with meekness and fear, of the hope that is in him." He should take his side, and valiantly keep it. All this is proper and necessary, but it is a different thing to our reducing religion to a mere matter of controversy. How many are there whose whole godliness is a mere contest for a creed, or a church, without their having any true faith in Christ, or their being members of the church which he has purchased with his blood! What multitudes are now fierce for Protestantism, who have never embraced with their whole hearts one great and true Protestant principle! Oh that men were more anxious to practise Christianity than controvert about it! That they were as zealous for holiness as they seem to be for truth, and as anxious to imbibe the spirit and exhibit the image of Christ in their temper, character, and conduct, as they are concerned to embody his doctrines in their creeds! Young men, be ardent lovers of the truth, diligent seekers after it, constant followers of it, and impassioned admirers, valiant defenders, and zealous promoters of it: but at the same time, not pugnacious, restless, bitter, and bigoted disputants for it.

Having received, upon satisfactory evidence, the system of doctrine which you believe to be Scriptural, do not allow your convictions to be shaken, or your faith to be staggered, on account of any difficulties with which it may seem to be attended; nor by any cavils and objections brought against it, which you may not be able to answer. It is of great importance for you to remember, that there is no truth, however evident and certain it may be, against which an ingenious and dexterous sophist may not advance some plausible objections; and in connexion with which, its most assured believers may not see some difficulties which they are not able to explain. Mathematical science is the only department of human inquiry which excludes all doubt and difficulty. Even the experimental philosopher sometimes finds many difficulties in his path which he is unable to clear up; some ultimate laws which perplex and confound him; and some results which baffle him. Does he abandon himself to scepticism? Certainly not. He credits his proofs, he relies upon his ascertained facts, and says, "I am puzzled, I see a difficulty which I cannot yet explain, but I hold fast my conviction of the truth of what I have proved, and wait for further light to clear up what is now dark. I cannot give up evidence, because of difficulty, and thus relinquish what I do know for what I do not know." Is not this perfectly rational and entirely philosophical? In this way I am anxious that you should act in reference to religion, its doctrines, and its controversies. Receive whatever truth revelation makes known, and because it makes it known, no matter with what difficulty it may be attended, and wait for further light to enlighten what is now dark. By difficulty, I mean something that you cannot perfectly understand: something that you cannot entirely harmonise with your previous notions; something that you cannot make quite to agree with some other portions of divine truth; something which may have been objected to by others, whose objections you feel yourselves in some measure unable to answer. If convinced that any doctrine or fact is revealed, let not any difficulty connected with it confound you or shake your convictions. It may be well sometimes, when startled and perplexed with difficulties on one side of a question, to look at the difficulties on the other side. Suppose you reject a doctrine, or a system, because of something that you cannot explain, should you not encounter difficulties far more formidable in the opposite system? Have you not more evidence and less difficulty on the side you have taken, than you would find if you were to pass over to the other side? There is a one-sided way of looking at these matters practised by some people, which you should avoid. In very many cases, conviction must rest upon the balance of evidence and difficulty, there being some seeming proof and some sound objection on each side, and our business is to determine which side has more of the former, and less of the latter. I cannot, therefore, give you a more important piece of advice than this, never abandon evidence to follow difficulty, for it is like turning away from a lantern, somewhat dim it may be, but still a steady light; or from the moon, in a mist perhaps, to run after an ignis fatuus. And at the same time, do not allow yourselves to be driven from your convictions, because you cannot refute all the arguments, or remove all the difficulties, or meet all the objections, which may be brought against them. There are men, I repeat, of such subtle minds, of such logical power, and so clever in argument, as to make the worse appear the better cause; who can by fallacy and sophistry sustain the most palpable error, and make that truth doubtful which has to you the luminousness of the sun. Never be ashamed to say to such an opponent, " I cannot refute your arguments, nor meet your objections, but I am unmoved by them." And I would reiterate the advice I have already given, avoid controversy. Having found what you believe to be truth, believe it, love it, enjoy it, practise it, but do not be eager to dispute about it.

Whatever may be your convictions of the truth of the religious opinions you have embraced, cultivate with a love of truth, a spirit of charity. There is a medium which it should be your anxiety to discover, between indifference to truth and a distempered zeal for it: between latitudinarianism on the one hand, and bigotry on the other. There are some who make truth everything in religion, others who make it nothing: the former are the advocates of an unsanctified orthodoxy, the latter of an equally unsanctified charity: the one are the worshippers of a creed, the other, the iconoclasts of all creeds: the former say, " No matter how well a man acts, if he does not hold these opinions;" the others reply, " It is no matter what opinions he holds, provided he acts well." Both are wrong. There can be no right belief of the truth which does not lead to holiness: and there can be no holiness which does not spring from right belief of the truth. Be you, therefore, the zealous advocates of truth, for error is sin. Error cannot sanctify. If a man may disbelieve one truth, and be innocent, he may disbelieve two; if two, ten; if ten, half the Bible; if half the Bible, the whole. Affect no false candour, no spurious charity, as if all sentiments were equally unimportant. This is treason against truth, and the God of truth.

Let not all the various sects, denominations, and creeds, appear in your eye as the beautiful colours of the rainbow. It is a false and bad figure, and the very germ of infidelity. But, at the same time, guard against the opposite extreme of a want of charity towards those who differ from you. It is not your business, nor mine, to fix the boundary line of religious opinion which divides those who will be saved from those who will be lost. The Church of Rome, with insufferable arrogance, and a daring invasion of the prerogative of Heaven, has fixed that line in the pale of her communion. Imitate not this impious assumption. And while you avoid this highest of all pretensions, of determining who shall or shall not be admitted to the kingdom of heaven, guard against the lesser mischiefs of controversy; I mean that bitterness of spirit and exclusiveness of feeling which we are but too apt to cherish towards those who in lesser matters differ from us. Charity is as much a part of truth as doctrine. No man believes the Bible who rejects charity. The want of charity is as truly a heresy as a disbelief in the divinity of Christ. The want of charity will as certainly exclude a man from heaven, as the want of faith. "Now abide faith, hope, charity, these three; but the greatest of these is charity." With one hand, lay hold of faith; with the other, lay hold of charity; then and then only, may you cherish hope.

And now, Young Men, let me endeavour at any rate, to impress upon you the infinitely, eternally, and therefore inconceivably, momentous nature of that subject about which all these controversies are carried on. Oh, what interests and what issues, beyond the compass and the power of any mind, but that which is Infinite, to grasp, are comprehended in that word, Religion! Science, art, literature, politics, law, medicine, all appertain to time, to earth, to the body; but religion relates to the soul, to heaven, to eternity. What are all the questions which have been asked, the parties that have been formed, the controversies which have been carried on, in reference to the former of these classes of subjects, but matters of momentary interest and trifles light as air, compared with the latter? Of what importance are all the questions, the sects, the parties, the controversies, of an earthly nature, to "the congregation of the dead," to the inhabitants of the unseen world, to the spirits of just men made perfect, or to the lost souls in prison? What will they all be to you a few years hence? what may they be to you next week? But the great controversy about religion has in all three worlds, heaven, earth, and hell, an interest that will continue through all eternity. This is a controversy in which you, each one of you, are personally interested. It involves your eternal destiny, and will be a matter of infinite moment to you millions and millions of ages hence. Surely, surely, this consideration, if anything can do it, will throw over your mind an air of deep and solemn seriousness. The levity and frivolity you carry to other questions; the carelessness and half-heartedness with which you regard other controversies, must be checked here. You must ask the question, "What is truth?" with a mind looking up into heaven, down into the bottomless pit, and abroad upon eternity. And with a recollection that, various as are the answers to that question returned from those around you, your torment or your happiness for ever and ever will be influenced by the answer to it on which you decide. Oh, if you would but enter thus seriously, anxiously, and prayerfully, into the subject, there would be little danger of your going wrong on this momentous topic.

Still you must expect, notwithstanding all your solicitude, to be the subject of some perplexity, as long as you are an inhabitant of this world. Be thankful, however, that what is essential to salvation is so plain, that he that runs may read. Repent, believe, love, be holy: Is there any mystery here? How many sects agree in this! Of how many creeds this is the essence! How much of the strife of controversy lies outside of this circle! How many minor truths a man may not believe, and yet be saved, if he believe these great fundamentals. How many lesser errors he may have unhappily embraced, and yet not be lost, if he is in no error here! He that keeps his eye upon the pole-star and the greater constellations, will steer his vessel safely, though he may not be intimately acquainted with the stars of lesser magnitude and brilliancy. To adopt, in conclusion, the directions and words of Saurin: " Buy the truth, which requires the sacrifice of dissipation, of indolence, of precipitancy, of prejudice, of obstinacy, of curiosity, of the passions. We comprise the matter in seven precepts :

" Be attentive.

" Do not be discouraged by labour.

" Suspend your judgment.

" Let prejudice yield to reason.

" Be teachable.

" Restrain your avidity of knowledge.

" In order to edify your mind, subdue your heart."

But shall we always live in shades and grope in darkness? Will there always be a veil between the porch and the sanctuary? Will God always lead us between chasms and gulfs? Shall we for ever dwell near the battle-field of religious controversy, and be within sound of its artillery and the range of its shot? Shall we always hear the confused noise of its warriors, and the cry of defeat, mingling with the shouts of victory? Shall we always have to struggle with argument from without, and with doubt and suspense within? O, no! Presently this night of our ignorance, this dark night, will end, and we shall enter into that blessed world where there is no need of the sun, because the Lamb is the light thereof. In heaven we shall know all things by blessed intuition. We shall repose around the fountain of celestial radiance, where the sound of controversy will be as unheard as the din of arms. In heaven, we shall understand all mysteries in nature, providence, grace, and glory. All difficulties will be solved. All objections will be silenced. How will this perfect light fill us with perfect joy! How delightful will it be to drink knowledge for ever from its divine source, with the assurance that it is pure from any admixture of error! How blissful thus to spend eternity! "This is the revelation of God to us, and there is not in religion a more joyful and triumphant consideration than this perpetual progress which the soul makes in the perfection of its nature, without ever arriving at an ultimate period. Here truth has the advantage of fable. No fiction, however bold, presents to us a conception so elevating and astonishing as this interminable line of heavenly excellence. To look upon the glorified spirit, as going on from strength to strength; adding virtue to virtue, and knowledge to knowledge; making approaches to goodness which is infinite; for

ever adorning the heavens with new beauties, and
brightening in the splendours of moral glory, through
all the ages of eternity, has something in it so transcendent and ineffable, as to satisfy the most unbounded
ambition of an immortal mind." Young men, have
you this ambition? If not, take it up from this moment; it is the noblest which God can inspire, or the
human bosom receive.

CHAPTER VI.

THE CHARACTER OF JOSEPH.

How can I do this great wickedness and sin against God? GENESIS xxxix, 9.

THE Bible, viewed apart from its highest character as a revelation of divine, eternal, and immutable truth, and from its design as intended to make men "wise unto salvation," is the most instructive, entertaining, and interesting volume in the world, uniting, as it does, every species of writing, every variety of subject, and every style of composition. Hence the testimony of Sir William Jones, a man who, by the exertion of rare intellectual talents, acquired a knowledge of languages and literature which has seldom been equalled, and scarcely, if ever, surpassed. "I have carefully and regularly perused the Scriptures," says this truly great man, "and am of opinion that this volume, independent of its divine origin, contains more sublimity, purer morality, more important history, and finer strains of eloquence, than can be collected from all other books, in whatever language they may have been written." Such a testimony, borne by a scholar who was intimately acquainted with twenty-eight different languages, and with the best works which had been published in most of them, deserves attention, and must carry weight with every considerate mind. The page of Holy Writ on which we open in this chapter justifies this eulogy: for where is the judge of literary composition who will not pronounce the history of Joseph to be one of the most exquisitely pathetic narratives ever written?

Before I proceed to enter upon the character of Joseph, I will point out what, besides the exhibition of a splendid example of human excellence, appears to me to be the design of God in preserving his deeply interesting and eventful history. This narrative is a representation of Providence in miniature. Here we see God working out his wise and benevolent schemes by means and instruments the most varied, the most unlikely, and seemingly the most opposite; and by a series of events, which as they arise singly and separately, appear to favour the designs of the bad and to oppress the good, but which are all made to terminate in the triumph of virtue and piety. Here, on a small scale, we see a wonderful and complicated mechanism, numerous wheels moving in opposite directions, but all made to subserve one wise and holy purpose, and thus to furnish an historical and beautiful illustration of the declaration, that " All things work together for good to them that love God." In many parts of Scripture we hear Providence speaking, but here we see it acting; and making evil, without altering its nature or excusing its agents, subserve the good man. Here we see that though truth and holiness for a while may be trodden down by the iron heels of falsehood, vice, and power, they shall at length lift up their heads with joy, and be crowned with glory and honour.

But we now take up the other purpose of this beau-

tiful narrative, and that is, to exhibit, for admiration
and imitation, an extraordinary pattern of human excellence. Much of the Bible is historical and biographical.
It is a gallery of portraits, both of good and bad men ;
some merely sketched in outline ; some showing part
of the figure only, and some drawn at full length.   This
makes the Scriptures at once interesting and instructive.
We see sin in living shapes, depraved, leprous, beastly,
diabolical, and learn to hate it.   We see holiness, fair
and beautiful, though by no means perfectly angelical
and heavenly, and we are by such examples taught to
love it, and helped to acquire it.   Let us, then, now
contemplate the character of Joseph.   It is not my
intention, for it is not in my power, in a single chapter
to enter very much at length into details of his touching
history.   I must take for granted your acquaintance
with them, and can do nothing more than give you so
much of the narrative as shall help you in studying his
character.

And, first of all, let us look at Joseph in that situation where the germ of all his future excellences began
to develope, his father's tent.   There, were laid, in his
fflial piety and his true religion, the foundations of that
noble and lofty character which all nations and ages have
delighted to contemplate.   It is unquestionably true, and
should ever be borne in mind by parents and children,
that the rudiments of character are formed in early life,
and at home, and then and there those seeds of good
or evil are sown which bear in future years their appropriate fruits.   He was the favourite child of his father,
who in a manner most injudicious in itself, most dangerous to the object of his preference, and most
destructive of his own peace, displayed his partiality by

" the coat of many colours," and other marks of parental distinction. This partiality, though unwisely manifested, was grounded in part on Joseph's exemplary conduct, for he was a most dutiful son, and one that feared God. At the same time, however, he was the object of hatred and envy to his brethren. This was caused partly by his father's partiality; partly by his artless simplicity, not perhaps untinctured by vanity which had been increased by indulgence, and which showed itself in relating his dreams; and partly by the information which he gave of the misconduct of his brothers; for all these things tended, doubtless, to increase and exasperate their ill-will. But their enmity was produced chiefly by his good conduct and blameless character. They hated him because " their own deeds were evil and their brother's righteous." It was the enmity of the wicked towards the good. He was their constant reprover by the silent reproach of his holy example. I scarcely know a situation more trying, or requiring more firmness, humility, meekness, wisdom, and caution, than that of a pious and dutiful child, loved by his parents on account of his excellence of character, and surrounded by brothers of an opposite description. If any of you are in that situation, pray earnestly to God to make his grace sufficient for you. With the murderous conspiracy of Joseph's cruel and unnatural brothers you are well acquainted. I shall draw no picture of his cries and entreaties, when he was seized by them, and cast into a pit to be left to starve; but I will for one moment suggest how in that horrible situation he must have been sustained and comforted by the religion he had learnt at home; and what else could meet his case? What a situation for one who had never till now been from beneath the protection of paternal care and tenderness; whose face the wind of heaven had never, hitherto, visited too roughly; whose spirit, mortification had never galled; whose heart, affliction had never yet pierced. But his gracious God and his easy conscience were with him there; and in those mournful and desolate circumstances he found that he was not alone. O religion! thou divine and seraphic companion and comforter, thou wilt never leave us, however forlorn our condition or gloomy our prospects.

I also pass by the successful intercession of Judah for his life, and the providential arrival of the Arabian caravan, and follow Joseph down into Egypt, to witness his conduct in the house of Potiphar, to whom he was sold as a slave. Instead of cursing his lot, yielding to sullen despondency, and making his master angry by hopeless misery, he accommodated himself, by the aid of religion, to his circumstances, and applied all his faculties to serve his master, to secure his confidence, and conciliate his kindness. And he was successful. You see how wise it is, instead of giving up all for lost in unfavourable circumstances, and sinking into absolute despair, to resolve, by God's blessing, to do all we can to improve our condition. Learn, young men, to bear up with patience, fortitude and hope, against adverse circumstances. It is always too soon to despair in this world. It was an old Greek proverb, "We ascend downwards." And in Bunyan's inimitable allegory, the "Valley of Humiliation" lay in the direct road to exalt-ation. If by any cause you are brought into a less favourable situation than you have been accustomed to occupy, go diligently and cheerfully to work, and determine, by God's grace, to make even this bitter experience subservient to your future welfare. It may be necessary to prepare you for something higher and better. Never abandon hope. The mainspring of exertion is broken when this is gone.

Joseph's conduct in the house of Potiphar was so exemplary for diligence and fidelity, that it drew upon him, first of all, the favour of God, and next, the esteem of man, for he was soon advanced to a high place of trust and honour in the establishment of his master. The reason of Potiphar's conduct in thus promoting his Hebrew slave is given by the historian in the following words: "He saw that the Lord was with him, and the Lord made all that he did to prosper in his hand." Here is one of the ten thousand instances which corroborate the declaration of the apostle, that "Godliness is profitable for all things, having the promise of the life that now is, and of that which is to come." True piety is the parent of every virtue which is either useful to man or pleasing to God; and when confirmed and illustrated by a faithful life, is the best recommendation a youth can offer to one whose confidence he wishes to secure. Few men are so blind to their own interest as not to know the value and to appreciate the services of an able diligent and faithful servant, and rarely does it happen that such a servant, where there is room for it, is not promoted. Depend upon it, there is a buoyancy in talent and virtue which will make them rise to the surface. "Seest thou," says Solomon, "a man diligent in business, he shall stand before kings." "I," said Benjamin Franklin, "can attest the truth of that, for I have transacted with five monarchs in my time." It was as a servant that Franklin commenced his wonderful career, and by the fidelity and diligence he displayed in that capacity, he laid the foundations of his future fame. Innumerable instances have occurred of eminent and excellent servants becoming partners and proprietors of the establishments in which they once acted in a very subordinate capacity.

In the chapter entitled " Entrance upon Life," I reminded you that sincere, heartfelt and very decided piety is necessary to prepare for those sudden, violent, and unexpected temptations which often beset the young traveller on life's eventful journey; especially in circumstances of promotion and prosperity. Joseph soon experienced the truth of this. He was, we are informed, a young man of such personal appearance as was likely to attract the attention and excite the passions of an unprincipled and flagitious woman. Beauty is the production of God, and, as one of his gifts, is, like every other, to be considered good in itself, and to be received with thankfulness: but how often does it prove a snare to its possessor, and a temptation to others! It had nearly proved more fatal to Joseph than even the envy of his brothers. This last threatened only his body, but that endangered his soul. His virtue was vehemently and perseveringly assailed. Every thing combined to give all but irresistible force to the assault. Its nature, so adapted to the passions of youth: its source, a person who by her favour could aid his promotion, or by her malignity, which was sure to be roused by disappointment and resentment, could ensure his ruin: its secrecy, which would cover the crime from every spectator, but that One who is the witness of all deeds: its repetition, carried forward from time to time: its violence, as if she would carry her purpose by

assault, all rendered it every thing but certain that
Joseph's integrity must yield. Who does not tremble
for him? Who would not tremble more for himself in
such a case? His destiny is suspended upon the manner in which he meets that fierce assault. If he fall,
he will in all probability never rise. But if he stand, he
will in all probability never fall. If he resist, he is safe
for ever after. If he consent, one criminal act will lead
to another, till he becomes an abandoned profligate.
A first wrong step will render all wrong afterwards, and
be an entrance on the road to ruin. Yes, there are
cases in most men's moral history, when their whole
character and destiny depend upon their decision
regarding one single act. Joseph was victorious.
Wonderful! How was this triumph of virtue over
vice, of youthful innocence over all but irresistible
temptation, achieved? First, by a deep sense of honour.
He replied to the seductress, "There is none greater in
this house than I; neither hath he (my master) kept
any thing from me but thee, because thou art his wife."
Shall I thus abuse his confidence and requite his kindness? Noble youth! All generations since have done
thee honour! But whence this delicate sense of honour?
From infidelity? No, for David Hume taught that
adultery was but a little thing if known, and if unknown, nothing. Infidelity! Where is the infidel who
would not have laughed at the squeamishness of a conscience which would have hesitated, in such a situation
as this? No: it was religion that made Joseph
virtuous in himself and honourable to his master; for
he immediately added, How shall I do this great wickedness and sin against God? Yes, that was his safeguard.
All guards but one were absent, and that One, though

invisible to sense, now stood revealed to the eye of his faith in this the most perilous hour of his existence, and threw over him the shield of omnipotence, which averted the shafts of the tempter, preserved his chastity unsullied, and inspired deep abhorence of the sin to which he was so perilously exposed. Yes, it was his religion, his realizing sense of the Divine presence, that in this crisis of his history determined the purpose that saved him from ruin. He acted under the potent and protecting influence of the consideration, Thou God seest me: and endured as seeing him who is invisible. How solemn a reflection,

> "Within thy circling power I stand,
> On every side I find thy hand;
> Awake, asleep, at home, abroad,
> I am surrounded still with God.
> O may these thoughts possess my breast,
> Where'er I roam, where'er I rest,
> Nor let my weaker passions dare
> Consent to sin, for God is there."

Young Men away from home, removed from beneath the vigilant eye of parental superintendence, and exposed to temptations of this or any other kind, look at the power which preserved Joseph, and which can also preserve you. See where your strength, your safety, and your happiness lie. There are temptations so strong, so violent, so fascinating to our corrupt natures, that all other restraints but those of true piety will be swept away before them, like cobwebs or chaff by the force of a tempest. It is beautifully said of the good man, "The law of his God is in his heart; none of his steps shall slide." Seek this support guidance and protection, and you will be safe and happy in dangers as imminent as those which hung over this holy and honourable man.

Voluptuous and profligate youth, votary of licentious pleasures, thou that deridest the prudish scruples of Joseph, place thyself in imagination on the bed of death, at the judgment seat, on the brink of the fathomless abyss of punishment. Through the flames of the bottomless pit seek those persons of whose crimes thou hast been the witness, the accomplice, perhaps the author. Behold the pleasures of a moment succeeded by the sufferings of eternity. Or look up into heaven, where the present mortification of sin is followed by everlasting ages of holiness without effort, and happiness without alloy, and say, which thou wilt then wish thou hadst chosen on earth, the love of sinful pleasure, or the love of the holy God.

There is another lesson of momentous consequence for the young, and indeed for all, to learn from the conduct of Joseph in this assault; and that is, that while some temptations are boldly to be encountered and resolutely overcome, there are others only to be conquered by flight, and to be disarmed by removing to a distance. Joseph fled from the company and solicitations of this shameless woman. He that carries gunpowder about him should not stay and endeavour to protect himself from the fire, but should instantly get as far from it as he can. So should it be in many cases of temptation; to parley is to be in danger, to listen is to be in jeopardy, to linger is to fall. He that enters with his eyes open into temptation, or remains in it voluntarily, is already vanquished.

As Potiphar's wife could not corrupt Joseph's virtue, she determined to blast his reputation and effect his ruin, and brought forward the memorial of her shame

as the proof of his guilt. Appearances were unquestionably against him, and show how even the most spotless
purity may sometimes be slandered amidst circumstances
calculated to excite suspicion, and may for awhile lie
under the imputation of crime. "And here again,"
says an author, "we have a fresh instance of his greatness of mind. He chooses rather to incur his master's
groundless displeasure, and to sink under the weight
of a false accusation, than to vindicate his own honour
by exposing the shame of a bad woman; and he leaves
the clearing up of his character, and the preservation
of his life, to that God with whom he had entrusted
still higher concerns, those of his immortal soul. And
thus the least assuming, the shamefaced, feminine
virtues, temperance, and chastity, and innocence, and
self-government, are found in company with the most
manly, the heroic qualities, intrepidity, constancy, and
contempt of death." This is very finely put, but it is
not quite certain that the silence of the historian proves
also Joseph's silence in defence of himself; nor is it
quite clear that either chivalry or trust in God should
have made him willing to bow down to such an accusation. Perhaps, however, he saw that as he could bring
no witnesses, and that the matter rested wholly between
himself and his tempter, it was useless to reveal the
facts, and better to leave his vindication to the Providence of God, who would bring forth his righteousness as the light, and his judgment as the noon-day.

Joseph was imprisoned, but he was infinitely happier
there, with his smiling conscience, than was his slanderer
amidst all the luxuries of her mansion, tormented as
she must have been by her own reflections. No place
is frightful to a good man but the dungeon of an ill

conscience. Free from that, Joseph is at large, though in prison. Nor can any place be pleasant to one tormented with remorse; that will convert a paradise into hell. Here again in this seemingly hard condition, we see Joseph maintaining his self-respect, his confidence in God, his benevolent activity, his obliging disposition, and his general good conduct. By this course of action, he subdued even his jailor, and conciliated the friendship and affection of one who may be supposed, from his occupation, not to have possessed the gentlest nature. He made friends everywhere, and of everybody, but her whose favours would have been his ruin. This was accomplished by the union of piety, general excellence of character, a cheerful disposition, and obliging demeanour. The same course will be followed in other cases with the same effect.

While suffering unjustly in prison, the inspiration of God came upon him in the interpretation of the dreams of two of Pharaoh's officers, and this after two weary years of ungrateful and criminal forgetfulness on the part of one of them, led to his liberation. But in this ingratitude of the chief butler we see the Providence of God, for had he spoken earlier of the poor captive whom he ought to have remembered, the king might have given Joseph his liberty; but probably none of the events which followed would then have taken place, and to have been numbered among the wise men of the land, might have been the greatest honour to which he attained. How conspicuously Providence appears in all these incidents! The envy of Joseph's brethren; the lasciviousness of his mistress; the misconduct and dreams of his fellow-prisoners; and the ingratitude of one of them; all bad in themselves, yet all meeting, strange to think, in one point, the elevation of Joseph to be the second person in all the land of Egypt, inferior to the king alone. Remove one link, and the chain is broken. God is wonderful in counsel, and excellent in working.

The dreams of Pharaoh, and their interpretation by Joseph, under inspiration by God, made way, not only for his liberation, but for his advancement to the highest dignity which the monarch could bestow, next to the crown. Instead of the fetters which bound him, he receives Pharaoh's ring of office. Instead of his prison clothes, he was dressed in the fine linen of Egypt, worn only by the great. Instead of the confinement of a prison, he dwells in a palace. Instead of being the servant of a jailor, he is first minister of a monarch, never appearing in public but to be seen in a chariot of state preceded by a herald, calling upon the people to bow the knee. A change so sudden; a transition so great; an elevation so lofty; usually intoxicates the mind, corrupts the heart, and mars the character. It had not this effect upon our true hero. Joseph's dignity, his courage, his humility, his clemency, on this trying occasion, were astonishing, and are all to be traced up to his piety, which dictated and produced them, and caused him to maintain, when the prime minister of state, the same fidelity and prudence which he exhibited in the house of Potiphar and in the prison. His holy excellences, as the circle of his influence widened, increased their power, and multiplied their effects, till they pervaded the greater sphere as completely as they had done the less. Potiphar's base and flagitious wife, his tempter and calumniator; the ungrateful butler; his own wicked and murderous brethren; were all now at his mercy; he had an arm long enough to reach, and strong enough to crush, them all; but with generosity untinctured by a single particle of malice or resentment, he determined that the sun of his glory should shine forth without a spot. "Joseph was but thirty years old when he became the prime minister of Pharaoh; seventeen of which had been spent under the wing of a fond, indulgent parent; and the other thirteen, at that period when the heart is most devoted to pleasure, he had lingered away in all the variety of human wretchedness, but in all the dignity of virtue, all the superiority of wisdom, all the delights, pure and sublime, of true piety; and now, at an age when most men are only beginning to reflect and act as reasonable beings, we see him raised, not by accident nor cabal, nor by petulance, but by undisputed merit, to a situation which one part of mankind look up to with desire, another with awe, and a third with despair." See him, young men, now as a minister of Pharaoh, serving his royal master during the years of famine and plenty, with a zeal surpassed only by his honesty. What an opportunity did he now possess to amass for himself, by selfishness and peculation, incalculable wealth! But his fidelity was as signal and illustrious as his situation. He has been blamed by some for taking advantage of the famine, first to impoverish and then to enslave the Egyptians. I have not time to examine this charge at any length, nor to enter minutely into the circumstances of this part of his conduct: and perhaps we may not be able to come to any satisfactory conclusion upon it, for want of more information than is contained in the Scriptural account. There are some expositors who are of opinion that there was nothing in this transaction which reflects discredit on Joseph's character. That he had no selfish view is evident; and as regards Pharaoh, it must be borne in mind, the government of Egypt, before the famine, was despotic and arbitrary. If there were in this affair nothing but a display of ministerial adroitness, in ungenerously employing his superior skill and address in planning or carrying out a system of despotism, let it be viewed as a dark spot on the disc of his glory: but it is believed by many that this was not the case. It is said, in his defence, that it is clear that after the expiration of the famine, he restored to the people their lands and their liberties, upon condition of their paying to the king, for the purpose of government, a fifth part of their produce, which was a kind of corn tax in lieu, it should seem, of arbitrary exactions, and was a tax which in that fertile country they could easily pay. That Joseph was not an oppressor is evident from the sentiments of gratitude which the Egyptians expressed, "Thou hast saved our lives;" and from the veneration and love with which his memory has ever been cherished among them. Instead of enslaving the people, he was the first, say his defenders, that in Egypt limited the power of the crown, settling by a formal ordinance, that portion which alone the king could touch.

Before we pass on, let us just pause for a moment to mark the changeful condition of man upon earth. Compare, or rather contrast, the situation of Joseph now as prime minister of Egypt, and second only to Pharaoh himself, with his condition as first the slave and afterwards the prisoner of Potiphar. How soon may the most brilliant scene be enveloped in the darkest clouds, and the calm be succeeded by the storm; on the other hand, how soon may the dark clouds roll off and exhibit the orb of day in more than previous splendour, and the storm give way to a brighter and a sweeter calm. Amidst such vicissitudes, let us indulge neither a careless and confident security in prosperity, nor a settled and gloomy despondency in adversity; but seek that true piety and that humble trust in God, which shall preserve us in cheerful and tranquil equanimity of mind, and make us feel independent in one condition and hopeful in the other.

We now turn from Joseph as prime minister of state, to contemplate his conduct as a brother and a son. I do not profess to be able to explain how it came to pass that all this while he made no inquiries after his father and brethren. There is a chasm here which I cannot fill up. That it arose neither from resentment nor alienation, seems evident from his subsequent conduct. Perhaps he thought he could not communicate the details of his history without inflicting a deeper wound upon his father's heart, by an account of the unworthiness of his other sons, than could be healed by the information of his own life and elevation. Or God, whose counsel he sought in all his ways, may have given him an express revelation, directing him at what time and in what manner to make himself known to his family. For the account of Joseph's conduct to his brethren, I refer you to the inimitably touching narrative preserved in the book of Genesis. To many readers, doubtless, there will appear to be a somewhat unseemly sporting with their feelings, a want of sincerity in the disguise he assumed and the accusations he preferred, and a degree of profanity in the somewhat heathen language which in one or two instances he employed. I will not contend that in all his conduct he was perfectly blameless. There may have been spots in his character, and after comparing it very closely with Scripture, some may be discovered; and we must disapprove of what is wrong wherever and in whomsoever it is found. Sacred history exhibits its characters just as they were, not in all respects as they should have been. Dark spots are most easily discovered upon the whitest garments, and foul blemishes in the fairest reputations. There were, however, obvious reasons for the general conduct of Joseph. He knew the former wicked character of his brethren, and had experienced their murderous cruelty towards himself; and as he very likely foresaw that this interview and renewed intercourse might lead to their coming down and settling in Egypt, he wished to ascertain how far their present character would, from its improvement, warrant his encouraging such a step. What might appear, therefore, to others as unnecessary cruelty, was in his intention the wisdom and severity of love. It was as the test of fire to the metal, to prove of what sort it is. He wanted to know how far they repented of their sin towards himself, and he therefore placed himself in a position to ascertain this, a position in which he could look into their hearts, without discovering his own. His love yearned over them, and he longed to tell them how fully and freely he forgave them; but with a prudence and strength of mind which proved not only how good, but how wise and great he was, he laid a stern restraint upon his feelings till the proper moment of disclosure arrived, and the end of postponing it had been fully answered. The whole scene is of such exquisite pathos, as is not to be equalled in the creations of fiction.

At length the full evidence of contrition and

amendment having been obtained, and the purpose of his disguise having been accomplished, his heart could endure no longer the torture of concealment; the pathetic speech of Judah, the sight of his own beloved brother Benjamin, the frequent mention of his father's name, raised such a torrent of filial and fraternal love in his soul, that he suddenly lets fall the mask, and exclaims, "I am Joseph. Doth my father yet live?" Who can describe, who can imagine, their feelings at this discovery? If they had in his early life actually put him to death, and his ghost had now started up before them, their feelings could not have been greatly different. A little mind might have enjoyed the triumph which he had now gained over those who once hated him. He saw their distress, he beheld them dumb with amazement, petrified with terror, tortured with apprehension, and he instantly dissipated their fears; calmed their perturbation; became their apologist, instead of their accuser; and directed their attention to that Providence which had over-ruled their conduct, not only to procure his advancement, but also for the preservation of the lives of thousands. A less generous noble and delicate mind, would have talked much of his forgiving them, but he entreats them to forgive themselves.

Revengeful and implacable men, whom the least offence inflames, who never forgive an injury incomparably less than that committed against Joseph; who, with a serpentine cunning, a blood-hound scent, and a leonine ferocity, pursue the object of your malice, and at last take a demon-like pleasure in his tortures as he writhes under the inflictions of your revenge, how little, how contemptible, you appear, when compared with this hero of fraternal love! Pause, young men, upon this instance, and say if there is not more true greatness in this act of forgiveness than in all the sanguinary heroes of history or romance?

You have seen Joseph as a brother, now contemplate him once more as a son; I say once more, for we have already seen him in his youthful days, the comfort of·his father's declining years. The boy has become a man, the man has become illustrious, and the illustrious man has become the minister of a foreign court; and does he still remember and love ‚his father, the old shepherd of Canaan? Has filial piety outlived his injuries, his changes, his reverses, his elevation? Or, has Joseph wished and contrived, amidst his brilliant fortunes, to forget the hoary patriarch? Again, I say, read the beautiful history, and see how this best of sons shall answer, by his own conduct, this question. How abrupt the transition in that gush of feeling! "I am Joseph, doth my father yet live?" How beautiful the exhortation, "Ye shall tell my father all my glory." How exquisite the admonition, "Haste ye, and go up to my father, and say unto him: Thus saith thy son Joseph, God has made me lord of all Egypt; come down; tarry not. And thou shalt dwell in the land of ‚Goshen, and thou shalt be near unto me, thou and thy children's children, and all that thou hast, and there will I nourish thee. Ye shall haste and bring down my father hither."

The joyful news being conveyed to Jacob, he immediately removed with all his family to Egypt. I attempt not to describe the raptures of that interview, when father and son, clasped in each other's arms, found not only words, but tears and sobs, too weak to express the overwhelming ecstacies of that scene and that moment in which Jacob could find nothing better fitted to give utterance to his emotion than this: "Now let me die, since I have seen the face of my son." Would you behold the greatest triumph and the richest trophy of filial love, turn to that glorious spectacle, when the prime minister of Egypt, the man next to Pharaoh himself, led the poor old shepherd of Canaan, leaning upon his arm, into the palace, and before the whole circle of courtiers, introduced him to the monarch, exultingly exclaiming, "My Father." "O nature, nature! How honourable thy empire, how glorious thy triumphs." There may be a more splendid example of filial love than this, but I know not where to find it. While Joseph was indulging in all this luxury of affection for his father, he did not forget his brethren; and though encircled with the splendours of a court, and invested with its richest honours, he was not ashamed to own, as his brothers, those whose occupation was odious in the estimation of the Egyptians, and to regard as his greatest distinction, his descent from the herdsman, who was the friend of God.

Here, young men, is the example of a son, which I commend most earnestly and affectionately to your attention and imitation. Be each of you a good son, not only in youth, but in manhood, and as long as the old man, your father, lives. There can be no moral excellence where filial piety is wanting. You cannot love your Heavenly Father, if you do not love your earthly one. In the sterile ground, where this virtue grows not, nothing good can grow, but only a few miserable weeds. Let it be to you a matter of tender solicitude and constant vigilance that all your conduct

may be such as to give comfort to your father's heart.
Ask how every thing will affect his peace, and thus
imbibe the spirit of the noble Epaminondas, who being
asked what he esteemed the happiest circumstance of his
life, replied, " That my father and mother were living
when I gained the victory of Leuctra." Or if you
want a more modern instance of strong filial affection,
take Dr. Samuel Johnson's example, borrowing, in his
extreme poverty, six guineas, to comfort the death-bed
of his poor dying mother, and paying the expenses
of her funeral with the proceeds of the sale of the
manuscript of " Rasselas." And especially remember
the solemn and incumbent duty of maintaining this
affection through every change of circumstances. Some
have dropped their affections for their relatives as they
rose in life, and having arrived at wealth and worldly
honour, have blushed to own the connections whom
they left below. I can conceive of cases in which virtue
itself may make a son blush to own his father; I mean
when the wretched parent has, by his misconduct, not
only disgraced himself, but his family : but for a child
to be ashamed of a father, simply on account of his
poverty, is a disposition of which it is difficult to say
which is the greatest, the meanness, the folly, the
cruelty, or the wickedness; it is, however, enough to
say, it is a compound of all those detestable ingredients.

I hasten to contemplate the closing scenes of Joseph's
history. He had welcomed his aged father to Egypt,
and by dutiful and loving behaviour had so cheered his
latter days, and had crowned his hoary head with such
glory and honour, as, during the seventeen years that
Jacob enjoyed his son's society, must have almost

obliterated his recollection of his past deep sorrows. Joseph had settled his brethren in Goshen, and lived beloved and respected by them. Pharaoh and his court continued to him their confidence, and the Egyptians their gratitude and veneration. Jacob at length died, and Joseph gave proof that neither his sensibilities as a man, nor his piety as a believer in God, had been dried up under the tropical sun of his wonderful prosperity. He fell on the lifeless corpse of his father, wept and kissed him. It was Jacob's dying request to be buried not in Egypt, but in the land of Canaan; a request that expressed his faith in the promise of God, which ensured the possession of this country to his descendants. This request was most scrupulously complied with by Joseph, and, to do honour to his father's memory, he followed his remains to Canaan, accompanied in the funeral procession by a retinue suited to his high rank as the prime minister of Pharaoh.

It now remained to be proved, as Joseph's brethren thought, whether his forgiveness had been granted to them out of mere respect to their father, or from the generous impulse of his own feelings. They first sent, therefore, in the most supplicating terms, to implore his pardon, enforcing their request by the sacred name of his father, and his father's God; and then came and prostrated themselves before him, thus fulfilling the dreams of his youth, which had excited their envy and hatred. They knew not, even yet, the depths of his generosity, and formed their opinion of him from themselves. He wept over their submission, cheered them with assurance of his continued kindness, and said to them, "Fear not, for am I in the place of God? But as for you, ye thought evil against me, but God meant it unto good. Now, therefore, fear not; I will nourish you and your little ones. And he comforted them, and spake kindly unto them." Noble-minded Joseph! What a brother! What a beautiful example of holy charity!

Joseph lived fifty-four years after this, and year succeeded year with unvarying splendour, but the events of his life, which were to interest and instruct all ages, were over, and his remaining history is comprised in a few sentences. He diffused happiness around him, and saw his father's house and his own descendants greatly multiplied. But as neither station, nor power, nor wealth, nor piety, nor all these combined, can preserve from the stroke of death, Joseph laid down his honours at the feet of the king of terrors, and was gathered to his fathers. " Grief finds a cure, usefulness a period, glory a decay, and pride a destroyer, in the grave." So he found it. The piety which had been the guide of his youth, the guard of his middle life, and the prop of his old age, sustained him to the last, and he died with firm faith in the promise of God, requesting that his bones might be preserved in order that they might be carried to Canaan, whenever the Lord should visit his people, and restore them to the land of promise. This request, similar in nature and design to that of his father, like that was sacredly fulfilled; for when the Israelites, nearly two centuries afterwards, left Egypt, notwithstanding the hurried circumstances of their flight, they repaired to his sepulchre, exhumed his bones, carried them with them, as a precious legacy, amidst all their wanderings in the wilderness, and at length interred them in that sacred spot where already reposed the dust of Abraham, Isaac, and Jacob.

It is scarcely necessary to remark, that the character of Joseph is a deeply interesting one, which combines the sobriety of truth with the charms of fiction. The variety of incident, the scenes of true pathos, the constant vicissitudes, the vivid contrasts of character, the unexpected turns of fortune, the struggles of exalted piety with temptation, and the signal victories of truth and virtue, the workings of the various passions and the play of the diversified affections of humanity, together with the intermixture of supernatural interposition with the ordinary courses of nature and events, which it contains, all invest this history with a fascination which nothing can surpass. Every one who has ever read it has confessed its power. "The peasant and the philosopher," it has been truly said, "the child and the adult, the believer and the infidel, the men of all nations and all ages, have admired, delighted in, and been edified by, a story, which, clothed with all the graces of eloquence, conveys the purest and sublimest lessons of piety and morality."

This is a real history and not a fiction. I do not deny that even examples which are merely the creations of genius and the offspring of imagination, have some power over the mind; or that truth and holiness, even in fable, may inspire affection and stimulate imitation ; but it is with a power far less commanding than that of fact. Whatever effect such exhibitions of virtue and vice may have, it is weakened, both at the time and in recollection, by a secret whisper, "It is all unreal." The perusal of such descriptions, however strongly it may excite the imagination, has little hold upon the conscience, and is rarely followed by any lasting results upon the character. The effect of moral fables and moral facts upon the mind respectively is not unlike that of a picture which is a work of pure fancy, as compared with a painting of real life. Now the character of Joseph is a reality.

It is a scriptural character, on which the hand of God has been specially employed, both in its production and in its exhibition. God has not only lavished upon it the riches of his power, wisdom, and grace, in forming and finishing it as one of the most beautiful specimens of his divine art and workmanship, but he has also set it in the gorgeous frame of inspiration, and suspended it in his own Scripture gallery of portraits of holy men of old, where he exhibits it for admiration, and for imitation, as fresh, though now nearly four thousand years old, as when it was just finished by the Divine pencil.

It is a character which countless millions have beheld with admiration, and multitudes of them with anxious, studied, and successful imitation. It has been held up before the youth of all nations, and all ages, to whom the Bible has gone. How many have been fortified in their struggles against sin, and made victorious over temptation, by the holy exclamation of this noble youth, "How shall I do this great wickedness and sin against God?" It comes therefore to you recommended and sanctioned by the experience of numbers.

The basis of this beautiful specimen of sanctified humanity was laid in true religion. All that lofty and noble structure of excellence which this history exhibits, rose upon the foundation of the belief and fear of God. It began in the house of his father Jacob, while he was yet a boy, and it was on this account that the patriarch cherished the partiality which he so unwisely displayed.

Joseph "remembered his Creator in the days of his youth." The fervent, consistent, and triumphant piety which he manifested abroad, he gained while under the parental roof. Those seeds of excellence, which grew up and protected and adorned him, when a young man from home, were sowed by the hand of his father at home. What security is there for moral excellence without religion, and what security for religion, except it be taken up in youth? It was religion, I repeat emphatically, that was the substratum of all Joseph's excellence.

The character of Joseph is as symmetrical as it is well based. There is a beautiful harmony and proportion in it. You do not see one excellence flourishing amidst many imperfections like a flower amidst many weeds in a wilderness, but a garden of beautiful plants, all exhibiting their colours and mingling their fragrance; nor like a single column rising amidst ruin and surrounding desolation, but a majestic temple, with all its parts in all their orderly arrangement and all their exquisite proportions. Here we see the son, the brother, the servant, the master, the ruler, each in its single and separate excellence, and all combined and harmonised in one glorious and lovely character. Here are no eccentricities; no anomalies; no deficiencies; no extravagances; there is no need to excuse great irregularities in some things, by as great excellences in others; no balancing of virtues against vices; but we see admirable consistency, beautiful uniformity; in short, that exquisite completeness which strikes the eye of the observer from whatever point of view it is contemplated. How inflexible was Joseph in temptation; how cheerful and active in adversity; how modest, humble, dignified, and holy in prosperity! In him were united the sagacity of the statesman, the penetration of the prophet, the firmness of the believer, and the purity of the saint. Goodness came first, greatness followed; and the former remaining uncorrupted by the latter was heightened by it like a jewel set in gold.

Young men, what a character is here : how worthy of your study, it sets forth to you the dangers which you may have to encounter from excessive parental indulgence; from injurious treatment; from living away from home in a corrupt state of society; from violent and unexpected temptation; from being entrusted with the interests of others; from coming into possession of great wealth, exalted station, and public honour. What a host of perils! And here you learn in Joseph's piety, meekness, integrity, diligence, economy, dignity, sympathy, forgiveness, filial regard, and dependence upon God, the many excellences you should imitate; and the means by which these perils are to be vanquished. Nor less strikingly do you see in his end the rewards that follow a holy and virtuous life; you see virtue crowned with safety, with peace, with riches, with honour, with usefulness, with heaven.

It is possible that curiosity may lead some of the Parents of the youths who may purchase this volume to look through its pages; and should this be the case, let the following remarks arrest their attention.

How momentous a duty is it, on their part, to give sound religious instruction to their children at the earliest period in which they can receive it, and endeavour, by the most judicious, affectionate, and persevering methods, to form their character by religion!

Of what great consequence it is, in order to promote the peace of families, to avoid the manifestation of partiality for any one child, by any unwise marks of distinction !

Parents, you know not how early your children will be removed from you, and this is an additional motive to train them up in the fear of God, that they may leave home fortified by true piety, to encounter the temptations of the world, and to endure the trials of life.

It may be that a child long lost to you may be restored under circumstances of such delight as more than to compensate for his absence, and your suspense concerning him. The pious son, removed from your family at a tender age, and for a long time having no share in your affairs, may prove to be the main pillar of your house, when there is no other person to prevent its fall.

It is possible, and even probable, that the piety of one child may become in following years the means of reformation and conversion to many others in your family, who had neglected pious instructions in their early years, and fallen into the ways of vice and wickedness.

Many a parent whose heart was at one time well-nigh broken by the circumstances of his family, has lived to see the tide of his domestic sorrow turned, and has ended a cloudy and stormy day by a calm and beautiful sunset.

A pious child is a father's best companion, next to God himself, amidst the infirmities of old age, and in the chamber of sickness and death.

But it is you, my young friends, and you especially, Young Men, who should consider this history. Often peruse the history as it is recorded in the book of Genesis. It is of unequalled beauty and pathos. Give yourself time to study it, and seek grace to imitate it, as far as the principles on which it is founded, and the virtues which compose it, shall apply to your own circumstances. And when you have thus studied it for its importance, admired it for its beauty, and copied it for your own advantage, ascend from it to the contemplation of that still more glorious, perfect and august example which is given us in our Lord Jesus Christ, of whose personal history it furnishes, though not perhaps a type, yet a parallelism, which is most singularly striking. Joseph envied by his brethren; sold into Egypt; degraded to the condition of a servant; exalted from the dungeon to the neighbourhood of the throne; invested with power; drawing his perishing kindred to him; and bestowing upon them a possession in the best of the land; at any rate reminds us of Him, if it does not actually prefigure Him, who was hated by the Jews; sold by one of his apostles; crucified by the Romans; and having thus been made of no reputation; was in the end raised from the cross to a throne above the skies. Behold Him ascending on high; receiving gifts for men; attracting millions to Him for salvation: and conferring upon them an inheritance incorruptible, undefiled, and that fadeth not away. Thus unite the Old and the New Testament histories, and combine in yourselves the character of Joseph with the mind of Jesus.

CHAPTER VII.

THE STUDY OF THE BOOK OF PROVERBS RECOMMENDED.

The Proverbs of Solomon, the son of David, King of Israel.

To know wisdom and instruction; to perceive the words of understanding.

To receive the instruction of wisdom, justice, and judgment, and equity.

To give subtilty to the simple, to the young man knowledge and discretion. PROVERBS i, 1-4.

In the subject we have to now consider, we have another proof and illustration of the opening sentiment of the last chapter; I mean the variety, beauty, and usefulness of the Holy Scriptures. In that chapter we saw and felt the fascination of sacred narrative; in this we shall see no less prominently, and feel, I hope, no less powerfully, the value of Scripture proverbs: and if that presented to us a chain of gold, in which each event was a distinct link, yet all were so conjoined as to form a complete ornament: this will present a string of the richest pearls of which each by itself is a separate and valuable jewel.

Proverbs are short sentences containing a maxim of wisdom, or expressing an instructive truth or fact ascertained by experience or observation. Shrewd rules for practical life, meaning more than the mere words express. They have ever been favourite vehicles of instruction, especially in countries of little civilization, where books were few or unknown, and men depended for their knowledge upon tradition. Among such people this method is more likely to produce effect than any other, for it assumes, as Bishop Lowth remarks, not to argue or persuade but to dictate. In order to render their precepts more pleasing, as well as more powerful, the instructors of mankind have ever illuminated them with metaphors, comparisons, and other embellishments. Proverbs prevailed much among the Hebrews, and continued to the latest ages of their literature. But they have also been adopted by people far advanced in refinement; indeed, by all nations upon earth. The prevailing characteristics of a good proverb, are brevity, that it may be easily remembered; point, that it may stimulate; and elegance, that it may please. And how all these apply to the Proverbs of Solomon you know full well. Let us then enter on a consideration of this admirable portion of Holy Scripture.

I. We will consider its author. It opens with ascribing this honour to Solomon. The tradition of the Jews represents him as having written the Canticles in youth, and the Book of Proverbs in middle life, and it considers the book of Ecclesiastes to be his confession as a penitent, mourning over his early dark and winding aberrations from the path of truth and holiness. Several of the sages, or wise men, of Greece, were rendered illustrious by a few well-known maxims; but though posterior to Solomon, how limited in this respect was their wisdom, to that which blazed forth from his wonderful

genius, "to whom God gave wisdom and understanding exceeding much, and largeness of heart, even as the sand that is on the sea shore. And Solomon's wisdom excelled all the wisdom of all the children of the east country, and all the wisdom of Egypt; and his fame was in all nations round about: and he spake three thousand proverbs, and his songs were a thousand and five." Considering the early age of the world in which he lived, he was probably the most extraordinary genius that ever appeared on earth. "Magnificence was his identifying attribute. And alas, alas, for the weakness of humanity, the dangers of knowledge, and the pride of intellect, wealth, and power, even when he sinned, as most awfully he did, it was with a high hand, on a large scale, and with a kind of royal gusto: he did not, like common sinners, sip at the cup of corruption, but drank of it, 'deep and large,' emptying it to the dregs: and when he suffered, his groans seemed to be those of a demigod in torment. He stood like a pyramid, the shadow he cast in one direction was equal to the light he received in the other. An example his which proves that any great disproportion between gifts and graces, renders the former as fatal as a knife is to the suicide, or the power of writing to the forger. We ardently hope that Solomon became a true penitent. But if he did not, his writings, so far from losing their value, would gain new force; the figure of their fallen author would form a striking frontispiece, and these solemn warnings would receive an amen, as from the caves of perdition. A slain Solomon! since fell Lucifer the son of the morning, what more impressive proof of the power of evil."*
It is clear, from information contained in the book

* Gilfillan's "Bards of the Bible."

itself, that Solomon did not publish the whole during his life. The latter part, from the twenty-fifth chapter, forming an appendix, was collected after his death, and added to what appears to have been more immediately arranged by himself. What a production of one mind! and when we add to this the book of Ecclesiastes, we stand amazed at the intellect which could have poured forth such a fund of practical wisdom.

Of the Divine authority of this book, as a part of the inspired canon, there can exist no doubt. It is frequently quoted in the New Testament, and was evidently considered by the apostles as a treasure of revealed morality. Such, indeed, it is; a mine of divine wisdom, which may be ever explored and worked without being ever exhausted. What Cicero said of Thucydides applies far more truly to this work of Solomon, it is so full of matter that it comprises as many sentences as words.

II. It will help you, my young friends, better to understand this book if you consider its scope and design. " All Scripture is given by inspiration of God, and is profitable for doctrine, for reproof, for correction, for instruction in righteousness, that the man of God may be perfect, thoroughly furnished unto all good works." But this is a description of the Bible as a whole, and not of each separate part. One portion may be more full of doctrine, and therefore more important in reference to this, than some others. Another portion may relate more specifically to practice, and have more value as a rule of conduct, than those which speak only of doctrine. We go for information concerning the person, mission, and work of Christ, and the way of pardon and salvation, to the prophecies

of Isaiah in the Old Testament, and to the Gospels and
Epistles of the apostles in the New Testament; but the
book of Proverbs, while it supplies us with no information, or but a dim light on these momentous topics,
furnishes us with invaluable rules for our conduct in
this life. The beauty, force, and value of these admirable maxims lie in their practical design and character.
If we had no other book of Scripture than this, in vain
should we seek here for a solution of that problem,
" How shall man be just with God?" or for an answer
to that question, " What shall I do to be saved?" But
thanks be to God, we have other portions of Holy Writ,
and having learnt in them how as sinners we are to be
justified, and our peace with God is to be obtained, we
come back to this, as well as to others, to learn how the
pardoned and regenerated man is to conduct himself in
all his various relations, situations, and circumstances.
It is wholly a practical book, and teaches us " to deny
ungodliness and worldly lusts, and to live soberly,
righteously, and godly, in the present evil world." Nor
is this to be thought a low grade in the Divine scheme
of revelation. The truth as it is in Jesus is " a doctrine
according to godliness." Holy living is the end of all
truth : " Sanctify them," prayed our Lord for his
apostles, " by thy truth." The grand scope of the
Proverbs is (and can God propose, or man conceive, a
higher ?) to explain the nature of true wisdom ; to show
its importance ; to demonstrate its necessity ; to urge its
acquisition ; and to enforce its practice.

How lofty a place among the objects of human
pursuits has been assigned to wisdom ! What a stir in
the world of mind has that word made through all ages,
from the history of Egypt to that of Greece. All the

most gifted intellects of antiquity have started in quest
of this most precious acquisition. Every country has
been visited, every oracle consulted, every source of information explored, to find out wisdom. Yet all men
have searched in vain, as long as the inquiry was
conducted by unaided reason. When Pythagoras was
complimented by the tyrant of Syracuse as the wise
man, he modestly refused the flattery, declaring that he
was not the possessor of wisdom, but only its lover
seeking after it, a philosopher. You may see this
subject finely illustrated in the Book of Job, where, in
one of the sublimest chapters (the twenty-eighth,) of
that wonderfully sublime portion of Scripture, we find
the question proposed for the solution of the universe,
" Where shall wisdom be found, and what is the place
of understanding?" And when man, through ignorance,
is silent, and the depth says, It is not in me; and death
and destruction reply that they have only heard the
fame thereof; then God comes forth from his pavilion
of darkness as the divine teacher of wisdom. And what
is it that, after all the researches, and opinions, and
conflicting systems of philosophers, He proclaims to be
true wisdom? Not some profound secret of nature
which had baffled the inquiries of philosophers. Not
some great principle of political science which was to
regulate the affairs and change the destinies of empires.
Not some new theory of public economics, which was
to direct the stream of commerce and open new sources
of wealth to the nations. No: these were not the
communications most suited to the exigencies of our
nature: " To man he saith, Behold the fear of the Lord,
that is wisdom, and to depart from evil, that is understanding." It requires the revelation of God to settle

this question, "What is wisdom?" and he has settled
it once and for ever. This wisdom is religion. This is
man's highest wisdom as a rational, moral, and immortal
creature. It is his wisdom on earth, and will be his
wisdom in heaven. It is his wisdom in time, and will
be his wisdom through all eternity. Philosophers
of every country, hear it! Shades of Pythagoras,
Socrates, Plato, hear it! Divines and moralists, hear
it! And ye young men, the objects of my solicitude
and my address, hear it! "The fear of the Lord, that
is wisdom, and to depart from evil, that is understanding." This is the subject and design of the Book
of Proverbs, it is ever recurring to the glorious theme,
and again and again personifies wisdom and represents
her disclosing her nature and teaching her lessons,
in piety towards God, and all the moralities, charities, amenities, and courtesies of social and domestic
life. Here the basis of all sound morality is laid
in the fear of God. On this broad, deep foundation
of religion, is raised a superstructure of morals, which
combines the duties and the excellences of the good
monarch, the good subject, the good neighbour, the
good master, the good husband, the good son, the good
servant.

III. It may help you better to understand this extraordinary book if you are enabled to perceive the parts
into which it is divided; and which, though not notice-
able at a superficial glance, do yet really exist. These
parts are three. The first includes the first nine
chapters, in which wisdom, or the practical knowledge
of God, is set forth with great copiousness and variety
of expression, as the only source and foundation of true
virtue and happiness. This portion seems to be prin-

cipally addressed to, and intended for, youth. The sins, temptations, and dangers, incident to this period of life, are exhibited in the most striking descriptions and the most glowing colours. All the beauties of diction and of metaphor, all the charms of eloquence and the ornaments of poetry, all the persuasion of tenderness, all the expostulations of love, and all the commands of authority, are employed to induce the young man to turn away from sin and to practise holiness.* This part may be designated " A manual for youth."

The second part extends from the tenth to the end of the twenty-fourth chapter, and comprises precepts which seem intended for those who have advanced from youth to manhood, and relate to all the duties of social life. Here the transactions of secular business are alluded to, and whatsoever things are true, and just, and honest, and pure, and lovely, and of good report, are stated with a minuteness, and enforced with an earnestness, the most edifying and impressive. This may be called " A direction for the man of business."

The third part begins at the twenty-fifth chapter, and goes on to the end of the book, and contains an appendix of miscellaneous Proverbs, collected after Solomon's death. The two last chapters, written very probably by separate hands, but under Divine inspiration, and preserved by Divine care, were added to the sacred book. And they may not inappropriately be called " A mirror for females."

IV. But let us enter upon a general (and it can be but general,) examination of the contents of this book.

* Mr Bridges' admirable exposition of the Proverbs supplies a few of the remarks of this chapter.

1. I would direct your attention, first of all, to the very appropriate and impressive terms which Solomon has selected under the direction of the Spirit of God, to set forth the principal subjects of the book; I mean Folly and Wisdom. These two words are of course to be understood in a practical sense, as referring to moral rather than intellectual subjects, as designating sin and holiness. By the fool we are to understand, the man not of weak understanding, but of bad heart and vicious conduct: and by the wise man, the individual not of large knowledge, but of genuine religion. It is true in many places, the words wisdom and folly are employed by the sacred writers to denote the possession or the want of some specific excellence, but for the most part they have the generic meanings of religion and wickedness. This is plain from that admirable definition, "The fear of the Lord is the beginning of wisdom," and from that other text of an opposite nature, "Fools make a mock of sin." All sin is not only wicked, but it is foolish; and every sinner, whatever may be his intellectual attainments, is not only a transgressor, but a fool. Nothing is considered more reproachful than this appellation; hence many, more jealous for their intellect than for their heart, would rather be called knaves than fools. Sin then is folly, it is declared so by God, it is thought so by all holy angels and men, and is proved to be such by the experience of mankind, in the consequences of poverty disease shame and misery which it often brings after it in this world, and the certain destruction with which it is followed in the world to come. Look at the prodigal, wasting his substance among harlots and in riotous living, the idle profligate, the extravagant

spendthrift, the besotted drunkard, the diseased debauchee, the dishonest servant, the maddened gamester,
how wicked is their conduct, yes, and how foolish also!
Is it not folly to wage war against Heaven, to contend
with the Almighty, to barter away the joys of immortality for the pleasures of sin, which are but for a season;
and for the gratification of a moment, to incur the
bitter pains of eternal death? On the other hand,
if there be holiness in religion, there is also wisdom. To
secure the favour of God, to be saved by Christ, to have
a title to eternal glory, to have peace of conscience, to
control the passions, to be comforted in sorrow, to
secure the germ of every virtue, and the death of every
corruption, in short, to be wise unto salvation hereafter,
and to have that which will best promote all our interests
here, is to be wise indeed. This is the truest, the
noblest, the only, wisdom. What is the wisdom displayed in amassing wealth, acquiring fame, or gratifying
appetite, compared with this? Surely that must be the
deepest folly which ruins estate body and soul, and that
the highest wisdom which saves them all.

2. I next select a few single proverbs for the sake
of holding them up and showing their beauty and their
value. But I can only pluck a few flowers at random
from a garden enlivened by the bloom, and perfumed
with the odour of a thousand others, as beautiful
and as fragrant as those I gather. How tender how
lovely or how wise are such sayings as these: "The
path of the just is as the shining light, which shineth
more and more unto the perfect day." "The memory
of the just is blessed." "The mouth of the righteous
is a well of life." "Hope deferred maketh the heart
sick." "The heart knoweth its own bitterness, and a

stranger intermeddleth not with its joy." "A merry
heart doeth good like a medicine." "Even in laughter
the heart is sorrowful and the end of that mirth is
heaviness." "Better is a dinner of herbs, where love
is, than a stalled ox, and hatred therewith." "The
beginning of strife is as the letting out of water, therefore leave off contention before it is meddled with."
"Faithful are the wounds of a friend, but the kisses
of an enemy are deceitful." "As a bird that wandereth
from her nest, so is a man that wandereth from his
place." "As iron sharpeneth iron, so doth the countenance of a man his friend. "A foolish son is the
grief of his father, and bitterness to her that bare him."
"Open rebuke is better than secret love." Such are but
specimens, taken almost indiscriminately from this vast
and all but inexhaustible storehouse of wisdom. What
mind of the least perception or taste must not, does not,
admire the point and the elegance of these beautiful
aphorisms? I can only allude to the principal topics
on which the wisdom of Solomon was employed in this
collection of golden sentences. Here are innumerable
sayings on all the duties of religion towards God, on
filial affection, on the right use of speech, and the
government of the tongue; on ability, diligence, industry, honesty, and honour in business; on prudence
in domestic affairs; on friendship and companionship;
on forethought and anticipation of the future; on contracts and suretyship; on the obligations of kings and
subjects, of husbands and wives, of masters and servants: yea, what subject is there connected with social
existence, not only in its greater concerns, but in all its
minute and delicate ramifications, in reference to which
we may not find some sententious remark, some pithy

saying, which, if remembered, would be of vast service
to us! Rules for the house of God, for our habitations,
for the shop, the parlour, and even the kitchen, may all
be found here. The character of every individual,
whatever be his rank, station, or social relation, may
find a mould here in which it may be cast, and from
which it would come forth beautiful, useful, and
admirable.

3. But leaving particular and isolated proverbs, I
go on to select and exhibit a few of the beautiful
allegories, or perhaps more properly, personifications,
which are scattered over this wondrous book. Metaphors and similes abound, in seemingly grand and endless
confusion, like the single stars of the firmament;
while allegories, which are but extended metaphors, are
to be seen here and there standing out like magnificent constellations, amidst the single stars. I can
mention only two or three of these, for they are too
numerous to be all of them considered, as Solomon
seems to delight in the use of allegory. And first
of all, let me direct your attention to the personification
of religion in the first chapter. " Wisdom crieth without, she uttereth her voice in the streets; she crieth in
the chief place of concourse, in the openings of the
gates : in the city she uttereth her words. How long,
ye simple ones, will ye love simplicity, and the scorners
delight in their scorning, and fools hate knowledge?
Turn ye at my reproof; behold I will pour out my
Spirit upon you, I will make known my words to you."
How finely is this wrought, when religion is thus seen,
not retiring to the cloister or to the cell, not even
confined to places of worship, but going through the
streets, standing in the gates, entering into public

assemblies, and delivering her instructions, breathing out her expostulations, urging her counsels, administering her rebukes, and denouncing her threatenings, to the congregated multitudes, the mass of the people.

Nothing can be conceived more apt, more beautiful or more sublime, than the personification of Wisdom, which he introduces in the eighth chapter, exhibiting her not only as the director of human life and morals, as the inventor of arts, as the dispenser of wealth, of honour, and of real felicity, but as the immortal offspring of the Omnipotent Creator, and as the eternal associate in the Divine counsels.

> "When he prepared the heavens, I was present;
> When he described a circle on the face of the deep;
> When he disposed the atmosphere above;
> When he established the fountains on the deep;
> When he published his decree to the sea;
> That the waters should not pass their bounds;
> When he planned the foundations of the earth;
> Then was I by him as his offspring:
> And I was daily his delight:
> I rejoiced continually before him:
> I rejoiced in the habitable parts of the earth,
> And my delights were with the sons of men."*

" It is a difficult thing to personify an attribute well; and to sustain it through a simile or an apostrophe is not easy; but to supply a long monologue for the lips of Eternal Wisdom! This Solomon has done, and not degraded the mighty theme."†

Turn now to another of these beautiful personifications, to one which will come more home to your own condition and circumstances.

* Lowth's translation. I must express my conviction that this chapter is intended as a personification of wisdom, and not as a prophetic description of our Lord Jesus Christ.

† Gilfillan.

"Happy is the man that findeth wisdom, and the man that getteth understanding."

"For the merchandise thereof is better than the merchandise of silver, and the gain thereof than fine gold."

"She is more precious than rubies, and all the things thou canst desire are not to be compared unto her."

"Length of days is in her right hand, and in her left hand, riches and honour."

"Her ways are ways of pleasantness, and all her paths are peace."

"She is a tree of life to them that lay hold upon her; and happy is every one that retaineth her."

Such, young men, is religion, for wisdom you know is religion, as here set forth by a striking mixture of metaphor. She is represented as a queen coming forth from her palace and her treasury, with both hands full of blessings, which she is holding out, ready to drop them into the lap of those who will submit to her government, and become her subjects. To represent the influence of religion, even on the interests of earth and time, she is seen holding in one hand health, and in the other riches and honour, which often are the fruits of that godliness which is profitable for all things, having the promise of the life that now is, as well as of that which is to come. But what are her ways? A lonely rugged path across sandy deserts, or through gloomy passes and frowning precipices, where no verdure springs, no sun-beams play, no birds carol, and where neither streams nor fruits are found? So the enemies of religion, the men who dwell in the fools' paradise, would represent: but how different the description in God's Word of Truth! This tells of "ways of pleasantness and paths of peace." It is indeed a narrow and somewhat toilsome way, but every step is lighted by the bright shining of the Sun of Righteousness; is strewed with the promises of God; is a step of happiness; and a step to heaven. Yes, even what are called the austerities of religion are more joyous than the pleasures of sin. The yoke of Christ is far lighter than that of Satan. And in the tree of life, that wonderful ornament and glory of the garden of Eden, in the branches of which sang the birds of Paradise, whose roots were watered with the rivers of God, in whose shade Adam basked, and of whose fruits he ate as the sacramental pledge of immortality, there, I say, is the emblem of heavenly wisdom. She is a tree of life growing up from a branch brought out of Eden, when sin had barred our access to the original stock, and caused it to decay; a tree whose branches bend down upon this world of sin and misery, and whose clusters hang within the reach of even the youngest child. Young men, what think you of this beautiful description of wisdom's blessings? It is no fancy picture, no mere creation of human genius, no mere poetic garniture of the page of revelation. How many have proved all this to be a divine reality! O, come, come, to this tree of life, and take of its twelve manner of fruits, and live.

I pass by, with only a glance at it, the personification of wisdom in the ninth chapter, building her house, preparing her feast, and sending out her invitations to collect her guests: a beautiful representation of the blessings of true religion.

4. I now turn to a few of those graphic sketches of character with which the book abounds. Scarcely has it opened, before we find the character of the Tempter described in the following language: "My son, if sinners entice thee, consent thou not: if they say,

Come with us, let us lay wait for blood; let us lurk
privily for the innocent without cause; let us swallow
them up alive as the grave, and whole as they that go
down to the pit; we shall find all precious substance,
we shall fill our houses with spoil. Cast in thy lot
among us, let us all have one purse." How true this is
to the life, as a description of the conduct of those who
tempt others to evil! The earnest invitation, the
secrecy of the plot, the prospect of advantage, the
promise of a share in the booty, how accurate! It is
true that in your situation and circumstances the
temptation will not be to deeds of blood and rapine;
but there will be much the same urgency of enticement,
the same promise and prospects of gain, and the same
ensnaring representation of companionship. Sinners
are ruthless and zealous in the dreadful work of temptation; they want companions to assist them in accomplishing their evil deeds, and sometimes they equally
need, and earnestly seek, associates to maintain their
courage. Guilt, till its subject becomes hardened and
desperate, is cowardly, and gets rid of its fears by multiplying its companions. If sinners then entice you, do
not yield, or even harken to their solicitations. Consent
constitutes the sin. Turn a deaf ear to every entreaty.
Let no prospect or promise of gain or pleasure induce
you to listen for a moment to their solicitations. Flee
from them as you would from a serpent or a lion. You
need not yield. You cannot be forced to sin. Repulse
the tempter at once, and with a frown. Do not parley
with him for a moment. His look is the fascination
of the basilisk's eye, his words are snares, his breath is
pestilence, his presence is destruction. The moment he
asks you to sin, flee, instantly flee. And while I warn

you against being ensnared by the tempter's arts, let me, with still more emphatic importunity, entreat you never to employ them. No character is so like that of Satan, who is called by way of eminence, the Tempter, as he who entices another to sin. This is the most truely diabolical act ever perpetrated in our world. Turn with horror from the thought. If you must and will sin, sin alone, have no partner in your crime. If you will sink to the bottomless pit, drag no others down with you into that fiery gulf. Emulate not the fate of Achan, of whom it is said, " This man perished not alone in his iniquity." What an eternity of torment is that man preparing for himself, as well as for others, who is ruining the souls of his fellow-creatures by soliciting them to sin! How will those victims of his wiles avenge themselves upon him by their execrations in the world of woe!

Next I direct you to a very striking description of the tempted. I can only allude, delicacy forbids more, to the vivid description of the unwary youth caught in the snares of the abandoned woman, contained in the seventh chapter. This picture is to be looked at with half-averted eye, for warning only. It is painted with a master's hand, and with exquisite fidelity of colour. Was ever the harlot's likeness more accurately taken? Her sallying forth in quest of her prey in the evening, her position at the corner of the street, her unmistakeable dress, her tempting speech, her plausible suggestions, her impudent face, all show the harlot's false and mercenary heart. There is no vice against which you have more need to be warned than sensuality. It is that to which your age, your situation, and your temptations expose you. Imitate the conduct of that noble youth whose character we contemplated in the last chapter, and say, when tempted to sin, " How shall I do this great wickedness and sin against God !" How true is human nature at all times, even in its corruptions, to itself. The corners of the streets of our modern towns and cities exhibit the same night scenes now, just as those of Solomon's time. Three thousand years, with all their warnings and experience, have not banished the " strange woman " from society, nor driven the female tempter from our streets. Everything in the description is impressive and instructive. Trace the sad end as set forth here, to its beginning. Was not idleness the parent of this mischief? The loitering evening walk, the unseasonable hour, the vacant mind, all bringing the youth into contact with evil company; was not all this courting sin, tempting the tempter? How awfully true the representation of the tempter's success, " He goeth after her straightway as an ox goeth to the slaughter," unconscious of his fate; perhaps dreaming of rich pasture; or " as a fool to the correction of the stocks," careless and unfeeling, " till the dart strike through his liver," or " as a bird hasteth to the snare, and knoweth not that it is for his life." Young men, set a guard upon your senses. Go not in the way of sin. Enter deeply into our Lord's beautiful petition, " Lead us not into temptation." He that would not fall into sin, must not go into the way of temptation. Keep from the harlot's company, and speech, her private haunt, and public walk, as you would from contact with a person infected with the plague.

I now direct you to the description of the end of the profligate; who after running his course of dissipation, looks back with remorse and regret, amidst poverty and disease, upon his polluted and ruinous career; "And thou mourn at last when thy flesh and thy body are consumed, and say, How have I hated instruction, and my heart despised reproof; and have not obeyed the voice of my teachers, nor inclined mine ear to them that have instructed me. I was in almost all evil in the midst of the congregation and assembly." Here is the fruit of sensuality set forth in awful terms. Disease preying like worms upon the body, and remorse, like a vulture, gnawing at the heart. Yes, there are sins which set their loathsome brand upon the outer man, while they fill with the poison of their guilt the inner one; sins which pollute the blood, disfigure the countenance, destroy the health, and turn the whole frame into a mass of corruption. How many martyrs of intemperance and licentiousness prove by a bitter experience the truth of the apostle's words, "He that soweth to the flesh shall of the flesh reap corruption;" and realise the description of Zophar, "His bones are full of the sins of his youth, which lie down with him in the dust." Oh, to sit down amidst wasted fortunes with a body half destroyed by profligacy, and the voice of conscience telling of slighted opportunities, abused privileges, stifled convictions! Young men, think of this "mourning at last," when it will be too late to mourn, and when the mourning will be the more bitter the longer it has been delayed. Impenitence does not put away sorrow, but only postpones it to a future period, when mercy shall have fled for ever, and nothing remain but a fearful recollection of past sins, and a still more fearful foreboding of wrath to come. How will neglected warnings,

despised sermons, and slighted counsels, then rise like
spectres from the grave of oblivion, each repeating that
dreadful sarcasm, "Son, remember."

I hold up now another portraiture, I mean that
of the Drunkard. "Who hath woe? Who hath
sorrow? Who hath contentions? Who hath babbl-
ings? Who hath wounds without cause? Who hath
redness of eyes? They that tarry long at the wine;
they that go to seek mixed wine. Look not thou at the
wine when it is red, when it giveth its colour in the cup,
when it moveth itself aright. At the last it biteth like
a serpent, and stingeth like an adder. Thine eyes shall
behold strange women, and thine heart shall utter
perverse things. Yea, thou shalt be as he that lieth
down in the midst of the sea, or as he that lieth upon
the top of a mast. They have stricken me, shalt
thou say, and I was not sick; they have beaten me, and
I felt it not: when shall I awake? I will seek it yet
again." This is perhaps the most graphic and vivid
description of drunkenness ever given to the world.
The drawing is perfect, and not less so the colouring.
It has been often called, and with great truth and justice,
"the drunkard's looking-glass, in which he may see his
own face." It is said that amidst all the splendid
furniture and ornaments of our gin palaces no mirror is
found; the vendors of poison not being very willing
that the miserable victims should see their own suicidal
act, in gulping the fatal dram, reflected. In default
of a looking-glass, I wish they could be compelled to
have the passage just quoted painted in large and
flaming characters, and hung up in the most conspicuous places of those human slaughter-houses. Observe
the description of the drunkard. The quarrelsome

temper which liquor produces, the fights in which it involves the man who quaffs it, and the wounds he gets in his affrays; his babbling discourse on subjects which he does not understand, and is then unfitted to discuss, when blasphemy is wit, treason courage, and ribaldry eloquence; his going on, when inflamed by wine, to the gratification of other lusts, and the commission of other sins; his insensibility to injury and danger when his brain is stupified; his returning to the indulgence of his vicious appetite when awakening up from his drunken slumber; his intense misery and woe produced by his remorse of mind and wretchedness of body, these are all set forth in this wonderful passage with a graphic power that nothing can exceed. Begin life, Young Men, with an extreme dread of this vice. There is ground for alarm. Drunkenness was never more prevalent than it is now. Myriads and myriads sink every year into the drunkard's grave, and lower still, into the drunkard's hell. One-half of the lunacy, two-thirds of the pauperism, and three-fourths of the crime of society, are said to spring from this desolating habit. Beware, then of this dreadful appetite and propensity. Be afraid of it. Consider yourselves liable to it. Abandon all self-confidence. Avoid everything that leads to drinking. Abjure tobacco in every shape. Shun bad company. Never cross the threshold of the tavern for the purpose of conviviality. Practise total abstinence. All the drunkards that are, or ever have been, were moderate men once. I do most earnestly entreat you to abstain from all intoxicating drinks. You do not need them for health, and to take them for gratification is the germ of inebriety. Total abstinence will conduce to health, to economy, to prosperity. You will one day bless me if this chapter should lead you to adopt this practice. I do not say that this will ensure the practice of every virtue, and the enjoyment of all prosperity, but I know nothing in the order of preparatory means more likely to be followed with such results.

And now, I ask, what is it that leads to all other sins? Idleness, and I therefore now direct you to the last picture which I shall present in this chapter. " I went by the field of the slothful, and by the vineyard of the man void of understanding, and, lo, it was all grown over with thorns, and nettles had covered the face thereof, and the stone wall thereof was broken down. Then I saw and considered it well; I looked upon it and received instruction. Yet a little sleep, a little slumber, a little folding of the hands to sleep; so shall thy poverty come as one that travelleth, and thy want as an armed man." This, too, is fine painting: the late riser, the lover of sleep, the drowsy drone, lifting up his half-opened lids weighed down with sleep, grumbling at the person who has disturbed him, turning away from him on his bed; and settling himself down again to slumber. And then the broken fence left without repair, the thorns and nettles covering the field and choking the vineyard. How true to life. Idleness is a complicated vice, yes, I say vice. First it is a most wasteful habit, it wastes time, which is more precious than rubies, it wastes a man's mental faculties, and dooms the noblest machine on earth to stand still: it wastes property, and should compel the sluggard to put down in his expenses a large sum per annum lost by neglect. It is disgraceful, for how reproachful is it in a being made to be active, to spend life in doing nothing, and to throw away his mental powers in sloth. It is criminal, for God has commanded us to be active, and will call us to account for the sin of killing time. It is dangerous; doing nothing is next to doing ill, and is sure to lead to it. From its very inaction it ultimately becomes the active cause of all evil; as a palsy is more to be dreaded than a fever. The Turks have a proverb which says, "The Devil tempts all other men; but the idle man tempts the Devil." Idleness is the stagnant pool that deposits mud, and breeds all kinds of vermin; but running water is clear, sweet, and wholesome. Idleness is wretchedness. An idle man, as I said in a former chapter, is the most miserable of all God's creatures: and woe be to the man who is doomed to bear the pain and penalties of a slothful disposition. Employment is not only a source of excellence, but of enjoyment. Young men, be industrious. It will be a source at once of pleasure and profit. If you study the Book of Proverbs for nothing else, study it for the purpose of promoting industry. No man who ever made this book the subject of his study and the rule of his life, failed to ensure a competency; while multitudes who have acted thus, have attained to respectability, honour, and wealth.

Let me now, in conclusion, enumerate a few general points, which are suggested by a consideration of this interesting portion of holy Scripture.

We see the benevolence of God, in not only providing the means for our glory, honour, immortality, and eternal life in heaven, through the mediation of our Lord Jesus Christ, but in giving us, in this valuable book, the most minute directions for all the details of our earthly life. He not only wills our salvation hereafter, but our convenience and comfort here. He acts like a good and rich father, who, while he makes

his son heir of all his estate, consults in the minutest
particulars, his well-being and enjoyment, through the
period of his boyhood and education. How exquisitely
beautiful it is to see God thus managing our mean
affairs ; intent even upon our success in trade ; promoting our pleasant intercourse with our neighbours ;
providing rules for our conduct everywhere ; and sup-
plying us with the means to secure a thousand little
enjoyments, and to protect ourselves from a thousand
little annoyances on our road to our Father's house in
heaven. To me the Book of Proverbs proves the
condescension of God's goodness, while the Gospels and
Epistles of the New Testament exhibit its grandeur and
sublimity. Arising out of this, I would observe, what an
inestimable volume and priceless treasure is the Bible,
which thus proclaims to us the goodness of God, and
carries out his gracious purpose towards us. I want,
young men, to endear to your hearts this book of books,
and therefore will embrace every opportunity presented
by these chapters, to commend it to your attention and
regard. I want to fortify you against the seductions
of infidelity and false philosophy. I want to show you
the injustice to yourselves, as well as the wickedness
towards God, and the hypocrisy, as well as the cruelty,
of those who, under the pretext of liberating your mind
from thraldom, and exalting you to the dignity of men
of reason, would deliver you from what they call the
dominion of superstition and the trammels of the Bible.
It is their delight to represent the Bible as teaching
only a system of priestcraft; as prescribing only a
round of religious ceremonies ; and forming a character
fit only to dwell in a monastery, or to worship in a
church. Ask them if they have ever deigned to read the

Book of Proverbs. If not, they are unfit to pronounce an opinion upon the Bible; and if they have, tell them that by such misrepresentations they lie against their own knowledge; for here is a part of the Bible which, they must know, follows us into the social haunts of men, to the family, to the shop, to the market and exchange, in order to dictate truth, kindness, and meekness, in our words, and justice, honesty, and honour, in our transactions; which regulates all sales and purchases upon the principles of equity; gives validity and efficacy to all contracts; prohibits all wrong, and sustains all right. A single perusal of this book would convince them that if it were universally possessed believed and practised, human laws would be almost unnecessary, courts of justice would be forsaken, and jails untenanted. Take up this volume with the simple question, "What kind of man shall I be if I follow the rules herein contained?" Hold fast your Bibles then, till infidelity can find you a better rule of conduct for this life, a brighter revelation, and a surer hope for another. Ask it what it has to offer you in exchange for doctrines so sublime, morality so pure, precepts so wise, promises so precious, prospects so grand. And what has it to offer? A dreary, blank, and hideous negative, no God, no Redeemer, no salvation, no heaven : no, nor anything even in this world to save you from the dominion of vice, or to guide you to the practice and enjoyment of virtue; this is all that infidelity has to give you as a substitute for the Bible. Say to it with surprise, indignation, and abhorrence, "Avaunt, lying spirit! Curse not me with your discoveries of nothing. Is this all you have to give me in exchange for that volume which is profitable for all things, having the promise of the life that now is, as well as of that which is to come? You have nothing by which I may steer my course across the stormy ocean of this life; and nothing at the end of the voyage but the black rocks of annihilation on which I must dash, and be for ever lost. Begone, with thy creed of wretched negations, to him who is fool enough to be cajoled out of his Bible by thy miserable sophistries." Sometimes the mind is more impressed with the atrocity of an intended felony, by examining the articles one by one, which it would have purloined, than by looking at the whole in a mass. So it is in judging of infidelity, take up book by book of Scripture, examine each separately, and say, "The felon infidel would rob me of this, and this, and this." Yes, Young Men, he would cheat you, among the rest, out of this Book of Proverbs. He would tell you that this is imposition, and no revelation from God at all. Or if he consented to leave it in your hands, he would, by taking away its divine authority deprive it of all power to bind your conscience as law, and merely submit it for your adoption as advice, which you are still at liberty to reject if you do not like it.

This book shows us the connexion between true religion and general excellence of character. This was noticed in the last chapter, when we contemplated the character of Joseph, and is now repeated in this general analysis of the Book of Proverbs. It lays the foundation broad, deep, and strong, in that wisdom which is the fear of God. It anticipates the apostolic injunction "Add to your faith, virtue." The foundation of the temple of virtue is religion; the golden ornament upon its dome is all that is gentle in spirit and graceful in demeanour. Hence is to be derived that completeness of character which this book is intended and calculated to form. It begins with the heart, and forms a holy mechanism there, which guides the hands in regular movements round the dial-plate of life. It implants right principles of action. It communicates a hidden life, it sanctifies the inner man, and thus fashions the outer man, and does not merely paint a picture or carve a bust. Here man in all his relations and all his interests is consulted, as a creature of God, as a citizen of the state, as a member of society, as an inmate of the dwelling, as a creditor or a debtor, as a buyer or a seller; in each and all these he is contemplated, directed, and encouraged. It has been beautifully observed, that " we want religion to be to the character what the soul is to the body, the animating principle. The soul operates in every member. It sees in the eye, hears in the ear, speaks in the tongue, animates the whole body, with ease and uniformity, without ostentation or effort." Thus let the good conduct of the citizen, the son, the husband, the father, the brother, the tradesman, be only so many operations of true piety, so many acts of this animating soul, so many developements of this hidden life.

Though there is much in this book which, properly understood and followed, would, in connexion with other parts of Scripture, guide the reader to heaven, and prepare him for its enjoyment, it must be confessed and remembered, that it principally aims to form the social character for the present world. What I have already said on this subject I repeat, that for a clear and explicit knowledge of the way of pardon and eternal life, we must read the New Testament. There we learn how Christ is made of God unto us "wisdom, and righteousness, and sanctification, and redemption." And there also we learn the great moral principles on which all the transactions of this world's business should be founded : but in this book of the wise king, principles of wisdom and virtue are given in detail for every relation of social life. It is the commercial man's vade mecum. It may lie upon his desk by the side of his ledger, and that in a thousand instances would have been in a better state, had this been more constantly consulted. It is my firm belief, that no man who reads this book through with close attention and earnest prayer, once a year, will fail, either in this world, or in reference to that which is to come. It is designed and adapted to form the industrious, prudent, honourable, and successful man of business, and is therefore eminently suited to this great commercial country. Napoleon Buonaparte, when in the zenith of his power and pride, called this country, more in a spirit of mortification and envy than of contempt, a nation of shopkeepers. If in that term he comprehended our merchants and manufacturers, he did not inaptly describe us. We are not ashamed of our commercial character and greatness ; and provided our merchandise be carried on upon the principles of this book, and we thus inscribe upon it, Holiness to the Lord, it is our glory and defence.

In this book is disclosed the secret of true happiness, which, if really put into practice, will make happy individuals, happy families, happy neighbourhoods, happy nations, and a happy world. All the errors which men have fallen into on this subject ; all the delusive shadows, the polluted springs, the deleterious ingredients, which have misled and injured so many, are here detected and exposed; while the nature, the source, and the means of true felicity, are as clearly pointed out. Here in the favour of God; in the mortification of our corruptions; in the restraint of our passions; in the cultivation of our graces; in the performance of our duties; in promoting the good of our neighbours; and in the hope of immortality, are the materials of human blessedness. Here, happiness is set forth, not in the heathen forms of Bacchus, Venus, or Momus; not by such descriptions as those of Horace, Ovid, and Anacreon; not in such riot and revelry as the lovers of pleasure in every age would recommend. Quite the contrary. In this book, happiness is seen descending from heaven, her native place, and lighting upon our orb in the seraph form of religion. She is clad in the robe of righteousness, arrayed in the garment of salvation, and adorned with the ornament of a meek and quiet spirit. Like the king's daughter of old, she "is all glorious within, her clothing is of wrought gold." Joy sparkles in her eye, and peace reposes upon her brow. Her conscience is rendered easy by a sense of pardon, and her heart is light through purity. The song of the seraphim is upon her lips. Her hand is alternately lifted up in adoration to God, and stretched out in mercy to his necessitous creatures. Her feet ever carry her with willing steps, either to the house of prayer, or to the abodes of sorrow. Her excellences are described, and her praises are sung, not in the odes of licentious poets, at sensual orgies, in strains inspired by lust and wine; but in the hymns composed by prophets and apostles, resounding in the temples of devotion, or chanted by good and holy men in the circles of their friends, or the homes of their families. Such is the happiness set forth in this book, the only thing which deserves, the only thing that can prove itself worthy of, the name. That seraph form alights, Young Men, in your path, and with her own angelic, divine, and heavenly smile, beckons you to follow her to the well-springs of delight, repeating, at every step, the beautiful language of this book, "Happy is the man that findeth wisdom."

CHAPTER VIII.

*He becometh poor that dealeth with a slack hand; but
the hand of the diligent maketh rich.* PROVERBS X, 4.
*In the day of prosperity be joyful, but in the day
of adversity consider.* ECCLESIASTES vii, 14.

THINK not, Young Men, that in selecting subjects
for the last two chapters and a previous one, from the
books of Proverbs and Ecclesiastes, I am drawing your
attention away from the New Testament to the Old,
and investing the latter with an importance superior to
that of the former. By no means. Both the portions
of the sacred volume belong to the one divine system
of revealed truth, and they stand related to each other
as the two great lights of the moral world, the sun to
rule the day, and the moon to rule the night. The Old
Testament, with lunar effulgence borrowed from the yet
invisible orb of spiritual day, shone forth upon the
Jewish Church during the night season of its existence;
while the New, with its own brightness, constitutes the
day of our Christian dispensation. But though the sun
of righteousness has arisen, the moon is still a valuable
member of our spiritual system. Let us then hold fast
both parts of the Bible, not neglecting the Books

of Moses, David, Solomon, and the Prophets, but delighting most to study the gospels and epistles, because of their clearer revelation of everything that stands connected with the moral character of God, the person and work of Christ, the way of salvation, and the glories of immortality.

The book of Ecclesiastes, when properly understood, is an important portion of Sacred Scripture. It is on good grounds ascribed to Solomon, and is supposed, as I stated in the last chapter, to have been composed after his recovery from his deplorable apostacy, and to have been intended by him to be a record of his own experience, and a warning, or at any rate a lesson, to mankind. Its chief design seems to be to answer that momentous inquiry, prompted at once by the misery and the ignorance of fallen humanity, " Who will show us any good ?" Man is made for happiness, and is capable of it : but what is it, and how is it to be obtained ? To possess and enjoy it, he must be furnished with some good, suited to his nature, adapted to his condition, and adequate to his capacity and desires.

The nature of the chief good has been, in every age, the interesting subject of most earnest philosophic inquiry. But how various and opposed have been the conclusions at which the inquirers have arrived on this important subject. Varro, a learned Latin writer, who died about thirty years before Christ, reckoned up more than two hundred different opinions on this subject; thus plainly evincing man's ignorance of his own nature, circumstances, and wants. Not perceiving what it is that has made him miserable, he cannot know of course what will make him happy. Unacquainted with, or rather overlooking, the disease, he cannot know the remedy. He feels an aching void within, an unsatisfied craving after something, but knows neither the nature nor the source of the food adapted to meet and satisfy his hungry appetite. What human reason is thus proved to be too ignorant and too weak to decide, the Bible undertakes to settle ; that which no human authority can adjudicate upon, the oracle of God explicitly, imperatively, and infallibly, determines for all and for ever. Precious Bible, if only for this ! The vagrant spirit of man is seen wandering from God, the fountain of bliss, roaming through this " dry and thirsty land, where no water is ;" anxiously looking for happiness, but never finding it ; coming often to springs that are dry, and to cisterns that are broken, till weary of the pursuit and disappointed in its hopes, it is ready to give up all in despair, and reconcile itself to misery, under the notion that happiness is but a name. In this sad and hopeless mood, the victim of grief and despondency is met by the Bible, which takes him by the hand, and leads him to the fountain of living waters. Such is the design of this extraordinary book, to show first of all what will not make man happy, and then what will. Upon all the most coveted possessions of this world, it pronounces the solemn and impressive sentence, " Vanity of vanities, all is vanity." It interrogates singly every coveted object of human desire, and asks, " What are you ? " only to receive the melancholy answer, " Vanity." Or if, deceptively, they return another answer, it turns to the man who has possessed and proved them all, and he contradicts their testimony, and mournfully cries, " They are vanity."

In the beginning of the book, Solomon gives this out as the first part of his subject, and then twenty times repeats it, and oftener still alludes to it in the course of his details; and when he has finished his proofs and illustrations, he formally re-announces it in his peroration. He does not by this sentence intend to pass any censure on the works of nature, the dispensations of Providence, or the arrangement of man's social existence. All things are good in their nature, relations, and designs as God originally made them; but man's sinfulness renders all corrupt to him; he makes those things to be ends which were only intended to be means; rests in what is subordinate instead of going on to that which is supreme; and abuses that which is granted him only to use. Solomon shows in this book, that nothing on earth can satisfy the soul of man, as its supreme good. Three thousand years nearly have passed away since he wrote. Science has multiplied its discoveries, art its inventions, and literature its productions; civilization has opened new sources of luxury, and ingenuity has added innumerable gratifications of appetite and of taste, unknown even to Solomon; every domain of nature has been explored, and every conceivable experiment been made, to extort from her new means of enjoyment, and new secrets of happiness; but still the heart of man confirms the testimony of the king of Israel, and the experience of the human race prolongs the echo of his words, " Vanity of vanities, all is vanity."

This, however, is only the negative view of the subject, if all these are vanity and not good, what is good, and is there any thing which really deserves the name? There is, and it is the design of this portion of Scripture to reveal and to declare it. What is it? What, that is to settle the question, and reveal to the children of men the nature and the source of happiness? What, that is to terminate the weary pursuits, to revive the languid hopes, and to gratify the anxious desires, of the destitute and sorrowing children of men, hungering and thirsting after bliss? What? Wisdom. That wisdom of which I spoke in the last chapter, as constituting the subject of the book of Proverbs: between which portion of Scripture and this Book of Ecclesiastes there is so close a resemblance of design and construction. But what is wisdom? He himself declares in the last chapter, where he sums up the whole of what he had said, "Let us hear the conclusion of the whole matter: Fear God and keep his commandments, for this is the whole duty of man." The first six chapters of the book give negative views of happiness, and are intended as illustrations of the declaration, "All is vanity:" the remainder is devoted to the illustration of the nature, excellence, and beneficial effects of true wisdom or religion. This then, after all the inquiries of philosophers, is the chief good, true religion. This suits the nature, meets the wants, alleviates the sorrows, satisfies the desires, of the human soul, and is its portion for ever. This finds man depraved, and makes him holy; finds him little, and makes him great; finds him earthly, and raises him to heaven. This leads the human spirit through the mediation of Christ, into the presence of the infinite, eternal, omnipotent, and all-sufficient Author of its existence, and by the teaching and aid of the Holy Spirit, impels and helps him to say, "Thou art my portion, O my God. Thy favour is life, and thy loving kindness is better than life. Thon art the centre, the rest, the home of my heart."

Perhaps we shall better understand this book "if we suppose that the author at every step is meeting the arguments of an objector, who contends that appearances, in the present world, are such as to exclude the idea of a superintending Providence, to confound together, without discrimination as to their fate or fortunes, their merit or desert, the wise and the foolish, goodness and sin; thus destroying all rational hope for the future, and leaving nothing better to man than that he should eat and drink, and enjoy himself here as well as he can. The author meets, examines, and answers these objections, by exposing the unsatisfactoriness of mere pleasure, and insists on the regality and supremacy of duty." This view of the design and the construction of the book will remove that appearance of an atheistic spirit which seems, in the view of objectors, to characterise some passages.

Having considered the design of the book, and thrown, I hope, some light upon what appears a little enigmatical, I will proceed to take up the subject of this chapter, and consider success or failure in business.

I will suppose the case of two young men setting out in life with equal advantages as to capital, connexions, and prospects. They have gone through their term of apprenticeship, and the intermediate stage of the shopman or the clerk, and have commenced business for themselves. One of them succeeds, a propitious gale seems to fill his sails, and a favourable tide to flow in, to help him onward in his course from the very time of sailing. He makes a prosperous voyage, and enters safely into harbour with a rich cargo. His business flourishes, his capital increases, he rises to competency, to respectability, perhaps to wealth. His influence and his rank in society keep pace, of course, with the increase of his opulence. Such cases often occur in this trading and commercial country. It is only a few days since I was visiting a friend in a town not very remote, who has recently taken a large house and beautiful grounds, having come to the town with only a few shillings in his pocket. While in this humble condition, one day on gazing at a mansion and its surrounding lawn through the opened gates, he felt the kindlings of desire and ambition in his soul, and said to himself, " I will one day possess such a place as that if I can." He was an industrious young man, got on in life; became a true Christian, a prosperous tradesman, and now is dwelling in elegance in the house and enjoying the grounds which excited his desires; and what is still better, is giving God the glory of all, and sanctifying his prosperity by Christian liberality. He is also the deacon of a Christian church. I might mention another pious individual, of large fortune, and a member of parliament, who was once a boy in a Sunday-school. And indeed, such instances of success are numerous.

There is, however, a dark reverse to all this, which sometimes occurs, I mean an early failure. In this case the vessel has no sooner left port than it encounters unfavourable winds, is tossed upon the billows by tempests, and dashed upon the rock, or stranded upon the shore, becomes a wreck. The business commenced with hope terminates in disappointment, and the young tradesman is soon converted into a young bankrupt. This, in such a country as ours, is no uncommon case. May it, Young Men, never be yours. It is important to inquire into the causes for this difference of result. I put aside the idea of chance. There is no such thing in our world, none in nature, none in human affairs. We must not explain the matter by saying,

" It was just as it happened. One was a lucky man and the other an unlucky one." Luck, if it mean nothing more than an event of which the cause is not apparent, is a term that may be employed without error; but if it means, as it generally does, an event which has no cause at all, a mere chance, it is a bad word, a heathen term. Drop it from your vocabulary. Trust nothing to luck, and expect nothing from it. Avoid all practical dependence upon it or its kindred words, fate, chance, fortune. True it is, that success or failure in business, as in other things, depends often upon a concurrence of circumstances, which no human prescience could foresee, and no human sagacity could arrange; but this is not chance, luck, fate, or fortune, but Providence. There is much of Providence in every man's history, and more of a favouring Providence in some men's history than in others. " The lot is cast into the lap (or urn, the usual way of drawing lots,) but the disposal thereof is of the Lord." Providence no doubt gives advantages to some which it does not bestow upon others. Scripture is full of instances of this kind. How conspicuous was Providence in the history of Joseph! How manifest in the life of Moses! How remarkable in the advancement of David and Mordecai! In ordinary life we see the same kind and unexpected interpositions on behalf of some favoured individuals. Throughout the whole range of Scripture, prosperity is spoken of as the gift of God, as matter of prayer where it is desired, and of grateful acknowledgment where it is possessed. " The rich and the poor meet together, but the Lord is the maker of them all :" not merely as men, but as rich and poor. Therefore believe in Providence. " In all thy ways acknowledge Him, and He shall direct thy paths. It is the blessing of the Lord that maketh rich." Look up for that blessing by constant, earnest, believing prayer. Enter upon life devoutly believing in God, as the God of Providence. Do nothing upon which you cannot ask his blessing, and then seek his blessing upon everything you do. Never forget your dependence upon Him. He can exalt you to prosperity, or sink you into the lowest depth of adversity. He can make everything to which you set your hand to prosper, or to fail. Devoutly acknowledge this. Abjure the infidelity that shuts God out of his own world.

There is a passage, however, which, as it seems to favour an opposite view to this, I will explain. "I returned, and saw under the sun, that the race is not to the swift, nor the battle to the strong ; neither yet bread to the wise, nor yet riches to men of understanding, nor yet favour to men of skill; but time and change happeneth to them all." The obvious meaning of this verse is, that while there are some so timid and desponding as to expect nothing from their exertions, there are others so sanguine, bold and self-confident, as to feel almost sure to succeed in everything : and while the preceding verse is intended to stimulate the energies of the former, by showing the benefit of exertion, this verse is designed to check the proud confidence of the latter, by reminding them, that the success of human efforts, is not always in proportion to their ability. "Time and chance happen to all." There are times propitious and unpropitious in the history of all, for the accomplishment of our purposes, over which we can have no command or control : and an endless variety of circumstances, which, as they could not be foreseen and cannot be controlled, may appear like chance, and which may frustrate the wisest plans, and render nugatory the most industrious exertions. All is Providence in determining results. So that from this well-known and frequently quoted passage, we are not to conclude there is no adaptation of means to ends; no correspondence between the qualities and actions of men and their results; that there is, in fact, no superior probability of success for the swift more than for the slow; for the strong more than for the weak; for the intelligent more than for the ignorant; for the skilful more than for the foolish. Far from it. For if this were the case, forethought, intelligence, industry, were all useless, a large portion of Scripture would be contradicted by itself, and the passage proved false by a reference to examples constantly occurring before us. The meaning evidently is, that though these qualities tend to success, they cannot actually ensure it. Such a passage is not intended to discourage industry, but only to check a spirit of proud self-reliance: not to repress the energies and the chastened confidence of the rational man, but to call into exercise the caution and the piety of the dependent one. It is ever to be remembered, that Providence works by means, and the means employed are those which possess an adaptation to produce the end intended. And since God has appointed means to be employed, we do as much homage to him in using them, as we do in depending upon him for their success; in the one we honour his wisdom, and in the other his power. Hence, therefore, we must, in ordinary cases, look for the means of success, and the causes of failure, in men's own conduct. This is true both in spiritual and tem-

poral things; and is as true in one as the other, for
the God of nature and providence is the God of grace,
and there is an analogy between the methods of his
procedure in these two departments of his action. In
each, second causes are employed; and in each the
means are adapted to the end. Let us then examine
into the causes of the two different results of success
and failure.

I. The possession or want of ability, cleverness, good
judgment, and tact, in trade, will often account for
success or failure. Success in any department of human
action, without a competent knowledge of the means
of obtaining it, cannot be expected, and ordinarily never
is obtained. It is true an unusual occurrence of what
are called fortunate circumstances, may, in some cases,
contribute to results not otherwise to be looked for:
but they form the exceptions, not the rule. It is unde-
sirable for some young persons to be acquainted with
such cases, as they may receive from them an unfavourable influence, leading them to trust to what they call
luck rather than ability. It is in the order of nature
for intelligence combined with industry to succeed, and
you should not let an occasional instance of prosperous
ignorance, happening now and then, shake your conviction of the necessity of skill. Though in these cases
the element of knowledge was in small proportion, the
other elements of success in some measure compensated
for that deficiency by their abundance: a combination
not to be expected in your case. A man must at all
times, especially in this age of competition, thoroughly
know not only his own trade, but the principles of trade
in general. Business is an art and a science too, and
to succeed he must be acquainted with both. He must

know how to buy and how to sell. He must be a judge of articles and prices. He must know the markets and the times. In order to this, young men, you must be thoughtful, observant, and diligent, as an apprentice and shopman. You must be neither lovers of pleasure, nor companions of those that are. Next to religion, it should be your aim to gain a complete mastery of your trade. Who are the men that usually succeed? Not the dolts, the ill-informed, or the half-informed, but the well-informed. Who are the men that fail? Usually you will find them not the well-informed, but the half-informed, or the ill-informed. Even religion itself, however eminent, cannot supply the want of the knowledge and the habits of a good tradesman. Godliness, it is true, is profitable for all things, having the promise of the life that now is and of that which is to come. But then it is not godliness without other things, but with them. A good and holy young man is not to expect to succeed by the favour of God, without either industry or ability. God's blessing is not to be looked for as a substitute for these. He does not bless pious dolts, in whom the want of ability is the result of neglect. God will not set aside the general laws by which he governs the social world in favour of religion, any more than he will those of the natural world. Even a seraph, where he incarnate upon earth, would, if he had no acquaintance with earthly affairs, make a bad farmer or a bad manufacturer. Nor will the countenance and support of friends lead to success, without the tradesman's own skill. Who can help an incompetent man? What foreign aid can be a substitute for personal ability? There are some cripples too feeble to walk, even by the help of others. So there are some persons too ignorant ever to be helped to succeed. Capital will not do without knowledge. The largest amount of this will be soon dissipated, where there is no skill to direct its employment, and beware of over-stocking and trading beyond your capital. A very frequent source of ruin to young tradesmen is their allowing travellers to force upon them too large purchases.

II. Success or failure depend a great deal upon a favourable commencement; a good start. This is true, as a general principle, in application to all things. Bad beginnings may be repaired, but they are not usually. A first wrong step is often, if not always, the beginning of a series of steps all wrong. Great care, caution, circumspection, and forethought, therefore, are necessary here. Many begin too soon, before they have sufficient capital or competent knowledge. They are impatient to be masters, before they are prepared for it. They are unwilling to "bide their time," and they also miscalculate their ability. They are better fitted to obey than to rule. It is not every good servant that will make an able master, though unquestionably the best preparation for the latter is the former. He that begins with little capital and less experience, commences with fearful disadvantages, and failure has often been the result. Our most successful tradesmen have been cautious, as well as able, men. They have begun perhaps with limited capital, but they did not over-trade with it. They were willing to creep before they walked; to walk before they ran; and to run before they fled. There is an old Latin proverb, which being interpreted, is, "We hasten by being slow." Beginning well is a great thing, next to ending well; and the one leads on to the other. Let there, then, be much reflection, much counsel, much prayer in such an important step as commencing business for yourself. As this, like marriage, is a step for life, let it be taken with care, and think no time lost, or too long, which is necessary to enable you to tread firmly and steadily at the outset. For one that has repented of beginning too late, ten have repented that they began too soon. Next to seeking counsel from God, by earnest and believing prayer, seek the advice of disinterested wise and experienced men. A young man came to me some years ago, to get an introduction to any friend whom I might know in the neighbourhood in which he wished to engage in business, and who would be willing to give him counsel on the probable success of a concern which he had some thoughts of taking. I gave him a letter to one of the most capable men in the country, who very kindly received him, and very wisely and earnestly advised him to abandon the project. But he had set his heart upon it, and, in opposition to the counsel which had been given him, entered upon the concern, from which he was very soon glad to escape without being utterly ruined. Do not first make up your mind, and then ask advice afterwards. Reverse this order, and go to the oracle first, and defer to its responses.

III. Success and failure are dependent upon diligence on the one hand, or neglect and indolence on the other. For proofs of this, I refer you to that invaluable book which was the subject of my last chapter, and to your own reason and observation. I have already quoted one passage from the Proverbs, which says, "The blessing of the Lord maketh rich." I now add to it another, "The hand of the diligent maketh rich."

Both are true, and they stand related to each other, as the instrumental and the efficient cause. Man's industry cannot be successful without God's blessing, and God's blessing is not bestowed without man's industry. The Lord's providential visits are never granted to loiterers. Moses, David, and the shepherds at Bethlehem, were all keeping their flocks, and Gideon was at his threshing floor, when God's revelations were made to them. How is slothfulness exposed, condemned, branded, in God's book. Let a man have ever so good a knowledge of his business; let him begin with all the advantage of capital, connections, and situation; yet if he be of an indolent or self-indulgent habit; a late riser; a lover of pleasure; a gossiping neighbour; a zealous political partizan, more busy in improving the State than in minding his own concerns; he will soon furnish another evidence of the truth of Solomon's words, " He becometh poor that dealeth with a slack hand." Weigh well, then, young men, the import of that momentous word, diligence. You remember the anecdote of Demosthenes, who, on being asked the first grace of elocution, replied, " Delivery." The second? " Delivery." The third? " Delivery." So if asked what is the first qualification of a successful tradesman? I answer, " Diligence." The second? " Diligence." The third? " Diligence." Write it upon your hearts. Keep it ever before your eyes. Let it be ever sounding in your ears. Let it be said of you, as was affirmed of that admirable and holy missionary, Henry Martyn, when he was at college, " That he was known as the man who never lost an hour."

IV. Method and system have much to do with failure or success. In this I include promptness, as opposed to procrastination. No habit can be more fatal to success than the wretched disposition of postponing till another time that which ought to be done, and can be done, at once. Procrastination has ruined millions for both worlds. There is a class of adverbs which some men appear never to have studied, but which are of immense importance in all the affairs both of time and eternity. I mean the words, "instantly;" "immediately;" "at once;" "now;" for which they have unhappily substituted, "presently;" "by and bye;" "to-morrow;" "at some future time." Young men, catch the inspiration of that weighty monosyllable "now." Yield to the potency of that word "instantly." But to use a still more business-like term, acquire a habit of "dispatch." And in order to this, do not only something immediately, but do immediately the thing that ought to be done next. Punctuality is of immense consequence. It has been humourously said, "Some people seem to have been born half an hour after their time, and they never fetch it up all their lives." In the present busy age, when business is so extended and complicated, and when, of course, one man is so dependent upon another, and oftentimes many upon one, a want of punctuality is not only a fault, but a vice, and a vice which inflicts an injury not only upon the transgressor himself, but upon others who have been waiting for him. "You have caused us to lose an hour," said a gentlemen to another, for whose appearance twelve persons had been waiting. "Oh, that is impossible," replied the laggard, "for it is only five minutes after the time." "Very true," was the rejoinder, "but here are twelve of us, each of whom has lost five minutes." He who keeps servants, customers, or creditors waiting, through his want of punctuality, can never prosper. This is as irreligious as it is injurious, inasmuch as the apostle has commanded us to "redeem the time." Order is no less essential to system and success than promptness and punctuality. Order, it is said, is heaven's first law, an aphorism as true of earth as it is of heaven, and as applicable to the movements of trade as of the stars. A place and a time for everything, and everything in its place and time, is the rule of every successful tradesman. A disorderly and irregular man may be diligent, that is may be ever in a bustle, a very different thing from a well-regulated activity, but his want of order defeats everything. The machinery of his habits may have velocity and power, but its movements are irregular and eccentric, and therefore unproductive, or productive only of uncertain, incomplete, and sometimes mischievous results. A disorderly man wastes not only his own time, but that of others who are dependent upon, and waiting for him; nor does the waste stop here, for what a useless expenditure of energy and a painful sacrifice of comfort are ever going on with him.

V. Economy has a most powerful influence in determining the failure or success of a young tradesman. This applies to personal trade and domestic expenses, and the man who would succeed in life must reduce them all to the lowest prudent level. In order to keep down the expenses of trade, he must do with as little purchased help as he can; and to accomplish this, he must be a hard worker himself, till he has attained to that pitch of prosperity, when he can do more with his eyes and his ears than with his hands and feet. As to personal expenses, let him avoid all unnecessary consumption of money in dress and ornaments. Let it be no part of your ambition, young men, to be noticed and admired for matters of this kind. It is a very grovelling ambition to be complimented for that with which the draper, the mercer, and the jeweller, may bedizen the veriest fool in existence. How mean and petty is foppery, compared with an enlightened mind, a dignified character, and the beauties of holiness. I am not an advocate for either meanness or slovenliness. Cleanliness and neatness border upon virtue, as excessive foppery and expensiveness do upon vice. It is unworthy of a female to be inordinately fond of dress; but for a man to love finery is despicable indeed. Avoid also the love of pleasure, for "he that loveth pleasure shall be a poor man." Never were truer words uttered. The man who is bent upon what is called "enjoying himself," who will have his boon companions, his amusements, and his frequent seasons of recreation; who is fond of parties, entertainments, the gaming table, the ball room, the concert, and the theatre; is on the high road to poverty in this world, and to hell in the next. Let the lover of pleasure read the history of Sampson in the Old Testament, and of the Prodigal in the New; and also let him turn back to the illustrations contained in the last chapter. If you would have economical habits as a master, cultivate them as a servant. Begin now and persevere. But you must carry out the principle of economy into your domestic establishment. Frugality in the house is a virtue, and extravagance a vice. If you would have elegance and luxuries at the close of life, be content with necessaries at the beginning of it. He that must have superfluities at the beginning, will in all probability have scarcely comforts at the end. Let your furniture, your style

of living, your whole domestic establishment, be all
arranged upon the principle of a rigid, though not mean,
economy. Never aim to cover over poverty by extravagance, nor adopt the false principle that dash is
necessary to success. Such conduct often defeats its
own end, by exciting suspicion and undermining credit.
Wise creditors have keen and vigilant eyes, that look
not only at the shop, but penetrate into the dining and
drawing room, and thus watch the mode of living as
well as of doing business. They deal more readily and
upon better terms with the frugal man, than with the
extravagant one. The basis of credit is laid in economical simplicity and plain living, not in unsubstantial
splendour; just as the foundation of a house consists
of unadorned bricks and unsculptured stone, and not
of carved and gilded wood. It is the diligent and frugal
man who is considered the trustworthy one. But while
I recommend economy, I would with equal force condemn meanness; and reprobate, with stronger language
still, a want of principle. There have been men of fine
talents, and otherwise excellent character, who have well
nigh ruined themselves by a spirit of mean and starvel-
ing economy, which grudged the very means of success.
There have been even professing Christians, and some
of great benevolence too, who, from education or habit,
have been so mean in some of their pecuniary transactions, as to throw a dark shade over their character.
Economy, when rigid, has not unfrequently degenerated
into sordid avarice. Hence the necessity of your
being on your guard against the meanest of all vices,
the most despicable of all passions, and the most insatiable of all appetites, an excessive love of money. It is
very striking to observe how seemingly opposite disposi-

tions are balanced in the word of God. How is industry commended and slothfulness condemned in that precious volume; and yet in that same Book it is said, "Labour not to be rich;" "Labour not for the bread that perisheth;" "Lay not up for yourselves treasures on earth;" "They that will be rich fall into temptation and a snare, and into many foolish and hurtful lusts which drown men in destruction; for the love of money is the root of all evil, which while some have coveted after, they have erred from the faith, and pierced themselves through with many sorrows." Does not this look like contradiction? If it does, it is not so in reality. These seemingly opposing passages are intended to teach us that we are neither to despise money nor to be fond of it. I know it is difficult to define covetousness; to draw the line with precision between the idolatry and contempt of wealth; and to state that exact regard to money which industry requires to stimulate and reward its energies, and which both reason and revelation justify. When, however, wealth is considered as the chief end of life, and is sought exclusively, to the entire neglect of religion; when it is pursued at the expense of principle and honour; when it is the first thing coveted, and the last thing relinquished; when it is loved for its own sake, instead of its uses; when it is hoarded for the sake of mere accumulation, instead of being diffused for God's glory and man's benefit; when it is regarded as the standard of individual importance both for ourselves and others; it has then become the tyrant of the soul, which it has enslaved, it may be with fetters of silver and gold, but which is not the less a miserable bond-slave because of the splendour and value of its manacles.

VI. Perseverance is also necessary to success. Without this nothing good or great can be achieved in our world. Success is not so much a creation, as a gradual formation; a slow deposit. In business it usually proceeds on the principle of arithmetical progression, till at a certain stage, and in some few instances, it changes its ratio of increase to that of geometrical progression. The ascent in life is usually the reverse of that of a mountain. In the latter case the steepest part is near the summit; in the former, at the base. Both, however, require perseverance. He that would succeed, must not expect to reach his object by a light, easy, and elastic bound, but by many a successive and weary step, and occasionally, perhaps, by a step backwards. He must go on sometimes amidst discouragement, and always with labour. There are some who cannot succeed, because they will not wait for it. If success does not come at first, they will not follow after it. They are as impatient as the foolish child that sowed his seed in the morning, and went to bed hopeless and crying because he did not see it springing up before sunset. Be ever hopeful, prayerful, and persevering. " In the morning sow thy seed, and in the evening withhold not thy hand, for thou knowest not whether shall prosper either this or that, or whether they both shall be alike good." " Behold the husbandman waiteth for the precious fruit of the earth, and hath long patience for it. Be ye also patient."

VII. The possession or the want of religion will have considerable influence in producing success or failure. Not that I mean to say all religious persons will be prosperous, and that all irreligious ones will sink to adversity. But that piety contains most of those qualities which tend to success, while sin, where it leads on, as it frequently does, to vice, tends to ruin. God has better promises than of wealth and honour for his people, even of glory everlasting; but then, godliness, as I have often said, has the promise of the life that now is, as well as of that which is to come. Wisdom, as we saw in the last chapter, has riches and honour in her right hand for many who submit to her sway. It is quite certain that those who have come to poverty and ruin have been dragged down by iniquity, while many have succeeded who owed their prosperity to their piety. We have examples of this in holy Scripture. Religion made Joseph prosper in the house of Potiphar, and raised him to the eminence he obtained in Egypt. Religion elevated David to the throne of Israel. Religion made Daniel prime minister of Babylon. Religion made Nehemiah governor of Judea. And although we should not expect such rewards, it may still bring prosperity. It is the parent of virtue, the protector of health, the nurse of economy, the patron of industry, the guardian of integrity, the prompter of knowledge, and thus the guide to success and the helper of prosperity.

And now let me set before you the two young men whom I have supposed to set out in life together, the one actually failing, and the other succeeding, in business. Failure is a word, in such an application of it, pregnant with terrors. What a variety, complication, and depth of sorrows, are there in that very simple, and not uncommon expression, "He has failed in business." You are happily unable by reflection, may you never be able by experience, to grasp that comprehension of wretchedness. Now, young men, I present the fearful subject, the dreadful possibility to you, first of all, to excite a desire, an anxiety, an earnest solicitude, that in your case it may never be realized. Prevention is better than cure. It is easier to avert ruin by industry and economy, than to bring back prosperity when it has once departed. Be this easier task, then, your first care and endeavour. For you, ruin is yet, happily, only pictured; a scene for the imagination to contemplate: except, indeed, as the reality is seen in the history of some acquaintance. Though it is not well to fill your mind with dark imaginings and gloomy forebodings, lest such thoughts become predictions, and the predictions verify, by fulfilling, themselves, yet is it well to look at the dreadful picture, in order not indeed to quail before it, but to bring up your mind to this determination: " By God's grace upon my own intelligence, industry, economy, and perseverance, this shall never be my lot; but if, in the mysteries of Providence, it should befall me, it shall not be made more dreadful by the venom of self-reproach, it shall come from the ordination of God, and not from my own misconduct."

Still I will suppose that you may, and that some of you will, fail. What then? The answer to this depends upon the causes of the disaster. I will not deny that this, in some cases, is to be traced entirely to the dispensations of Providence, without any blame to the individual himself. I would not break the bruised reed, by heaping censure upon one who is an object of pity and sympathy. I would not pour vinegar into the wounds of his lacerated heart, and quite crush his broken spirits, by telling him that his misfortunes are his faults. If, after exercising the abilities and virtues of a good tradesman, after struggling hard and long, it should be your lot to be compelled to yield to difficulties utterly insuperable by skill and labour, in that case, first of all, bow with submission to the will of God. Indulge no hard thoughts of God. Keep down a gloomy hopelessness, a sullen despondence, a comfortless grief. Call in religion to your aid. Open your Bible. Pour out your heart in prayer. Believe in God, in Providence, in Christ. Take it as a matter to be relied upon, that there is some wise and merciful end to be answered by these painful events. Perhaps your were setting out in life forgetful of God. You were striving to make yourself happy without Him. You were entering upon your career in a state of practical atheism. Success in business would have been your spiritual ruin. The gain of the world would have been the loss of your soul. God spake unto you in what you thought was your prosperity, and you would not hear; and now he calls to you in harsher tones, and says to you in the language of the text, Consider. Consider the Author of your troubles, that they come from God: their cause, that sin is the bitter fountain of every bitter stream: their design, to do you good: and their impressive lesson, to teach the vanity of all things earthly, and the necessity of a better portion for man's heart. Ah! young man, you have indeed sorrowfully proved the uncertainty of all things earthly. How soon and suddenly has the beautiful prospect, which expanded before your admiring eyes, been covered with mist and gloom! How have all the ardent hopes which such a scene inspired, withered in your soul and left it bleak and desolate! Well, amidst the fragments of your broken cisterns, now look up to the great fountain of happiness, pouring out its never-failing streams before you. Earth has failed; now turn to heaven. The world has disappointed you; now turn to religion. The creature has forsaken you, now turn to the Creator. All is not lost. Besides, you may yet recover. You have failed, but it is in early life, not in its decline. You have the main portion of existence yet before you, and have health and vigour on your side and in your favour ; and, in the case I am supposing, with your character unimpaired and your principles unsuspected. It may be only a step back to spring forward with greater vigour. It may be prosperity postponed, not put off for ever. This painful experience might be necessary for you. It may be to prevent a sudden plethora which would have been fatal to you. Abandon not hope then. Do not let the main-spring be broken. Give not yourself to despair. The sun is not gone down, but is only veiled with a cloud. Begin afresh, make good use of your experience. Look up for God's blessing; and you will have it.

But where the failure is the result of blameworthy conduct, what shall be said? Even here I would not be harsh, severe, and reproachful; but would blend tenderness with fidelity. Be humble before God. Your want of attention, industry, and economy, is a sin to be confessed to Him, as well as a matter to be bewailed on your own account. You have neglected God's commands, as well as your own interests. You have abused the gifts of Providence, as well as trifled with your own happinesss. And you cannot be in a right state of mind without penitence, humiliation, and confession. God is displeased with you; and you must seek his forgiveness through faith in our Lord Jesus Christ. You must take care to blame yourself, not God, for your present situation. Especially must

you be careful not to apply to wrong sources of relief.
Misfortune and misconduct have led, in thousands
of instances, to drinking. Broken in fortune, and
equally broken in spirits, men have endeavoured to gain
a momentary oblivion of their sorrows in the exhilara-
tion or stupefaction of intoxicating liquor. Dreadful
resort! What is this but to add crime to misery; and
when the effect of the poisonous draught is over, to
overwhelm the miserable dupe of intoxication with
sorrows envenomed by the stings of remorse? It is,
indeed a horrible idea, but one that is often realized,
that drunkenness should select some of its many victims
from the ranks of misfortune, and thus complete the
ruin which incompetency or indolence had begun, by
depriving the subject of it of all power and all disposition
to retrieve his position.

But I now, in contrast, take up the case of those
who succeed; a happy, and I rejoice to think, not a
very small class. It is a delightful, and to you, my
young friends, an encouraging thought, that success,
varied of course in degrees, is the rule, and failure the
exception. Conceive then of the man who, by the
blessing of God upon his ability, industry, and economy,
makes good his ground, and advances in life to respectable competency; perhaps to affluence. The Scriptures
call upon him to be joyful, a state of mind, in which,
without such call, he is likely to be found. A Christian
is to be joyful not only in, but for, his prosperity. His
joy, however, should be a religious, not a sensual, joy.
He is not to express his delight by conviviality, extravagance, splendour, and all the other delights of sense
and taste. He is piously to trace up all his prosperity
to God. He is not boastfully to look round upon his

possessions, and say, " My own hand hath gotten me this :" and thus, to use the language of the prophet, " Sacrifice unto their own net, and burn incense to their drag, because by them their portion is fat, and their meat plenteous." Let your joy be subordinate to a higher and nobler felicity, I mean the felicity derived from true religion. Prosperity, if it has its joys, has also its snares. It is, as regards the moral character, the interests of the soul, and man's eternal destiny, a most perilous condition. " How hardly shall they that have riches enter into the kingdom of God. It is easier for a camel to go through the eye of a needle, than for a rich man to enter the kingdom of heaven." " The prosperity of fools shall slay them." Multitudes have lost their souls in gaining a fortune. Their wealth has been their curse : their gold, the weight that dragged them down to perdition. And after all, " What shall it profit a man, if he gain the whole world, and lose his own soul ?" The whole world is no more compensation for the loss of the soul, than a feather or a grain of sand. " Seek first the kingdom of God and his righteousness, and all these things shall be added to you." Be made happy by religion. " Rejoice in the Lord, and again, I say rejoice."

But the best way to use, to enjoy, and even to pre-serve prosperity, is to sanctify it by true religion, and to employ it for Christian liberality. Set out in life with the intelligent, deliberate, and fixed determination, that if you should succeed in business, your prosperity shall in due measure be consecrated to the cause of God and man. Already make up your mind to this opinion, that the chief design and highest enjoyment of wealth, is diffusion rather than accumulation. Instead of admiring

the men whom you see living in splendid houses, rolling
about in gay equipages, and faring sumptuously every
day; but who all this while are known by their grandeur,
but not by their public spirit, liberality, and good works;
fix your delighted gaze upon those nobler spirits, who
while sustaining with propriety, yet simplicity, the rank
which Providence has assigned to them in society, are
economical that they may be liberal, and are redeeming
time from business, ease, and elegant retirement, to
glorify God and bless their species. Look at the Howards,
the Wilberforces, the Thorntons, the Wilsons, the Rey-
noldses; men who gave their talents, their influence,
and their lives, for the benefit of the slave, the prisoner,
and the debtor; who renounced in some cases, the gains
of business, for the pursuits of benevolence; and in
others, carried it on to have larger means to assist the
cause of humanity and religion; who lived for others
rather than for themselves; and who had far more
enjoyment while they lived, and will ever have far more
honour after their death, than the sordid and selfish,
whose wealth, while it did little to make them happy or
respected upon earth, will neither preserve their names
from oblivion, nor yield them a fragment of reward in
heaven.

But wait not till you are rich before you begin to be
benevolent. Let the beginnings of your success be
consecrated by the beginnings of your devotedness. I
knew a christian philanthropist who set out in life by
consecrating a tenth of his income to God. He did
this when he had but a hundred a year. He became at
length possessed of eight thousand a year, and having
no children, he did not then satisfy himself with the

tithe, as he had commenced, but spent less than two thousand a year on his own simple and elegant establishment, and gave all the rest away.* How much happier, as well as holier, was that christian man than those who hoard for they know not who; or than those who lavish their wealth on splendour, luxury, and pleasure: and, oh! the different reception he will meet with at the bar of God where wealth must be accounted for; and in eternity, where the successful, but irreligious worldling will remember, and be punished for, his unsanctified prosperity!

And now let me remind you that this alternative of failure or success exists also as to the great trial ever going on in this world, and which must issue in the ruin or the salvation of your immortal soul. You are here upon a probation for eternity. Your chief business is religion, your supreme object should be immortality. He that is enabled to repent, to believe, and to lead a holy life, notwithstanding the temptations by which he is surrounded; who thus obtains the salvation that is in Christ Jesus, with eternal glory; though he should fail in everything else, may look round upon the wreck of all his hopes, prospects, and fortunes, exulting even now in the greatness and the grandeur of his success, and shall stand at the last day, upon the ashes of the globe, after the general conflagration, exclaiming, "I have lost nothing." While he who so far succeeds as to gain everything else that is dear to ambition, to avarice, and to sensuality, but fails to obtain the one thing needful, the salvation of his soul, stands now, amidst all his prosperity, a miserable instance of failure in all the

* Mr. Broadley Wilson.

great objects of man's immortal being, shall be seen in the day of judgment, a ruined and lost immortal, and shall wander for ever through the universe, with this awful exclamation, " I have voluntarily, deliberately, and irrecoverably incurred a failure, which it will require an eternity to understand, and an eternity to deplore."

CHAPTER IX.

EMIGRATION.

Whither shall I go from thy Spirit? Or whither shall I flee from thy presence?

If I ascend up into heaven, thou art there; If I make my bed in hell, behold thou art there.

If I take the wings of the morning and dwell in the uttermost parts of the sea, even there shall thy hand lead me and thy right hand shall hold me.

PSALM cxxxix, 7-10.

GOD made this world to be inhabited, and did not intend that it should always remain an untenanted house, or be occupied only by beings without minds to understand his nature, hearts to love him for his favours, and tongues to speak his praise. To man as well as to the inferior creatures he said, "Be fruitful and multiply and replenish the earth." And yet at this period of our planet's history, nearly six thousand years after the fitting up of the globe for man's residence, there are vast tracts of the earth, amounting to islands and continents, till lately occupied only by birds, beasts, and reptiles. The fact however of these desolations subserves a moral purpose, inasmuch as it corroborates the chronology of the Bible; for upon the acknowledged principles of the increase of population, the date of the commencement of our race could not be much otherwise than that assigned to it in revelation. These now un-peopled regions must have been long since filled up, had the present earth been much older than it is according to the chronology of the Bible. Upon the same prin-ciples it is evident that it cannot continue for an indefinite period, at least without some depopulating process different from any that has hitherto occurred in the world's history.

Our earth has yet to "yield its increase," the Trans-atlantic world, capable of sustaining half the present population of the globe, but till lately tenanted only by savages in the north, and a half-civilized race in the south, and four centuries ago unknown to all the other people on the face of the globe; the island continent of New Holland, with only a scattered sprinkling of savages from its aboriginal inhabitants; the Polyne-sian Archipelago; and all the yet uninhabited spots of earth where means of support and occupation for man can be obtained, are to be covered with an intelligent, busy population: and where now the forest throws its dark shadow over its innumerable flying or creeping tribes, or the wilderness is the range of herds of untamed beasts, or the jungle affords a shelter to the tiger, the elephant and the serpent, there shall the dwellings of men and the sanctuaries of God be seen, and the hum of commerce, and the anthems of religion be heard.

The replenishing of the earth never went forward more rapidly than in the day and from the country in which we live. Colonization and emigration are two of the grandest features of our age. Infant states are being born to Britain, and our country is becoming the mother of nations. Myriads and myriads, year after year, are wafted, not only in ships, but I may almost say in fleets, to the shores of America, Australia, and New Zealand. The vast tide of population is flowing out to relieve our overcrowded town and cities, and to found new towns and cities in the wilds of those distant regions. Thus are carried out the plans of Providence, to have a peopled world instead of a wilderness; and thus are the predictions of holy writ accomplished, which assure us that the knowledge of the Lord shall cover the earth. Everything falls in with the current of God's gracious purposes towards our dark disordered world; everything indicates human improvement and the progress of social existence; everything tends to the diffusion of the Bible, and harmonizes with its tendency, design, and announcements; everything is making way for the universal spread and triumph of religion, for the reign of Christ, for the millennial glory and the jubilee of the world.

Some of my readers may, by joining the multitude of emigrants, be instrumental in this great work of re-plenishing the earth with people, and, if possessed of religion, of carrying the light of divine truth to the ends of the earth. This, then, is the subject of the present chapter: Emigration. In treating this subject I shall consider

I. The decision. I will suppose the resolve is taken, the plan laid, the purpose unalterable. But what has led to it? There are various and very different motives and grounds for such a step. In some cases it is obedi-ence to the stern dictate of necessity. Misconduct at home renders it matter of compulsion rather than of choice, to go abroad; it is a flight rather than a voluntary departure. Reputation may have been lost, and lost also the hope of retrieving it here. This is a painful case, but not a hopeless one. If this be your condition, you will have abundant and most favourable opportunities for rectifying what is amiss, without being subject to the suspicion, neglect, rebukes, and frowns of those who knew you in your better days. On your voyage reflect upon your conduct, review the past. Dare to look back. When pacing the deck at night, or lying in your hammock, or listening to the awful roar of the tempest, not knowing but you may be soon swallowed up in the billows raging around you, and every now and then breaking over your trembling vessel, repent before God, seek his pardoning mercy through Christ, and implore his Holy Spirit to help you first to resolve upon amendment, and then to carry out your resolution. Determine to begin a new life in a new world. Resolve to set out afresh. There is hope for you yet. Carry a Bible with you, read it, and make it your councillor, comforter, and companion. You have neglected religion, and your sins have found you out. You are in imminent danger of becoming worse instead of better for the change. Bad companions may have been your ruin. You will now be broken off from their circle, but, unless you are firm, you will find worse associates where you are going. You have neglected religion, and this has been your bane. Now take it up, and it will not only reclaim and reform you, but it will be your friend in reference to things seen and temporal, as well as things eternal. If you are wise, you will turn this dire necessity of leaving your country into a means of obtaining the signal blessing of the salvation of your soul. I knew a youth, the son of an eminent, holy minister, who ran a profligate course till his crimes cast him as a convict upon the shores of a foreign land, but he then reflected upon his course, became penitent, and died, I hope, a sincere Christian. Nor is this the only case of the same kind I have known. Even our penal colonies, notwithstanding the enormities of the trans- portation system, have thus furnished instances of re- claimed convicts, who have risen to respectability and wealth. The veriest outcast of society may recover. Reformation is not impossible in the worst of cases.

But there may be another kind of necessity that is driving you away from your native shores. You have failed at the outset of life. Your prospects have faded, and now, with the hope of repairing your broken fortune, you are going to a foreign land. If this has happened through your own misconduct, you too must be humbled before God, and invoke his forgiveness; and when you have done this, but not till then, you may seek his blessing upon the step you are taking. Employ much of your time also in a severe inquiry into your habits. Detect, as you easily may, the cause of failure, and de- termine to remove it. The same cause, if carried to a distant land, will produce the same effects there. Change of country will not be of the slightest benefit to you without a change of conduct. Indolence and extrava- gance will as certainly bring ruin in Austral Asia as in England. You must alter, and you may. A new sphere of action will present an opportunity for alteration, and new motives for effort. But should your failure be the result of no fault of yours, trust in God. Earnestly pray for his help and blessing. Leave your country with hope. It may be that you too neglected religion in your happier days. If so, now take it up. I say to you also, carry with you a Bible, and a few religious

books. Have the moral courage not to be ashamed
of being seen with those silent companions. You will
find many on board who will ridicule you, but shall
they laugh you out of your convictions? Will you be
afraid of a sneer, when your soul and salvation are at
stake? Do not put off the subject of religion till you
land. This will be to ensure the neglect of it. Your
mind will then be so hurried in seeking employment,
and be so taken up with the novelties of a foreign country,
as to have little leisure or inclination for attending to
spiritual things. With religion in your heart, you may
step ashore in New Zealand or in America, with the
hope that God will befriend you in the land of your
adoption; and that the tide of your affairs will there
turn in your favour.

But by far the largest class of emigrants is composed
of those who go out with a spirit of adventure, with the
hope of doing better for themselves abroad than at
home. Every department of action is here so crowded,
competition is so fierce, and situations of advantage are
so rare, that they have little hope of success at home,
and turn their attention to one or other of our rising
colonies. I know not that such persons are to be blamed;
and yet is it a step to be taken with much deliberation,
caution, and prayer. Where a young man has an opor-
tunity of doing well for himself in his own country,
there seems no reason, except it be inordinate ambition
or a love of adventure, to lead him to another land.
Neither of these impulses is a very sufficient one for
expatriation. There will always be found an adequate
number of those who really are not doing very well here,
and could do a great deal better abroad, to keep up the
stream of emigration, without those going who are doing

well at home. There is great wisdom in the advice, to "let well alone." A love of change is a dark portent in the character of any young man. He that goes abroad for this, will soon come back again from the same impulse. There is nothing which a young man should more earnestly dread, nothing he should more assiduously watch against, nothing he should more resolutely resist, than this versatility : it will be fatal to all his hopes and prospects. Still there are very many cases in which it is not only justifiable, but even commendable, to emigrate : and when the character and conduct are good, where there there are those qualities of mind which are likely to make the individual a blessing to the land to which he is going, as well as a benefit to his own family and fortune, I cannot but approve the decision.

II. Having thus distinguished between the different classes of emigrants, I shall now speak of their trials. In most cases there is the separation from friends. Not unfrequently the emigrant has to tear himself from the arms and fond embrace of a loving and beloved mother, and from the warm grasp of an affectionate father; and he who has outgrown or outlived all sensibilities of this nature, gives poor evidence of right feeling of any kind, and holds out faint hope of being likely to obtain God's blessing upon his future course. Adieu is always a sad sound, when parents and children, brothers and sisters, are parting; but especially when, in all probability, they are parting for ever. And besides this, is it nothing to expatriate ourselves from our native land? Why, the irrational creatures love the spot of their birth, and their early dwelling; and this is an instinct which man shares with them. It is long before the charms of those expressions cease to be felt, " My country and my father's house." I can fancy the thoughtful emigrant watching from the deck of his vessel, with tearful eyes and intense feeling, the receding shores of his native land; seeing her green fields and white cliffs, her steeples and her houses, becoming more and more dim; straining his eyes still to see the last speck of land that is distinctly visible; and then looking upon the mighty waste of waters, till in an agony he exclaims, "I have seen the last of the land of my fathers!" Then the voyage, its length, its inconvenience, its hard fare and want of accommodations, its sea-sickness and other indescribable annoyances, its often disagreeable companions and uncongenial society. These things end, only to be exchanged, in many cases, for trials of another kind. Oh, for a man to light upon a new world, alike unknowing and unknown; to be a stranger in a strange land, with no one to recognize or smile upon him; to be informed that some whom he expected to welcome him on these distant shores are either dead or removed to another place; and to meet no one to stretch out the hand of friendship, or to give the kiss of love; to have to seek employment where perhaps the labour market is overstocked, and to be long without finding occupation; to see his little stock of money well-nigh spent without any means of replenishing it; to find all his dreams of colonial prosperity nothing but dreams, and see all his hopes of immediate success, so long and so confidently cherished, vanish like the baseless fabric of a vision; to discover too late, or at any rate to begin to think, he has made a mistake in leaving his native country; these, all these, are among the trials which many of our emigrants have to endure. And even where their trials are not altogether of so dreary an aspect as this, yet are they except in rare cases, many more and far greater than the most sober calculation had expected. A very large proportion of settlers have their lot cast in such thinly peopled spots, as to be miles from their nearest neighbour, and have to endure so many privations as to be reduced to the barest necessaries of existence. If the man be a Christian, who loves the house of God, the means of grace, the ministry of the Word, the oversight and conversation of a faithful pastor, and the fellowship of saints, he feels in addition the deprivation of all these.

To hear a sermon, he must travel miles, and to break the bread of communion with the saints, he must travel still further. Such are but a few of the trials of an emigrant's life. I could tell a tale of woe connected with some who have gone out from my own church, which would harrow up your feelings to a degree of intense suffering. Not however that affliction often falls with such weight as in the case to which I allude. Such things should make you cautious how you determine to encounter them, and should prepare your mind for the struggle, by laying up a good store of consolation for the evil day. And what can this be but religion? The trials of very many emigrants are fewer and lighter than I have described; and I have drawn the picture thus darkly, not to prevent emigration, or to fill the mind which has resolved on it, with dark misgivings, but to check that proneness to think a foreign shore a fairy land, in which so many indulge. The danger lies on the side of thinking too lightly of the trials of such a life, and not preparing for them, rather than on the side of having too gloomy an apprehension of them.

III. It is the part of fidelity to remind you of your dangers. It would not be kind to attempt to fill your mind with the perils of the ocean, and the dangers of shipwreck, or the other casualties of a voyage. Nor is it probable that you will be called to a calamity so fearful. I know not the proportion of fatal voyages to successful ones, but I should suppose they are not as one to a hundred. So that apprehension of this kind need not greatly alarm you. Still, your vessel may founder at sea, or be wrecked on some foreign shore, and it is well, by sincere and humble piety, to be prepared for the worst. Religion will enable you to meet death at sea in the storm, as well as in the calm on dry land. An eminent Christian minister, in the prospect of a voyage, when contemplating the possibility of shipwreck, recorded thus his feelings under the possibility of such a catastrophe: " How willingly should I embrace that wave, which instead of landing me at Liverpool, should land me in heaven." Mr. Mackenzie, who was lost in the Pegasus, on his way from Leith to London, was seen when the vessel was sinking, divested of all fear for himself, calmly directing the minds of his perishing fellow-passengers to look by faith to Jesus, and thus prepare for that eternity on which in a few moments they were about to enter. See what religion can do for its possessors amidst the roar of the tempest and when the ocean is opening its mouth to swallow them up. Could you thus hopefully and peacefully descend into a watery grave? But death sometimes comes on board an emigrant ship which escapes the tempest. To die at sea is no uncommon thing. Death, like its Omnipotent Lord and Conqueror, often walks the waves, and approaches the affrighted mariners, and steps on board the vessel, but not as in the case of Jesus on the lake of Gennesareth, to relieve, but to confirm, the fears of those who watch his approach. To a good man there is nothing very terrible in this. True it is that the ocean is not the house, nor a ship the chamber, in which any one would choose to endure his last sickness and meet the last enemy. But a believing sense of God's presence and love, and the prospect of a glorious immortality, can make a death-bed easy even there. And the real Christian can endure without dismay the thought of sleeping in the bottom of the ocean, amidst the monsters of the deep, instead of in a sepulchre on dry land, assured that at the resurrection morning, "the sea will give up the dead which are in it."

These, however, are not the greatest or most imminent dangers to which you will be exposed; or those of which you should be most afraid; or against which you need to be most impressively and anxiously warned by your friends. Perils of a moral kind, and fearful ones, will beset your path. What a mixture of society is to be found in every emigrant ship that floats its living cargo to a distant shore. There you will probably find the vicious of both sexes; the infidel, the debauchee, the gambler, the drunkard; the men of all principles, and of no principle; the men of bankrupt fortune, and, what is worse, of bankrupt character. And not unlikely "the strange woman" will be there, "whose lips drop as a honey-comb, and whose mouth is smoother than oil, but whose end (to you as well as to herself, if you are ensnared by her) is bitter as wormwood, sharp as a two-edged sword; whose feet go down to death, and her steps take hold of hell," with those also whom she inveigles. In the best appointed ships will be found persons who, if you associate with them, will imperil your morals, and may ruin your character and your hopes for both worlds. An association of this kind once formed, you cannot avoid its contaminating influence for a single day. You cannot get away from it if you would. The tempter is ever in sight, always at your elbow and your ear. There is no wider range for you to move in than the vessel which contains you both. The danger is thus greater than can be described or imagined. It will follow you ashore; it will affect your character and conduct when you land, and influence all your future destiny. If then you have the least regard to your welfare, be vigilant, be cautious. Go to the scene of danger aware of it, and look up to God to preserve you. Pray to him to spread over you the shield of his omnipotence.

Should you, however, escape this danger on board ship, it will meet you on your landing. Our colonies are not only a field of enterprise for adventurers, whether they be the sober and industrious seeking a legitimate and ample scope for their energies and their hopes, or the reckless and desperate, throwing the dice for their last chance; but also the retreat of the prodigal and the profligate, where they may hide their shame and pursue their vicious career, unknown and unob-structed. In addition to this, there is in our penal colonies the infection diffused by the convicts. In these situations a young man viciously disposed will have every opportunity for gratifying his animal appetites, unrecognised by friends, and unrestrained by strangers.

But there are also dangers of another type than these. In a country, the population of which, even as regards its better portions, are to a certain extent a vast company of adventurers, who are all beginning life afresh and struggling hard amidst many difficulties to root themselves in the land of their adoption, there is likely to be acquired a peculiar hardness and selfishness of character, very unfriendly to the tender affections of the heart, the amenities of life, and the feelings and purposes of religion. The thorns of worldly cares, and the stony ground of earthly-mindedness, are but too common every where, but especially there, and they prevent the growth of the good seed of piety and virtue. Failures are common, sound principle is soon undermined, and in the hard struggle and anxious effort for success, every object but such as pertain to the present world, is lost sight of. The flattering pictures of colonial life and prosperity, which the imagination of many had drawn, in which they dreamed of immediate and certain success, without fear and almost without labour, are all found to be illusions of the fancy, and they are ready to lie down in despair, or to adopt any course, however dishonourable or even dishonest, not, indeed, to gain a fortune, which was once their expectation, but a bare living, which is now their highest, indeed, only hope. How unfavourable is such a situation to the cultivation of piety, or even of virtue !

To all this must now be added the new temptations and perils which the discovery of the gold deposits has thrown in the way of emigrants. The stream of population, swollen and quickened in its course, is flowing with dangerous rapidity towards the auriferous regions, floating some to prosperity, but more to ruin for both worlds. It will prove a fatal maelstrom to multitudes. Guard against the influence of these new visions of wealth. Let not your imaginations be filled with the

day-dreams and fascinations of this modern El Dorado;
nor allow yourselves to be allured with eager anticipations to its golden shores. That Providence has some
great ends to be answered by this new chapter in our
world's history there can be no doubt; and that some
must be employed as instruments to work out its plans
is equally clear. But be you not in haste to press into
its service. Let the tales of hardship, and of disease,
and of death, and of failure, which come from the
" diggings," cool the ardour produced by the reports
of sudden wealth, and balance the gainful side of the
account. Think of the peril to character which is produced by such a state of things; the lust of gold, the
selfishness of disposition, the jealousy and envy, the
grasping covetousness, or the reckless extravagance, and
the all but certain neglect of every thing but gold,
which even success is likely to produce. Such a state
of society is the worst possible mould in which character
can be formed. Avoid it, therefore, and be contented
with avocations which, if they are far less lucrative, are
at the same time far less perilous. If, however, your
course should seem to lie that way, enter upon the
scene of dangers duly aware of its perils, and looking
up to God for protection, and combining watchfulness
with prayer. To persons in such a situation the question applies with awful and alarming force, " What
shall it profit a man, if he gain the whole world and
lose his own soul, or what shall a man give in exchange
for his soul?" What carries the danger of all this to
the highest pitch is the absence, in many parts of our
colonies, especially in the gold regions, of the means
of grace, the ordinances of public worship, the fellowship
of saints, and the oversight of ministers. How difficult

is it here, even in this highly favoured land, by the aid of all these, to keep down sin and to maintain a due regard to the claims of religion and morality! But how much worse would things be without this! There can be no question that the observance of the Sabbath, the power of the pulpit, and the restraint of Christian example, tend greatly to moralise and purify the life even where they do not renew the heart, to restrain the sinner where they do not convert him, and to keep down the overflowings of ungodliness where they do not spread out the beauties of holiness. It is true that through the voluntary energies of almost all denominations of professing Christians, the deficiency of the means of grace, in our principal colonies, is being in some considerable measure supplied. But still how many emigrants are there who go out into the wild, who are not within a day's journey of a place of Christian worship, and scarcely hear a sermon in a year!

> "Oh, think of those who pine to hear,
> Far from their native shores exiled,
> A pastor's voice amidst the wild."

What is there in such circumstances to aid the struggles of the soul after good principles and habits here, or salvation hereafter? And even where the means of grace are within reach, they are, it must be confessed, too often of that feeble and inefficient character, which renders them neither attractive nor influential. Such, then, are some of the dangers to which the emigrant is exposed.

IV. I now proceed to offer him some counsels and directions. There are, as regards religion, two distinct classes of emigrants. There are some who are not living under the influence of true religion. Some of you, who read these pages, answer too justly to this description. You know you are not yet brought to repentance towards God, and faith in the Lord Jesus Christ: that you are not yet led to acknowledge God in all your ways, to live habitually in his fear and favour, and to enjoy the comforts of the Holy Spirit. Going out from your own country to a foreign land, without the guidance of religion! Going to encounter the perils of the ocean and the dangers of shipwreck, without the support of religion! Going to quit the home of your fathers, and sojourn in a strange land, without the companionship of religion! Going to encounter all the trials perplexities and difficulties of an emigrant's life, without the consolations of religion! How forlorn a condition! How desolate a lot! No acknowledgment of God; no trust in him, no prayer to him, no communion with him, no expectation from him! No preparation of mind to see his immensity shadowed forth in the boundless expanse of the ocean; to hear his awful power grandeur and majesty proclaimed in the tempest, the thunderstorm, and the water-spout; to trace his wisdom and goodness in the varied products of new countries; to contemplate his glory and realise his presence everywhere! Unhappy man! You are indeed to be pitied. The world is all before you, but Providence is not invoked to be your guide, and direct you where to choose. Oh, pause and ponder upon your condition, and the ways of your feet. Will you, dare you, can you, go out without God? Without God to guide and protect and bless you? And if without God as a friend, with him as an enemy. Do you forget it is God's world you live in, and God's country to which you are going? And

how can you think of going to it without asking his
leave, imploring his guidance, and seeking his blessing?
Recollect you are dependent every moment upon him,
and all your future destiny is to be decided by him.
He can raise you to prosperity or depress you to the
lowest adversity. He can frustrate or promote all your
schemes; disappoint or realize all your hopes. Before
you quit your native shore then, yield yourselves unto
God, " Remember your Creator, now, in the days of your
youth, before the evil days come." You are busy in preparing for the voyage, and are engaged in the cares of
the outfit. Religion, true, vital, experimental, decided
religion, is the best preparation, the most important
outfit. Determine, by God's grace, not to leave your
country an enemy to him, lest he send the whirlwind as
his messenger to arrest you on the sea, or ruin to overtake
you on the dry land. Go forth rather as his servant,
his friend, and his son, that to you may be applied the
beautiful language of the poet :

> " His are the mountains : and the valleys his :
> His the resplendent rivers : his to call
> With a propriety that none can claim,
> But he who lifts an unpresumptuous eye,
> And smiling says, ' My Father made them all.' "

Let the voice of friendship prevail, and the anxiety of
ministerial fidelity be successful, in persuading you
immediately to be reconciled to God through faith
which is in Christ Jesus. Present, in sincerity and
earnestness, the prayer of Moses, " If thy presence go
not with me, carry me not up hence." You shall not
ask in vain, for the answer will come, " My presence
shall go with thee, and I will give thee rest." You will
leave all other friends behind you, but your best Friend

will go with you, and he will be more to you than father, mother, brother, and sisters. Should you determine to act upon this advice, then all which will now be addressed to the next class of exiles will also appertain to you.

Many emigrants are already true Christians, and will go out as such. To this class I now address myself, with affectionate solicitude for your welfare in both worlds. First of all, I would make a few remarks in the way of consolation. In your present circumstances you need it, and you may have it. I trust you have the peace which arises from the testimony of your conscience, that in leaving your country you are following the leadings of Providence, and that you see the cloudy pillar moving before you: that it is a lawful object you are pursuing and one on which you may confidently ask God's blessing. This settled, you have in that one thought, "I am where God led me," a world of consolation. In the wreck of either your vessel or your fortunes, you may then be calm and satisfied, for no remorse will increase your terrors or aggravate your sorrows. Next you may, and should, reflect with comfort upon the omnipresence of God. This is one of the main props of all religion, whether in the way of holy fear or sacred pleasure; whether with angels in heaven or with man upon earth. It was the saying of a Jewish Rabbi, "If every man would consider God to be the great eye of the world, watching perpetually over all our actions, and that his hand is indefatigable, and his ear ever open, possibly sin might be extirpated from the face of the earth." This is going too far, but it is impressive. Yes, God is everywhere present, though invisible to us. Were the emigrant to leave his God, when he left his country, what crowds of sinners would flee from the presence of the Lord, and escape from the vigilance of his watchful eye, but what Christian would go? Pious youth, God goes with you, wherever you go, he is there before you in all the glory of his attributes, in all the tenderness of his love, in all the faithfulness of his promises, and in all the watchfulness of his providence. Be this your comfort, you cannot flee from his presence. And as God goes with you, so does your gracious Redeemer, in all his offices, characters, and endearments. So does the Holy Spirit with all his influences, so does your Bible, so does the throne of grace, so does the fellowship of saints, at least to most places. You thus carry your best friends, your richest treasures, your dearest comforts, your safest protection with you. Without these no sun would be bright: no scenery beautiful; no air balmy; no society agreeable; and no success joyful; but with these, consolation may be found on the most desolate shores, and in the most dreary scenes of nature or of Providence. All places are equally near to heaven, and all equally accessible to the falling rays which even now descend from its glory. On board the ship, amidst a wicked crew and noisy passengers, he can be with you; and equally so in the rough population of some colonial town, or in the dreary wild of some colonial desert. In the deepest solitude you may use the language which the poet has put into the lips of Alexander Selkirk, when dwelling alone on the island of Juan Fernandez:

> "There's mercy in every place,
>   And mercy, (encouraging thought!)
> Gives even affliction a grace,
>   And reconciles man to his lot."

You remember perhaps the anecdote of Mungo Park, the African traveller, which I have given in my work entitled, " The Young Man from Home." He was in the heart of Africa, alone and unprotected. He had just been robbed and stripped by ferocious banditti, and the following is the account he gives of his feelings and his relief : " After they were gone, I sat for some time, looking around me with amazement and terror. Whichever way I turned, nothing appeared but danger and difficulty. I saw myself in the midst of a vast wilderness, in the depth of the rainy season, naked and alone, surrounded by savage animals, and men still more savage. I was five hundred miles from the nearest European settlement. All these circumstances crowded at once on my recollection, and I confess that my spirit began to fail me. I considered my fate as certain, and that I had no alternative but to lie down and perish. The influence of religion, however, aided and supported me. I reflected that no human prudence or foresight could possibly have averted my present sufferings. I was indeed a stranger in a strange land, yet I was still under the protecting eye of that Providence who has condescended to call himself the stranger's friend. At this moment, painful as my reflections were, the extraordinary beauty of a small moss, in fructification, irresistibly caught my eye. I mention this to show from what trifling circumstances the mind will sometimes derive consolation ; for, though the whole plant was not larger than the top of one of my fingers, I could not contemplate the delicate conformation of its roots, leaves, and capsule, without admiration. Can that Being, thought I, who planted, watered, and brought to perfection, in this obscure part of the world, a thing which appears of so small importance, look with un-concern upon the situation and suffering of creatures formed after his own image? surely not! Reflections like these would not allow me to despair. I started up, and disregarding both hunger and fatigue, travelled forwards, assured that relief was at hand : and I was not disappointed. In a short time, I came to a small village, at the entrance of which I overtook the two shepherds who had come with me from Koama. They were much surprised to see me; for they said they never doubted that the Foulahs, when they had robbed, had murdered me."

But let me now offer you some counsels. Taken away from the means of grace, to which you have been accustomed, you will be in danger of resembling a child weaned at too early an age, which droops and sickens for want of its mother's milk. On your voyage you will find nothing around you to sustain your faith and godliness, but everything adverse to them. For months your Sabbath exercises will perhaps be nothing more than listening to a few prayers, or a sermon formally, coldly, and carelessly read. You will perhaps meet with no one who can talk with you the language of Canaan, and fan by his conversation and prayers the languid flame of your devotion. You will therefore be in im-minent peril of losing much of your religion on the voyage. To guard against this, it is well you should take a calm and intelligent view of your situation. In this case, as well as in others, to be fore-warned is to be fore-armed. Be much in prayer, in earnest, wrestling, and believing prayer, before you step on board. In-tensely long to be kept, and then you will be kept. God can and will make his grace sufficient for you. He can preserve you, and will, if you desire it, though there is not another Christian in the ship. He will be the lifter up of your head, will sustain you by his power through faith, and will put his glory upon you.

Do not be ashamed of your religion. Much of future annoyance and embarrassment will be prevented by a bold and honest, yet meek and humble, avowal of your principles. The first check given in a new phase or aspect of life is that which is most to be dreaded. Decision, maintained with firmness but gentleness, will soon subdue opposition. Your persecutors, if such you should have, will not be slow to find out that their ridicule is expended to no purpose on one who is not affected by it, and who always returns good for evil. But for this moral and spiritual courage, you must be much in prayer. "Of the ichneumon it is stated, that when wounded by the serpent with which it is in conflict, or previously to renewing the conflict, it retires by instinct to a particular herb, for expelling whatever venom it has received, and to be invigorated with fresh strength for obtaining the victory. Sanctify the thought by your frequent retirement to God for aid in the war-strife in which you may be engaged with sin in its various forms around you, and its most subtle insinuations in your own breast."* Fear not, then, to be seen with your Bible and other good books. Let your piety be neither ostentatiously obtruded, nor timidly concealed. At first it would be well to say little about it to others, till you have gained their confidence and affection. Let there be no bustling and officious zeal, no attempt to take the ship's company by storm, nothing like parading your religion and proclaiming your in-

* "The Christian Emigrant," by Dr. Leifchild.

tention to convert all on board. This will defeat your purpose by raising up resistance. Your light must shine before your fellow-passengers, by your good works, and your religion must be seen in all its loveliness and consistency before it is heard. Be known as the humble, meek, and gentle follower of the Lamb, the friend of every one, the enemy of none .If you can find men of like mind on board, cultivate their acquaintance, and live in sweet fellowship with them. If they have their peculiarities, as probably they will have, bear with them in love. Let there be the best understanding between you and them; for the quarrels, or even the coolness, of professing Christians, will do immense harm.

Take especial care that your conduct be uniformly consistent. When it is known, and known it ought to be, that you are a religious man, you will be watched by the malignant eyes of those who wait for your halting, and whose ingenuity will be taxed to lay snares for your feet. One wrong step will destroy all your influence, by defacing the beauty and impairing the strength of your example, and will subject not only yourself, but all religion, to the suspicion of hypocrisy. You may hope by acting in a blameless and harmless manner, to be the means of doing good to some of your fellow-emigrants. You may discover some pensive and sorrow-stricken heart, prepared, by deep sorrow, to receive the consolations of the gospel. Or you may find some prodigal already beginning to ponder with remorse on his wanderings, in whose relenting heart you may fasten conviction, penitence and faith. You may be honoured of God thus to "convert a sinner from the error of his ways, to save a soul from death, and hide a multitude of sins." Should you escape the moral dangers of the voyage, and land upon a distant shore unharmed in soul, you must not consider that all, or even the greatest, perils are over. There still remain all the trials to which you will be exposed in the struggle to be carried on for establishing yourself in the colony. Many have escaped the shipwreck of the sea, only to incur the more fearful one, not only of their fortune, but of their character. Professors who have stood well at home, have miserably failed abroad. In the eager strife which you will perhaps carry on for success in your new locality, where so many are striving with you and like you, there is a fear lest the ardour of religious affection should be quenched in a flood of earthly-mindedness; and lest the purity of religious principle should be debased by the love and the prospect of Mammon's pelf, especially in the gold regions. It has been said, with what truth I will not take upon me to determine, that very lax principles of morality govern the trade of some of our colonies ; and that many professing Christians are carried away by the stream of commercial dishonesty. Doubtless many have therefore damaged their characters, however they may have improved their circumstances. " The transplanted tree may exhibit as flourishing a foliage in the new soil where it is fixed ; but if its fruit become dwarfed, insipid, and tasteless, the change is one that will ever have to be deplored. Let your piety, on the contrary, take a deeper root, and strike out wider its fruit-bearing branches in the locality where you may be destined to spend the remainder of your days."

A Christian ought to be anxious to promote the moral and spiritual well-being of the colony to which he emigrates. The best way to preserve his own religion is to keep it in action. Still water, as I have previously remarked, breeds filth and vermin, but the running stream is clear and pure. Neither our soul's health, nor our body's, can be preserved without exercise. But there is another reason, my young friends, which I press upon your attention, why you should be active in diffusing religion where you go, and that is, the future destiny of the colonies. What is a colony? Now, indeed, the collection from various parts of the earth of comparatively few adventurers settling down upon the coast with a view to retrieve their fortunes or their characters, or to start in life with advantages there which they could not command at home; but what will it be a century or two hence? It is an infant state, a nation in boyhood, which, when, full grown, may be a rival of the land that gave it existence. A little more than two centuries ago, a few outcasts and fugitives from this country, flying from the demon of persecution, landed from the "Mayflower," on a bare and barren rock on the northern coast of America. The country all around was bleak, desolate, and wild, and inhabited only by tribes of Indians and herds of buffaloes. There was a colony. What is it now? The greatest, the strongest, the most flourishing republic ever founded upon earth; a republic which is already the rival in trade of the fatherland, and which has more than once been engaged with it successfully in war. It is thought by some that England has passed the zenith of its glory, and that the British empire is destined to decay and fall; that its population will remain stationary or recede; its courage abate, its wealth diminish, and its ascendancy disappear; till at length the Queen of the Waves will sink into an eternal, though not forgotten, slumber. And the question has been asked, whether at some

future period in our world's history, and amidst the
changes which take place in its affairs, some traveller
from New Zealand or Australia may not sit down upon
a broken arch of London Bridge, to depict the ruins
of St. Paul's Cathedral; or place himself where he shall
delineate "the towers of York Minster, rising in dark
magnificence amid an aged forest; or go and trace the
red deer sporting in savage independence round the
Athenian pillars of the Scottish metropolis." All this
is not very probable; but if it should be in the decrees
of heaven and the destinies of earth, let it be your care
who go as christian emigrants to these future nations
which are to be exalted in majesty over the ruins of their
parent country, that they shall be so educated in their infancy as to rise up christian states in their manhood. Go
out with the holy and noble ambition of carrying on the
work of evangelisation, civilisation, and refinement. Be
the patriots of your new country; and have your names
enrolled among those to whom its future generations
shall look back with gratitude and respect. Carry out
the principles of civil and religious liberty, and never
forget that as you are joining with others in laying the
foundations of civil polity, it should be done with care
and skill, and so that they shall bear a superstructure
in which God shall dwell with man upon the earth. A
high and holy object of ambition is thus presented to
you. Seize in all its grandeur and extent the conception that you are assisting in constructing the basis
of future nations, and let not even the modesty and
humility which are the natural result, and should be
the accompaniments, of your comparatively humble
circumstances in life, dispossess you of it. Even the day
labourers who worked at the foundations of the Pyramids

had a share in raising a fabric which has been the admiration of all ages, and will probably last till the end of time. So the humblest emigrant that lands on the shore of Australia, if he be a man of piety, virtue, and active benevolence, is doing something towards the wealth, the power, and the moral glory of the future state that may rise in that now comparatively unpeopled wilderness.

In connexion with all this, and indeed for its realization, it is necessary you should attend to some other things. I refer you to the last chapter for what you will need as a man of business, and what is essential to your success. The knowledge, industry, economy, system, and perseverance, there recommended, necessary for all, are pre-eminently so for you. Without your determining to act thus, there is not the remotest hope of your success. If you expect to do without these endowments in a foreign land, you are mistaken. Give up at once all notion that less qualification for success is necessary in the colonies than at home. The earth does not bring forth her fruits spontaneously there even in a virgin soil, any more than here. The ground is cursed for man's sake all over the globe; and to earn your bread by the sweat of your brow is the condition of your existence in Australia and New Zealand, as well as in England.

You must make up your mind to hardships unknown at home. He that expects to carry to a new settlement, at least in some parts of the world, all the luxuries, or even comforts which he may command here, and who is not prepared to endure much self-denial, had better remain where he is. It is true, in the towns already formed in some of the colonies most of the usual comforts of life may be commanded, as well as in this country; but an emigrant cannot always choose his abode, and may be called to go beyond the circle of population where he will have to construct his own dwelling, to make great part of his own furniture, to cook his own food; and you should consider well whether this will suit you, or you it. A spirit of adventure, where it exists, a buoyancy of spirits, a love of enterprise, and a hope of success, will carry a man through all these difficulties, but have you these qualifications?

Guard against a reckless spirit of speculation. Do not make haste to be rich. This is one of the dangers of colonial life, dangerous alike to moral principle and to commercial prosperity. There is great room for it abroad, and many temptations to it. It has made a few, but it has ruined many. Some have endeavoured to leap the chasm or ford the river, without patiently going round by the bridge, and have succeeded; while others in making the same attempt have been dashed to pieces or drowned. Speculation is a game at hazard. Do not play it. One throw of the die may win a fortune, but the next may lose it. Be contented to plod on slowly, but certainly. What is gained by patient industry usually wears better and lasts longer than that which is won in a lottery.

Especially watch against a want of commercial principle. In the fierce conflict for success in a young settlement, this is one of the dangers to which all who enter into it are exposed. Go out determined to follow the "whatsoever things are true, honest, just, pure, lovely, and of good report." Make up your mind to the truth of God's Holy Word, that " Better is the little that a righteous man hath, than the riches of many wicked." Failure is to be infinitely preferred, when it comes with a good conscience, than success procured by iniquity. As a general principle it will be found true that " honesty is the best policy."

Keep up a correspondence with your native country, especially if you have left friends in it who take an interest in your welfare. There is something immoral and unchristian in a disposition to forget the home and the friends of your childhood, and something positively cruel, in keeping your parents, or your brothers and sisters, ignorant of your circumstances. This is sometimes not sufficiently thought of by those who leave their country. But the soil in which early and home affections all wither and die, cannot be favourable to the growth of piety or virtue; it is cold and stony.

Be very cautious about choosing your companions. Characters of all varieties, and many of them of the worst kinds, are to be found in the colonies. How many are obliged to emigrate, and find in those distant retreats a shelter from the finger of scorn, the tongue of reproach, and, in some cases, from the visitations of justice; men who go out unreclaimed, and who carry all their bad principles and evil dispositions with them. Many of them are clever, specious, and plausible; but they carry the serpent's cunning and venom under the variegated colours of his skin. Never give your company, your ear, your hand, or your confidence, to any one, till you have proved that he is worthy of them. A stranger in a strange land, you will feel your loneliness, and in your craving after social intercourse, will be in danger of falling into the snares of those who lie in wait to deceive. One of the members of my church,

who carried out with him a considerable sum of money,
gave his confidence, and with it a considerable portion
of his property, to one who professed for him great
friendship; and but for most determined proceedings
would have lost it. Men prowling about society to prey
upon the unwary, are to be found everywhere, and they
are not wanting in the colonies.

And now let me direct your attention to what the
apostle has said of the holy patriarchs of Canaan,
" These all died in faith, not having received the promises, but having seen them afar off, and were persuaded
of them and embraced them, and confessed that they
were strangers and pilgrims on the earth. For they
that say such things declare plainly that they seek a
country. And truly, if they had been mindful of that
country from whence they came out, they might have
had opportunity to have returned. But now they desire
a better country, that is, an heavenly : wherefore God
is not ashamed to be called their God : for he hath prepared for them a city." Be this the view you take
of your earthly sojourn, as a pilgrimage to the skies;
and this the spirit you cherish in reference to it. Your
circumstances forcibly remind you of it. By faith in
God's blessed Word, look up to that better country
which is above and beyond the boundaries of earth and
time : the land of the holy, the good, and the blessed;
where there is no more sea, and where there shall be no
more death, or sorrow, or crying; neither shall there be
any more pain, for the former things shall have passed
away; where the fears, the anxieties, and the labours
of this world have no place, and the turmoil of life, and
the strifes of business are unknown; where the wicked
cease from troubling and the weary are at rest; where

temptation will be over, and conflict will cease. Blessed country! Be it your chief solicitude to emigrate to that joyful and glorious land. From this world you must depart. No choice is left you. The hour of departure draws on; but whether it will be in youth, in manhood, or in old age, is known only to God. Shall there be no preparation for that voyage and settlement? How much your thoughts are now occupied about the new country to which you are going, and how anxiously busy you are in preparing for the voyage and your future residence; and shall less thoughtfulness, less preparation, less anxiety be given to the emigration to eternity? You have exercised much thought in choosing the colony where you mean to settle for life. There are but two places of settlement beyond the grave, heaven and hell; between these lies your choice; to one or other you must soon depart; which will you choose? Which?

CHAPTER X.

And Lamech lived an hundred eighty and two years, and begat a son: and he called his name Noah, saying, This same shall comfort us concerning our work and toil of our hands. GENESIS v, 28, 29.

And the king was much moved, and went up to the chamber over the gate and wept: and as he went, thus he said, O my son Absalom, my son, my son Absalom! would God I had died for thee, O Absalom, my son, my son! 2 SAMUEL xviii, 33.

WHEN Lamech, one of the few antediluvians mentioned in the fifth chapter of Genesis, selected a name for his son, he determined to call him Noah, which signifies "rest;" for he said, "This same shall comfort us concerning our labour." The history of this Lamech is involved in impenetrable obscurity, which no conjecture can remove. But you are not to confound him with the Lamech mentioned in the preceding chapter, who was a descendant of Cain. It is probable that in naming his son, Lamech the father of Noah was guided by a reference to some circumstances of disquiet and discomfort connected with his own life, of which no mention is made in the Scriptures. Whether the selection of the name was the result of prophetic inspiration, or merely of parental solicitude and hope, we cannot tell. The event, however, justified the selection, and the life of Noah answered to his name. With his early history the Author of revelation has left us almost entirely unacquainted. All that is said of him before he is introduced to us as the patriarch of the new world's inhabitants, is, that "Noah walked with God, and was perfect in his generation." In the midst of a corrupt age he dared to be singular, and was not ashamed or afraid to avow his piety amidst the scoffs of the impious. For five centuries his parents lived to witness his holy conduct and his high calling, as the preacher of righteousness, and the preserver of the human race from utter destruction. What a lengthened period of parental enjoyment !*

A melancholy contrast is presented to all this, in the history of Absalom. His name signifies, "the father of peace." Alas, alas, what a contradiction was there between his history and his name. He was evidently his father's favourite son. We discern and condemn the

* We are not permitted to know all God's reasons for the extreme longevity of the Patriarchs of the antediluvian world. But we can see that it tended, by oral tradition, to preserve, uncorrupted, the original revelation made to our first parents in Paradise. At that time, most probably, alphabetic writing was unknown ; and it was important that the transmission of the account of creation ; of the origin of the human race; of the primeval prophecy concerning the seed of the woman; and of the divine institution of sacrifices, should pass through as few hands as possible. It is not absolutely certain that this extreme longevity was granted to any but the persons mentioned in the book of Genesis ; if it was, there may have been reasons for this extraordinary length of human life before the flood, with which we are not acquainted. This is one of the many things of revelation, which we must take upon its own well-accredited testimony, without making our experience or observation a standard by which to try them, or a reason for rejecting them.

weakness of David, whose partiality was, in all probability, called forth by the extraordinary beauty of
Absalom, an unworthy motive. He gave him a name
expressive of his fondest wishes and affections. He
watched with more than ordinary interest and regard,
the development of his beautiful form, the increasing
attractions of his winning and fascinating manners, the
nobleness of his bearing, and the displays of his genius.
Even Solomon was, at that time, little thought of compared with Absalom. In this favourite David's hopes
at one time centred more than in all his other children.
But this bright blossom of parental fondness and expectation, soon exhibited signs of blight, and the sequel
became another instance and proof of the effects of a
father's injudicious and misdirected partiality. With
Absalom's personal beauty, was associated a most vicious
character, which wrung his father's heart with anguish.
He manifested one enormity after another, till his misconduct rose to a climax, by rebellion and parricide in
intention, and brought him to an untimely end. What
a bitter and cruel disappointment of parental hopes was
there! The darling, the beautiful Absalom, proved a
libertine, a murderer, a rebel: a character which, notwithstanding all his father's lingering affection and fond
precautions, brought the unhappy son to his grave in
infamy and blood. Instead of his remains reposing in
the splendid mausoleum which his vanity had constructed, and by which he ambitiously hoped to perpetuate his fame to future generations, they were buried
under a heap of stones, with no funeral obsequies to do
honour to his rank, and no inscription to perpetuate his
name. But how much does it take to wear out a
father's love, and to quench his fondness for a favourite

child! No sooner were the tidings announced that Absalom was dead, than all his crimes were forgotten, and the poor afflicted father rushed into his chamber, and uttered one of the most simple and pathetic lamentations which grief ever dictated, or language ever expressed, in those moving words, "O my son Absalom, my son, my son Absalom! would God I had died for thee! O Absalom, my son, my son!" With these two cases, as an historical introduction, I enter upon the consideration of my subject: "The disappointment or fulfilment of parental hopes."

I shall reverse the order of the texts, and dwell first upon the conduct of him who defeats the expectations which have been indulged by those who were the authors of his being. Parental hopes are usually strong. The words of our Lord are according to nature, "A woman when she is in travail hath sorrow, because her hour is come: but as soon as she is delivered of the child, she remembereth no more her anguish, for joy that a man is born into the world." Who but a mother can tell the feelings of that moment when her new-born babe is first laid in her bosom; and who but a father can know the emotions which are excited when he sees, for the first time, his own image reflected from the countenance of that little unconscious creature, whose infant cry, as he takes him in his arms, seems to say, in inarticulate language, "My Father!" From that moment parental hopes begin. The child brings them with him into the world. How fondly the parents watch their treasure as he is dandled in a mother's lap, or sleeps in the cradle. How often they muse together over his future destinies, saying to each other, "What manner of child shall this be?" As the babe grows to

a child, the child to a youth, the youth to manhood,
what expectations are raised, what conjectures are
formed, what prognostications are uttered! The mother
hopes her son will be her comfort, and the father his
help, and both make him their boast. As his faculties
develope, they see, or think they see, and the fond
illusion can be forgiven them, the marks of ability and
the traits of excellence. Freaks of childish passion,
instances of waywardness of temper, and not unfrequent
acts of disobedience, which to others hold out painful
portents, are either unnoticed, or do not disturb the
pleasing vision, or lower the expectations of future excellence, if not of eminence. Hope is predominant in
the father's heart; all children, he says, have their follies
and faults, and his not more than others. He sends his
son to school, where he trusts he will improve his mind,
and prepare for future life: apprentices him to some
trade or profession by which he expects he will do well
in the world: he starts him in business, and thus en-
ables him to provide for himself and a family. How
many hours of his private conversation have been spent
with his wife over this son of theirs! What pictures
have been drawn of his future career! Surely such
talents, so cultivated, and with such advantages, must
succeed. Under the burdens of life, and the cares and
labours which their family bring upon them, they look
forward, during the infancy of their children, to future
years, anticipating the pleasures to arise from the obedience, gratitude, and usefulness of those who they think
will be the prop of their old age, and the supporters
of each other, when they are gone to their rest. Pleasing reflections! Joyful anticipations! But in many
cases, vain illusions! How wisely is it ordered that

man should not be able to lift up the veil of futurity and foresee the history of himself and of his children. It is enough to know the ills of life as they arise, without contemplating them in the distance. What a misery to have all these hopes end in bitter disappointment, like beautiful blossoms cut off by a nipping frost! I speak not now of that disappointment which is occasioned by the dispensations of Providence, in the early death of children. This often comes, but how many, under a bitterer disappointment still, have lived to wish their children had died in infancy. And amidst the sins and follies of the after years of their children's lives, have mourned with grief of heart, and exclaimed, "Oh, that my son had died from the womb, and that the cradle had become his coffin, rather than that he should have lived to distress and dishonour me as he has done."

But what is it that will disappoint parental hopes? Undutifulness, and want of affection, will do this. Parents have a right granted by nature, confirmed by reason, and enjoined by Scripture, to the obedience, honour, gratitude, and love of their children. They look for their due, and expect from their offspring everything that can thus conduce to their comfort. And to receive rudeness instead of respect; disobedience instead of submission; contempt instead of esteem; and cold indifference, or manifest dislike, or cruel unkindness, instead of affection and gratitude! How cutting is this! Well did Solomon say, "A foolish son is a grief to his father, and a bitterness to her that bore him." "Oh, how often," do they say together, "has our authority been affronted, and our love slighted for a mere trifle. We expected better things, and naturally supposed that so much love as we have lavished upon him would have brought us back some love in return. Is this the reward of all our study and efforts to make him happy and do him good?" Oh, who can tell, " How sharper than a serpent's tooth it is, to have a thankless child." I believe that deep filial reverence is often the basis of that higher principle, the fear of God; and that, on the contrary, a manifest want of good disposition and good conduct towards parents, must ever be attended with irreligion, and vicious dispositions and habits.

Indolence, want of application, and carelessness about general improvement, must, of course, produce the disappointment I now speak of. After a good school has been selected for a youth, and afterwards a suitable situation for acquiring a knowledge of business; when improvement in general knowledge, and especially the acquisition of a trade, is naturally looked for, then to see nothing but indolence, ignorance, and stupidity; money, time, exhortation all wasted; the youth going forth into the world ill-informed, unskilled in matters of trade, unfit for any situation of importance as a servant, and equally unfit to manage a business as a master! How mortifying, how disappointing, is all this to a father! How distressing for him to find all his schemes thwarted; all his anticipations frustrated; and while other young men are making their way in life, to see his son neither able nor willing to do any thing for himself! He may not be vicious, but he is idle, a habit which is next to actual crime, and generally leads to it.

Versatility of disposition also, wherever it exists, defeats the hopes of parents who judge wisely. It is good counsel which Solomon gives, where he says,

" Meddle not with them that are given to change."
To change, when it is from bad to good is always right;
and it is a part of wisdom to know when and how to
change for the better. This is a different thing from
being "given to change." I repeat what I said in the
last chapter, that there is nothing against which a young
man ought more assiduously to guard than versatility
of disposition. There is as much truth as beauty in the
proverb, " A rolling stone gathers no moss." Reuben's
character should be a beacon to all young men, " Unstable as water, thou shalt not excel." The man who
tries many things, without keeping to any thing, is
absolutely certain to do nothing. A tree may sometimes be better for one removal, but it can never flourish
under a frequent transplanting. How annoying is it to
a father to find that he has scarcely introduced a son
into a good situation ere the youth grows tired of it and
leaves it, and comes back again a dead weight upon his
father's hands, till, tired out with his perpetual changes,
the good man is compelled to throw him upon his own
resources, in which case he generally comes to ruin.*

* A very lamentable instance of the disappointment of parental
hopes, occasioned by an unsettled and roving disposition, happened
in the family of that distinguished theologian, the late Rev. Andrew
Fuller. His eldest boy was a youth of this character. His father
obtained for him a good situation in London. He at one time thought
of the ministry, and was then, of course, a moral, and, apparently, a
religious, young man. His father, however, soon recorded this
remark in his diary: "Alas, alas, I have seen that in the conduct
of my poor boy which has almost broken my heart, whose instability
is continually appearing. He must leave London, and what to do
with him I know not." Another situation was procured in his native
town, but his restless disposition soon discovered itself, and he
enlisted into the army. In a little time, being understood to be an
apprentice, he was discharged. Another situation was found for him,

Failure in business, however it occurs, must of necessity prove a very painful disappointment to parental hopes. When a father has started his son in business, and advanced capital for the purpose, and expected to see him prosper, it must be a source of very great

but in vain: for he enlisted a second time; into the marines. His father, in compliance with his wishes, procured his liberation; and in about a month he left his new place and friends. Perceiving there was no hope of his settling to business, his sorrowing parent procured him a situation in a merchant ship: but being on shore one Lord's day, before he joined the ship, he was laid hold of by a press-gang, and carried to sea. It was soon reported that the poor boy had been guilty of some offence; had been tried, and sentenced to receive three hundred lashes; that he received them, and immediately expired. Under this trial, Mr. F. thus wrote to a friend, "Oh! this is heart's trouble! In former cases, my heart found vent in tears; but now I can seldom weep. A kind of morbid heart-sickness preys upon me from day to day. Every object around me reminds me of him! Ah, he was wicked, and mine eye was not over him to prevent it; he was detected, tried, and condemned, and I knew it not; he cried under his agonies, but I heard him not; he expired without an eye to pity or a hand to help him. Oh, Absalom, my son, my son! would I had died for thee, my son!" The report however was incorrect, yet some time afterwards he deserted, and suffered so severe a punishment as to be totally unfitted for service, by the effect it had upon his health. He was again discharged. He in some measure recovered his health, and a situation was about to be provided for him; but he again absconded, entered a second time into the marines, went to sea, and his friends never again saw him. He died off Lisbon after a lingering illness, and, there is some reason to hope, confessing and lamenting the error of his ways. "This narrative," remarks Mr. Fuller's biographer, "contains many things painful to surviving friends, which they would gladly have buried in oblivion, and which I would never have inserted had they absolutely forbidden me. But the strong room there seems to be to hope that so affecting an account may be, under the Divine blessing, the means of reclaiming some unhappy youth under similar circumstances, or of deterring others from rending a parent's heart with anguish, and involving themselves in misery, has induced them to yield to my wish for its not being suppressed."

distress to find that all his efforts to serve him are abortive. Where this is the effect of causes over which even industry and ability could have no control; which involve no blame; and which therefore must be resolved into a dispensation of Providence, there is not the aggravation of sorrow which is produced by incapacity indolence or extravagance. In such a case a judicious and kind father will comfort his unfortunate son, and cheer him onward, by sympathy and promise of assistance, to make other efforts, though it is of course a trial, and a heavy one. But where misconduct has led to the sad result, how bitter is the cup of parental sorrow! For a father to occupy the dreadful post of observation, darker every hour, as he watches the downward progress of a son negligent of his business, and giving himself up to habits which must end in his ruin! Oh, miserable son, and miserable parent! He who should, and might, have been a flourishing tradesman, becomes a bankrupt, and instead of rising to respectability, sinks to indigence and contempt. How many fond anticipations are terminated, how many bright visions are dispelled, how many joyous expectations are prostrated by that wreck! And as the hopes of past times are defeated, none can be indulged for the future. Had it been the result of misfortune, the son might have recovered himself; but as the ruin came by misconduct, what ground of hope is left to the disconsolate father?

Profligate conduct is the bitterest disappointment of all. To see a young man who has been religiously educated, and brought up in the fear of God, so far forgetting the instructions, prayers and examples of his father, and the tears and affectionate entreaties of his mother, as to "walk in the counsel of the ungodly, to

stand in the way of sinners, and sit in the seat of the
scornful:" to see him forming bad associations, neglecting business, indulging his evil propensities, wandering
off, like the prodigal, into the paths of vice and
profligacy, the slave of lust and wine, how distressfully
disappointing is all this! Unhappy parents! You who
have been called to endure this trial, and you only, can
tell what this means: and even you know it better than
you can tell it. "Oh," says the christian parent, "is it
then come to this, that all my solicitude, my prayers, my
tears for my son, end in his profligacy! That all my desires and expectations that he would become a child of
God, terminate in his being a prodigal! All my hopes
of his being a servant of Christ, disappointed in my
seeing him a slave of Satan! How carefully have I
watched him, how diligently have I instructed him, how
earnestly have I prayed for him, how anxiously have I
waited for his yielding himself up to God and coming
into the fellowship of his Church! And are all my
prayers and tears as water spilt upon the ground? In
all that I have done for his conversion and salvation I
have been labouring in vain, and spending my strength
for nought, yea, worse than in vain: for every instruction, correction, and reproof, has aggravated his guilt
here, and will increase his misery hereafter; so that
while, in intention I was acting the most kind and
tender part, I was, in the result, only treasuring up for
my son wrath against the day of wrath. Alas, alas!
Woe is me. 'O my son, my son!'"

How tenfold more dreadful are these reflections if the
son has died in his sins, a case by no means uncommon.
How painful are the father's tears that his child has
fallen into a state of everlasting ruin. "Oh," will the

afflicted parent say, " how comparatively light would be my sorrows, if, while looking on his breathless corpse, and mourning the disappointment of my hopes as to the present life, I could by faith look forward to the world of glory, and see the branch of my family, which is cut off from earth, transplanted thither and flourishing there. Joy would then mingle with my paternal sorrows, and praises with my tears. But alas! I have reason to fear that it was cut down that it might be cast into ever-lasting burnings. On the former supposition, I might have comforted myself with the thought of meeting my child again, and of meeting him on terms of infinite advantage, to be no more separated from him. But alas! now I have lost my child, and lost him for ever. Nor is this all. It would be mournful to me to think I should meet him no more; yet as the matter now stands, even that would be some alleviation to my distress; but the immutable decree of God forbids it. I must meet him at the bar of God, and oh! what a dreadful inter-view will it be. Must I be a witness against him? How terrible an office! To bear my testimony for the con-demnation of one whom I tenderly loved, of one whose soul I would have died to deliver. Oh, that if no shelter must·be allowed him, God would hide me in the grave till this tremendous scene of His indignation be over-past; lest the anguish of a parent mingle with the joys of a rising saint, and to me overcast the triumphs of the day."*

This disappointment may, however, take place where none of the former causes exist. There may be no pro-fligacy, no versatility, no indolence, no want of clever-

* Dr. Doddridge's " Sermons on the Reflections of a Pious Parent over an Ungodly Son."

ness in business, but the very opposites; still there may be, as we have seen in a former chapter, amiability without religion; the possession of all other good things, yet the want of the one best thing. To a really christian parent, the want of this in his children is a severe trial, a heavy affliction. This is the chief object of his desires, his prayers, his efforts, and his hopes. Till they are savingly converted to God by his grace, and are brought to live a life of faith in God and in Christ, he is, and must be, disappointed. He longed, above all things, for their salvation, and hoped to see them members of the church of Christ and useful in setting up his kingdom in the world: and in the absence of this, though they should gain wealth, rank, or fame, he is a disappointed father. He cannot but rejoice and be thankful that his sons are not profligates; but as long as they are not true Christians, his chief joy is not fulfilled. He looks upon their success, their respectability, their worldly comfort, with the inward reflection, " Ah, this is all very well, and I am truly thankful for it, but it reaches no further than the grave; and what I have coveted for them, prayed for, and sought, is, ' glory, honour, immortality, and eternal life.' I wanted them to be united with me by ties which would last for ever, and make us one in heaven as well as upon earth. Notwithstanding their worldly prosperity, then, I am, by their want of personal religion, a disappointed father."

This disappointment of parents in regard to their children may be aggravated by several circumstances. Where unusual care has been bestowed upon their education, and it might have been expected that a proportionate degree of excellence would have been the result: where considerable talents have been possessed, and early indications of genius have exhibited themselves so as to awaken expectations; where virtue at one time began to bud, and piety to blossom; where friends congratulated the parents, and the parents felicitated themselves, on the promising appearances of their children: where, in short, for a while all seemed to hold out the most auspicious omens, and to justify the most favourable conclusions: in such cases, to have all these hopeful beginnings terminate unhappily, and the anticipations raised upon them disappointed; how bitter, how painful, how overwhelmingly cruel! Think of a parent mourning over the wreck of such hopes, and bewailing such a failure.

Young men, let me plead with you on behalf of your parents. Are there not some of you who are thus disappointing every hope which they have formed concerning you? Does not the reflection grieve and shame you, and ought it not to overwhelm you? Let me appeal to your sense of obligation. Ungrateful youths! Have you no idea of what you owe to them? Are these the returns you make them for all their bounty, tenderness, and care, to be a sword in their vitals, and to pierce their very hearts? Did they expect such scenes as these when you hung upon your mother's breast, reposed in her lap, and grasped in childish fear her hand to protect you from danger: when you returned their smiles with your own, and cried with your faint accents of endearment, " My father, my mother?" How can you endure the thought? How without embarrassment can you converse with them, and still daily receive unnumbered favours at their hands, when you are behaving in a manner that looks as if the more

they love you, the more they must be afflicted and ter-
rified by you? Do, do have compassion upon them.
Or if that will not move you; do have compassion on
yourselves, for your own interest is much more nearly
concerned than even theirs. It is not yet too late, even
though till now you have pursued this course of disappointing them. There is time to repair the mischief.
Repentance and reformation will yet heal the wounds
which misconduct has inflicted, and the joy of receiving
back the prodigal will almost compensate for the sufferings occasioned by his wanderings and his errors. Say
then, and say it at once, " I will arise and go to my
father, and say, 'Father, I have sinned against heaven
and in thy sight; forgive and receive thy once sinning
and ungrateful but now penitent child.' " Such a confession, followed by fruits meet for repentance, will bind
up hearts all but irreparably broken, and will transfer
you to the class I am next to describe.

II. I speak of the young man fulfilling the hopes
of his parents. And it will take very much to do this.
Much to reward a mother's pangs in child-birth; her
months of anxious care by day, and often sleepless
vigilance at night; all which involuntarily prompted her
to say, " Surely I shall have a rich reward one day for
this." Much that will be accounted an adequate reward
for a father's incessant toil to provide for his family;
his deep concern to select the best school, and the most
suitable business, and all his wakeful and ceaseless
solicitude for the welfare of his sons. How often, when
bearing the heat and burden of the day, has he wiped
away "the sweat of his brow," and exclaimed, with the
smile of hope, " Well, my boy will one day reward me
for all this. I am now sowing in hope to reap one day

in joy!" And there are sons who realise all these expectations. How?

By their dutiful conduct. "There," said a father, "is a son who never gave his father's heart a pang." I knew the son while he lived, till full of years, and Christian virtues, and public esteem, he no long time since ascended to glory, and left behind him a name never to be repeated but with esteem. Other sons of the same family had wrung their father's heart with anguish; but he, by his uniform obedience, general good conduct, and amiable character, was nothing but a delight to his parents. How sweet is it to a parent's heart to see a child so considerate for his comfort as to be ever studious to avoid everything that would for a moment distress him, and to do anything that could yield him the smallest pleasure. A parent does expect, has a right to expect, all this; and how ineffably sweet is it to his heart to be able to say, "In all that is dutiful, obedient, reverential, respectful, and attentive, my son is all a son should be or can be. He has equalled all the ideas I had formed in my most sanguine moments of filial excellence. My hopes are more than realized."*

* A beautiful memoir of that most saintly man and eminent clergyman, the late Mr Bickersteth, has just appeared from the pen of his son-in-law, Mr Birks; and among the other virtues for which that holy servant of Christ was distinguished, filial reverence sustained a very high place. The early history of Mr Bickersteth exhibits one of the most lovely and striking exhibitions of this excellence which I have ever met with. One scarcely wonders at the eminence he attained to as a Christian and a minister, when we read of his conduct as a son. I am persuaded that much of the neglect of the fear of God for which so many of the young men of the present day are notorious, may be traced to a defect of filial reverence. [The Editor cannot help recording here that a very strong mutual attachment existed between Mr Bickersteth and the Author.]

High mental culture and attainments will do much
to realize parental hopes. The most affectionate and
amiable disposition, coupled with the most dutiful conduct, will not answer parental expectation if, at the
same time, there be a want of application to mental
improvement and general knowledge, and also a stolid
ignorance, or a deplorably low and grovelling taste. In
this extraordinary age every man is expected to fill up
his place with credit to himself and advantage to others.
Society never had stronger claims upon young men than
it has now. It is a high satisfaction to a parent blessed
with a promising son to be able to say, "There is one
who has repaid all the expense incurred by his education. While at school he received the most honourable
testimonials for diligence and acquisition. He scarcely
ever returned without a prize. He has assiduously improved himself since then, by reading and thinking, and
now that he is entering upon life, he is evidently quali-
fied to take a high standing for respectability and usefulness. He will not be one of the multitude who are
ciphers. I certainly feel some glow of heartfelt delight,
occasionally rising, unless well watched, into pride, as I
see how he is acquitting himself already, and is noticed
by others; and can predict the eminence to which he
will rise, and the esteem with which he will be regarded."

Next come industry, diligence and aptitude for business. For nothing without these will be sufficient to
satisfy parental desire. A son may be dutiful and
intelligent, but if he has not devotedness to business,
habits of industry, he must occasion disappointment to
his parents. Happy is the father who sees in his
son a constantly expanding germ of the diligent and

thriving tradesman. With what pleasure does he mark the indefatigable application, the growing skill, the sharpening sagacity, the increasing tact, of his boy, in reference to business. "Ah," says he with gratitude, "I see he will make a good tradesman. He will make his way, and if I am not mistaken, will rise in life. He will be something." The youth rises into the man, and having learned his business or profession, commences it, and displays, as a master, the qualities he learned and exhibited as an apprentice and a shopman. Success crowns his efforts. His business prospers. His father follows him through his successful career with secret delight. He is never afraid to visit his son lest he should find him playing truant from his shop, neglecting his business, with all things in confusion, and ruin looking in at the window. It is always a pleasure to him to go and see the beautiful order, the established system, the well-formed habits, the crowded scene, of a well-conducted business. How gratifying to hear from himself the report of his continued success, of his trade extending, his capital accumulating, and his property gradually increasing! The father's solicitude is over; his son is thoroughly established, and has attained a degree of prosperity which at one time could not have been looked for. How peaceful and pleasant are the reflections of the parents of such a son in their private intercourse: "We are happy in being released from the pressing and painful anxieties of some families. Our dear son is obviously doing well. We never had much fear of his success; his steadiness and ability forbade this; but what little anxiety we felt is all gone. Prosperity has begun to dawn upon him, and promises to shine more and more. We have but one anxiety now, and that is, that he may settle well in marriage." This anxiety is natural and wise. It is God's arrangement and intention that man should marry, for he sees that it is not good for him to be alone. It was not good in Paradise, it is not good now. It is not good for his morals, his comfort, or his prosperity: and all judicious parents have a wise solicitude that their children should in proper time marry, and always marry suitably. Indiscreet and unsuitable marriages by children, are a source of unutterable grief to parents. Hence the joy which is felt when others of an opposite nature are contracted. That anxiety, in the case I am supposing, is soon relieved. The prudence and propriety that have characterised the conduct of this good son in other things, do not forsake him in this. He is cautious and wise: selects a woman who, by her sterling excellence, good sense, and amiable qualities, is worthy of him. She is one of whom the wise man saith, " She looketh well to the ways of her household, the heart of her husband doth safely trust in her, so that he shall have no need of spoil." The parents see with delight a prosperous business, a rising family, a happy home.

But still we have not reached the summit of a good man's wishes; for though all this is very pleasant, and to a worldly man would be quite sufficient to realise his uttermost expectation, and fulfill his richest hopes, yet it is not so with the Christian. He has learned that, for himself, religion is the " one thing needful," without which he neither attains to true happiness on earth, nor answers the great end of existence, nor is meetened for the felicity of heaven; and what he is supremely anxious for on his own account, he desires above all things for his children. It would be unnatural and cruel if he did not. If religion be all-important to him, it can be no less so to them. Hence, whatever else they may gain, if they neglect this, he is, as I have already said, and I now repeat it, by way of emphasis, still sad at heart.

But I am now supposing a case in which the Christian parent sees his deepest anxieties relieved, and his fondest hopes realized, in the religious character of his sons. Aware that they are exposed to greater temptations than his daughters, and much more in danger of neglecting religion, he is proportionably thankful when they become decidedly pious. The first symptoms of a serious attention to the momentous concerns of eternity awaken the liveliest emotions of delight, not unmixed with solicitude, lest it should be only as "the morning cloud or early dew, which passeth away." He prays more intensely than ever, and watches more anxiously for decision of character, and shields the bud of hope by his most assiduous care. As the bud expands into the blossom, and the blossom sets in fruit, his hopes and fears alternate, till at length the doubtful case is decided, and his child becomes first a Christian, and then a professor. What a load of parental anxiety is removed! What an accession is made to his parent's delight! If the youth has been away from home, and the intelligence of his conversion is conveyed by letter, the good man's heart is too full to hold, and, weeping over the welcome tidings, he hastens to his chamber to pour out his gratitude to God, the author of this new rich mercy; a mercy in his esteem far greater than the appointment of his son to a lucrative and honourable situation, or his success in some matter

of business. And the gratitude of the father is equalled,
if not surpassed, by that of the mother. "What, my
son a true Christian! My boy, for whom I have suffered so much deep and painful solicitude; who when he
left home wrung my heart with agonising fears, because
he was going forth as a lamb among wolves; what, he
become a sincerely religious man, a child of God! May
I indeed believe the blissful intelligence? A happy
woman am I now become, to be the mother of one who
shall glorify God, and enjoy him for ever."

The religion of this young man proves itself sincere,
consistent, and active. It preserves him from the snares
to which a youth away from home is ever exposed, and
affords another illustration of the declaration that "godliness is profitable for all things, having the promise
of the life that now is, as well as of that which is to
come." He connects himself with the schemes of usefulness which are so numerous in this day of Christian
activity, and becomes a blessing to the church and
the world. His religion goes with him into his future
character, situation, and circumstances, as a husband,
a father, a master, and a tradesman. He is seen
habitually among the Christian philanthropists of the
age, uniting his influences and energies with theirs, to
bless his species, and glorify his God. His assistance
is willingly granted to all that is going on for the moral
renovation of the world. By his prayers, his example,
his property, his intelligence, and his labours, he acts
up to the metaphorical description of the righteous,
where our Lord says to his disciples, "Ye are the light
of the world; ye are the salt of the earth." His family
are brought up in the fear of the Lord, and are likely

to be his imitators in all good things, and thus hand forward religion as an heir-loom to their descendants.

What a beautiful scene is this for Christian parents to witness, if, indeed, they are still alive to watch the growing piety, prosperity, happiness, and usefulness of this their son! How blissful are the feelings, how delightful the intercourse of the happy couple as they sit and talk of this their beloved and holy child! If he live at home with them, how uninterruptedly agreeable is their intercourse with him. They have nothing to complain of or to reprove ; and he nothing to explain, defend, or excuse. They have common objects, common delights, and common topics. Their spiritual tastes, their highest and most momentous pursuits and pleasures, are alike. How it rejoices them to be the witnesses of his piety and activity, and to hear the testimonies of others to his respectability, importance, and usefulness. How many congratulations they receive on the character and conduct of this their son. They see old age coming on upon them, but here is the bright star in the evening sky of their life. Here is no disappointment, but on the other hand, the fulfilment of their brightest hopes. Here is the rich reward of all their parental labours and anxieties, the abundant answer of all their prayers.

It may be that these parents are called, according to the order of nature, to descend first to the tomb. During a long decay, they are cheered and comforted, if their son live at home, with his presence, his prayers, and his conversation. If he live away from home, they are refreshed by his letters, and by his occasional visits. His conduct has planted no thorns in their dying pillow, but has softened it till it has rendered it even downy. They feel that separation from such a child is, indeed, bitter and painful to nature : but then his piety assures them they are not parting for ever. As he comforts them by his holy suggestions and devout petitions, they are ofttimes in a strait, like the apostle, desiring to depart to be with Christ, and yet, on the other hand, desiring, for the sake of those they are leaving, to remain. No painful but necessary warnings issue from their lips, wringing their hearts with anguish, as they solemnly abjure an ungodly son to forsake his ways. No bitter tears roll down their cheeks as they grasp his hand and entreat him to repent, and thus mitigate the sorrows of death, the only sorrow they know. On the contrary, all are words of consolation, expressions of gratitude, and effusions of joy, that they shall soon meet again. They are ready to repeat the words of Simeon, "Lord, now lettest thou thy servant depart in peace, for mine eyes have seen thy salvation, not only upon myself, but upon my children also." Happy parents, and happy son !

But if, on the other hand, this son after his father's own heart should, by an inversion of the order of nature, be called first to descend to the grave, with what feelings do his pious parents hang over his couch of sickness, and watch the progress of decay and the advance of death, how different from those of parents who have to wait around the death-bed of an ungodly son ! True they are disappointed by his early removal from our world. To see such a blossom, yea fruit, of parental hope cut off, and sent to the grave, is indeed a trial ! One so dutiful, so good, so holy, so promising, so useful, to be carried off from them, from the church, from the world; how mysterious an event, how great a calamity. Yes, but then his deep submission, his strong faith, his joy unspeakable and peace that passes understanding, his holy converse, his words of consolation to them, how tranquillising all these! No agonising fears about his spiritual state distress their minds. All is safe for eternity. He dies, but they can trace him to the realms of glory. To lose such a son is, of course, a severe trial of their faith and patience : but the recollections of his past character and conduct, the soothing influence of his dying testimony, the assurance of his heavenly bliss, the anticipations of their final meeting and ever-lasting association, reconcile them to the stroke, and enable them to feel that after all, this their disappoint-ment is inconceivably lighter than that of many who are afflicted by the conduct of a living profligate. In one case the affliction brings its own comfort with it, but in the other it is unmixed wormwood and gall. To the language of condolence which they receive from sympathising friends, they are ready to give the answer which the Duke of Ormond did in similar circumstances, " I would rather have my dead son than half the living sons of all Christendom."

There have been cases where the realisation of parental hopes has come after a season of protracted, anxious, and even agonizing fear and disappointment. The ex-quisitely beautiful parable of the prodigal son, in its close as well as in its beginnings, has, in a few instances, and perhaps but a few, received its accomplishment in the children of the godly. There have been youths whose erratic career of folly and sin has half-broken a father's and a mother's heart, but whose ultimate recovery came just in time to save them from being entirely crushed.

I heard of one young man of this description, who, though the son of religious parents, and therefore, the child of many prayers and much instruction, had wandered far, and wide, and long, from the path of piety and morality. Through his dark and winding course he was followed by a father's prayers and a mother's tears. Every means which ingenuity could suggest, had been tried to reclaim him, but in vain. To parental remonstrance while under his father's roof he was deaf, and to all letters sent to him in his distant vagrancies he was insensible. As a last means of restoring him, after a long suspension of intercourse, his father, who could not forget his truant and wicked son, nor alienate his heart altogether from him, called together in the vestry of the chapel, where, if I mistake not, he laboured as a minister, a few friends to pray for his penitence and restoration. After several had poured out their hearts in fervent supplication, the father gave utterance to his own feelings, in a strain of most tender supplications, which melted all present to tears. During these exercises a poor wretched creature was seen wandering round the window, and listening at the door of the vestry; and no sooner had the prayer of the good man for his son ended, after which the meeting was about to break up, than the listener, who was indeed the subject of all these prayers, entered, fell upon the neck of his father, and simply sobbed out, "O, my father, forgive me." It is unnecessary I should describe the scene that followed; you have it in the parable of the prodigal son, "Rejoice with me, for this my son was dead and is alive again, he was lost and is found." He lived a new life, and realized in the end, the hopes of his parents, after long disappointing them. What an encouragement this to parents to continue instant in prayer! And what an encouragement to prodigals to say, "I will arise and go unto my father, and say, Father, I have sinned against heaven, and in thy sight, and am no more worthy to be called thy son." If any whose eye shall glance over these pages shall be still in the land of their wandering, to them would I say, Return, return. It is not yet too late. You may still realize the hopes of your parents. You may still repent, reform, and lead a new life. The grace of God which brings salvation may teach you to deny ungodliness and worldly lusts, and to live soberly, righteously, and godly in this evil world. You may be respectable, happy, and useful even yet. Abandon despair. There is no need of it even in your case. If returning prodigals are few, be you one of the few. Let me recommend, earnestly recommend, you to read the fifteenth chapter of the gospel by Luke, which is one of the most beautiful and touching portions of the whole Bible. It is full of instruction, of tenderness, of encouragement; and will, if you have not extinguished every spark of feeling in your soul, melt your heart to compunction and your eyes to tears. It describes your character, suits your condition, represents your father's heart towards you, and will perhaps, by God's grace, recover you from your present condition. Read it, read it, till this blessed effect is produced. Read it with earnest prayer, that you may be indeed a reclaimed, restored prodigal, and even yet bind up the heart which you have nearly broken, and not bring down a "father's grey hairs in sorrow to the grave." Or if your parents have gone to the world where "the wicked cease from troubling and the weary are at rest," and perhaps have been hurried to their grave by your misconduct; if they left our earth with hearts broken by disappointed hopes, and breathed out their last feelings for you, exclaiming, " O my son, my son, must we part for ever?" if in this world there was not, by your good conduct, any reward of their prayers, their tears, their example, and their labours, carry it to them, by your present repentance and reformation, and by your thus following them thither when you die. If nothing but disappointment was felt by them here, let the reward of their trouble be granted to them there. Though they left you in your sinful wanderings when they ascended to their glory, and feared they had lost you for ever, let them by your forsaking your evil courses, find you in Paradise. What a meeting will you then have in that happy state. How will it enhance even their heavenly felicity, after having given up all hope of your salvation upon earth, to have the assurance of your salvation by seeing you in heaven. Richly will it repay them for all their sorrows and anxiety, and infinitely more than compensate for all they have endured on your account.

And now, young men, let me close this chapter by a few more words of affectionate yet earnest expostulation and persuasion. It is cruel under any circumstances, to frustrate wilfully and wantonly, by any part of our conduct, the hopes of our fellow creatures; and the cruelty is in exact proportion to the strength, the propriety, and the justness of the expectations which are so defeated. If persons who have no right to expect anything from us, make us out of mere choice the subject of foolish and unwarranted anticipations, we have no great need to concern ourselves about the matter; and any disappointment which we may occasion is rather a punishment for their folly than a reproach upon us. But where by a kind of necessity we become to others the objects of their well-founded and rational expectations; where these expectations are very large and authorised by every consideration; where their disappointment must be followed by great misery; and the accomplishment of their wishes must secure them great happiness; and where it is in our power to bring about either of these alternatives, it is most cruel wantonly to sport with the hopes thus suspended upon our conduct. A generous and sensitive mind does not like to occasion disappointment even to a dumb animal. Think, then, of the hopes of parents in reference to their children. I appeal to your generosity on their behalf. Have they not a right to entertain hope concerning you? Does not the very relationship give them this right? Fancy your mother thus addressing you, " I am a mother and have all a mother's affections, anxieties, hopes, and rights. Next to God and my husband, in whom should I hope so justly as in my child, whom I have borne in my womb, nursed at my breast, fondled in my arms? For whom I have given the sleep of countless nights, and the labour of countless days. Whom I have taught to walk, to speak, to think, to act. Whom I have loved with a mother's love, watched around his couch in sickness, wept when he wept, and smiled when he smiled, heard his complaints, and soothed his sorrows, borne with his waywardness, and gently reproved his faults. Whom as an infant, a child, a youth, a man, I have anxiously cared for, as I have watched with solicitude each successive development. Whom I have prayed for, instructed, warned, encouraged. O, my son, my son, had not thy mother a right to hope that all this would be rewarded at some period when it should be all understood? I saw thy infant smiles as thou turnedst thy eyes upon her that fed thee from her bosom, and which seemed at that time silently to thank me for thy sustenance. I heard thee call me thy 'dear mother,' as thou madest thy first essays at articulate language. I beheld thy opening talents and virtues, as they appeared to be then, and interpreted them into signs of future excellence, and had I not a right to hope for much at thy hands, and wilt thou disappoint it all, and thus reward thy mother's care? Shall hopes so early awakened, so fondly cherished, so long sustained, so justly founded, that rose so high, and anticipated so much, be all doomed, by thy misconduct, to disappointment? O, my son, my son." And then your father too, think of him: that kind, good man, who when he first took you in his arms, felt the new and strange emotions of that rapturous moment all kindle into hope, as he looked upon your face, and for the first time cried, "My child!" How did that hope grow with your growth, and strengthen with your strength: rising higher and sinking deeper at every advanced stage of your life. His hope of your future excellence was his prospective reward for all the labour he sustained to support, to educate, and provide for you. Often as he wiped away the sweat of his brow amidst the heat and burden of the day, and began to think his labours almost too severe, his hope of your future good conduct checked the rising feeling of hardship, and compelled him to say, "It is for my children: and it is my hope that they, by their affection and general good conduct, will one day make me as thankful that I endure all this for them, as their mother already does."

Young men, have you generosity, gratitude, nobility of soul? If so, let me ask you, what do such ties, such benefits, such feelings, and such conduct, deserve at your hands? Can you be insensible to such an appeal? One should imagine it would be your study and delight to acknowledge and discharge, in the most effectual and satisfactory manner, obligations which you began to contract before you had the ability to understand and appreciate them; and which, from that time to the present, have never ceased to accumulate. Above all things upon earth your parents have the largest claims upon your consideration, and though there are higher motives to the cultivation of all moral excellence, than even a regard to their happiness, yet this ought never to be left out of view, and never will be, by any generous, dutiful, and affectionate son.

CHAPTER XI.

*The children of Issachar, which were men that had under-
standing of times, to know what Israel ought to do.*
1 CHRONICLES xii, 32.
Can ye not discern the signs of the times? MAT. xvi, 3.

IN the first of these passages, the Israelites who were
of the tribe of Issachar, in the time of David, received a
high encomium for understanding the times, and knowing
what it became the inhabitants of the kingdom to do.
They were thoughtful, intelligent men, who studied and
who understood the signs of the times; were well versed
in public affairs; knew the character of the age that was
passing over them, and what was best to be done for
the exigencies of their nation; and perceived that it was
the duty and the interest of Israel to advance David to
the throne. In the second passage, our Lord reproves the
Pharisees for their not being able to discern the signs
of their times. The signs of the times are the character
and aspect of the passing age. Every age has its characteristic signs impressed upon it by the hand of God. To
discern these is to mark and comprehend them. Such
attention and discrimination are our duty, and the neglect of it subjects us to the rebuke of Christ. Among

many extremes to be avoided, there are two which are suggested by the subject of the present discourse; I mean too great individuality of feeling on the one hand, and being too much the citizen or the cosmopolite on the other; or, put in other words, too selfish a regard for our own personal affairs, or too absorbing an interest in the affairs of the state or the world. There are some persons, though they are not many, whose whole world is self. They have surrounded themselves by a very narrow boundary, within which they endeavour to keep their attention closed, and occupy themselves strictly in their own business, with as little inquisitiveness about, or connexion or sympathy with, the great world without as possible. Now this is wrong, for, as they are members of the community, they owe it some duties, which they cannot rightly discharge without knowing its condition. It is foolish, because their individual lot is influenced by the general one. It betrays a gross insensibility not to look up when Providence is passing by, and notice its stately march. It prevents their getting good, as well as doing good, for God is ever teaching us lessons by public events. It is very true, there may be the opposite extreme of being so occupied by watching the progressive development of the great drama of Providence, as to forget and neglect our own individual concerns, and our immediate duties. We are placed in a very busy world, full of men and works; of transactions and events, and of vast varieties of human character and action. We may be acquainted with all that is going on, by reading, conversation, and observation. We are in the midst of the throng, and are moving on with it. It is of vast importance, then, to attend to two things: first, not to let our attention be too much drawn off from our own private matters to public ones; and secondly, to take care that our notice of public events be carried on wisely, so as to turn what we observe to profitable account. Our Lord's reproof to the Jews contained in the text, condemns the habitual disregard of passing events in all ages of the world and in all periods of its history. But there are times when it is still more to be repro- bated. Providence is always at work, and we, after all, are poor judges of the comparative importance of its operations, since preparations may be going on in its secret recesses, of which the stupendous dispensations that we witness are but the first manifestation. Still there can be no doubt of the wonderful character of our age, nor any danger of our unduly magnifying its importance. It is obvious that the world is becoming a far more active, agitating, changing, tumultuous scene, than formerly. Discoveries and inventions; intelligence and events; omens and alarms, come upon us not singly, but in troops; not in showers and streams, but with the rapidity, the copiousness, and the force of an inundation. In such an age, to be swallowed up in our own individual concerns, and to be such religious recluses, literary solitaires, mercantile devotees, or do- mestic exclusives, as to have no sympathy with the actors and operations of the age, is sanctioned neither by religion nor reason, but is contrary to both.

I. Let us inquire into the characteristics of the age in which we live. Almost every age has something in common with other ages and something peculiar to itself. What then are those peculiarities of the present times which should be pointed out to the inquiring and observant mind? If we speak of the age as regards its intellectual character, we cannot fail to notice an intense excitement and inquisitiveness. The human mind was never so active and so exploring in all the regions of thought as now. The discoveries of science are wonderful, and, as might be expected, the inventions of art are proportionate. The two must ever move together, being reciprocally helpful to each other. What surprising disclosures of the secrets of nature are going on, under the scrutinising researches of experimental philosophy! Men seem to feel as if there were no limits to human inquiry, and as if there was nothing knowable which they could not and would not know; as if nothing would satisfy them till they had reached the furthest boundary of knowledge. How rapidly and how widely is the circle of universal knowledge expanding. We are grown so familiar with the wonders which have been of late years achieved by the human intellect, that we now do not think anything too wonderful for man to attempt or expect. Hence the magnificent, but somewhat presumptuous, title of his last publication by Humboldt, "Cosmos," "The World;" as if he had laid open all the globe to our knowledge, and not only our planet, but the great universe itself, with all it comprehends.

If we regard the age in its social aspect, we see the same proof of its extraordinary character. "The pervading connecting principle of community, throughout mankind as one immense body, has become much more alive. It is now much more verified to be one body, however extended, by the quicker, stronger sensations which pervade the rest of it, from what affects any particular part." Intercourse is so facilitated, quickened, and extended, that men begin to feel less

and less the interposing geographical and political bar-
riers, which separate them from each other, and are
approximating to universal neighbourhood; great social
principles are also in operation, which are breaking
down national prejudices and antipathies. The evils
of war are being denounced in loud and emphatic terms,
and schemes of universal brotherhood are put forth,
which, if not likely to be immediately successful, are
the harbingers of the approaching reign of love, and
the shadows which coming events cast before them.
The subject of slavery, the treatment of criminals, the
foundation of government, the theory and practice
of law, the physical condition of the people, the
temperance reform, national education, the principles
of international trade, the grand questions of civil and
religious liberty, are all agitated and discussed with an
inquisitiveness and an eagerness which look as if society
were absolutely and resolutely bent on self-improvement,
and was going on towards a point immeasurably in
advance of anything it has yet reached. Nor should
we forget the extraordinary impetus that has been lately
given to colonization and emigration, by which new
additions are being made to the great family of nations,
and new experiments instituted in the principles of human government.

The political character of the age, especially if we
take in the whole of the present century, is almost
unparalleled for the number, rapidity, extent, and magnitude of its revolutions. In what a state has Europe
existed during this period! Almost every kingdom but
our own has been the seat of war, and most of them
the scenes of changes of dynasty and government. We
have seen monarchs driven from their thrones; sceptres

broken, and crowns rolling in the dust. And though the great earthquake at present (1851) has ceased, and there is a lull in the tempests that have been raging; yet with four millions of men under arms at this moment, and nations jealously watching each other; with France uneasy and restless within itself, and containing the elements of mischief fermenting both in its capital and in its provinces, who can say how soon the spark will fall which may cause another explosion? Depend upon it, the next convulsion, come when it may, will be more tremendous than any that have preceded it. The liberties of Europe have yet to be established by the subversion of many of its old governments, who seem not disposed to gain wisdom by experience. The nations are panting for freedom, and the despots are resolved they shall not be free; and ere long the slaves will break their fetters and the sceptres of their tyrants, in the same furious struggle and in the same awful hour. Young men, you know not and cannot conceive what you may be called to witness. Happily you live in a country where whatever the many have to gain from the few, it will be won by reason and not by force.

The moral aspect of this age is no less impressive than either of the preceding. If asked to describe in one or two words this aspect of the age, I should say, first of all, it is the age of conflict. The struggle always going on in our world between truth and error, good and evil, has assumed a character of earnestness, not to say fierceness, as if both parties were preparing for a last and decisive battle. The four great religious controversies are becoming more and more determined. There is the conflict which is maintained by infidelity

in all its forms (including atheism, pantheism, and
deism) against Christianity: that which is carried on
between those foundation truths which (as held by all
the chief denominations of Christendom) may fairly be
called orthodoxy, and heresy: that which is sustained
by the advocates and opponents of State establishments
of religion: and that mighty struggle which is becoming
more determined every day between Popery and Protestantism. Never was the war of opinions so general
and so determined as it is now. To a contemplative
mind it is a somewhat awful exercise of thought, to look
over this vast field of conflict, where such forces are
contending for supremacy over the moral destinies of the
present and all future generations of mankind, and to
watch the movements of the armies, and their alternate
victories and defeats.

Happily there is also another feature of the age,
which, though in one sense it bears the aspect of conflict also, is sufficiently distinct from it to admit of
separate consideration; I mean the evangelising spirit,
now manifested by professing Christians of all denominations. This though it may be unpraised, and even to a
considerable extent unnoticed, by "the children of this
world," wise as they are in their generation, is the
grandest and most hopeful sign of the times. If then
asked for a second characteristic of the moral aspect
of the times, I reply without a moment's hesitation,
benevolence. Yes, and that not a mere sentimental
compassion, the benevolence that can weep before the
pictures of imagination, but will do nothing to relieve
the miseries of real life. Nor is it the benevolence
that only builds alms-houses, hospitals, dispensaries;
which would combat the ills that flesh is heir to, disease,

poverty, and hunger, though I do not think lightly
of this, nor is the age wanting in it; but the benevolence
which characterises this age, and in which I most
delight, is that which lighted upon our orb from heaven
in the person of our Lord Jesus Christ, who came to
redeem man from sin, and death, and hell. That which
lived and moved and had its being in apostles, when
they went everywhere preaching the gospel, "to turn
men from dumb idols to serve the living and true God."
That which in modern times is embodied in the character
of the devoted and self-sacrificing missionary, who, for
the love of Christ and pity for immortal souls, quits the
comforts of civilized society to dwell among savages,
amidst the deserts of Africa or the ices of polar regions.
That, in short, which aims at the salvation of souls, the
rescue of the human mind from the chains of ignorance
and the emancipation of the heart from the bondage
of its lusts. This, this is the noblest characteristic
of our age, a religious zeal to diffuse the blessings of the
gospel over the face of the whole earth, more intense,
more active, and more comprehensive than any which
has existed since the apostles' days. The missionary
spirit, as manifested in the various organisations which
it has called into existence, the numerous missions which
it has established, and the triumphs over barbarism,
idolatry, vice and cruelty which it has achieved; stamp
upon this age its most beneficent, most important, and
most sublime character. Christianity is the world's
best friend. Apart from its being the means of eternal
life in another world, it is the best benefactor of man in
all his relations to the present world. " It maintains an
incessant struggle against all that is selfish, barbarous,
and inimical to human happiness, and comprehends in

itself the seeds of endless improvement; and it is this which rising upon us like a finer sun, has quickened moral vegetation, and replenished our country with talents, virtues, and exploits, which, in spite of its physical disadvantages, have rendered it a paradise, the delight and wonder of the world." How great, then, and how noble an enterprise is that which attempts to make this the religion of the world, and thus to supplant all the vices and crimes which degrade the intellect, pollute the heart, deform the character, and fill the life with misery!

Such, then, Young Men, is the age in which you are called to exist; and such the signs, omens and portents by which it is distinguished: and to them may be added the reflection, which gives the consideration its most intense force and importance, that your lot is cast in the country which is placed by Providence at the centre of the intellectual, social, and moral interests of the world. It is something more than an effusion of national vanity, to affirm that England, beyond all countries on the globe, is at present the temple of religion, the hall of science, the school of learning, the citadel of liberty, the refuge of distress, the mart of commerce, and the seat of power. On her depend more closely than on any other nation, the intellectual, social and moral destinies of the world. The nations of the earth and all coming ages and generations have more to hope from her, than from any other country under the sun. Her decadence would be more their loss, as her continued glory and greatness would be more their gain, than the adversity or prosperity of any other state on the face of the globe. It is not then allowed to you to look on from afar upon passing events, without being permitted to guide or influence them. You are in the midst of them, and can touch the springs of activity which are in motion around you. You are not only permitted, but invited; and not only invited, but commanded, to bear a part in all that is going forward for the world's improvement.

II. I therefore consider the character of the men that are wanted for the age. This will lead me to state what you should be. Men of the age, and for it. Men worthy of it, that can avail themselves of its opportunities for getting good, and doing good; that catch its spirit, and receive its impress; that can even do something to improve it, as well as be improved by it; that are wiser, holier, more benevolent, more active, than their fathers; that, like those of the tribe of Issachar, "understand the times, and know what Israel ought to do."

As the basis of everything else, of all the talents and the virtues by which you can act most beneficially, I mention of course personal religion. Maintaining, as I do, that real religion is the chief element in the world's well-being, as well as in the happiness of each individual, I ought to mention it as the first thing essentially necessary in him who would benefit the age in which he lives. I have as high an estimate as any one of the value and importance of the sciences, literature and the arts; I am as strenuous an advocate of liberty as can be found; but I contend that they will never renew the human heart, or restore it to peace. It is religion more than these things, or than all other things, that the nations need for their repose and felicity; and he that would do most to bless his species, must seek to spread the blessings of Christianity. When I speak of religion

being the world's best friend, I mean religion as we
have it pure in the Bible, and in the hearts and lives
of its true believers; and not as it is presented in the
corrupt forms which it has assumed in the creeds,
churches, constitutions, and professions of some that
call themselves Christians; I mean the religion of repentance, truth, holiness, and love; the subjugation of
the heart and life to the law of God; "the wisdom
that is first pure, then peaceable; full of mercy and good
fruits; gentle and easy to be entreated; without partiality, and without hypocrisy." I see with pleasure the
ever advancing tide of knowledge : but I am quite sure
it is not upon this, but upon the stream of religion,
that men must float into the haven of sound morals and
permanent peace. The best benefactor of his race is
not he who teaches them something they did not before
know, though even he is entitled to their gratitude, but
he who delivers them from the dominion of their
passions, and the slavery of their vices. Hence, no man
can serve his age so effectually as he who fears God, and
under the influence of motives derived thence, seeks to
benefit his fellow-creatures by implanting in their hearts
the principles that sway his own. The worshippers
of knowledge award to the philosopher the palm which
is due to the Christian philanthropist, as the world's
best friend. Hence, my young friends, I tell you that
you are not men for the age, if you are not religious
men. Neglect religion, and you may by your vices
become the world's bane and curse. Possess it, and
you not only promote the moral interests of the age,
which are its highest ones, but you also give the best
guarantee, and use the best means too, of serving it
in every other way.

It becomes you to be observant, thoughtful, reflective : for who in such an age as this can be in harmony
with the times without such a disposition? Rise above
the folly of those young men whose frivolous spirits,
taken up with the levities, trifles and petty imperti-
nences of little minds, seem incapable of serious reflection; men who would wonder what strange mysterious
power was operating upon them, if at any time they
found themselves in a pensive mood, and, in ever so
slight a manner, moralising on passing events : men
who seem to think they are born to talk, and smoke,
and laugh, rather than to think. Despise such men.
From these gay and thoughtless triflers society has
nothing to expect. They may have their brief day
of sunshine and pleasure : they will then die, vanish,
and be forgotten, as though they had never been. Belong, my young friends, to the class so characteristically
described as "thoughtful men;" men who, knowing
they were made for thought and reflection, fix their eyes
on the currents of events, to see which way they are
flowing; who not only make themselves acquainted with
the surface of things, but who look beneath it, and
endeavour philosophically to trace events backward to
their causes, and forward to their consequences; who
not only exercise their curiosity in knowing what is
taking place, but their reason in judging of its tendencies and influences; who read the histories of past times,
as well as the chronicles of the present age, to form
opinions founded upon examination, comparison, and
legitimate deduction. Endeavour to discern the connection of events, and their influence upon the great
interests of social happiness, liberty and religion. And
especially let the speculative contemplation of human

life and passing events be combined in you with active energy. Let observation constantly be converted into reflection, and reflection into action. Let your thoughtfulness be something more than musing. Be not like one who watches the swelling tide in a dreamy mood, and sees it rise and fall as a mere object of curiosity; but be as one who is waiting for it to reach a certain elevation, when he shall throw in a net or embark in a boat. Stand amidst passing events, asking the question, "What does all this mean generally, and what does it require me to do? What practical teaching is there in all this? What must I rise from this scene to perform for myself, for society, or for the church of God? What is it that Providence, by what is now passing before me, calls on me to attempt?" I do not by all this mean to impose upon you a premature gravity, an unnatural solemnity and taciturnity. I do not mean to depress the buoyancy and check the sprightliness of youth, to stiffen your manners into repulsive formality, and to transform a modest, humble youth, into a "Sir Oracle." Nothing of the sort, but still I entreat young men to be sober-minded.

Here, again, I bring in mental cultivation and robustness of intellect, as of great importance. Thoughout the whole of this work I have insisted much on this, being well-assured that though religion is the first thing, as an object of human pursuit, it is not every thing; and that other things being equal, he is likely to be the most useful and happy man, who is best taught and best disciplined. I say to you most emphatically, "Seek ye first the kingdom of God and his righteousness;" but I then add, Seek next a well-informed, well-cultivated mind. In an age like the present, so cultivated, so enlightened, no man can make way in the world, so as to gain respect, influence others, and do good, who has not some power of character, and some store of intellectual wealth. Character does something, I know, even where the jewel is not set in the gold of brilliant knowledge: but how much more when it is! He who is ambitious to be useful, and it is a noble ambition wherever it exists, and it ought to exist in all, must not neglect to improve his mind. Who in such an age as this will hearken to the talk of ignorance, or bow to the puerilities of weakness, or revere even real excellence, if it be associated with imbecility? One of the characteristics of the age is, as we have considered, active benevolence; and another, the diffusion of knowledge. Many have taken part in the former, without being careful to take part in the latter, and thus have failed in doing all the good they wished.

I recommend the adoption of certain great principles, which ought ever to be present with you when looking abroad upon the course of events and the general history of mankind; and which every one who properly discerns the signs of the times will assiduously cherish.

Recognise, in the current of human affairs, the scheme and operations of an all-wise, all-controlling Providence. Behold in all events the permission or the appointment of God. Renounce not only the atheist's creed, but his mode of thinking and speaking of passing events. The transactions and affairs of the day, though brought to pass by a vast multitude of free and accountable agents, fulfil God's counsel, and contribute to the perfecting of his plan. Be the signs of the times therefore what they may, they are such as he has stamped

upon them, and are significant of something pertaining
to him and his purpose. Believe that the will of God
controls all events. In looking over the scenes of history, as well as those of nature, realize the thought that
all you see is governed by one controlling will, one
infinitely wise and benevolent mind. This gives additional interest and grandeur to the view. There is no
beauty, no interest, no pleasure, in the idea of chance.
It is not only an irreligious and unphilosophical, but it
is also an unpoetical thing, a repulsive negation, a
sterile, hideous conception. On the contrary, how
delightful it is to look upon the revolutions of empire,
the discoveries of science, the inventions of art, the
conflict of systems, the progress of society, and realize
in all these the operations of an Ever-present, Omniscient Intellect: and thus to feel ourselves in the great
workshop or laboratory of the all-wise, all-good, all-
powerful Artificer, and surrounded with the glorious,
though as yet unfinished, productions of His consummate
skill.

Another great principle to direct us in considering
the events of the age, is that truth is far more excellent
and important in matters of morality and conscience,
than in matters of science or mere intellect; or in other
words, that religion and virtue are superior to science,
literature, and the arts, as to all that affects the well-
being of man. All truth is important; but all truth is
not equally important. Man's moral is above his intellectual nature. The intellectual is for the moral, rather
than the moral for the intellectual; and as the intellectual is for the moral, so the moral is for the eternal.
I have glanced at this, in a former chapter; and renew
the consideration of it here on account of its import-

ance. It is, as I have already said, as a moral agent that man is farthest removed from the brutes that perish, and approximates nearest to God. The lower animals have moments of reason, but they have no susceptibility of moral ideas. Piety and virtue are loftier qualities of character in themselves, and far more productive of happiness, than merely intellectual acquisitions; they alone fit the soul for communion with God now, and for presence with him hereafter in heaven. The extension of knowledge alone, without religion and morals, even if every barbarian in existence were made a philosopher, would fail to make men happy; but moral qualities will make man happy in any state of society, in any condition of life. The Greenlander amidst the never-melting ices and long nights of Arctic regions, the Red Indian amidst his boundless prairies and interminable forests, the Hottentot amidst the vast African deserts, or the Negro subjected to the yoke of slavery, may, by the external blessings of the gospel, and the internal graces of a holy mind, be happy. One would imagine, from much that is said and done, in the present age, that knowledge was the bread of life which would satisfy every desire of the soul hungering after bliss; the panacea which would heal every wound of diseased humanity; the crown of glory to our nature; the chief felicity of our present existence; and all we need for our happiness in another world. This is however a lamentable and fatal error, but one in which nearly the whole civilized world is involved. Education, apart from religion, is, it seems, to do everything for man. Ideas, ideas, ideas, are alone needed to renew, reform, and bless the human race. Let but mankind be admitted to the tree of knowledge, and they will find

nothing but good to be the result. It is the darkness
of the intellect only, that is the cause of the depravity
of the heart; and only let in the light of science, and it
will set all right. Such is the deplorable error of the
moral quacks of the age, whose nostrum for the cure
of all diseases is knowledge. Deluded men! They
would rectify society without religion, and govern it
without God. Have they forgotten all history, especially
that of Greece and Rome? Have they ever read what
the apostle says, "For after that in the wisdom of God,
the world by wisdom knew not God, it pleased God by
the foolishness of preaching to save them that believe."
It is something for the moral nature that man needs for
his happiness; and you may offer mere intellectual
knowledge to a man whose limbs are dislocated, or
whose flesh is corroded by disease, as that which will
give him health and enjoyment, as reasonably as you
can offer it to the unholy man, as that which will give
him holiness, ease, and contentment. While then, you
concede to knowledge all that is contended for on its
behalf, short of its being the supreme good, and the
supreme means of good; and while you go on seeking
it for yourself, and diffusing it among others, ever remember that religious and moral truth is infinitely more
important than science and the arts; and give your most
zealous interest to those institutions which promote it.
You see on every hand restlessness and dissatisfaction.
Amidst the advances of society in all that can exalt and
dignify man as an intellectual being, amidst all the
wonders which his noble intellect is producing, amidst
all the homage he is ever receiving from his fellows and
from himself, he is still as far from happiness as ever,
and still lifting up the anxious inquiry, "Who will show

us any good?" The nations of the earth, notwithstanding their marvellous advancement in physical
knowledge and refinement, are still as ignorant of the
nature, and as short of the attainment, of true bliss as
ever. Yes, and they ever must be so, as long as any
truth is set above that which is divinely revealed in the
Word of God, and as long as the seat of happiness is
supposed to be the intellect rather than the heart.
Young men, be it your felicity to discover what it is
that man needs to make him happy, and then to join
those who are labouring to diffuse "the excellency of the
knowledge of Christ," which by renovating the moral
nature, roots out all that can degrade and disturb it,
and plants all those seeds of piety and virtue which can
elevate, adorn, and bless it.

As another principle to guide you in your views conduct and relations in this important age, let it be your
conviction that all social changes are subservient to the
kingdom of Christ. In all difficult problems, and complicated schemes, it is a vast advantage to be furnished
with a key to unlock the whole. Now this advantage
we possess in the knowledge furnished by the Bible,
concerning not only the tendency, but the actual design
and final result, of all events to promote the advancement of Christianity on the earth. It is not at all
necessary to prove to those for whom I am writing, that
the universal diffusion of the Christian religion in its
purity, would be a great blessing to the human race.
What curses are Paganism, Mohammedanism, and
Popery! What a withering blight has come from those
sources over the moral interests of the globe! What a
jubilee for the world would the universal reign of our
Lord Jesus Christ be! How many evils would flee be-

fore him : war, slavery, tyranny, anarchy, and vice in all its branches ! How many blessings would follow in his train; peace, liberty, good government, just laws, universal brotherhood ! The diffusion of Christianity is the greatest thing that can happen in and to our world. Nothing can for a moment be put in comparison with it : nothing can be conceived more worthy of the Divine Being, as the supreme end of his government. Hence it is very delightful to know that all which is taking place is subservient to this end. How grand is the position of a true Christian, a believer in revelation ! He stands upon the mount of prophecy, and sees all the various operations of science, literature, art, history, commerce, navigation, all widening the channel and deepening the bed of the " River of Life," which is flowing from the throne of God and the Lamb, for the salvation of the world. He sees statesmen, warriors, travellers, philosophers, merchants, mechanicians, engineers, while pursuing their own separate objects, and never dreaming of promoting Christianity, actually carrying on this great work. Is it not an immense advantage, in looking abroad upon the millions of events of all kinds that are ever occurring, events which seem to have no connection with each other, and no end and design in common, to be furnished with the knowledge of the centre in which all these lines meet and converge? We are told that Christ is Head over all things to his church. There is the secret, the grand glorious and blissful secret. In looking upon the progress of science and the arts, the question is often almost involuntarily asked, " Where will it all end? What will it all come to ?" The Bible answers the question : In the setting up in our world of Christ's

kingdom of truth, holiness, and happiness. Take this
conviction with you through life. Look abroad upon
this wonderful age, with the knowledge of this still more
wonderful and glorious fact; and while the unreflecting,
the irreligious, the sceptical, or the atheistic philosopher,
is revelling in the discoveries of science, but stopping
there; do you go on to that nobler cause, the universal
diffusion of religion, of which all the sciences are the
hand-maids, and he himself, though he knows it not,
nor does his heart think so, is but an unconscious
instrument.

The last principle I would request you to take up
and apply to the age, is this, Social reform must be
brought about by individual regeneration. This principle
is as important as it is true. We hear a great deal in
various directions about the improvement of society, and
a noble idea it is, whether politically or morally viewed.
Social evils are so numerous, so deeply seated, and so
pernicious, that it is desirable and important that they
should be removed by extensive reform. But it is
forgotten, even by those who declaim most loudly
against them, and call most earnestly for a better
direction to be given to the masses, that the best, and
only way to improve the whole, is by seeking the improvement of each part. Individual regeneration is the
only method of general reformation. It is all well
enough to talk about the latter, and to join in combined
efforts to promote it; but it will end in talk, as long as
there is no concern for each man to improve himself.
Public and confederate evil must, I know, be publicly
and jointly attacked; but the assailants must begin
with reforming themselves, and come to the assault on
others with clean hands and pure hearts. It is of vast

importance to set out in life with this view of things. He is the best reformer who begins with the reformation of himself; and no systems will be effectual for public amelioration which leave out of consideration the necessity of individual excellence. A deep sense of personal responsibility should lie on every man's conscience. Every man is a part of the existing generation, and does something by his own character and conduct to form the character of the age. Each ought therefore to resolve, What I would have the age to be, that I will endeavour to be.

No man can rightly appreciate his age who does not cherish Public Spirit. This, at all times incumbent, is especially so in the present day. By this I do not mean a noisy obtrusive and restless desire to obtain notoriety by a seeming zeal to rectify public evils, and to promote the public good; a disposition to associate with those who are given to change; but I mean, a determination, founded upon conscientious conviction, associated with deep humility and modestly expressed, to do all the good you can, and to leave the world the better for your having lived in it. No man "liveth to himself" is the dictate of reason, as well as the command of revelation. Each man, not being like Alexander Selkirk, the solitary inhabitant of a desolate island, is, as a member of society, a debtor to the community from which he receives benefits, and is under corresponding obligations to it. Every man can do something to benefit other men, and what he can do he ought to do. If this is his duty at all times, it is especially so at the present time. Benevolence, as I have already shown, is one of the noblest and most identifying moral features of the age. Never was so much doing for the well-being of mankind. It is a glorious thing, and makes one grateful for the present, and hopeful for the future. Men are everywhere stepping out of the centre of selfishness into the broad circumference of the general good. It is an age of action, of action in the cause of God and human happiness. Public spirit has become with multitudes a principle, and with multitudes more a fashion. Selfishness acquires at such a time peculiar enormity, whether it be the selfishness of avarice, which will give no money for the public good; of indolence, which will give no labour; or of literary or scientific taste, which will give no time. Under the influence of public spirit the world is improving; ignorance, vice, and misery are yielding to its influence; and knowledge, truth, holiness, and happiness are bringing on the millennium. The religious institutions of this age are its own glory and the hope of every other yet to come. They are preparing the earth for its emancipation from the thraldom and misery under which it has been groaning for nearly six thousand years, and for the glorious liberty of truth, holiness, happiness. At such a time will you be torpid at the centre of universal activity? Will you now refuse to sympathise with philanthropists, reformers, and evangelists? · Never, no never, were the youth of any preceding generation called to a work so great, so noble, and so beneficent, as is offered to the young men of this generation. Never had they such an opportunity of signalising themselves by active benevolence, or were they in such danger of disgracing themselves by selfishness and indolence, as in the present day. "Begin early then to cherish a public spirit, because if you do not possess this disposition in the morning of life, you probably never will. This is a virtue that rarely springs up late in life. If it grow and flourish at all, it must be planted in youth, and be nourished by the warm sunshine and rain of the spring season of existence. He who cares only for himself in youth, will be a very niggard in manhood, and a wretched miser in old age."*

A young man rightly impressed with the circumstances of the age, will guard assiduously against its evils, for every age has its peculiar dangers, and the present one forms no exception to the general rule. I can only briefly enumerate those perils.

He will check and restrain an excessive love of pleasure, which in many cases leads to dissipation, in others unfits for business, and in far more altogether indisposes the mind for sober thought mental culture and true religion. This is one of the growing tendencies of the day in which we live, and threatens infinite damage to the present and eternal welfare of mankind, by bringing on an age of frivolity, sensuality, and practical atheism. Find your pleasure, young men, in the improvement of your mind, in attention to business, in true piety, and in active benevolence. Is there not scope enough for enjoyment here? "Wisdom's ways are ways of pleasantness, and all her paths are peace."

Excessive worldliness is another of the dangers of this age. In a country, compared with which Phœnicia, Tyre, Carthage, and Corinth, viewed as commercial nations, were mere pedlars; and in an age, compared with which every other that has preceded it, was a time of stagnancy; there is most

* Dr. Hawes' Lectures to Young Men.

imminent peril of sinking into the mere worldling, and living only to get wealth. Never was competition so fierce, and never was there so great danger of having the conscience benumbed, the moral principle prostrated, the heart rendered callous, and even the intellect rifled of its strength, or sharpened only into cunning and duplicity by the love of money, as in the age in which we live. Wealth is the god of Britain's idolatry just now; and you, without watchfulness and prayer, are in danger of bowing devoutly at its shrine, becoming its worshippers, and immolating your souls as a burnt-offering on its altars.

Pride of intellect, leading to scepticism and infidelity, is a most fearful source of peril in this age. I have already alluded to the conflict now going on between the various forms of unbelief and Christianity. The struggle is eagerly maintained by both parties; and though to the sincere believer in Christianity there is no doubt how it will terminate, yet in the meanwhile there is great reason to fear, from the boldness and subtlety of the attacks of infidelity, that some, and not a few, victories will be gained by the opponents of Christianity. The natural bias of youth is almost always to infidelity. And such is the case, not merely because, as Bacon says, "a little philosophy inclines us to atheism, and a great deal of philosophy carries us back to religion;" but youth has an intellectual bias against religion, because that would humble the arrogance of the understanding: and a moral bias against it; because it would check the indulgence of the passions; and these two causes will account for the prevalence of infidelity among so many young men of the present day. In an age when the mind of man is pouring out its prodigies in such profusion, there is imminent peril of believing it almost omnipotent omniscient and all-sufficient, and of man's accounting himself his own God, and feeling as if he needed no other. The tendency is to that Pantheism which, instead of saying nothing is God, says everything is God. Man-worship is the idolatry of the day, as well as money-worship. And yet notwithstanding the prodigies of intellect which man can and does accomplish, how little way does all go to make him either holy or happy. The profoundest philosopher and the noblest son of science, as much need a revelation from God to guide them in matters of religion and morals, as the peasant or the child.

Superstition, leading to formalism in religion, instead of the religion of the intellect, the heart, the conscience, and the life, is with some, though not so much with you, a danger of the age. Yet though it is chiefly among that portion of our race most under the influence of passion and imagination, that superstition gains its victories, it is evident from many facts that even the most masculine minds of your sex are not proof against the seductions of Popery and its cognate systems. And when we see over what mighty intellects this dreadful system has cast its shade or thrown its spell, and what gifted minds it has induced to drink of the Circean cup of its enchantments, we must not speak too strongly on the probability that none but the feeble or the imaginative will yield to its sorceries.

Young men, study then, seriously consider, and be duly impressed with, the dangers that characterise the age in which you live, dangers by which you are surrounded. I speak not now of the ordinary perils which apply to every age alike, the dangers arising from the ardour of passion, the pruriency of imagination, the influence of example, the love of companionship, the temptations to sensuality, to intemperance, to dishonesty, to extravagance, which beset the young man's path at all times: these have been already considered in the previous chapters. But I now speak of those which appertain to the age in which it is your lot to live. Do not be ignorant, insensible, or indifferent, in such a situation: nor treat the subject with carelessness or levity. Ponder, devoutly ponder, the subject. As your protection from these perils, possess yourselves of personal religion. This, and this only, is your adequate defence. This is your shield and buckler. Watch and pray, that you enter not into temptation. Put your trust in God. With his fear before your eyes, and his love reigning in your hearts, you are safe, and will escape unscathed from all these perils to which you are constantly exposed.

Reflect, then, upon your condition. Here you are in being, existing not by your own choice, but by the appointment of Providence, in one of the most eventful eras that ever elapsed in the history of the world or the flight of time. For you, all preceding nations, ages, and generations, with all their mightiest men, and their greatest discoveries, events, inventions, and exploits, have existed. Whatever valour has won, science explored, art contrived, labour achieved, suffering purchased, has come down to you. For you, heroes have bled in the field, martyrs suffered on the scaffold or at the stake, philosophers studied in the closet, monarchs reigned on the throne, statesmen legislated in the senate, and travellers crossed the desert or the ocean. All the light and experience of nearly six thousand years concentrate in your history. You receive the full benefit of the art of printing, the revival of letters, the Reformation of the sixteenth century, and the English Revolution of the seventeenth. For you, America has been disclosed in its secret solitude between the two great oceans. For you, the British sway has been established in Asia and Africa. For you, civil and religious liberty has been matured in its most unrestricted form. For you, Bible Societies, Missionary Societies, Tract Societies, and all the other institutions of Christian benevolence, have been established and made ready to your hands. All nations, all ages, all generations have laboured, and you have entered into their labours. You stand surrounded with all the spoils of time, the wealth of nations, the achievements of humanity, and the gifts of Providence. And I now ask, " What manner of men ought you to be."

So much for the past and the present, and then the future. What a future ! Which of the seals is breaking for the next century. All men are fixing an eye of inquisitive curiosity and anxious expectation upon the unfolding of the scroll which contains the history of the next century. What may we not expect from and for humanity within that period ! What may not be hoped for from science, the arts, learning, and religion ! All, all, under God, depends upon you and your coevals. Into your hands, as the next generation that is to be, must come the destinies of futurity. You, and others of your age, must cause the wheels of the world's progress to roll backward or forward. You, you are to determine the character of the next age, for you are to form it. Look over the world's intellectual and moral condition, its civilization and evangelization ; look over the civil and religious interests of your country, its government, its laws, its liberties, its institutions; look over the state and extent of the church of Christ, the world's illuminator and regenerator; and recollect that all these interests are soon to be in your hands. You cannot escape from this trust, and the responsibility which it involves. Providence has fixed it upon you, and you cannot throw it off. For the manner in which you sustain these interests you are accountable not only to futurity, but at the bar of God. "You must exist, you must exist in the midst of society, burdened with the weighty responsibility that grows out of the relations you sustain to the living beings around you, and to the generations that are coming after you; and you must take the eternal consequences of living and acting in these deeply interesting circumstances."

Young men, is there nothing here that deserves and demands reflection? Perhaps you have never thought of it as you should : have never seriously considered the obligations imposed by the peculiar features of the age: and have never revolved the fact that the value, importance, and accountability of human life are to be measured, not by a fixed, but a variable scale, and that they rise and fall according to circumstances. In innumerable cases, one man can now do in the common arts and manufactures, what ten or twenty men could not do a century ago; and this is as true in regard to the operations of benevolence, as it is to those of trade, and thus the value of existence, and the importance of individual existence, are far greater than they once were. A man is a man at all times, but he is more of a man as regards power and achievement at one time than another. In such a day as this, then, not only as

related to the past but to the future, I again ask, and
with all possible emphasis, "What manner of men ought
you to be?" I want you to be worthy of what the
past has done for you, of what the present confers upon
you, and of what the future will demand from you. I
am solicitous that you should not prove ungrateful to
the one, or unfaithful to the other. I tremble lest the
current of improvement which has flowed so strongly to
you, should flow languidly from you. I press again and
again that question, What manner of men ought you to
be? Yes; and I add to this question the apostle's
words, "in all manner of holy conversation and godliness." For this, and this only, can prepare and fit you
to become blessings in the highest sense of the term, to
the age in which you live, or to those which follow. It
is this you need for yourselves, above all arts and sciences. Religion has done more to exalt human nature,
and does exalt it more wherever it is possessed, than all
other endowments combined. It is the noblest element
of mental and moral growth, both in heaven and earth.
Indeed, no man can be truly great, unless his mind is
enlarged and his heart purified by its sacred power.
This was the grace and glory of our first father when
he came glowing in moral beauty from the hand of his
Creator. It gave elevation and grandeur of soul to
prophets and apostles; sacred heroism to martyrs; and
in modern days it placed high in the scale of being such
men as Newton, Milton, Boyle, Locke, and Pascal.
And while it is your own highest dignity and richest
happiness, it will prove your mightiest instrument
of power for the well-being of others. That which
makes you Christians, is that which would make you
philanthropists. Do you wish to benefit and bless the

world in the most extensive and most lasting manner, aim at its subjugation to the power of religion. The world is to be converted to Christ, the beauties of holiness are to cover every region, and the song of salvation is to float on every breeze. It is not science that is to hush the deepest groans of creation, nor the arts that are to wipe away the bitterest tears of humanity; these triumphs are reserved for religion. Many an humble follower of the Lamb who has paced the walks of the Crystal Palace, and surveyed with but partial knowledge, its teeming wonders and indescribable beauties, shall do more to bless his species in the way of direct moral and religious benefit, than any of the skilful artificers whose productions attracted the eyes and excited the admiration of gazing millions. One human soul possesses a value compared with which the unrivalled glories of that wonderful collection are but a thing of nought: the loss of one such soul would be an infinitely greater calamity than the destruction of that whole building and all its contents by fire : while its salvation would be to him who obtains it a greater treasure than his possession of all that wealth of nations, and to him who achieves it a greater honour in the world of spirits, than to have contrived that palace, and to have crowded it with its matchless and innumerable wonders. What a motive to seek our own salvation first of all, and then to obey our high and noble calling to seek the salvation of our fellow-men. Rise, my young friends, to your high, your holy, and your beneficent calling, live for the present age, and send forward an influence through all future ages. Live for glory, honour, and immortality, and let nothing satisfy you, either for yourself or for others, but that which is eternal.

CHAPTER XII.

EARLY DEATH, OR THE REVIEW OF LIFE IN OLD AGE.

*One dieth in his full strength, being wholly at ease, and
quiet.* Job xxi, 22.

*Now when he came nigh unto the gate of the city, behold,
there was a dead man carried out, the only son of his
mother, and she was a widow.* Luke vii, 12.

*We spend our years as a tale that is told. The days
of our years are three-score years and ten: and if by
reason of strength they be four-score years, yet is
their strength labour and sorrow: for it is soon cut
off, and we fly away.* Psalm xc, 10.

You remember, perhaps, the incident recorded of
Xerxes, the Persian monarch, that when reviewing the
mighty host, with which he was then invading Greece,
and which numbered more than two millions of men, he
burst into tears upon the reflection that when far less
than a century had passed, not an individual of all those
multitudes would remain alive. Pity that he had not
thought how many myriads of them his mad ambition was
hurrying to the grave by the devastations of war! With
like pensive, but more practical feelings, let us look over
the population of our globe, and consider that, according
to the average term of human life, nearly a thousand
millions of immortal beings pass from our world to their

eternal doom every thirty years. What a conqueror is
death! What an evil is sin, which is the cause of this
mortality! What a world is that beyond the grave,
where all these countless millions assemble! And what
a being is God, who is the Author of their separate
existence, pursues each one through his whole individual
history, and will not suffer one to be left forgotten in
the grave, overlooked in the judgment, or left without
his just and appropriate doom in the retribution of eternity! Are you in want of subjects for reflection and
useful moralising? What themes are these! Man is
born to die: death is ever doing its work; and the tide
of mortality is ever setting in upon the shore of eternity,
bearing with it all that belong to the human species.
In looking at the race of Adam only in this aspect of it,
in seeing one generation follow another to the grave in
endless succession, like the various vegetable and animal
tribes, we are ready to ask the question of the Psalmist,
"Wherefore hast thou made all men in vain?" And
truly if there were no other state of existence than this,
there would be reason in the inquiry; for, apart from
immortality, life is a dream, and man a shadow. Comparing the nobleness of his faculties, with the shortness
and uncertainty of his life, and the vanity of his pursuits, he would, if this world only were the sphere
of his existence, seem to cast a reflection upon the
wisdom of his Creator, who had invested him with the
powers of an angel, and yearnings after immortality,
merely to mind earthly things. But with the eternal
world thrown open to our view, and its state of rewards
and punishments disclosed to our faith, how momentous
are that term and condition of existence which are
granted us here as a discipline and probation for im-

mortality! With far other feelings than those of contempt or complaint, I now echo the inquiry, "What is
your life?" Death is an agent that works by no rule
or order with which we are acquainted; sometimes
passing by the aged to take the young: leaving the
sickly to seize upon the healthy: removing the useful
and sparing the worthless. This brings me to the
subject of the present chapter, Early Death or the
Review of Life in Old Age.

Let us consider the first alternative. The young
man may die. Indeed the fact recorded in the text is
often repeated. It is in the order of nature for the
aged to die, and for the young to live : but this order is
not always observed. More deviations from it take place
in the human race than in any other tribe of creatures.
But few of the young of the inferior animals die
of disease, compared with those of the human race.
Life seems to be precarious in proportion to its value.
What multitudes of young people die annually in this
country of consumption, that bane of English youth!
It is mournful to me to recollect how many beautiful
flowers I have seen thus cut down in spring. I have
during my ministry followed to the grave young persons
in sufficient numbers, were they all still living, to form
a congregation of no inconsiderable size. And what
has been, still is, and ever will be, in respect of the
mortality of youth. There is always something affecting in the death of a young man. In some cases it
realises the scene described by the evangelist in one
of the texts at the head of this chapter, "Now when he
came nigh to the gate of this city, behold there was a
dead man carried out, the only son of his mother, and
she was a widow." Her only comfort is removed, and

the last light of her tabernacle is put out; her one tie to life is cut, and she feels left alone upon a bleak and desolate shore. In other cases it is the son of wealthy parents, whose brightest prospects hung suspended upon that one precious life, the termination of which causes them to repeat in sorrow, not perhaps unmixed with complaint, the words of Job, " He destroyeth the hope of man." In other instances it is the death of a youth of great promise; he had finished his education, served his apprenticeship, and with talents that excited the liveliest hopes of success, and with virtues that had already ensured admiration, was just about to step upon the stage of active life. He had formed, perhaps, a connection of chaste and tender love with one worthy of him, and with whom he expected soon to share the cup of connubial happiness; and then, when all was smiling around him, and he was returning so joyously its smiles, he is smitten down by death. Oh, to see that noble flower, when nearly full-blown, droop its head upon its stalk, wither, and die! How many tears are shed, how many hopes are disappointed, how many sorrowful voices exclaim, " What would he not have been had he lived!" When the aged man, who has lived out his term, expires, we are not surprised; we expected it, and were prepared for it. But for the young to die, for whom no fears nor dread anticipations were cherished, strikes us, not only with grief, but with astonishment.

I will now put two cases before you.

I. That of the young man who dies a true Christian. He has remembered his Creator in the days of his youth, repented of sin, believed in Christ, lived in the fear of God. He has not forgotten or neglected religion.

This was his mode of life, when death came upon him. For the king of terrors pays no more respect to piety than to talent. Many a bright blossom of the church, as well as of the world, is nipped off by his relentless hand. The Christian youth has often been removed, as well as the irreligious one. In such a case, when he found he must die, he felt serious, solemn, and at first somewhat sorrowful, on looking round on all he was parting from, on seeing the mists of the dark valley rising over the landscape which he had been accustomed to survey with so much delight, and on witnessing all his prospects suddenly fading before his eyes. But when his faith came to his relief, bringing with it the "everlasting consolation" of the Gospel, and "a good hope through grace, a hope full of immortality," he recovered his tranquillity, and in the prospect of that glory, honour, and eternal life, to which he believed he was going, he could then serenely look "On all he's leaving, now no longer his." We are ready to say, what hopes are buried in his tomb, what expectations of himself, his parents, and his friends! He was permitted to see, and even to touch, many things that were attractive and alluring, but to grasp nothing. He was conducted to an eminence whence he could survey a beautiful prospect as his seemingly destined possession, and then closed his eyes in death. He had but a fragment of existence, and what made it all the more mournful was, that the fragment indicated how precious the whole would have been, had it been spared. Did he not live in vain? No, he did not live in vain. He answered the highest end of existence, as certainly as if he had lived out the threescore years and ten, or fourscore years, of man's existence; as if he had entered upon business and succeeded in obtaining wealth; as if he had married and had raised a numerous and respectable family; as if he had obtained rank, station, and influence in society, or renown. For what is the highest end of human life? The salvation of the immortal soul, a preparation and a portion for eternity, a meetness for heaven. Man's chief end is to glorify God and enjoy him for ever. Now, the truly pious person has accomplished this end, has secured this object as completely, though he die at the age of twenty, as if he had lived to that of seventy. He says on his death-bed, " True there are some things I could have wished to live for and I feel that in not being permitted to remain and accomplish them, I am giving up some of the secondary and inferior ends of existence, but I have fulfilled the one great end of life. I have obtained the one thing needful, even the salvation of my soul. I have accomplished the loftiest and most benevolent purpose of God in sending me upon earth. I have not lived in vain. He who is made for immortality, and has everlasting ages of pure delight before him, need not regret the loss of a few years of pleasure mixed with pain. I am upon the threshold of eternity, and have attended to that which will prepare me for an eternity of bliss. I am disappointed in the hope of some little things, but I am not disappointed in the pursuit of far greater ones, and in the eternal fruition shall forget the momentary pain. I am parting from friends dear as life, but I am going to others still dearer. I am turning away from bright prospects, but infinitely brighter ones are opening upon my view. I am going away early from earth, but am going as early to heaven : and my existence in the former is shortened only that my existence in the latter may be extended. The connections whom I am leaving pity me for my early death ; the angels in Paradise congratulate me on so soon quitting a vale of tears, and so early retiring from all the trials, temptations, and dangers of this scene of conflict. I am now within sight of glory, and am all but absolutely certain of being safely brought to it. Who can tell but I am taken home to escape perils which might have been too great for my strength. I therefore die without murmuring, and depart with cheerful submission, though I die in youth, since it is to be with Christ, which is far better." Happy youth ! Yes, happy, to have thy warfare thus early and successfully accomplished, to win the victory at the very commencement of the battle ! So soon to gain and wear the crown !*

II. But I must now turn to a class of young persons the reverse of all this : I mean those who die in youth, but die without religion. Alas ! alas ! what an idea ! How sad, how mournful, how awful ! To die without religion ! To go out of the world without

---

* I will give an illustration of this by a scene, part of which I witnessed myself. One Lord's-day, after the morning service, I was requested to visit a gentleman who was alarmingly ill, at one of our inns, on his way to Scotland. It is not my custom, for want of strength, to visit the sick on Sabbath-days, but this case was urgent, and I went. I was introduced to the sick chamber of a remarkably fine young man, of considerable worldly respectability, who was attended by two anxious sisters and a brother. They were bearing him home with many apprehensions that he would die on the road. My visit was one of solemn and mournful delight, for I found him a real Christian, expecting death hourly, but expecting it in the most serene and hopeful frame of mind, as his kind deliverer from the burden of the flesh. Since then I received from one of his sorrowing sisters the following account of his peaceful dismissal :

comfort in death, and without hope beyond it! And usually those who live without religion, die without it. Death-bed repentances are in most cases little to be thought of, and less to be depended upon. True repentance is never too late, but late repentance is rarely true. Religion is not like the act of a man who in a shipwreck is cast into the sea, and there in the greatest alarm, as a matter of necessity, lays hold of and grasps a plank as a means of saving himself from being drowned. But, on the contrary, it resembles the conduct of one who deliberately and by choice steps on board a vessel or a boat, to convey him on some gainful or pleasurable voyage. And, therefore, those who live without religion, I repeat, generally die without it. Everything renders the death of a young man who dies without religion peculiarly melancholy. He has no comfort in death; on the contrary, he has most melancholy reflections. Comfort in death can come only from religion. The petrifying process of a stoical philosophy, or of a hardening infidelity, may, and sometimes does, so turn a man's heart into stone, that he may acquire a stupid insen-

"* * * He suffered greatly the last three weeks, but was enabled to bear all with much patience, feeling it came from the hand of a loving Father. His growth in grace was very rapid: he seemed to enjoy largely the teaching of the Holy Spirit. The Lord was most gracious in the support and comfort he vouchsafed to him. He often seemed lost in adoring wonder, contemplating the amazing love of God in Christ Jesus. Although he had much to make life to be enjoyed, he left earth without regret; indeed he said he should not like to return again to the world, except from one desire, that he might be honoured in doing something for the Saviour. When in much suffering, some hours before his death, it was said to him, 'Soon will this be ended, and then, happy, happy spirit!' he faintly replied, 'Happy even now.' Amongst his last words were, 'Peace, peace.'"

Are you, if called to die in youth, prepared to die so happy?

sibility even in death; but actual comfort can come only from religion. It is the hope of immortality alone which can be as a lamp in the dark valley of the shadow of death, and the man destitute of it, passes through the gloomy region, either in perturbation and mental agony, or in sullen indifference. In this case, there are also the vexation, disappointment, and distress, of giving up life so early. A feeling of mortification springs up, akin to that of a person reluctantly called away at the commencement of a pleasurable scene which he intensely wishes to see completed, while others are left behind still to enjoy it after his departure. For a while he resists and resents the thought of dying. He clings to life with a tenacity which looks as if he could not, would not, dare not, die. He sends for his companions, who endeavour to cheer him, and persuade him he will yet do well, and he talks with them of plans of future enjoyment, when he shall recover. Disease, however, progresses, and extinguishes these hopes: and at last comes, first the dreadful fear, and then the still more dreadful certainty, that he cannot live. Thoughts such as these are in his mind, although he may be afraid to give utterance to them in language. " It is really a very hard case to die so young. Before I have well tried what life is, to be thus hurried out of it! To have ties so tender, and only just formed, severed! To see all my hopes so soon, and so suddenly cut off, and all my prospects shut up! To have the cup of pleasure dashed from my lips, just as I had begun to sip it, and before I had taken one full draught! To see others of my own age in full health, pursuing their schemes, and likely to live and prosper, while I am dying and going down to the grave! How cruel is inexorable fate! How I almost wish I had never been born! For what has this short life proved to me, but a a disappointment? My existence has been rather a shadow than a substance, a mockery rather than a realisation of hope. I have lived only for this world, which I am now leaving for ever, and have made no provision nor preparation for that on which I am about to enter. I have neglected my soul and have forgotten God. I am wrecked at the commencement of the voyage of life, and shall perish, with all that belongs to me, both as a mortal and immortal creature." How distressing to meet death in such a frame as this, so cold, so hopeless, so comfortless, and cheerless! A young man dying without religion is, according to his own views and reflections, cut off, without having seen known or enjoyed much of life. He has not had his share of life's business enjoyments and possessions. His views of his case are quite correct. He is withdrawn from the gay circle, and the scenes of business, as soon as he entered them. And as he had lived without religion, and secured the possession of nothing else, he has lived in vain. His case is the very opposite of that which we have considered in the former part of this chapter. He has not sought the one great end of ex- istence, the salvation of his immortal soul, and all the secondary and inferior ends are failing him. The supreme objects of our being, which God proposed to him, he turned away from; and the inferior ones, which he proposed to himself, are turning away from him. He lived only for this world, and the deity to which he consecrated his life has left him almost immediately after the surrender. He has had no time to gain worldly wealth or distinction, and has wilfully put away from him the opportunity which he once possessed, to lay up treasures in heaven; and there he now lies, with all his hopes of time a wreck, and no hope of heaven and immortality rising up in their place. Follow him on to eternity. No compensation is found there for what he has lost here. It is not in his case as it is in that of the religious young man, whose early death is so much taken from earth to be added to heaven; for he has not sought heaven, and has no portion there. He has lost the possession and enjoyment of both worlds at once; his few fleeting pleasures on earth are not followed with the fullness of joy which is at God's right hand, and the pleasures that are for evermore in his presence. He has been suddenly hurried away from the springs of earthly delight, and no fountain in heaven, no "river of water of life, clear as crystal, proceeding from the throne of God and the Lamb," comes in to supply their place. Earth rolls from beneath his feet, and heaven stoops not to sustain and receive his sinking spirit. He rises not to glory as does the young departing Christian, exulting as he looks on the fading scenes of terrestrial beauty, and exclaiming, "I have lost nothing." It is his, on the contrary, as he resigns his spirit, mournfully to confess, "I have lost everything. I am early driven out of earth, and the portals of heaven open not to receive me." Nor is this all; for the death of an irreligious young man reaches the climax of its distress and misery in the consideration that his early removal is so much time taken from the occupations, possessions, and pleasures of earth, to be added to the bitter pains of eternal death, the inconceivable torments of the bottomless pit. To the religious man who dies in youth, whatever he may part from, still death is gain. He gains infinitely more than he can lose; but the irreligious young man not only loses all he had, and all he hoped for on earth, but gains nothing in return but the loss of his soul's salvation with it, and has in his miserable condition the agony of contrasting what he had left on earth with what he has gained in the dark world of hell. He will not have the poor, wretched, meagre satisfaction, if such it can be called, of reflecting that on his way to perdition, he had his fill of earthly pleasure and business, and, like the rich man, lived long and fared sumptuously every day, before he descended to that place of torment. On the contrary, he will have through eternity to reflect that he received nothing in exchange for his soul but the vices and follies of youth, and sacrificed his immortal interests for the pleasures of sin, confined, as in his case they were, to the brief season of his short life. O! how mean, how insignificant a price this, for which to barter away immortal bliss! How far below even the folly and impiety of that profane man who sold his birthright for one morsel of meat!

These things, young men, are submitted for your most serious consideration. Presume not upon long life. Millions die in youth every year. How know you that you will not be included in the millions of this year? You are 'in robust health. What says the patriarch Job? "One dieth in his full strength." Accident may crush you in a moment. Fever may seize you, and, after a few days' delirium, during which no place may be found for repentance, may send you to the bar of God. Or the seeds of consumption may already be sown and germinating in your frame. Death may have selected you for his victim; the arrow may be fitted to the string, the aim taken, and the shaft about to fly to the mark. Should you die as you now are, will yours be the death of the religious or the irreligious young man? Which? Let that question sink deeply into your heart.

Still, it must be conceded to you that you may live to old age: and I will now take up the other alternative, and suppose that this privilege, if privilege it may be called, will be granted to you. I will imagine that by the ordination of Providence you will number threescore years and ten, or fourscore years. You will then have to review life. Memory will naturally revert to the past. Who arrives at the top of a hill without turning to look back? Who ends a long journey without reconsidering its incidents? And who comes to old age without some thoughts of the years that have elapsed, and the scenes that have intervened between infancy and senility? Memory cannot be inoperative, unless, indeed, it has altogether perished amidst the wreck of the faculties which old age sometimes produces. It will look back, it must. What kind of an old age would you like to have? How, and with what reflections and reminiscences, would you wish to spend the close of life? Would you have it bright and serene, with pleasant and peaceful recollections, and "calm as summer evenings be;" or rendered cloudy, dark, and stormy, by a painful retrospect and a troubled conscience? I am aware that there are some persons so little given to reflection, others so stupified by the paralysing influence of old age, and some so fully occupied to the last with the pursuits and cares of this world, as to go out of life, even at its most advanced period, without serious consideration of either the past or the future. But what a melancholy spectacle is an un-reflecting old man, a human being coming to the close of a long earthly existence, and yet not looking back with the question, " How have I lived, and what have I done with all those years which my Creator has given to me?" Such cases, however, one would hope, are comparatively few.

The retrospect of life is in every view of it a solemn affair; indeed, the most solemn except the account to be rendered at the judgment-day. Each portion of existence as it passes, every year, month, week, day, demands a retrospective survey, with the question, " How has it been spent?" How much more a whole life ! Man has but one life on earth, and that one can never be recalled, whatever mistakes may have been made. Oh! what momentous interests are bound up in that one life; and then it must all be accounted for to God! What an impressive spectacle is that of an old man spending the evening of life in turning over the leaves of his history, and reading those records which are to be the ground of his condemnation or acquittal at the bar of God, before which he must soon take his stand! How solemn a position is it to be placed where childhood, youth, manhood, and old age, with all their good or evil, will pass before, not only the memory, but the judgment and the conscience, in a series of dissolving views !

Oh ! how much is comprehended in the term of only one man's lengthened existence ! How many, various and momentous acts, scenes, and events, pass before the mind of the aged man, in reviewing his pilgrimage on earth. There is time, with all its scores of years, its hundreds of months, its thousands of weeks, its

myriads of days, to say nothing of its minutes and
moments. There are the end and purpose for which
the whole was given. There are all the means of grace
and the opportunities of salvation which have been
granted him; the Bible, with all its doctrines and
duties, promises and precepts, invitations and threatenings; thousands of Sabbaths and sermons and sacramental seasons; the instructions of his parents, the
counsels of friends, the ministrations of his pastor, and
the books he has read; the strivings of God's Spirit,
and the remonstrances of his own conscience. There
are all his opportunities of doing good and getting
good neglected or improved; all he has done, and all
he has not done, which he might have done. There
are the sins or virtues of his childhood, youth, manhood,
and old age. There is his conduct as a tradesman
in getting money, whether by good or bad means.
There is the manner in which the relations of life have
been discharged by him, and his behaviour as a son, a
brother, a husband, a father, a master, or a servant.
There is the use that he has made of prosperity or
adversity. There is his kindness or cruelty to others.
There is the manner in which he has disappointed or
fulfilled the expectations that were formed concerning
him. There are the recollections of the temptations
which he has thrown in the way of others, or which
he has been exposed to himself, and which he has
resisted or yielded to. What a landscape to look over,
what a road to turn back upon, what a scene to survey,
what a history to read! How much of all this is
crowded into threescore years and ten! What an
employment is the review of life! To spend the long
evening of old age in conference with our conscience

over our past existence of probation, and our future state of retribution! Oh! to see the unrepented, unforgiven sins of threescore years and ten occupying the lengthened space, and to hear voices from within and without, saying, " You have lost your life, your soul, your God, your all!" In that situation there will be many things that will alike appear to all. All will be impressed with the brevity of life. All will echo the language of the apostle, "What is our life? It is even as a vapour that appeareth but a little while, and straightway vanisheth away." All will look back upon a chequered scene of light and shade, though some have had more light, and some more shade than others. All will have proved, more or less, the uncertain and unsatisfying nature of what is earthly, though some have made better use than others of their knowledge. But still there is a strange and melancholy difference of character and of feeling with which the impressive survey of life is made.

Consider the infidel reviewing life : if indeed there be a man who can persist in his creed of negations till he has reached threescore years and ten. What has he to look back upon? He has cut himself off from the prospect of immortality, and reduced himself to the idea of a mere ephemeron, which having fluttered through its brief day, is about to sink into the darkness and the sleep of eternal night, into nothing. Behind him in the past is mere animalism : before him in the future is annihilation. He has lived without faith, and is dying without hope. He would have no God, and he will have no heaven. Life with him has been spent (O what a pursuit !) in persuading himself, and en-deavouring to persuade others that man is only a rational brute. He has worn out a long term of years in hostility to the Bible, and in enmity to religion. He has ever been at war with that which others have counted their richest honour and their dearest bliss. His business delight and endeavour have been to oppose the Bible, to dash the cup of consolation from the lips of the mourner, to rob the widow of her last possession, to take from youth its safest guide, and from age its strongest prop. Humane and beneficent purpose! Miserable man, to have grown grey in attempting to put out the light of the moral sun, and to die, after all, in despair of that result being ever accomplished; and to die, not without occasional and horrible fears, and still more horrible forebodings, that he has been fighting against God. May this dreadful retrospect never be yours!

Now contemplate the aged man of pleasure. And here the picture shall be drawn from life, and shall be no imaginary portrait. You shall hear the testimony of one, " by whom the world, with its fashions and its follies, its principles and its practices, has been proposed in form to Englishmen, as the proper object of their attention and devotion. Lord Chesterfield has avowed as much with respect to himself, and by his writings said in effect to it, ' Save me, for thou art my God.' He has tendered his assistance to act as priest upon the occasion, and conduct the ceremonial. At the close of life, however, his God he found was about to forsake him, and therefore was forsaken by him. You shall hear some of his last sentiments and expressions, which have not been hitherto, so far as I know, duly noticed and applied to their use, that of furnishing an antidote, (and they furnish a very powerful one) to the noxious poisons contained in his volumes. They are well worthy your strictest attention. ' I have seen,' said this man of the world, ' the silly rounds of business and pleasure, and have done with them all. I have enjoyed all the pleasures of the world, and consequently know their futility, and do not regret their loss. I appraise them at their real value, which is, in truth, very low; whereas those who have not experienced always overrate them. They only see their gay outside, and are dazzled with their glare: but I have been behind the scenes. I have seen all the coarse pullies and dirty ropes which exhibit and move the gaudy machines: I have seen and smelt the tallow candles which illuminate the whole decoration to the astonishment and admiration of an ignorant audience. When I reflect back upon what I have seen, what I have heard, and what I have done, I can hardly persuade myself that all that frivolous hurry, and bustle, and pleasure of the world had any reality; but I look upon all that is passed as one of those romantic dreams which opium commonly occasions; and I by no means desire to repeat the nauseous dose for the sake of the fugitive dream. Shall I tell you that I bear this melancholy situation with that meritorious constancy and resignation which most people boast of? No, for I really cannot help it. I bear it because I must bear it, whether I will or no. I think of nothing but killing time the best way I can, now that he has become mine enemy. It is my resolution to sleep in the carriage during the remainder of the journey.' When a Christian priest speaks slightingly of the world, he is supposed to do so in the way of his profession, and to decry through envy the pleasures he is forbidden to taste. But here, I think, you have the testimony of a witness every way competent. No man ever knew the world better, or enjoyed more of its favours, than this nobleman. Yet you see in how poor, abject, and wretched a condition, at the time when he most wanted help and comfort, the world left him, and he left the world. The sentences above cited from him, compose in my humble opinion, the most striking and affecting sermon upon the vanity of the world, ever yet preached to mankind."* Such was the confession in his old age, to a son, (who afterwards died by his own hand,) of Lord Chesterfield, the oracle of fashionable life, and no mean statesman. Would you spend the evening of life thus?

You may now turn to the old age of the unreclaimed prodigal. He who in youth settled to no business, practised no virtue, feared not God nor regarded man, but, bursting through the restraints of parental authority, and trampling under foot the laws of prudence and morality, gave himself up to the indulgences of passion, and plunged into the depths of vice. Such was his youth. His manhood was little better, it had the addition of being a constant struggle against the poverty and want, which were the consequences of his misconduct. The wonder is that he lived so long; that human nature could survive what he had passed through. The wintry season has come upon him, and oh, what a winter, how bleak and desolate! His circumstances, how deplorably necessitous; his mind, how intolerably wretched! In some cases the poor creature is dependent upon the bounty of friends; bounty never bestowed but with reluctance, because bestowed upon one so unworthy, and rather flung at him in anger, than given

* Bishop Horne's Sermons.

with courtesy and kindness: in other instances, he is driven to the necessity of picking up, by various mean and discreditable artifices, a poor and precarious living. Destitute of all but necessaries, and having few comparatively of them, his miserable existence seems protracted for no purpose but to show what a wretched old age is made by vicious youth. To him appertains the language of one of Job's friends, "His bones are full of the sins of his youth, which shall lie down with him in the dust." But his poverty is the least part of his misery, for he has, and can have, no peace of mind. When he reflects at all, his thoughts prey, like vultures, upon his peace, and he is unable to drive them away. For him the retrospect is indeed most painful. Life with him has been worse than a blank. On what a dark and winding course has he to turn his affrighted gaze! What follies and what sins meet his eye at every turn! Childhood, youth, and manhood, are all alike distressing in retrospect. Not one bright or verdant spot presents itself to his survey in either. Oh! that some oblivious draught could drive the whole from his memory, and that, with the recollections of the past, could be extinguished the anticipations of the future. He is as little respected by others as he respects himself. No eye beams upon him with affection, no countenance greets him with a smile, no voice addresses to him the language of respect, no heart yields to him its sympathy, no door is thrown open to welcome him. He is an outcast from society, a burden to his friends, (if he has any left,) a torment to himself, and a nuisance to the earth on which he walks. He is one of sin's most miserable slaves, one of Satan's most degraded vassals, and one of hell's most fitting denizens. Of all the spectacles upon earth, the most melancholy, therefore, is such a wicked old man. Look at it, my young friends, and tremble.

I next exhibit the aged worldling, the man who has lived exclusively for wealth, who has realised his wishes, and who spends the evening of his life in thinking upon his treasures, and the toil and anxiety it has cost him to acquire them. And what are his reflections? In some cases, I have no doubt, there is a feeling of gratification at his success. He traces his gradual rise and prosperity in life with gleeful delight, and compares himself with other less happy adventurers. His imagination revels in his wealth, and he thinks how much he is leaving to his heirs. Poor creature, and this is all! No gratitude to God; no recollection of money got by his blessing, or spent for his glory; no testimony of his conscience, that he has honoured God with his substance; no plea-surable reminiscences of good done with his property; no expectation of hearing God say to him, " Well done, good and faithful servant." No, nothing but the re-flection that he has been what the world calls a fortunate man, and has amassed so many thousands of pounds. What a bald, meagre, and wretched retrospect, that he has scraped together so much money, and will be said, whenever he quits the world, to have died rich! But there are others whose thoughts go deeper than all this, and who are not privileged (if the phrase may be used) with so much insensibility. Their review of life is far more painful, as their folly in living only to get money comes out to their view. " I have been success-ful," will such a one say, " I have worked hard, even as I have lived long; and have been a thriving man. I shall certainly leave much behind, but what is it now to me? I am an old man, and must soon be a dying man. I am not permitted to remain with it, nor can I take it with me. The only pleasure now left me, is to say whose it shall be when I am gone. Is it for this I have lived and laboured? Have I not been too busy in getting wealth, either to enjoy it, or to employ it? Have I not laid up treasure on earth, instead of heaven? Have I not been so much taken up for myself, as to forget God and my fellow creatures? Am I prepared to give an account of this property? Have I not too much reason to ask the solemn question, ' What shall it profit a man if he gain the whole world and lose his own soul, or what shall a man give in exchange for his soul? Can I not, do I not, enter painfully into Solomon's experience, when in disgust and penitence he looked back, and seeing the sins, the follies, and pleasures of his apostacy, exclaimed, Vanity of vanities, all is vanity?' " Would you spend old age in indulging such reflections? Is this the retrospect you would have?

I present one more character looking back upon life's eventful journey, and that is, the aged Christian. He too reviews life, and with adoring wonder, gratitude, and joy. He has no fear of the past, no dread of the future. How calm and how peaceful are his reflections ! How pleasant is the retrospect, and how much more bright and glorious the prospect ! " Blessed," he exclaims, " be the God and Father of our Lord Jesus Christ, who hath led and guarded me all my life; who having been the guide of my youth, and the benefactor of my manhood, is now the support of my old age. I adore him with unutterable gratitude, for calling me early, by his grace, to be a partaker of true religion, which has been a source of happiness, a means of prosperity, and an instrument of usefulness, to me, through a long and chequered life. Through Divine goodness, I have been kept from vice and folly, and have risen to respectability and usefulness; and I owe it all to religion. I have corrupted none by infidel principles, nor seduced any from the path of integrity by immoral conduct; but on the contrary, while I am deeply humbled that I have not better improved my opportunities and my talents, I hope I have done some good by my example, my property, and my prayers. Life with me has not been a blank, either as regards myself or others. I know that as a man, and a sinful man, I must rely for salvation exclusively upon the infinite merit of the Saviour; but still I rejoice to be able to say, as a Christian man, 'I have fought a good fight; I have finished my course; I have kept the faith. Henceforth there is laid up for me a crown of life, which God, the righteous judge, will bestow upon me in that day.' Providence has given me a long life, and grace has made it a comfortable, and I hope a useful, one: and now I can lay it willingly down under the influence of a hope full of immortality." Venerable saint! "Thy hoary head is a crown of glory, being found in the way of righteousness." How cloudless and majestic is thy setting sun. Recollecting thy holy, blameless, and useful life, all respect and many love thee. The young delight to show thee reverence, and the aged to manifest esteem.

My young friends, which of these characters would you be in the evening of life? Which kind of old man would you be? With which class of these reflections would you survey life from the extreme verge of your earthly existence? How would you look forward to

eternity at the close of a protracted existence? With
the dread of punishment for all the unpardoned sins
of three score years and ten; or with the anticipation
of gracious reward for all the holy actions of that long
period?

Life is before you now. Ask the question seriously,
solemnly, frequently, "What is my life?" Soon it will
be behind you. Consider it well, its chief purpose, its
brevity, its uncertainty; the smallness of its available
portion for any useful end; its relative proportion to
eternity, and its moral influence and bearing upon
eternity. Life is probationary, and the whole of probation. All that follows belongs to retribution. It is
the causal period, and the only period of causation.
Everything beyond is effect. It is the little pivot
of existence, on which turns the immense and immeasurable whole. It is preparatory. Here we sow,
here we are always sowing, and here only we sow.
Hereafter we reap, and shall for ever do nothing but
reap. It is a term for which we have to account, and
the judgment to come will be founded on it. Though
we shall be accountable beings as long as we exist, yet
it is this short prefatory portion of our existence that is
to determine the character of all the rest. The actions
of this little life decide for eternity. This is a consideration of unparalleled power and weight. Let it be
contemplated and felt. We are acting for eternity :
ages of retribution will answer to this hour of probation.
How circumspectly then ought we to live! If such be
the consequences of life, how frugal ought we to be
of all its moments! A little care and effort now, and
all will be safe for ever. A little providence and pains-
taking, through the short period of your earthly

existence, and you will have made your fortune for immortality.

How momentous then is life! How important to think of this when it is commencing! Who should not prepare to live? Life, the day of salvation, the harbinger of death, the season of grace, the subject of the judgment, the preparation for eternity, the opportunity for heaven, the pathway to hell! What a solemn exercise to review life at its close! First to ask ourselves, "What have I done with life?" and then almost immediately afterwards to hear God saying, "What hast thou done with life?"

Behold the Judge standeth at the door! And,

"This is the summons that He brings:
Awake! for on this transient hour,
Thy long eternity depends."

THE YOUNG MAN FROM HOME.

"Thou, God, seest me."

"In all thy ways acknowledge him, and he shall direct thy paths."

"Wilt thou not from this time cry unto me, My Father, thou art the guide of my youth?"

INTRODUCTION.

A YOUTH leaving home! There is something not a
little melancholy in the idea. Home is one of the most
delightful of words, and it is no wonder that it should
have become the subject of poetry and song. There is
music in the sound; and in every heart that is not yet
corrupted, there is a chord that vibrates to the note. It
will ever awaken a long train of associations and recollections, painful or pleasant, as may have been the
conduct of the individual by whom the word is repeated.
It is at home that parents and children, brothers and
sisters, as long as Providence permits them to dwell
together, mingle in the sweet fellowship of domestic
bliss. But you, whose eye is ranging over these pages,
are leaving, or have left, your father's house. You are
going, or are gone, away from home. I sympathize
with you in the sorrows of that tearful hour of your
existence. Well do I remember, even at this distance
from the time, the scene which my own home presented,
when I finally quitted it, to embark on life's stormy and
dangerous ocean. My mother, one of the kindest and
tenderest that ever bore that dear relationship, unable
to sustain the parting, had retired to the garden; my
sisters wept; my father walked silently by my side to

the edge of the town, where I was to take horse and ride to meet the coach that was to carry me to London; while my own heart was almost overwhelmed with emotion, under the idea that I was leaving home, to encounter the anxieties, dangers, and responsibilities of a new and untried course.

In any aspect of the event, it is- no trifling or in-considerable matter to quit the scenes, friends, and guardians of our childhood; to leave that spot, with which are associated all our earliest reminiscences, and its dear inhabitants; to go from beneath the immediate inspection of a mother's anxious love, and the protection of a father's watchful care, and expose ourselves to the perils, privations, and sorrows that await the traveller on his journey through this world. You ought, as a child, to feel a pang as your mother presses you to her bosom, and sobs out her parting exclamation, "Adieu, my son." You ought to feel pensive and sad, as your father squeezes your hand, and turns from you with a heart too full to speak. You ought, as you cross the threshold of that habitation where you have been nurtured so tenderly, to cast a longing, lingering look behind. You would be unworthy of your parents' love, and of home's endearments, if you could leave them without emotion. Still, however, these feelings are to be guided and limited by reflection. You cannot always remain at home, to be nursed in the lap of domestic enjoyment. You have a part to act in the great drama of life, and must leave home to prepare to act it well. It is the appointment of God that man should not live in idleness, but gain his bread by the sweat of his brow; and you must be placed out in the world to get yours by honest industry. In some few cases, the son remains with the father, and prepares for his future calling at home; but in by far the greater number of instances it is necessary for young men to learn their trade or profession, and to procure their livelihood, by being placed with strangers at a distance from home. This is your case, and in kind solicitude for your welfare, this little volume has been prepared, and is now presented to you, with the prayers and best wishes of the author.

CHAPTER I.

CRITICAL, I mean, as regards his character. Yes, imminently so. You are aware that, besides attention to business, and acquiring a knowledge of a trade or profession, there is such a thing as the formation of character, or fixed habits of action, arising out of fixed principles. A man may be a good tradesman, and yet a bad man; though, generally, good moral character has a very favourable influence in forming the good tradesman. I wish you to direct your most serious attention to the importance of character, moral and religious character. What is everything else without character? How worthless is any man without it! He may have wealth, but he can neither enjoy it, improve it, nor be respected for it, without character. But it very rarely happens that those who begin life with a bad character, succeed in the great competition of this world's business. Multitudes, with every advantage at starting, have failed through bad conduct, while others, with every disadvantage, have succeeded by the aid and influence of good character.

Character for life, and for eternity too, is usually formed in youth. Set out with this idea written upon your hearts, in order that it may be ever exerting its

powerful influence on your conduct.   As is the youth,
such, in all probability, will be the man, whether he be
good or bad.   And as character is generally formed in
youth, so it is not less generally formed at that period
of youth when young people leave home.   The first year
or two after quitting his father's house, is the most eventful period of all a young man's history, and what he is
at the expiration of the second or third year after
leaving the parental abode, that, in all probability, he
will be, as a tradesman for this world, and as an
immortal being in the next.   This should make you
pause and consider.   Before you read another line, I
entreat you to think of it.   Perhaps you doubt it.
Attend then to what I have to offer in support of the
assertion.

Does not reason suggest, that such a transition as
leaving home cannot be negative in its influence?   You
cannot quit so many restraints, so much inspection and
guardianship, and come into such new circumstances, at
an age when the heart is so susceptible and the character
so pliable, without receiving a bias : it is impossible.
New temptations assail you, which, if not at once
and successfully resisted, will acquire a permanent
ascendency.

Your parents, who have gone before you in the path
of life, know the fact, and tremble.   It makes their
hearts ache to think of sending you away from home.
You know not, you cannot know, what was the deep
and silent trouble of your father's heart, the painful
solicitude of your mother's gentle spirit, in the prospect
of your leaving them.   They sat hour after hour by the
fire-side, or lay awake at night talking on the subject,
and mingled their tears as they thought of the youths

of their acquaintance, whose ruin was dated from the hour of their departure from home. "Oh!" they exclaimed in anguish, "if this our son should be like them, and become a prodigal too, and thus bring down our grey hairs in sorrow to the grave! Would that we could keep him at home under our own care, but we cannot." They then fell upon their knees, and by united prayer gained relief and comfort to their aching hearts, while commending you to Him, who has in ten thousand instances been the guide and protector of youth. While your mother, good woman! as she packed your trunk, dropped her fast flowing tears upon your clothes, placed the Bible among them, and sighed out the petition, "Oh my son, my son! Great God, preserve him from all evil."

Ministers have seen the danger of youths leaving home, most painfully exemplified in young men who have come from a distant town, recommended perhaps by parents to their care, and who for a while attended their ministry. At first their places in the sanctuary were regularly filled twice a day, and while the novelty lasted, they appeared to hear with attention and interest: this soon diminished, and they became listless and neglectful; then their seat was occasionally empty on a sabbath evening; then habitually so; till at length, giving up the morning, or only strolling in occasionally with some gay companion, they proclaimed the dreadful fact, that they had fallen into the dangers incident to young men upon leaving home: and the next intelligence concerning them, perhaps, was a letter from a heart-broken parent, confirming the worst fears of the minister, by asking him to make an effort to snatch their son from his evil companions and profligate courses.

Instances innumerable have occurred, in which youths, who, while dwelling under their father's roof, were the joy and the hope of their parents, have, on leaving home and entering into the world, exhibited a melancholy and awful transformation of character. Some by slow degrees have passed from virtue to vice, while others have made the transition so suddenly, as if they had resolved by one bound to reach the way of the ungodly : in either case, the bitterest disappointment has been experienced by those who have had to contrast the prodigal abroad with the sober youth at home.

Youthful reader, I assure you that this is no uncommon case, but, on the contrary, so frequent, as to make every considerate parent tremble at sending away his son, especially to the large provincial towns, and most of all to that mighty sink of iniquity, the metropolis. What, then, should be the state of your mind, and your reflections, upon reading such an account as this ? " Is it so, that on leaving a father's house, so many young men, who were once virtuous and promising, have become vicious and profligate ? How much then does it become me to pause and reflect, lest I add another to the number ! What was there in their circumstances and situation so dangerous to virtue, that I may not expect to find in mine ? Or what is there in my habits and resolutions, which was not, in their better days, in them ? Did they fall, and shall I be so confident of stedfastness, as to dismiss fear and despise caution ? Do I recoil from vice ? So did they, when, like me, they were at home. Do I shudder at grieving my parents by misconduct ? so did they, when, like me, they had their parents continually before them. Am

I going forth high in the confidence of my parents, and the esteem of my friends? so did they. Yet how cruelly have they disappointed every hope that was formed concerning them! and what is there in my habits and purposes that will prevent me from imitating their example? Oh if this should be the case! If I should add another to the victims of leaving home! If my reputation, now happily so fair, should be tarnished, faded, lost! If I, of whom hopes are entertained of my becoming a Christian, should turn out a prodigal, a profligate! Dreadful apostasy. Great God, prevent it!" Could I induce you thus to reflect, I should have hope of you; while a contrary spirit of self-dependence and confidence, would lead me to expect in you another proof that the time of a youth's leaving home is most critical.

CHAPTER II.

It is well to know what these are, and where they lie, that you may know how to avoid them. Ignorance on such a subject would be itself one of the chief dangers. In many cases, to know our perils is itself one way of avoiding them. Steadily, then, contemplate the following:

I. You are in danger of falling into evil, from the removal of parental inspection, admonition, and restraint. It must be admitted, that home itself is sometimes a scene of peril to morals and religion. In some homes, young people see and hear very little but what is calculated to do them harm; parental example is on the side of sin, and almost everything that is said or done is of a nature likely to produce impressions unfavourable to piety, and perhaps even to morality. Where this is the state of things, removal is a benefit, and not a few have reason to be thankful for having been transplanted from such irreligious houses into families where God is feared and religion is exemplified. If this be your case, rejoice in the dispensation of Providence, which has rescued you from such imminent danger, and planted you in a soil more congenial for the cultivation of true piety. Happy youth! to be thus snatched from the vortex

of perdition at home, and brought into the way of salvation abroad. O prize your privileges, and improve
your opportunities! Many a young man, who, at the
time of leaving home, wept over the necessity which
caused him to quit the scenes of his childhood, and to
go from beneath the wing of his parents, has lived to
consider it the brightest era of his life, inasmuch as it
took him away from scenes of moral danger, and led
him to the means of grace and the path of eternal life :
and in looking back upon the way of Providence, and
upon his own feelings and ignorance of what awaited
him, has exclaimed, " Thou bringest the blind in a way
that they knew not, and leadest them in paths that they
have not known ; thou makest darkness light before
them, and crooked things straight."

This, however, is not applicable to all families :
if there are some parents who take no care about the
religious or even moral character of their children, who
neither set them good examples, nor deliver to them any
instruction, nor impose upon them any restraint, but
who allow them the unchecked gratification of their
passions, and the unreproved commission of sin, there
are many others who act a wiser and a better part. In
most instances, parents are moral ; in many they are
pious : and while the former are anxious to keep their
sons from vice, and train them to virtue, the latter go
further, and endeavour to bring them up in the fear
of the Lord. Many who will read these pages know
this by experience. You have been brought up in
habits of rigid morality. Your parents have been solicitous to form your character on a right basis. You
have been long familiar with the voice of instruction,
admonition, and warning. You have been the constant

subject of an anxiety which you could neither be ignorant of, nor mistake. If you were seen in company with a stranger, or with a youth of doubtful character, you were questioned and warned. If you brought home a book, it was examined. If you stayed out at night later than usual, you saw a mother's anxious eye turned upon you, and heard a father's voice, saying, " My son, why so late, where have you been?" In short, you felt yourself within the range of an ever-present inspection, and under the pressure of a never-relaxing restraint. The theatre and other places of pollution were strictly forbidden, and indeed you felt little inclination to visit those haunts of vice. Morning and evening you heard the Scriptures read, and the voice of prayer ascend to God, and ascend for you. With such examples, under such instruction, and amidst such scenes, you had no opportunity, and felt no disposition, to be vicious. Sometimes you thought, perhaps, that the restraint was too severe, and the care too fastidious; but then you said, " It is all for my good," and you submitted to it.

All this is now over: you have left, or are leaving home. The moment has arrived, or is past and will never be forgotten, when those arms which sustained your infant frame were thrown around your neck, and pressed you to the bosom that nourished you, while a mother's faltering voice exclaimed, " Farewell, my boy;" and a father, always kind, but kinder then than ever, prolonged the sad adieu, and said, " My son, I can watch over you no longer. The God whose providence removes you from your father's house, be your protector, and preserve you from the evils of this sinful world. Remember, that, though my eye cannot see you, His can, and ever does. Fear Him." And there, young man, you now are, where your parents' hearts trembled to place you, amidst the snares and perils of this evil world; where your father's inspection cannot reach you, or your mother's tearful eye behold you. Perhaps you are in a family where no prayer is presented, nor even the form of religion observed; where you are left to yourself, little or no care being taken of your morals or religious principles; and where, provided you serve your employers with industry and honesty, you may choose your own companions, recreations, and places of resort. Or, if more favourably situated, and your lot cast in a religious family, still what is the instruction of a master compared with that of a father, or the care of a mistress compared with that of a mother? Away from home, a viciously inclined youth will find opportunities for the gratification of his evil propensities in situations the most friendly to virtue. His wicked heart, rejoicing in the absence of his parents, will make that absence an incentive to sin. Ever and anon the whisper will come from within, " My father is not here to see it; my mother will not know it; I am not under inspection now, restraint is over; I can go where I like, associate with whom I please, and fear neither rebuke nor reproach." O young man, think of the unutterable baseness of such conduct as this. Ought you not to despise yourself, if you can thus meanly, as well as wickedly, take advantage of a father's absence, to do that which you know would excite his strongest reprobation, and afflict him with the bitterest grief, if he were present. Yet multitudes are thus base and wicked, and have gone from their parents to ruin themselves for ever. Act, young man, act as you would do, if you were conscious that your father's eye were upon you.

II. Your danger is increased by the spirit of independence and self-confidence (connected, as of course it must be, with much ignorance and inexperience) which young men are apt to assume, when they leave their father's house, and go out into the world. " Paternal rule is now over; my parents are not at hand to be consulted or obeyed; and if they were, it is time for me to think and act for myself. I am my own master now. I am a young man, and no longer a child. I am capable of judging, discriminating, and determining between right and wrong. I have the right, and will exercise it, of forming my own standard of morals, selecting my own models of character, and laying down my own plans of action. Who has authority to interfere with me?" Such probably are your thoughts, and they are encouraged by many around you, who suggest that you are not always to go in leading strings, but ought now to assert your liberty, and act like a man. Yes, and how many have employed and abused this liberty to the most criminal and fatal purposes: it has been a liberty to destroy all the habits of virtue formed at home, to subvert all the principles implanted by their parents' solicitude, and to rush into all the evil practices, against which the voice of warning had been raised from their boyhood. Many young men have no sooner been freed from parental restraint, and become their own masters, than they have hurried to every place of amusement, resorted to every species of vicious diversion, initiated themselves into all the mysteries of iniquity, and with prurient curiosity to know what it is bliss to be ignorant of, have entered into fellowship with all the unfruitful works of darkness. Happy, happy had they been, had they considered that an independence which sets them free from parental advice and control, is the bane of piety, morality, and happiness, and has proved, where it has been assumed, the ruin for both worlds of multitudes of once hopeful youths. Wise is that young man, and blessed in all probability he will be, who, though he has left his father's house, and it may be has arrived at the age of maturity, feels it his privilege, as well as his duty, to look up to his parents as his counsellors, his comforters, and, in some respects, his rulers; who allows the restraints of home to follow him abroad; and who, amidst the dangerous intricacies of life, is thankful to accept the kind offices of a judicious father, to be the guide of his youth.

Independence of one kind, I mean as to his own support, is that which every youth, sensible of what is due to himself, as well as to his parents, will be eager to acquire. It is a noble and generous ambition that dictates the wish to be self-supporting. Some young men have disgraced themselves in the estimation of all who knew them, by hanging upon the industry and resources, and those but limited too, of parents, whose delight in their children made them willing to endure any labour and suffer any privations on their account. I know nothing more mean or cruel, than for a youth thus to take advantage of the strength of parental love, and to keep a father chained to the oar of labour, and to drain him of his last pound, to support himself in idleness, or to supply the means of his luxurious extravagance. Disdain, young man, the thought of living by the sweat of your father's brow, and the wear and tear of his flesh and blood, his bones and muscles. Be industrious and frugal, that as soon as possible you may be, in this respect, your own master, and your own supporter.

III. The numerous incentives to vice with which every place, but especially the metropolis and large provincial towns, abound, and the opportunities of concealment which are to be found there, are a source of great danger. At the head of all these must be placed the theatre, which is there to be found in all its most powerful attractions and most destructive fascinations. Nothing can be said too strong or too bad, of the injurious tendency of the stage ; nor too earnest or impassioned, in the way of warning young men from venturing within its precincts. It is emphatically and eminently the broad road and wide gate that leads to destruction. It is idle to talk of what the drama and the stage may, in the hands of moralists, become. I speak not of playhouses in the land of Utopia, but of such as now are to be found in ours, and of such as you, my reader, will attend, if you go to any. Dr. Johnson has very truly said :

"The drama's laws, the drama's patrons give,
And they who live to please, must please to live."

The staple matter of which the ordinary run of dramatic representations are composed, is altogether adapted to corrupt the youthful mind, by appealing to the most inflammable, powerful, and dangerous of its passions. Tragedy, with whatever fine passages and occasional lofty sentiment it may be adorned, is usually calculated to produce pride, ambition, and revenge ; while comedy, such as is most suited to the public taste, and therefore most in demand, is the school for intrigue, amours, and licentiousness. It is not, however, the subject matter only of the play itself that is corrupting, but the representation of it upon the stage, with all the accompaniments of the theatre. Not only is the lesson vicious, but the teacher and the schoolfellows are vicious too. It is bad sentiment, borrowing every possible aid to render it still worse: it is vice recommended by the charms of music, painting, architecture, oratory, and eloquence, with all that is fascinating in female beauty, and dazzling in elegant costume. Think of the audience: that many of them are honest, virtuous, and respectable members of society, I allow; but how large a portion of it is of a contrary description! Is there any where such a collection of the vicious, such a condensation of vice, as at the theatre? Is it not there that the dissipated meet to make their guilty assignations? Is not the profligate, of whatever grade or kind, sure to meet his fellow there? Is it not the harlot's resort, the place of convocation for those miserable beings, whose ways lead down to the chambers of death and the pit of destruction, and who there swarm in the lobbies, and crowd the benches?

It were easy to enumerate the evils, though they are many and great, to which frequenting the theatre will expose you. It is expensive, and will thus endanger your honesty. It leads to other expensive sins, such as drunkenness and debauchery, which, besides being evil themselves, will consume the fruits of your industry. It is sure to lead you into bad company. It generates a feverish imagination, and destroys a right balance of character. It raises the passions above their proper tone, and thus induces a dislike for those grave and serious subjects of life which have nothing but their simplicity and importance to recommend them. It kindles low and base appetites, and creates a constant hankering after their indulgence. It not only hardens the heart against religion, so that a theatre-loving man never becomes religious, until he is persuaded to abandon these amusements, but it gradually benumbs the conscience into an insensibility to good morals. Through the power of the morbid propensities, and ungovernable desires, which it produces, it often urges on to licentious conduct, so that a youth who frequents the playhouse is almost sure to fall a victim to the lips of the strange woman, for " they drop as the honeycomb, and her mouth is smoother than oil; but her end is bitter as wormwood, sharp as a two-edged sword. Her feet go down to death, her steps take hold on hell."

Myriads of young men have had to date their ruin for both worlds from the fatal night, when, against the dissuasions of parents, and the remonstrances of conscience, they first trusted their morality, till then uncorrupted, within the walls of a theatre. Let earnest, affectionate, importunate entreaty prevail then, to induce you to abstain from this road to perdition. If you will not take my testimony, hearken to that which is furnished by witnesses more competent, from experience, to give evidence. It is said of Sir Matthew Hale, one of the greatest and most upright judges that ever sat on the bench, " that he was an extraordinary proficient at school, and for some time at Oxford; but the stage-players coming thither, he was so much corrupted by seeing plays, that he almost wholly forsook his studies. By this he not only lost much time, but found that his head was thereby filled with vain images of things; and being afterwards sensible of the mischief of this, he resolved, upon his coming to London, never to see a play again, to which resolution he constantly adhered." Augustine, the celebrated Latin Father, confesses, with a noble frankness, that it was at the theatre he imbibed the venom which so corrupted his heart and polluted his life during his early years.

"There is no part of theatrical economy," says one, "with which I am unacquainted; and it is my personal and complete knowledge of that economy which forces upon me the conviction, that were another Ezekiel to arise, and another angel descend, to exhibit to him the greater and greater abominations of this land, he would reserve for the astonished and indignant prophet a display of the iniquities of a London theatre, as the last and most fearful chambers of imagery." "As I was one day walking out," says an American preacher, "for my accustomed exercise, a gentleman passed me in his carriage, and invited me to ride with him. He is a man of wealth and distinction, and of an elevated and pious character. He came to the city when young, without friends, without money, without reputation, without any extrinsic means whatever of getting started in business. Soon after I took a seat with him, two young men of dissipated air, with cigars in their mouths, dashed furiously past us in a chaise. 'There,' said he, 'are two young men going fast to ruin.' This incident turned our conversation upon the expenses and the ruin of young men. He remarked, that most of the young men who came to live in Boston (America) at the time he did, had already gone to ruin. I told him that the interest I felt in them prompted the inquiry, how it came to pass that he escaped, and by what means he had succeeded so well in life? He replied, that when he came to the city, he laid down some rules, which he had stedfastly observed. Among them were the following: That he would always attend public worship on the Sabbath; that he would never read loose and infidel writings, nor visit infidel meetings; that he would devote a portion of his time to some profitable study; that he would be always diligent and faithful in business, however discouraging things might look; that he would not frequent places for refreshment, unless for necessary food; that he would form no alliance with any individuals, for society or amusement, till he knew them to be safe and virtuous companions; and that he would not go to the theatre till he was forty-five years old, when he supposed he should be above the reach of any injury from that source. Long before he reached that age he became a pious man, and of course he now finds higher sources of pleasure than the theatre, a place he never visited. Another youth, who came to the city at the same time and from the same place with him, took lodgings at a house with some theatre-going young men, was prevailed upon to go for once, then again, and again; became loose in his principles and habits: one wrong step led to another, until he went headlong to ruin, and found an infamous grave! And this, he remarked, had been the sad history of many who entered on and began the career in life with him."

I have no need, after this, to add anything, except it be to advise you never to do as some have done to their destruction, and that is, to go once, in order to judge for yourself. Taste not the poison to ascertain how you like it, and to form an opinion of its deleterious power. Touch not the fang of a serpent, to ascertain by examination the sharpness of its tooth. These are matters which it is safer and easier to decide by testimony; and a cloud of witnesses can, and do depose, that of all the avenues to destruction, not one is more seductive or more direct than the theatre.

But besides the theatre, how many other species of corrupt and corrupting amusement are to be found. Need I mention gambling houses, brought down to the level of persons of slender means, where the excitement of cupidity, and the witchery of a love of play, is kept up, to the destruction of all sobriety of mind and industrious habits. Is it necessary to speak of the divans, or rooms where young men meet to smoke cigars? It may seem to some to be trifling, but I know it is not, to say, that the first cigar a young man takes within his lips may become, and often does become, his first step in the career of vice. A cigar is with young persons, the symbol of foppery, and swaggering, and conceit. I knew a youth, the son of a minister, who acquired such a passion for this species of gratification, that it contributed to the ruin of his circumstances, as well as of his character. His income was limited, yet he was at one time twenty pounds in debt for cigars to the tobacconist, at whose house he used to meet a company of youths, as idle as himself. I was assured it was a fact well-known, in Liverpool, that one man there spent a pound a day in cigars, which he had sprinkled with otto of roses before he smoked them. I always grieve and tremble over every young man of my acquaintance whom I see contracting this habit. It often leads to other and far worse things.

Then there are the public gardens, the parks, and the steam-boats to Richmond, to Gravesend, or to Greenwich, those alluring baits for sabbath-breaking, by which millions, as time rolls on, are caught in the snares of Satan, ever lying in wait to deceive and to decoy. "What harm can there be," it is said, "after we have been shut up all the week in a close street, hard at work, to go out on a fine summer day, to enjoy the clear sunshine, the fresh air, and the beauties of creation? Surely our Maker is not such a hard master as to refuse us gratifications so innocent and so healthful." And thus sabbath-breaking, which is a manifest violation of the laws of God, is defended by an appeal to his goodness. Probably there is no means of destroying religious principle, and of leading to immorality, more common than the neglect of public worship, and the desecration of the sabbath. Let this season be taken from devotion, and given to pleasure, and the character is from that time open to all the inroads of sin, without any check.

CHAPTER III.

BAD companions are a source of danger. Perhaps more young men are ruined by this than by any other means that could be mentioned. Many who have left home with a character unsullied, and a mind not only comparatively pure, but really ignorant of the crooked ways of vice, who, simple, artless, and without guile, would have shuddered at the temptation to any of the grosser acts of sin, have at length fallen sacrifices to the powerful influence of evil associates. Man is a social being, and the propensity for company is peculiarly strong in youth, the season when it requires to be watched with greater care than at any other, because of the greater force which it exerts in the formation of character. Now and then we meet with a youth who is so engrossed with business, so intent on cultivating his mind, or so reserved in disposition, as to have no desire for companions; but by far the greater number are fond of society, and eager to enjoy it; and, if not extremely careful in the selection of their friends, are in imminent peril of choosing such as will do them harm. It is next to impossible, young man, for you to remain virtuous in vicious society. Good morals cannot long be retained in habitual intercourse with those who are gay and dissipated. It is like carrying money into the company of thieves, who will be sure to rob you of it. Your good conduct will render them uneasy; it will reprove them, accuse them, and exasperate them; and they will never cease till they have made you as bad as themselves. The more agreeable, amiable, and intelligent they are, the more dangerous and ensnaring is their influence. A youthful profligate, of elegant manners, lively humour, amiable temper, and intelligent mind, is Satan's most polished instrument for ruining immortal souls. Once give your company to such an associate, and you are in the coils of a serpent, or at any rate in the spell of the basilisk's deadly gaze, from which nothing but Omnipotence can pluck you. You may for some time be kept from imitating him in his excess of riot, and prevented by the last efforts of a yet surviving conscience, from going all his lengths in sin, but you are in the track of his footsteps, following at a distance, while he is perpetually looking back, and by smiles and beckonings rallying your courage, and cheering onward your yet timid and reluctant feet.

No evil companions are to be so much dreaded, as those who dwell under the same roof; and how frequently is it the unhappy lot of young men piously brought up, and in every respect hopeful as to morality, and perhaps as to piety also, to be fixed in the same house, to eat at the same table, to sleep in the same room, as some youths of vicious and infidel principles. They are thus brought into immediate contact with sin, and exposed at once to all the virulence of its contagion; and what strength of moral constitution does it require to resist the danger! They breathe an infected atmosphere, and continually touch a pestilential person.

Take the testimony of one who left his father's house strictly moral, and with much veneration for religion, but whose dark and winding course led him at last into the vicinity of the gallows.

"In my master's house," says he, "there were three young men employed besides myself. One of them, a gay, respectable youth, was a great favourite with my employer. He was my bedfellow. Of course this led to intimacy, and from him I received the first disposition to extravagance and dress, which laid the foundation of my ruin. He was extremely prodigal in his habits; but from the respectability of his connexions, no suspicion was excited that his supplies were not equal to his expenses. By him I became gradually familiarized to scenes of pleasure and dissipation, which soon exceeded my means of support; but I never dreamed of having recourse to dishonest means to meet expensive indulgences. I soon found that I should be involved in great difficulties, and began to withdraw from his company, and associated as much as possible with my brother and a cousin of mine in the city.

"A circumstance, however, soon occurred, which threw the forbidden fruit in my way, and my integrity could not resist the temptation. After being about two years in my situation, I was sent, on one occasion, with a parcel to a gentleman, for which I was to receive the money, about two pounds. Such parts of the business had often fallen to my lot. On this occasion, however, in the hurry of business, without the least dishonesty of intention, I forgot to give the money to my employer, and did not discover the note in my pocket till some time afterwards, several weeks at least. I was much alarmed at the circumstance, and knew not how to act. I was afraid to mention the matter to any one. I determined to let the note remain where it was, and if no inquiry was made, at length to appropriate the money to myself. Thus I fell into the snare."*

And thus he commenced a career of dishonesty, the end of which will be related in the sequel.

I might mention another case, illustrative of the same fact, of the danger of a bad companion in the house; but happily the danger was escaped in this instance. I knew a youth, whose parents felt the

* The London Apprentice.

greatest solicitude for their child, whom they were about to place from home. He had been carefully educated, from his earliest years, in habits of morality and piety. His school had been selected with special reference to the plan laid down at home, for the formation of his character. But now this lovely youth (for he was most lovely) must leave home, and go out into the world. How anxiously did the father read the advertisements to find one which commanded all the advantages of a pious master and an attractive minister! He succeeded, and a most excellent Christian he found, with whom to place his son. The family was what a Christian family should be; and the other apprentice also was supposed to be all that could be wished as a companion for a youth just quitting the parental roof, for he was the son of a minister, and unsuspected as to his principles. Many months, however, had not passed before the minister received a letter from the heart-stricken mother, to say she had heard from her child, stating that his soul was in imminent peril. He had been under religions impressions, and in much concern about his immortal welfare; but his companion proved to be a concealed infidel, concealed, I mean, from his father and his master. Nightly, when they retired to rest, was this deceiver and tempter instilling into the mind of his younger companion his artful objections against Christianity, and endeavouring to poison him with infidelity. His mind was assailed by one cavil after another, as he could bear them, till the poor boy unable any longer to endure his state of mind, yet afraid to disclose it, wrote home to his mother, exclaiming in an agony, "Oh, mother, I am lost, I am lost, unless you pray for me." Horror-struck, she addressed the minister immediately upon the subject, and by their joint labours, and the blessing of God upon them, this youth was snatched from the fangs of the destroyer. He acted most wisely in making his parents acquainted with his situation, and imploring their counsel and help. A little longer, and he would, in all probability, have been carried off in triumph, and perhaps have been ruined for both worlds.

Oh that I could select words sufficiently emphatic to express my entreaties to you to beware of evil companions out of the house, but especially in it! Oh! could you see but a thousandth part of the miserable ghosts that have passed to the regions of unutterable woe by the influence of bad associates, what a comment would their damnation be upon the passage, " A companion of fools shall be destroyed !"

Vicious women are as much to be dreaded as bad men, and far more so. I have known some who have been in great jeopardy from female servants. It is of the greatest consequence that a young man should be upon his guard against this danger, and not allow himself to take, or receive, the smallest possible liberty that would intrench upon the most delicate modesty. Profligacy and misery to a vast amount have been the result of a want of caution in this matter. Towards young women of this description, be always kind, but never familiar; never joke with them; keep them at a proper distance, by keeping yourself so. Not a few have been lost to morality, by not watching against this danger. And then, how are our towns infested with those unhappy women, who, in many, if not most cases, are the victims of seduction, and horribly avenge themselves upon the sex of their betrayers, by becoming seducers in their turn. Youthful reader, be upon your guard against this peril to your health, your morals, your soul. Go where you will, this snare is spread for your feet. Watch and pray, that you enter not into temptation. Set a strict guard upon your senses, your imagination, your passions. Once yield to temptation, and you are undone : purity is then lost, and, sunk from self-esteem, you may give yourself up to commit all uncleanness with greediness.

Drinking parties, though not so common as they were, or as are some other snares, are still sufficiently prevalent to be pointed out as a source of danger. Happily for the morals of our country, a hard drinker is no longer regarded with éclat in the better classes of society. Still it is an object of ambition with some misguided youths, to be able to drink the bumper and the toast with convivial grace as a matter of course. What a low and sensual aim. Young man, as you would not lie down in the grave of a drunkard, worn out by disease, and closing your miserable .career in poverty and wretchedness, beware of the filthy, degrading, and destructive habit of drinking. Remember the words of the wisest of men : " Who hath woe ? who hath sorrow ? who hath contentions ? who hath babbling ? who hath wounds without cause ? who hath redness of eyes ? They that tarry long at the wine ; they that go to seek mixed wine. Look not thou upon the wine when it is red, when it giveth his colour in the cup, when it moveth itself aright : at the last it biteth like a serpent, and stingeth like an adder. Thine eyes shall behold strange women, and thy heart shall utter perverse things. Yea, thou shalt be as he that lieth down in the midst of the sea, or as he that lieth upon the top of a mast. They have stricken me, shalt thou say, and I was not sick; they have beaten me, and I felt it not: when shall I awake? I will seek it yet again." Study this inimitable and graphic picture of drinking and its consequences, and begin life with a horror of drunkenness; acquire an oinophobia, or dread of wine. It is calculated that fifty thousand drunkards die yearly in this country, and that one half of the insanity, two thirds of the pauperism, and three fourths of the crimes of the land, are the consequences of drunkenness. A large proportion of drunkards begin this dreadful habit in youth. I again say, and with all possible emphasis, Begin life with a horror of drunkenness. Watch against a love of wine. As one who has practised total abstinence for three years, I can, and do recommend it to all persons in health, and especially to youth. The young man who has acquired a relish for wine; who always drinks it when he can get it; who drinks as much as is given him, or he can afford to purchase; who avails himself of the dinner or supper party, to go as far as he can without actual intoxication, is already an incipient tippler; and if he do not stop at once, and practise total abstinence, or, at any rate, watch his propensity, and lay down rules of the most rigid temperance, will, in all probability, become a confirmed drunkard.

IV. Perhaps, the discomfort of your situation exposes you to perils. It is not to be expected by any youth who has had the blessing of a comfortable home, that hé should find the same degree or kind of provision made for his enjoyment in any situation in which, on going out into the world, he may be placed: oftentimes the very reverse occurs, and his new residence presents

a melancholy contrast to the house of his father.
Perhaps you, my reader, may be thus circumstanced.
Your place of abode is so utterly comfortless, that you
can scarcely think of home without tears. It is not
only that your fare is coarse, your lodging mean, and
your work hard: you could bear all this, if your privations were made up by the kindness and sympathy
of your employer, and your labours were softened by
his expressed or obvious satisfaction; but it happens he
is a tyrant, whom nobody can satisfy or conciliate, or
his wife is a termagant, whom nothing can please.
Many a time you retire to your hard bed, and ill-
furnished room, with a spirit discouraged, and a heart
half broken. Oh what a contrast is this cold unfeeling
and grinding conduct, to the love of a fond mother, and
the solicitude of a kind father! In such a situation,
you are in danger of several things likely to be injurious
to your moral welfare and future prosperity. Some
have been induced by the pressure of their misery to
abscond. In an unhappy hour, they have listened to
the voice of temptation, and have suddenly burst the
bonds which they could not unloose, and cast off the
yoke which they felt to be intolerable, and run away.
This is a desperate and dreadful remedy; and has, in
most cases, proved a ruinous one. Never let such a
thought be entertained by you for a moment. Bear any
unkindness oppression and misery, rather than do this.
A youth who runs away from his place, is usually a
blighted character for life. He is sunk in his own estimation, and in that of every one else. What anxiety
does such a step bring on his parents if they are living,
and on all his other friends! Remain then in your
place: your term of apprenticeship will soon expire; it

is not a captivity for life. Endeavour to sustain your ill treatment with courage and patience. Meekness may vanquish your oppressor.

But perhaps you are a clerk, and not an apprentice, and as you do not dwell in the house of your employer, you are not exposed to the same kind of discomfort and annoyance which those suffer who do. You live in private lodgings. Your perils are therefore of another kind. Instead of being now surrounded with all the dear companions of home, and delighting in that busy scene of genuine love and tender offices, you dwell solitarily among strangers. When the business of the day is over, you go to a cheerless and silent abode. No mother's smiling countenance welcomes you to the fireside; no father's cheerful voice tells or asks the events of the day; no brother or sister calls you by name, and blithely sports with you. Instead of this, you receive no attention but that which is bought with money. You enter your lonely room, eat your joyless meal, and in sadness think of home and days gone by. Now there is danger here: danger of seeking companions who may be unmeet; danger of going out to find amusement in places of vicious resort; or of adopting a course of reading that will only pollute the mind. It is impossible to overrate the peril of a young man who has lately left his father's house, and is living in solitary lodgings in one of our large provincial towns, and especially in the metropolis. If he has not piety to preserve him, or fixed moral principle, or a love of reading and a thirst for knowledge, so as to make books his companions, he is in great temptation. With all the sources of sinful pleasure open around him, and in the midst of a multitude hastening to drink their deleterious waters; with

all the seductions near that appeal to every sense, every
appetite, and every taste ; it is more than probable he
will be drawn from his gloomy abode, to those scenes
where blaze all the lights 'of fashion folly and ruin.
The first scruples of conscience being subdued, the
temptation being once successful, continuance and
advance seem almost necessary. In addition to the
dreariness of solitude, he has now the pangs of self-
reproach to bear. And can he sit there night after
night, to hear the accusations of that internal monitor
whose indignant rebuke he has provoked, and the
sentence of that severe judge whose condemnation he
has procured? No. He must go again to the sounds
of revelry to drown the voice, and to the scenes
of mirth to lose the sight, of his awful reprover. A
young man in lodgings is thus in a situation where
nothing but decided piety, or strong moral principle,
can be expected to preserve him from temptation.

V. There is another danger to which your new
situation may expose you, against which you should
be cautioned, and directed to exercise the greatest vigilance ; and that is, the violation of the rule of honesty.
If placed in a retail shop, money will be continually
passing through your hands, and much uncounted cash
will be within your reach. The temptation may, perhaps,
in certain circumstances arise, to appropriate a part
of this to your own use. It may be your supply
of pocket money is short, and you find yourself below
some of your acquaintances in the means of procuring
clothes books or amusements. When the prospect of
concealment presents itself, and the pressure of necessity
is urgent, especially if aided by the hope and intention
of refunding at some future time what you purloin,

you are in imminent peril of the sin of embezzlement. Many, very many, have fallen into the snare, and have had their character and prospects blasted for ever. Enter life determined, by God's help, to follow whatsoever things are honest true lovely and of good report. Let the fear of God, united with the love of the noble, honourable, and dignified, prevent you from ever appropriating to yourself a farthing of your employer's property. Even should you not be detected, how degraded will you feel, if you have in any instance acted the part of a pilferer! It is a painful thing for conscience to cry, "thief," though a man may be spared the degradation of public exposure. On the other hand, how pleasant will be the recollection through life, that though exposed to many and strong temptations, your hands were pure from dishonesty. Be this your prayer, "Let integrity and uprightness preserve me."

An eminent Christian minister,* in relating to me the events of his early life, mentioned, with a fervid glow of delight and thankfulness, the victory which he gained in youth over a strong temptation to commit an act of dishonesty. Some circumstances, which need not be here detailed, led him to the resolution of running away from the place where he was serving an apprenticeship. On leaving the house, which he did in the morning before the family were stirring, he had to pass through a small room in which his master usually sat. On the table lay a small heap of gold silver and copper, carelessly mixed together, from which, as he was quite sure it was uncounted, a small sum abstracted by himself would not be missed. He stopped and looked at it, and as he looked he coveted. The temptation was

* [The Rev. Samuel Lowell. Ed.]

strong. He was going out upon the wide world, with scarcely anything in his pocket. His stock of clothes was low, all he had was on his back, and in a bundle in his hand. He reasoned with himself about his scanty means, the certainty that anything he took would not be missed, and the probability of his being able to refund, in more prosperous days, what he might appropriate then, in the season of his necessity: but his better thoughts prevailed, and, gathering up his remaining principles of virtuous integrity, he exclaimed, "No, I am wronging my master enough in leaving his service; I will not take his money too." And with only half-a-crown in his pocket he went out to seek his fortune in the world; but still he had the testimony of his conscience, that, though a runaway, he was, as far as money was concerned, an honest youth. He assured me, that he had never ceased to reflect upon that triumph over temptation with pleasure and thankfulness. His future destiny, perhaps, hung upon that decision. Had he taken any of the money, his conscience might have been benumbed, his heart hardened, his self-respect lost, and his future character have become profligate and depraved. Reader, you may not, I trust you will not, be placed exactly in the same circumstances of trial as this young man; but opportunities of embezzling your employer's property will often present themselves to you, if so disposed, and I hope you will ever have the principle to resist them. There is nothing more likely to expose you to this danger than habits of extravagance. If you should unhappily acquire a taste for expensive dress, or amusements, or vicious gratifications, you are in peril. Dishonesty often begins in dandyism. A young man thinks he must be genteel, elegant, fashionable; he looks with envy on those whose means are more abundant than his own, and becomes restless and dissatisfied. He must, he will be equal to them in clothes ornaments and diversions; but his salary, or his father's allowance, will not meet his wants, and then comes the temptation to embezzlement. Extravagance must have resources; and if they cannot be found by honest means, they will by dishonest ones. A love of display in dress and diversions has led many to the gallows, or to Botany Bay, by prompting first to pilfering, and then to forgery. Be upon your guard then. Avoid extravagance. Dread all foppery. Determine to live within your income. Begin life with the resolution to be neat and respectable, but not a fine gentleman. Be it your fixed purpose never to have an article till you can pay for it.

VI. I close this fearful list of perils, by mentioning the prevalence of infidelity, and the zeal and wily arts of its abettors and propagators, as forming another source of danger to youth. There never was an age when infidelity was more busy than it is now; not that it is now more generally professed by the thinking and intelligent portion of the community; quite the contrary. Literature and science, rank and fashion, pay far more external, though it may not be sincere, homage to revelation, than they did in times gone by: infidelity as a profession is no longer the boast of those who occupy the high places of society. Religion is obviously gaining ground among them. But the efforts of infidels to diffuse their principles among the common people and middling classes are peculiarly energetic just now. The subtleties of Hume, the pompous deism of Bolingbroke, and the artful insinuations of Gibbon, have given place to the ribaldries of Paine, and recently to the absurdities of Owen. The system, if system it may be called, of the latter, is obtruded upon public notice under the guise of an attractive misnomer, and pushed forward with a zeal which reminds us of the activity of its parent, the father of lies. Absurd in its principles, contradictory to every man's sound judgment, and repudiated even by the conscience of its abettors, socialism cannot long impose upon the credulity of even the labouring classes, among whom it has yet been chiefly successful. Amidst a jargon of pretended metaphysics, at war with the first principles of sound logic and our moral constitution, it announces as its leading dogma, that man is entirely the creature of circumstances; is in no sense the author of his opinions and volitions; nor the founder or supporter of his own character. If this be correct, he is a mere machine, gifted with faculties which can be of no use to him; without freedom, without responsibility, without conscience; to whom it is useless to offer inducements, and on whom instruction is wasted; so circumstanced by necessity, that he can neither originate nor sustain any self-improvement; a being, in reference to whom law is mockery, sin impossible, and punishment injustice. As if it were not enough to shock the public mind by a system so monstrous, the public taste, and all our social feelings are outraged, by the unblushing avowal of its author, that it is his design and wish to abolish the institution of marriage, and reconstruct society upon the basis of the unlegalized association of the sexes and the unrestricted freedom of divorce. Absurd and demoralizing as such a system is, it is popular with many; the reason is obvious, its very immorality proves to them its recommendation. If they can believe it, they feel that, commit what crimes they may, accountability is gone, and remorse is extinguished: the blame rests not on them, for any sin whatever, but on the circumstances which led to it: a short way to be very wicked, and yet very easy. Young man, can you believe it? No, your reason revolts from it, and so would your heart, too, if you could witness the moral ravages it has committed. " Call it not socialism, call it devilism; for it has made me more a devil than a man," exclaimed a poor dying man in my neighbourhood, to one of our town missionaries who visited him on his death-bed. " I got into company that led me to socialism and to drinking. I rejected the Bible, denied the Saviour, and persuaded myself that there was no hereafter; and as the result, acted the part of a bad father, and a bad husband. I have the testimony of my master, that I was a steady and respectable man until I listened to the Owenites; but since that time I have become a vagabond, and they who formerly knew me, have shunned me in the streets. The system of the Owenites is worse than that of Paine." Such is the testimony of a dying victim and martyr of socialism, and a similar confession has been made by many others. I have seen man moral happy and useful, so long as he professed religion: and have seen him in misery poverty and ruin, since he has thrown it off: I have heard the impassioned accents of his heart-broken wife, so far as weakness allowed her to be impassioned, exclaiming, as she looked at her miserable companion, " O sir, he has been a changed man ever since he went among the Owenites!" Such is socialism.

It must be obvious, that between immorality and

infidelity there is a close connexion, and a constant reaction going on in some minds. A young man falls into temptation, and commits sin: instead of repenting, as is his duty and his interest, he in many cases attempts to quiet his conscience by persuading himself that religion is all hypocrisy, and the Bible untrue. His infidelity now prepares him to go greater lengths in sin: thus vice calls in the aid of error, and error strengthens vice, while both together lead their victim to ruin and misery. To guard yourselves against such dangers, study well the evidences of revelation; read Paley, Chalmers, and Watson, and the works on the Evidences, and the tracts on socialism and infidelity, published by the Tract Society: but above all, let the power of religion be felt in your heart, as well as the evidence of it perceived by your judgment. Religion in the heart is the only thing to be relied upon as a defence against the attacks of infidels, and the influence of their principles. But this will be insisted upon at greater length in a subsequent chapter.

Such are the most common and pressing dangers to which youth are exposed on quitting the protection of their parental habitation, and going from beneath the sheltering wing of paternal care. "I send you forth," said the Saviour to his disciples, "as sheep among wolves;" and the same remark may be made by parents to their children, substituting the term lambs for sheep, when they place them out in this wicked and ensnaring world. It has been a dark day in the annals of myriads of families, when a son bade adieu to his parents, and commenced his probation and his struggles in the great business of human life. The tears that fell on that occasion were a sad presage, though unknown at the time, of others that were to flow in long succession over the follies, vices, and miseries of that unhappy youth. The history of ten thousand prodigal sons; the untimely graves of ten thousand broken-hearted parents; and the deep and heavy woes of ten thousand dishonoured families, attest the fact of the dangers that await a youth on leaving home: and he is most in danger, who is ignorant of what awaits him, or who, on being informed, treats the subject with indifference, smiles at the fears of his friends, and feels no fear for himself. Young man, there is hope of you if this representation shall awaken alarm, produce self-distrust, and excite vigilance and caution. Inexperienced, sanguine, and rash, with all your appetites sharpening, and all your passions strengthening; with an imagination lively, a curiosity prurient, and a heart susceptible; eager to act for yourself, panting to try your scarcely fledged wings on leaving the nest, and perhaps ambitious of distinction, you are in imminent peril of the lusts of the flesh and of the mind. All but yourself are anxious. Pause, and consider what you may become, an ornament of the profession you have chosen, a respectable member of society, a holy professor of religion, a useful citizen of your country, a benefactor of your species, and a light of the world. But according to the height to which you may rise, is the depth to which you may sink: for as the bottom of the ocean is supposed to be proportioned in measurement to the tops of the mountains, so the dark gulfs of sin and perdition into which you may plunge, sustain a similar relation to the summits of excellence and happiness to which you may ascend. Your capacity for ruin is equal to what it is for salvation. Survey for a moment the sphere which you may occupy and fill up with misery, desolation, and ruin. See what opportunities of destruction are within your reach, and to what suicidal and murderous havoc sin may lead you, if you give yourself up to its influence and government.

You may destroy your physical constitution by a more slow but not less sure process, than if you swallowed arsenic, or discharged a pistol at your heart. There are vices of the flesh that bring their own immediate punishment in the diseases which they entail. The martyrs of licentiousness are far more numerous, and the amount of their sufferings inconceivably greater, than the martyrs for religion. Millions die annually, the victims of drunkenness and debauchery, who long before the grave receives them to its dark domain, present a hideous and loathsome mass of corruption. Your pecuniary interests may be ruined. Many on whom the morning of life dawned in brightness, and its prospects opened in beauty, have seen their sun suddenly go down, and all before them covered with clouds, and ravaged with the storms of adversity; not that Providence was against them, not that man was unjust to them, but they were the destroyers of their own interests, by habits of extravagance, indolence, and indulgence, acquired in youth. You can blast your reputation. After building up with great care your good name, for some years, and acquiring respect and esteem from those who knew you, "in one single hour, by yielding to some powerful temptation, you may fix a dark stain upon your character, which no tears can ever wash away, or repentance remove, but which will cause you to be read and known of all men, till the grave receives you out of their sight. You may render yourself an object of the universal disgust and abhorrence of the good, and be the taunt and scorn of the wicked; so that wherever you turn your eyes, you will find none to bestow upon you a single smile of complacency. How many in this condition, bitterly realizing that, 'without a friend, the world is but a wilderness,' have, in a paroxysm of desperation, committed suicide." Your intellect, strong by nature, and capable of high cultivation, may, like a fine flower, be suffered to run wild by neglect, be trodden down by brute lusts, or be broken by violence. Your affections, given to be your delight by virtuous exercise on right objects, may be all perverted so as to become like so many demons, possessing and tormenting your soul, because they are set on things forbidden, and indulged to excess. Your conscience, granted to be your monitor, guide, and friend, may be wounded, benumbed, seared, till it is insensible, silent, and deaf, and of no use in warning you against sin, in restraining or reproving you for it. In short, you may destroy your immortal soul; and what ruin is like that of the soul, so immense, so horrible, so irretrievable? You may break the hearts of your parents; make your brothers and sisters ashamed to own you; be a nuisance and pest to society; a bane to your country; the corrupter of youthful morals; the seducer· of female virtue; the consumer of the property of your friends; and, to reach the climax of your mischief, you may be the Apollyon of the circle of immortal souls in which you move, sending some to perdition before you reach it yourself, and causing others to follow you to the bottomless pit, where you will never escape the sight of their torments, nor the sound of their imprecations. How great the power, how malignant the virulence of sin, that can spread its influence so widely, and exert its force with such deadly effect, not only destroying the sinner himself, but involving others in his ruin! No man goes alone to perdition, no one perishes alone in his iniquity; a consideration which every transgressor should regard : he sustains the character not only of a suicide, but of a murderer, and the worst of all murderers, for he is the murderer of souls. What a critical position you now occupy, between the capability of rising to so much excellence; or sinking to ruin so deep, and misery so intense! Reflect. Oh that you were wise; that you understood this ; that you would consider your end.

CHAPTER IV.

THE SUCCESSIVE STEPS OF GOING ASTRAY.

IF it is a melancholy fact, which the history of innumerable families can verify, that many young men,
who leave home in every respect moral and respectable,
become vicious, and end their course in profligacy and
ruin, an inquiry presents itself as to the steps which lead
to this dreadful reverse of character and circumstances.
It rarely, if ever, happens, that the heart throws off at
once all the restraints of virtue, and plunges suddenly
into the depths of vice. It is not by one stride, that the
moral youth passes from sober habits at home to those
of an opposite nature abroad, but generally by slow and
successive steps. The judgment and conscience would
recoil from a temptation which proposed to him to become profligate at once; and if he ever be an adept in
vice, he must be led on by insensible degrees, and by
little and little make advances in the way of sinners, and
the counsels of the ungodly. This is what is meant by
the deceitfulness of sin.

What individual who ever attained to enormity of
wickedness, foresaw or conjectured the end of his career?
When the messenger of Heaven disclosed to Hazael the
Syrian, the darkness of his future character, he indignantly exclaimed, " Is thy servant a dog, that he should

do this?" It was a burst of honest indignation. At that time he was incapable of the atrocities which it was foretold he should one day commit, and his whole nature rose in an expression of sincere abhorrence. He knew not the deceitfulness of his heart, or the corrupting influences of ambition and power. He was led on by a gradual progress in his guilty career, till the events of his history surpassed in criminality the picture drawn by the prophet. Who that ever ended his days at the gallows, or in the felon's exile, would at one period of his life have thought it possible that he should ever be so hardened as to commit such crimes? Habit renders all things easy, even the most atrocious crimes ; and habits of vice, like other habits, begin with acts, many of them little ones. The most alarming view of sin therefore, and that which should excite the greatest dread caution and vigilance, is its progressive nature.

I have somewhere read of one who lived in the early ages of the Christian era, who, on being asked by a friend to accompany him to the amphitheatre, to witness the gladiatorial combats with wild beasts, expressed his abhorrence of the sport, and refused to witness a scene condemned alike by humanity and Christianity. Overcome at length by the continued and pressing solicitation of his friend, whom he did not wish to disoblige, he consented to go; but determined that he would close his eyes as soon as he had taken his seat, and keep them closed during the whole time he was in the amphitheatre. At some particular display of strength and skill by one of the combatants, a loud shout of applause was raised by the spectators, when the Christian almost involuntarily opened his eyes : being once open,

he found it difficult to close them again; he became
interested in the fate of the gladiator who was then
engaged with a lion. He returned home professing to
dislike, as his principles required him to do, these cruel
games; but his imagination ever and anon reverted to
the scenes he had unintentionally witnessed. He was
again solicited by his friend to see the sport. He found
less difficulty now than before in consenting. He went,
sat with his eyes open, and enjoyed the spectacle; again
and again he took his seat with the pagan crowd; till
at length he became a constant attendant at the amphitheatre, abandoned his Christian profession, relapsed
into idolatry, and left a fatal proof of the deceitfulness
of sin. Thousands of facts to the same purport might
be collected, if it were necessary, tending to illustrate
the insidious manner in which the transgressor is led
on, in his gradual descent into the gulf of ruin.

Let us gather up the substance of the preceding
chapters, and trace the wanderer through his sinful
course. Perhaps before he left his father's house he
was not only strictly moral, but was the subject of religious impressions; convinced of sin, and an inquirer
after salvation. He heard sermons with interest, kept
holy the sabbath, and made conscience of secret prayer
and reading the Scriptures. His conduct had awakened
the hopes of his parents, and raised the expectations of
his minister; but he was not decided; there had been
no actual surrender of his heart to God, through faith
repentance and the new birth. In this state of mind,
he left home. Instead of taking alarm, as he should
have done, at the dangers to which he was now about
to be exposed, he went thoughtlessly to his new situation, and encountered its perils without due preparation.

In his place he found little to encourage, perhaps something, or even much, to damp and discourage serious
reflection.   The preacher whose ministrations he attended was less impressive and exciting than the one he
had left.   The master whom he served took little care
of his spiritual welfare.   Amidst these circumstances,
his religious impressions were soon lost, and his concern
speedily subsided.   Still he could not at once give up
the forms of devotion, and for awhile kept up the practice of private prayer ; but having no separate room, he
soon became ashamed to be seen falling upon his knees
in the presence of gay or thoughtless companions, who
slept in the same apartment, and who perhaps sneered
at the practice.   This is a temptation to which many
are exposed, and it is one of the most successful in inducing young persons to give up the habit of prayer.
He could not, however, quite relinquish a practice to
which he had been accustomed from childhood, and
occasionally he stole away to his room, and spent a few
moments in devotion.   This too in time was given up,
and prayer wholly discontinued.   A great restraint was
now removed, and a barrier thrown down.   The fear
of God, even that small portion of it he seemed to
possess, was leaving his heart.   He now lives without
prayer, and stands exposed to the ten thousand snares
and temptations of the world, without a single defence.
Yet he fills up his place in the house of God; for he
cannot throw off a certain kind of reverence for the
sabbath, and a still lingering attachment to the sanctuary.   In the same house in which he lives are to be
found one, or it may be several, who have no taste for
sacred things, but are worldly and sensual.   He hears
their scoffs at piety, which at first shock him, and he

rebukes them, or expostulates with them, for he is not yet reconciled to profanity : he goes further, and points out the impropriety of their conduct in other things, and warns them of the consequences. By degrees, however, he becomes more tolerant of their sins, and less offended by their dissipation. They rally him, ridicule him, and flatter him by turns, and on some fine sabbath evening persuade him to accompany them in a ramble into the country.. After a little hesitation, he consents, enjoys himself and is merry, though not altogether without his conscience smiting him. In a sabbath or two the Sunday party is again formed, and the authority of God again resisted and despised. He now thinks once a day quite enough for public worship, that the morning being given to God, the evening may be given to pleasure, especially by one who is all the week shut up in a close town, and who has no opportunity except on a Sunday, to see the country or breathe fresh air. The same argument, once admitted to be valid, is soon applied to the morning service, and the whole sabbath is at length given by him to recreation.

Conscience, however, has not suffered him to go thus far without frequent stings and warnings. A letter from home occasionally disturbs him. His father has been informed of his altered conduct, and, in grief of heart, expostulates, entreats, and warns. First he is sorrowful, then he is angry, then inwardly uneasy ; but the jest of a sinful companion scatters every better thought, and he is determined to go on. He is now the constant associate of evil doers, who have gained an ascendency over him, and are leading him further and further astray. To calm the apprehensions of his parents, and to silence the remonstrances from home, he writes a penitential letter, and gives promises of amendment. Lying and hypocrisy are now added to his sins, and they are dreadful auxiliaries in benumbing the conscience and hardening the heart. A celebrated actor comes to the town, or is to appear at one of the theatres, and he is solicited to go to the performance; he is now prepared for this, and readily assents. Every thing fascinates him. His senses, imagination, heart, taste, are all carried away captive. His soul is in a state of mental intoxication. He acquires a passion for the stage, and as often as his means and opportunity will allow he is at the theatre. Intelligence again reaches home, and again his shocked and heart-stricken parents write, and entreat him to alter his conduct, or return to them: but he can now treat a father's advice with contempt, and a mother's tears with cruel indifference. The theatre, as we have already shown, is the resort of those unhappy women, of whom the wise man says, "their house is the way to hell, going down to the chambers of death." He is caught in the snare and ruined. He is horror-struck when reflection comes, and in an agony of expiring virtue, exclaims, "What have I done!" Conscience is not quite dead, nor shame quite extinguished. To still the remonstrances of the troublesome monitor within, he revisits the scene where so many are assembled like himself, to drown their sorrows, or to blunt remorse. The death of a friend or relative occurs, which renders it necessary that he should attend a funeral, perhaps hear a funeral sermon. The Book of God, and his faithful servant, now proclaim the sinfulness of sin and the sinner's everlasting doom. He trembles, but repents not. Revelation now haunts him like a spectre, and disturbs him in his course. If he persist in sinning, he must get rid of this troublesome interference. Is the Bible true? Some one of his companions is a sceptic, and now labours for his conversion to infidelity. Byron's poetry prepares the way for Hume's subtleties, Paine's ribaldry, or Owen's absurdities. Christianity is now called a fable; man's accountability, a mere dogma of cunning priests; and hell, only the picture of gloomy superstition, to hold the mind of man in bondage. He throws off the yoke of religion; exults in his liberty; yields his members servants to uncleanness; adds iniquity unto iniquity, and runs to every excess of riot. But whence come the funds to support his lusts? His father cannot supply them, nor can his wages; but secret pilfering can, and does. If he can escape detection, what has he to fear? "Man is the creature of circumstances," and his circumstances compel him to rob his master; and as to an hereafter, it is all a dream. Gambling is now added to his other crimes. Shame is lost, nay, he glories in his shame; and commences the trade of ruining others; corrupting the principles of one sex, and the morals of the other. With a character composed of every darkest shade of human depravity, let his closing scene be narrated in the next chapter, which, by a melancholy fact, confirms the representation here given. Not that I mean to assert that all who go astray in youth reach this climax; but many do, and all are in danger of it.

What, then, are the maxims arising out of this representation, which every young man should always bear in mind?

1. That sin is the most deceitful thing in the universe, as manifested by the insidious manner in which it leads on the transgressor in his way; and the excuses

with which at every stage of his progress it furnishes him.

2. Those who would not be found walking in the path of sin, should not take the first step in it. Avoid first sins: they always, or nearly so, lead on to others. It is far easier to abstain from the first sin than the second. No temptation of Satan has been more successful than the suggestion, "only this once." That once may be your ruin for 'ever. Acts may be repeated, and come to habits. No sin comes alone, but stands in close connexion with others which they teach us to commit, and often afford us an opportunity to commit.

3. Carefully avoid little sins, for they usually lead on to greater ones. No sin abstractly is little, but comparatively some sins are greater than others. It is by inducing you to commit these, that Satan will prepare you for and lead you on to practices of greater enormity. When under the influence of temptation, though it be to a seemingly trivial fault, always ask the question, "What will this grow to?"

4. Be very watchful against common sins. It is wonderful to think what boldness sinners often derive from this circumstance, and how hard it is to persuade them of the danger of what is common, and generally practised. Even good men are sometimes carried away by prevailing and epidemic sins. How frequent is the remark, "If this be sin, I am not singular in the commission of it; there are many others guilty as well as I!" Common sins lead to uncommon ones. If we follow others in what is evil in little things, we are preparing ourselves to follow evil examples in greater matters.

5. Take care not to be misled by names. Look at

things as they are, and do not consider them merely by the terms employed to express them. "Woe to them," said the prophet, "that call evil good and good evil!" This is often done: vice is called virtue, and virtue vice. Thus excess and intemperance are often called, and unhappily deemed by many, a social disposition and good fellowship. Levity, folly, and even obscenity, are called youthful spirit, boyish cheerfulness, innocent liberty, and good humour. Pride, malice, and revenge, are called honour, spirit, and dignity of mind. Vain pomp, luxury, and extravagance, are styled taste, elegance, and refinement. Under such disguises does sin often conceal itself, and by such means does it entrap the unwary, and conciliate their regard. Do not then be cheated out of virtue by the change of names; lift up the disguise, and ascertain the real natures of things. This deceit also discovers itself by its counterpart in disparaging true piety and goodness by the most opprobrious titles. Tenderness of conscience is called ridiculous precision, narrowness of mind, and superstitious fear; zeal against sin is moroseness, or ill nature; seriousness of mind is repulsive melancholy; superior sanctity is disgusting hypocrisy. Now, as nothing tends more to discredit goodness than to give it an ill name, and as not a few are led more by names than things, I cannot give you a more important piece of advice, than to admonish you to be upon your guard against this deception, of covering sin with the garb of virtue, and branding virtue with the name of sin.

6. Study well the peculiar temptations of the new situation into which you are introduced, and anticipate, so far as it can be done, by what snare you are likely to be tempted and led astray. Look around, and survey

your circumstances, that, ascertaining as far as possible by what door temptation will approach, you may be the better prepared to meet it.   Remember, it is of great consequence to your future conduct and character, how you act immediately on arriving at your new situation. The first steps in the path of goodness or of sin, are, I repeat with emphasis, frequently taken very soon after a young man leaves home.

CHAPTER V.

[This Chapter is omitted, as it consists of extracts of narratives (illustrative of the preceding chapter) quoted from "The Happy Transformation, or the History of a London Apprentice;" and from the Rev. Hubbard Winslow.]

CHAPTER VI.

BESIDES the formidable and appalling perils which have been already enumerated, as awaiting the young man on his quitting the house of his father, and entering on the business of life, there are others, which, if they do not expose him to the same moral jeopardy, are of sufficient consequence to his well-being to deserve attention. Character may be injured by many things which can scarcely be called immoralities; and misery, yea vice also, may grow out of indiscretions and imprudences.

I. Absence from home may beget forgetfulness of home, and indifference to it: and such a state of mind, where there is much at home worthy to be remembered and loved, is not only unamiable in itself, but injurious to its possessor. Home is not only the scene of enjoyment to the youthful mind, but it is the soil in which the seeds of the social charities and virtues are first sown and grow; so that the child who, with much reason for loving his father's house, is destitute of this affection while there, or loses it when he leaves the spot long trodden by his infant and boyish feet, is a most unpromising character. The young man, who, upon quitting the house that has sheltered him from

his birth, cuts the ties which ought to bind him to that
dear spot, and casts no longing, lingering look behind;
who suffers all its lovely images to sink into oblivion
amidst new and ever-shifting scenes; who can forget
father and mother, brothers and sisters, in his intercourse with strangers, and whose heart is never under
the influence of an attraction to the circle of all that is
related to him on earth, is destitute, at any rate,
of social virtue, and is in peril of losing all other principles of morality. Cherish, then, young man, cherish
a fond affection for your parents' house; it may be
humble, but it is home to you. You may be rising
higher and higher at every step above the lowly spot
on which your cradle was rocked, and may be out-
stripping in prosperity those with whom you inhabited
it, but still let it ever be sacred to you. Let not
your parents have to say to each other with tears,
when they have waited years for a visit, and months
even for a letter, " Our son has forgotten us." Let
them not have to exclaim, in bitterness of spirit, " How
sharper than a serpent's tooth it is, to have a thankless child! " Keep up a constant correspondence with
home by letters, an additional motive to which you
now possess in cheap postage, and let every line be such
as shall be music to a father's and a mother's heart.
As often as your engagements will allow, gladden them
with a visit. Convince them that neither time, distance,
nor prosperity, can lead you to forget them. How will
it delight them to see that neither new scenes, nor new
occupations, nor new relations, can ever alienate your
heart from them ! The preservation of a tender love
for home and its occupants, has proved in some cases
the last tie to virtue, and a last preservation from

ruin. When all other kinds of excellence were lost, and every other motive had ceased to influence, this one lingering feeling was left, and filial affection prevented the complete abandonment of the character to the desolation of vice. " What will my poor father and my dear mother say and feel, and. my brothers and my sisters too, who yet love me? and how shall I ever be able to face them again?" By this one question the spirit, about to swing off into the turbid stream of vice that was rolling by, held on, till time was given for other and more powerful influences to come, and the love of home saved its possessor from the perdition that seemed to await him.

II. In opposition to this danger, the love of home has been so strong, so fond, so effeminate in some, that they have been really injured by it, through all their future life. It has promoted, and even produced, such a softness and feebleness of character, as totally unfitted them to struggle with the difficulties of the world, and rendered them good for nothing, but to be nursed in the lap of luxurious ease. Parents have sometimes lent a helping hand to this mischief, and have cherished in their children a whimpering fretfulness after home, and such a feeling of dependence on its comforts, as has rendered them, through their whole existence, pitiable spectacles of querulous effeminacy and helpless imbecility. After what I have said, no one will suspect me of encouraging an indifference to home, when I call upon my youthful readers to be willing to leave it, for the sake of their future welfare. Act the part of a good child, in loving your father's home and its happy circle; and act also the part of a man, in being willing to quit it, for the sake of learning to perform your part

well in the affairs of life. Do not cherish such a
hankering after home as will make every situation uncomfortable, and inflict wretchedness upon you where-
ever you are. Let not your parents be made unhappy
by letters full of complaint, and tales of lamentation
and woe. Rove not from place to place in quest of that
which you will never find, a situation abroad that will
command all the indulgences of a father's abode. Acquire a manliness of character, a nobleness and firmness
of mind, that can endure hardships and make sacrifices.
It is desirable, of course, that your parents should procure a situation for you, or that you should procure one
for yourself, where as much comfort may be secured as
is usually attainable, for we have no need to court
annoyance, discomfort, and privation : but be not over-
fastidious about these matters, nor let your happiness
depend upon having your palate, your convenience, and
your ease, consulted and gratified even in the minutest
particulars. Do not set out in life the slave of little
things. No situation is without some inconveniences.
Human life is a journey ; all men are travellers ; and
travellers do not expect the comforts of their own house
upon the road. Cultivate a hardihood of mind, that
shall make you insensible to petty annoyances. Look
at great things, aim at great things, and expect great
things ; then little ones will neither engage, nor amuse,
nor distress you.

III. Among the minor perils to which you are exposed on leaving home, is the liability of acquiring an
unsettled, roving, and romantic disposition. Now and
then a boy of erratic mind and precocious vagrancy is
found, who is ever shaping new and strange courses for
himself, and laying schemes for adventure and enter-

prise, even in his father's house. These, however, are comparatively rare cases. But the spirit of roaming is not unfrequently awakened when a youth leaves home; then "the world is all before him," as he imagines, "where to choose:" but, without making Providence his guide, he begins to think of looking further for himself than his judicious friends have done for him. A useful and honourable employment is selected; good situations are procured for acquiring a knowledge of his business, perhaps at much cost and trouble. His friends rejoice in the idea of his comfortable and advantageous disposal. But ere long, home comes a letter of complaint, which banishes from his father's mind all these ideas of his son's happy position, and fills him with perplexity. Much against the hopes and wishes that his friends had formed, a change takes place, and the youth removes to another situation. Here he stays not, but removes some where else. At length he wishes to go abroad, and try his fortune at sea. This is done, and he embarks. One voyage is enough, and he returns home, weary of foreign travel and of the waves, and is now a dead weight upon his father's hands. He is not immoral. He commits no vice. He does not grieve his friends by profligacy. He is not indolent, but his versatile, unsettled, romantic disposition, makes them sick at heart, and convinces them that he will never be a comfort to them, or do anything good for himself. And he never does. Life is worn out by him in trying many things, and succeeding in nothing.

IV. It may not be unnecessary to caution you against a spirit of insubordination and disrespect towards your employers. It not unfrequently happens, that a young man has his comfort destroyed, and his character in-

jured, by constant collision with his employer. Sometimes the fault is all on one side; the youth has been
so petted and spoiled at home, has had his own way so
entirely, and been left so much to be his own master,
that the yoke of authority, however light and easy, is
felt to be galling and intolerable, and, like an untamed
bullock, he resents and resists it, to the annoyance
of his employer and his own injury. Young man,
if this has been your case, instantly change, or you
are undone. Such a disposition will not only be your
misery, but your ruin. No one can be prepared
to become a master, but by first acting as a servant;
and the way to govern is first to obey. Give up your
home habits and caprices: and the sooner the better.
Call into exercise your judgment and good sense. Give
over the contest with your master: he must be obeyed,
and it is as much for your interest as for his that he
should. But suppose that he is an austere man, a hard
master, an unreasonable employer; even in that case
carry your patience and submission to the utmost limit
of endurance. If there be absolute tyranny and cruelty,
or an intolerable severity, make it known to your
parents, after having mildly expostulated against it
without effect. Do not by impertinence, by obstinacy,
or by rebellion, make bad worse. The galled animal
which is urged on by a furious driver, and which cannot
escape from the reins and collar, avoids much pain by
quiet and patient submission: resistance only brings
more blows from his unrelenting master, and causes
deeper wounds by the fretting and friction of the har-
ness. Perhaps in most cases of disagreement, there is
a little fault on both sides. I know an excellent young
man who was apprenticed to a master in a respectable

trade, and of a tolerably good disposition, and who made a profession of religion; but he was a very bad tradesman, and had a wife who was gay, worldly, and exceedingly imperious in ordering the young men who were in the house. The youth I speak of saw the fault of his employer, and felt the haughty demeanour of the wife. Instead of submitting with a good grace to many things that were certainly very annoying, he was constantly in strife about little things, that kept him in perpetual wretchedness. Sometimes his aim was really to correct the blunders into which the master fell, and to avert the consequences of them; but he often did so pertly and disrespectfully, and therefore met with passion and rebuke in return. He complained to his friends, and made them wretched without relieving himself; and had he not been released from his situation, he might possibly have absconded, and been ruined. I have since heard him say that, much as his employer was to blame, and much cause as he had to complain, yet if he had himself possessed a little more patience and prudence, and less irritability and combativeness, he should have saved himself incalculable wretchedness, and averted much ill-will and opposition. Let this be a warning to you. In a former part of this volume, I have alluded to the discomfort of such a case, as one of the sources of moral danger. I have now dwelt upon it more at length to show that it is sometimes brought on by a spirit of insubordination, and that it may be in great measure avoided by an obedient, conciliatory, and submissive temper.

V. Entanglements in love, and the rash formation of attachments and engagements of this kind, are another snare into which young men away from home

are too apt to fall. Besides the love of society, and the
desire of companionship, there is a susceptibility, a
strange and restless emotion, seated deep in the heart
of youth, which pants for an alliance of the soul with
some dear selected object closer than is felt or found in
the warmest general friendship. The love of the sexes
towards each other is one of the instincts planted in our
nature by the hand of Him who formed it, and was
intended, like every other arrangement of Providence,
for benevolent purposes; and when this passion is
guided by prudence and sanctified by piety, it becomes
a source of felicity, which if it does not remove, at least
mitigates the woes of our fallen state. "It must, however, be a reasonable, and not a reckless passion. A
check must be given to these emotions, while immature
years are passed in the acquisition of knowledge, or in
preparation for some useful station in society. The
young, affections should be restrained until the period
arrives, when it will be honourable and safe to unfetter
them. For want of such restraint many a youth has
dashed his earthly hopes, and dragged out a miserable
existence." Attachments formed in boyhood have often
led to dishonourable dissolution of them, or a wretched
union. The heart grows faster than the judgment, and
should not be allowed in this matter to be our first and
only guide. A youth not out of his apprenticeship is a
poor judge of the fitness of a person as young as himself
to be his companion for life; and his mind should be
occupied by other things. "It is not to be denied that,
when circumstances justify it, a reciprocal affection
between the sexes, founded on virtuous and honourable
principles, is one of the purest sources of earthly happiness. It seems as if the Creator, in pronouncing upon

the sinning pair the curses which their disobedience so
justly merited, left them in pity for their calamities this
soothing, mitigating blessing." But early connexions,
especially if clandestine ones, formed and cherished
without the consent or knowledge of parents, have
rarely proved happy ones. In some cases the dissolution
of them at the imperative command of parental authority,
has been followed by an injurious influence over the
young man's future destiny, inasmuch as it has made
him either reckless or misanthropic. I have some
painful instances of this before my mind's eye at this
moment, some of which are of melancholy, almost
tragic interest.

VI. Where a youth has been much indulged at
home, and not trained to habits of persevering application and patient industry, he is in danger of sinking
into indolence, and then into vice. This tendency is
not always the result of parental neglect, but is occasionally found in youths, who have had the best precepts
to guide them, and the most stimulating examples to
quicken them. To whatever cause it may be attributed,
indolence is an evil of immense magnitude. There may
be no actual vice, nothing at present bordering on
immorality, but only a disgraceful and shameless inactivity. Nothing rouses the inert and creeping youth.
His employer frowns, scolds, threatens, or coaxes, stimu-
lates, and promises; but it is all in vain. Nothing
moves him. It is a difficulty to rouse him from his
slumber, or draw him from his bed; and when he is up,
he may almost as well be in his chamber, for of the
little he does, and it is as little as he can make it, he
does nothing willingly, and nothing well. It is more
trouble to get him to do any thing, than it is to do it

oneself. If one single abstract word may express his character, it is "laziness." What a pitiable and almost hopeless spectacle! A young man gifted by Providence, perhaps with a mind susceptible of improvement, and talents for business, which if cultivated would lead to eminence, dozing away the most precious period of existence, wasting his time, burying his talent and sleeping upon its grave, disappointing the hopes of his parents, tormenting by his incorrigible laziness the heart of his employer, and preparing himself, probably for vice, certainly for misery. "Indolence throws open the avenues of the soul to temptations, and the great fallen spirit, in his malignant march through the earth, seizes upon the occasion, and draws the unwary youth into his toils. 'For Satan finds some mischief still for idle hands to do.' By indolence the moral principle ' is weakened, and the impulse of passion is increased. It is the gateway through which a troop of evil spirits gain admission to the citadel, and compel conscience to surrender to base desire. Activity in honourable pursuits strengthens moral‍ principle, makes the conscience vigilant, and furnishes a breastwork of defence impregnable to the assaults of the tempter. Indigence has in some cases counteracted the causes of indolence ; and if there be a spark of youthful fire in the soul, the stimulant of necessity will operate as a spur to vigorous action. Hence it is, that from the low walks of life have risen some of the greatest statesmen, most learned divines, and gifted geniuses in every department of human action. Their poverty has been the spring of their exertions. Though denied in youth the advantages which wealth commands, they have found more than an equivalent in their own unconquerable aspirations. What seemed to be an obstacle became an impulse; and the impediments in their paths to usefulness and reputation, which would have frightened back less noble spirits, only seemed like the interposing Alps in the march of Hannibal, to make their victory more glorious and more complete. Oh that I could reach the ear of every youth in the land, wake up in his soul those generous desires, and urge him to those active exertions, which should be at once his safe-guard from temptation and the pledge of his success."*

VII. On leaving home and entering on the business of life, or preparing to enter upon it, young men are apt to form too high an estimate of the importance of wealth, and to make the acquisition of it the supreme if not exclusive object of existence. Ours is emphatically a money-making country. By far the greater part, if not the whole, of those who read these pages, will be found among the middling classes; young men who leave a father's house, not to seek fame or rank, but wealth. Their feeling is, "I am going out to learn and try to get a fortune: to take my chance in the world's lottery, with the hope of drawing a prize." To this they are directed, perhaps, and stimulated by their parents, who send them forth, virtually, with this admonition: "Go, my son, and get rich." Perhaps the son has seen no other object of desire or pursuit before the eyes of his parents, has heard no other commended, and has been placed in a situation where the attraction of no other could be felt. Money, money, money has been held up to him as the summum bonum of human life, and he goes out eager to obtain its

* "Considerations for Young Men," by the author of "Advice to a Young Christian."

possession. But even without being thus sworn in and consecrated in childhood on the altar of Mammon ; and when all that they have seen and heard in the house of their father is opposed to the notion, youth, in general, can with difficulty be persuaded that to learn to get money is not the only or the highest end of their leaving home. Riches are the bright vision, which, seen in the distant prospect, call forth their aspirations, and make them willing to sacrifice the endearments of their father's house. They have no ideas of greatness, of happiness, of respectability, apart from wealth, which is the standard of every thing valuable with them. The hope of being a rich man is the nerve of their industry, the spur to their energies, the reconciling thought that makes them wipe from their brow with joy the memorial of the curse of earth. And should we cut this nerve of effort, and paralyse these energies? Should we take from the heart this desire and expectation of success? Should we quench the ardour of youth, and make life a dreary wilderness, pathless, objectless, hopeless? No. Money has proper attractions. It is the gift of God. When sought in subordination to a higher end of life, by honest industry, and as a means of rational gratification and of benevolent effort, it is a blessing to its owners and to others. But when it is wealth for its own sake that is set up as the object of existence ; when it is loved for itself ; when that love is an absolute passion ; when it takes such hold of the inner man as to thrust out and cast down every moral principle, every noble sentiment, every honourable emotion, and every subject which relates to our immortal destiny ; then it is a low and sordid passion, a grovelling ambition, a contraction of mind, of itself unworthy a rational, much more an immortal being, and in its influence will benumb the conscience, harden the heart, and ruin the soul.

In a case where you cannot have experience of your own to guide you, be willing, young man, to profit by the experience of others. Is there a subject about which the testimony of mankind is more concurrent, or on which they have delivered their testimony more spontaneously and emphatically, than the insufficiency of wealth to satisfy the soul? Has not this been proclaimed by the contentment of millions who have had little, and the restlessness and dissatisfaction of thousands who have had much? Does not Solomon, as the foreman of that countless jury which has sat in judgment upon the world's claim, deliver the verdict in those impressive words, "Vanity of vanities, all is vanity." Not that I mean to say wealth contributes nothing to our felicity, either by lessening the evils, or multiplying the comforts, of life: it does contribute something, and it may be lawfully sought after for as much as it can yield. My remarks go only to prove that it is not the chief good, and to dissuade the young from considering and treating it as such in the outset of life. It may be useful as one of the golden vessels with which to serve yourselves, your neighbours, or your Lord; but it must not become a golden idol, to be set up and worshipped instead of Jehovah. I do not wish you to become careless or inactive in business, or even indifferent to the increase of your possessions; but what I aim at is, to convince you, that it is not the supreme end of life, and that it is infinitely less desirable than an inheritance laid up in heaven. If you make it the end of life, you may miss it after all, and

even in reference to your own selected object live in
vain; while if you succeed, you will still miss the end
for which God created you, and lavish existence upon an
idol, which cannot save you when you most need its
help.   You may cry to it in your affliction, but it will
have no ears to hear.   You may call upon it in your
dying hour, but it will have no power to commiserate,
and to turn the ebbing tide of life.   You may invoke it
at the day of judgment, but it shall be only to be a
swift witness against you.   You may think of it in
eternity, but it will only be to feel it to be "the gold
that shall canker," and the "rust that shall eat your
flesh."

Such, then, are some of the minor dangers, if indeed
I can with propriety call them so, when they entail
such consequences as I have stated : but what I mean
is, that they are not so directly and flagrantly immoral
in their tendency and effects as those previously enumerated.   Look at them, young men.   Weigh them
with deliberation.   And may God, in answer to your
earnest prayers, grant you his grace for your protection
and preservation.

CHAPTER VII.

THE MEANS OF SAFETY.

Such means there certainly are, if you will avail yourselves of them. Imminent as is the peril to which you are exposed, defence is at hand, and it will be your own fault if you are not preserved. Thousands have been kept amidst the severest temptations. In the beautiful, touching, and instructive history of Joseph, as recorded in the book of Genesis, a history which will never cease to be admired as long as taste or piety shall remain in the world, we have a striking instance of moral preservation amidst great danger, well worthy your attention. How fierce and seductive was the assault upon his morals! it came from a quarter, and in a form, the most likely to corrupt a youthful mind: yet how promptly, firmly, and successfully was it resisted! True, his virtue subjected him for a while to much suffering, for, defeated in her criminal intentions, his tempter, under the combined influence of disappointment, shame, and remorse, wickedly revenged herself upon the virtue she could not subdue; blasted his reputation by calumny and false accusation, and caused him to be cast into prison. But Providence, ever watchful over the reputation and interests of pious men, overruled all for good, and made the prison of this illustrious Israelite the way to his elevation. But for Potiphar's wife, Joseph had never been prime minister of Egypt; her guilt and its painful effects were rendered subservient to his advancement. Sooner or later virtue will bring its own reward. But what was the means of Joseph's preservation from the snare? Religion. "How can I do this great wickedness, and sin against God?" was his noble reply. Here was the shield that covered his heart. True, he had a deep sense of the duty he owed to his employer, and on this ground expostulated with the tempter, " Behold, my master wotteth not what is with me in the house, and he hath committed all that he hath to my hand; there is none greater in this house than I : neither hath he kept back anything from me but thee, because thou art his wife." This was faithful, just, generous, noble ; but there needed something else, something stronger, to resist such a temptation : morality alone would not have done it, and he called in the aid of his piety. " How can I do this great wickedness, and sin against God?" Thus armed with religion, he fought with the tempter, and came off more than conqueror. Let every young man mark this, and see the power excellence and benefit of piety, as a preservative against sin.

Amidst the snares to which you will be exposed, you will need something stronger and more trustworthy than those feeble defences on which some rely, but which in many instances are demolished by the first assault upon mere unaided virtue. You may leave your father's house with fixed resolutions to shun what is evil, and practise what is good; you may suppose that you have no taste for the vicious pleasures of profligate persons ; you may cherish a tender regard for the feelings of your parents, sufficient, as you think, to preserve you from every thing that would grieve their hearts; you may have your eye on future respectability and wealth, and be inspired with an ambition that makes you dread whatever would interfere with these objects of desire; you may be already moral and upright, and thus be led to imagine that you are prepared to repel every attack upon your purity and integrity; but if destitute of real religion, you may soon be exposed to temptations which will either sweep away all these defences as with the violence of a flood, or insidiously undermine them with the slow but certain process of a siege. Religion, true religion, young man, is the only defence to be relied upon; morality may, but piety will, protect you. What multitudes of instances could the history of the church of God furnish, of youths passing unconquered through the most corrupting scenes, by the aid of this Divine shield taken from the armoury of revelation; this shield of faith! I might mention names known and loved among the pious, of your own and other countries, who in youth went unbefriended and unpatronised from the country to the metropolis, and who, by the fear of God, were not only preserved from evil, but were raised to wealth, to influence, and usefulness, by the aid of religion. There are two or three questions concerning true religion which may with great propriety be asked, and which have, or ought to have, great force in recommending it to all. Whom did it ever impoverish, except by martyrdom? Whom did it ever render miserable? Who ever, on a death-bed, repented of having lived under its influence? On the contrary, how many millions has it blessed with wealth, with happiness in life, and comfort in death!

But what is religion? Give me your attention while

I attempt to answer this question. It is the most
momentous inquiry which can engage the intellect
of man. Literature, science, politics, commerce, and
the arts, are all important in their place and measure;
and men give proof that they duly, or rather unduly
estimate their importance, by the devoted manner in
which they attend to them. To multitudes they are
every thing. Yet man is an immortal creature, and
there is an eternity before him, and what direct relation
have these things to immortality? or what influence
do they exert on our everlasting destiny in another
world? Nay, do they make us either virtuous or happy
in this? Is there any necessary connexion between
any, or all of these things, with human felicity? They
call out and employ the noble faculties of the mind;
they raise man from savage to civilized society; they
refine the taste; they embellish life; they decorate the
stage on which the great drama of existence is carried
on, and give interest to the performance; but do they
reach the seat of man's chief pleasures or pains, the
heart? Do they cure its disorders, correct its tastes,
mitigate its sorrows, or soften its weightiest cares? Do
they comfort man amidst the wreck of his fortunes, the
disappointment of his hopes, the loss of his friends, the
malignity of his enemies, the pains of a sick̦chamber, the
struggles of a dying bed, and the prospect of a coming
judgment? No. Religion is that, and that only, which
can do this; and this it can do, and is continually
doing. Disbelieve, then, the calumnies that ignorant
men have circulated concerning it, who represent it as
degrading our intellect, and destroying our happiness.
On the contrary, a little reflection will convince you
that it is the sublimest science, the noblest learning, the

profoundest wisdom, the most consummate prudence. In its theory, it is called by way of eminence, truth; in its practice, wisdom; its essence, is love; its effect, even here, peace; and its ultimate reward, an immortality of joy. It is sustained by abundant and unanswerable evidence; it has engaged the attention and captivated the minds of men of the profoundest intellect : to speak only of our own country, I mention Bacon, Milton, Newton, Locke, Addison, and Johnson, and I might mention a host of others : and it is now preparing to subdue all nations to the obedience of faith. Is it not a subject, then, which demands and deserves attention ?

The question, however, still returns, What is religion ? To reply first in negatives : it is not merely being baptized in any particular church; it is not merely being educated in the profession of any particular creed; it is not merely being accustomed to observe any particular forms; it is not merely an attendance at any particular place of public worship; or the preference of any particular set of doctrines, however orthodox and Scriptural: religion is all this, but it is a great deal more; it includes this, but it goes much further.

True religion consists of repentance towards God. This is frequently enjoined in the New Testament. "Except ye repent, ye shall all likewise perish." "Repent, and be converted, that your sins may be blotted out." "Godly sorrow worketh repentance to salvation not to be repented of." From this last passage it clearly appears what repentance means, and that sorrow is but a part of it, yea, only the operative cause of it. The word signifies a change of mind with regard to sin : it is such a view of the evil of sin in general, and of the number and aggravation of our own sins in particular, as leads us to confess them to God, without reserve or excuse, to hate, and to forsake them.

But repentance is not enough: this is but a part of religion, and is not all that is necessary to salvation; for without faith, have whatever we may, it is impossible to please God. God has not left man to perish in his sins. Mercy has visited our world, and brought salvation to man. "God so loved the world, that he gave his only begotten Son, that whosoever believeth in him should not perish, but have everlasting life." When the jailer, expecting to perish, exclaimed, "What must I do to be saved?" the apostle replied, "Believe on the Lord Jesus Christ, and thou shalt be saved." We are "justified by faith;" we "purify our hearts by faith," "we walk by faith." Faith in general means such a belief of the whole of God's holy word, as leads us to observe and obey it. Faith in Christ signifies such a belief in the testimony borne to him in the Scripture, as the Son of God and Saviour of the world; as our Mediator between God and man; as our Prophet, Priest, and King; as our atoning sacrifice and justifying righteousness, as leads us to quit all dependence upon our own works for pardon, acceptance with God, and salvation, and to rely exclusively, and with expectation of eternal life, upon his propitiation and intercession. This is one great part of religion, and an essential to salvation. Faith is the saving grace; it is not that for which we are saved, as the meritorious cause, but that by which we are saved, as the instrumental means. The first effect of true faith is peace, the second love, the third holiness.

With faith is connected an entire change of heart,

conduct, and character. This is what our Lord calls, being "born again," being "born of water and the Spirit;" and the inspired evangelist designates it, being "born, not of blood, nor of the will of the flesh, nor of the will of man, but of God." It is what the apostle calls, "putting off the old man which is corrupt with his deeds, and putting on the new man, which is renewed in knowledge after the image of Him that created him." It is what is meant when he says, "If any man be in Christ, he is a new creature: old things are passed away; behold, all things are become new." It is that entire change of our moral nature, which is effected by the Spirit of God, through the word received by faith; when the corrupt and fallen nature which we inherit from Adam is taken away, and the holy and spiritual nature which we receive from Christ is imparted. This is the new birth, such a change of our hearts, as gives a new direction to our thoughts, feelings, tastes, and pursuits; and this direction is towards God, holiness, and eternity; whereas formerly it was towards sin and the present world. Now, the soul loves God with a supreme affection, and from this love springs a sincere desire to please him, and an endeavour to serve him with the obedience of affection, even as a son obeys the father whom he loves. Now he fears sin, hates it, and strives to avoid it, as that which God hates, and from which Christ died to redeem him. Now he has a tender conscience, and a jealousy over himself, lest he should offend God, and pollute his own soul. He watches and prays, lest he enter into temptation, and sanctification is his delight. Now he keeps holy the sabbath, reads the word of God, rejoices in the preaching of the cross, loves secret prayer, partakes of the supper of the Lord, joins the communion of saints, because these things are means of grace and ordinances of God. Constrained by the love of Christ, he now seeks to be useful, especially by diffusing that religion which he has found so beneficial to himself. He gives up all his former sinful amusements, the theatre, the card party, the ball, fashionable and dissipating visiting, for they do not now suit his taste; his delight is in God and his service, to which these things are all contrary. He is independent of them, and happy without them.

Such is religion, a personal, experimental, and practical thing. It is a thing of the heart, and not merely outward forms; a living principle in the soul influencing the mind, employing the affections, guiding the will, and directing as well as enlightening the conscience. It is a supreme, not a subordinate matter; demanding and obtaining the throne of the soul, giving law to the whole character, and requiring the whole man and all his conduct to be in subordination. It is an habitual, not an occasional thing; it takes up its abode in the heart, and not only sometimes and at particular seasons visiting it. It is a universal, and not a partial thing; not confining itself to certain times, and places, and occasions, but forming an integral part of the character, and blending with every occupation. It is noble and lofty, not an abject servile and grovelling thing; it communes with God, with truth, with holiness, with heaven, with eternity, and infinity. It is a happy and not a melancholy thing, giving peace that passeth understanding, and joy that is unspeakable, and full of glory. And it is a durable, not a transient thing, passing with us through life, lying down with us on the pillow of death, rising with us at the last day, and dwelling in our souls in heaven as the very element of eternal life. Such is religion, the sublimest thing in our world, sent down to be our comforter and ministering angel on earth, "our guide to everlasting life through all this gloomy vale."

CHAPTER VIII.

You need, young man, to defend you from the perils to which you are exposed, a shield always at hand, and impenetrable to the arrows of your enemies, and you may find it in religion. It does this by various means. It changes the moral nature, producing a dislike and dread of sin, and a love of holiness and virtue. Piety is a spiritual taste; and, like every other taste, it is accompanied with a distaste for the opposites of those things or qualities which are the subjects of its complacency. Sin is that bitter thing which the soul of a true Christian hates; it is the object of his antipathy, and therefore of his dread. He turns from it with aversion and loathing, as that which is offensive and disgusting. It is not merely that he is commanded by authority to abstain from sin, but he is led away from it by inclination.. He may have sinful propensities of his animal nature, but he resists the indulgence of them, for it is sin against God. Now what can be a more effectual protection from a practice or habit than an actual dislike of it, or distaste for it? Who does that which he dislikes to do, except under compulsion? When you have once tasted the sweetness of religion, how insipid, how nauseous, will be those draughts of vicious pleasure with which the sinner intoxicates and poisons his soul! When you have acquired a relish for the pure, calm, satisfying joys of faith and holiness, how entirely will you disrelish the polluting, boisterous, and unsatisfying pleasures of sin! When you have once drunk of the waters of the river of life, clear as crystal, proceeding from the throne of God and of the Lamb, how loathsome will be the filthy turbid streams of licentious gratification! The new nature, by its own powerful and holy instinct, will turn away your feet from every forbidden place, and every unhallowed scene. Panting after God, and thirsting for the living God, taking pleasure in his ways, and delighting in the communion of the saints, you will shudder at the idea of being found in the haunts of vice, or in the society of the vicious. It will be unnecessary to forbid your going to the tavern, the theatre, the house of ill fame, the gambling-table, or horse-race; your own renewed and sanctified nature will be a law against these things, and compel the exclamation, "I will not sit with vain persons, nor go in with dissemblers; I have hated the congregation of evil-doers, and will not sit with the wicked. Gather not my soul with sinners."

In addition to this, religion will implant in your hearts a regard to the authority and presence of God. "By the fear of the Lord," says Solomon, "men depart from evil." This veneration for God comes in to aid the exercise of love for holiness. By the fear of God I do not mean a slavish and tormenting dread of the Divine Being, which haunts the mind like an ever-present spectre, that is superstition, not religion; but I mean a fear springing out of affection, the fear of a child dreading to offend the father whom he loves. What a restraint

from sin is there in that child's mind! He may be absent
from his father; but love keeps him from doing what
his father disapproves. So it is with religion; it is love
to God, and love originates fear. He who is thus blessed
with the love and fear of God is armed as with a shield
of triple brass, against sin. The temptation comes with
all its seductive force, but it is repelled with the indignant question, "How shall I do this wickedness,
and sin against God?" And this awful Being is felt to
be everywhere. "O Lord, thou hast searched me, and
known me. Thou knowest my downsitting and mine
uprising, thou understandest my thought afar off.
Thou compassest my path and my lying down, and art
acquainted with all my ways." Yes, God is in every
place. Heaven and the earth are full of his presence.
A person once dreamed that the sky was one vast eye
of God, ever looking down upon him. He could never
get out of the sight of this tremendous eye, he could
never look up but this awful eye was gazing upon him.
The moral of this fearful dream is a fact. God's eye is
always, and everywhere, upon us. Who could sin, if he
saw God in a bodily form looking upon him? Young
man, could you go to the theatre, or to still worse places,
if you saw this vast and searching eye, with piercing
looks, fixed upon you? Impossible. " No," you would
say, "I must wait till that eye is gone, or closed, or
averted." But it is never gone, never closed, never
averted. This the religious man knows, and therefore
says, "Thou, God, seest me." Would you sin, if your
father were present? Would you enter the haunt
of vice if he stood at the door, looking in your face,
and saying, " My son, if sinners entice thee, consent
thou not; my son, walk not thou in the way with them,

turn thy foot from their path?" You could not so insult and grieve the good man's heart. But though your earthly father is not there, your heavenly Father is. Your father's eye does not see you, but God's eye does. This the religious person believes and feels, and turns away from sin.

Religion also presents a judgment to come. Yes, " God hath appointed a day in which he will judge the world by Jesus Christ." "We must all appear before the judgment-seat of Christ; that everyone may receive the things done in his body, according to that he hath done, whether it be good or bad." "And I saw a great white throne, and him that sat on it, from whose face the earth and the heaven fled away; and there was found no place for them. And I saw the dead, small and great, stand before God; and the books were opened: and another book was opened, which is the book of life: and the dead were judged out of those things which were written in the books, according to their works. And the sea gave up the dead which were in it; and death and hell delivered up the dead which were in them: and they were judged every man according to their works." What a description! What a day will be the judgment-day! The voice of the descending Judge; the cry of the archangel, and the trump of God; the bursting tombs, and rising dead; the conflagration of the universe, and the gathering of the nations to the Lord in the air; the separation of the righteous from the wicked; and the final doom of all; the closing of time, and the commencing of eternity; the going away of the wicked into ever-lasting punishment, and of the righteous into life eternal! Oh, what destinies! The good man believes all this, and acts under its influence. How many has the prospect of a day of judgment alarmed in the midst of their sins; how many has it checked; how many has it been the means of converting! I knew a lady in high life, one of the most accomplished women I ever met with, who, while living in all the gaieties of fashionable life, visiting in noble families, and fascinating them by her power to please, dreamed that the day of judgment was arrived. She saw the Judge, in awful majesty, commence the dread assize. Around him, in a circle, the diameter of which no eye could measure, were drawn the human race, awaiting their doom. With slow and solemn pace, he traversed the whole circle; whomsoever he approved, to them he gave the token of his acceptance by graciously laying his hand upon their heads. Many he passed, and gave them no sign. As he approached the dreamer, her anxiety to know whether she should receive the token of his acceptance became intense, till as he drew still nearer, and was about to stop before her, the agony of her mind awoke her. It was but a dream: a blessed one, however, for her. It produced, through the Divine blessing, a deep solicitude for the salvation of her soul. She became an eminent and devoted Christian; and some years since departed, to receive from Christ the gracious token of his approval, in his immediate presence, and in the regions of immortality.

You, too, young man, must be brought into judgment. You are to form a part of the circle drawn round Christ, to receive your sentence: he will approach you; he will give you the token of reception or rejection. Do, do consider that tremendous scene. How awful was the irony of Solomon! " Rejoice, O young man, in thy youth; and let thy heart cheer thee in the days of thy youth, and walk in the ways of thine heart, and in the sight of thine eyes: but know thou, that for all these things God will bring thee into judgment." You may go to places of vicious amusements, but you must go from thence to the judgment-seat of Christ: there is a path from every scene of sin to the bar of God. He goes with you as a witness; and conscience also goes with you as a witness: what witnesses these to be brought against you in judgment! "I will come near to you to judgment, and I will be a swift witness against all that fear not me, saith the Lord." Oh, did you realize this awful fact, did you keep your eye upon the judgment-seat, did you anticipate your appearance at the bar of Christ, which religious men do, and which religion would lead you to do, if you possessed it, how effectually would you be protected from the evils by which you are surrounded! Could you sin, with a voice sounding in your ears, "For all these things I will bring you into judgment?" No! here would be a defence to you, as it has been to many others, and is to many now. Adopt it as yours.

CHAPTER IX.

"Young men away from home must have something," you are ready to say, "to interest, to amuse, to gratify them. They have been called to sacrifice the comforts of their father's house, and to endure many hardships and much discomfort, and need something to enliven and divert their minds." True. But it should be of a kind that will not endanger their health, their morals, or their future interests, and especially their souls. To seek relief from the labours of business, the gloom of solitude, or the annoyance of an unpleasant home, by "the pleasures of sin, which are but for a season," is to recruit our wearied nature, and to enliven our dull frame, by drinking a sweet-tasted and effervescing draught of deadly poison. That young man is not only not pious, but scarcely acts the part of a rational creature, whose love of diversion leads him to seek such gratifications as are ruinous to all his interests for time and eternity. A love of pleasure, a taste for amusement, as such, is a most dangerous propensity. Business, young man, business is what you should attend to. There is pleasure in industry. Employment is gratification. But still you repeat, "We must have something which shall interest the mind when business is over;

which shall be a subject of hope and mental occupation, to fill up the interstices of thought during the day, and which shall be an object to which the eye may constantly turn for refreshment and relief amidst all that is disgusting and disheartening in the rough cares of our situation." Well, here it is! Here is a glorious object! Here is what you want, just what you want, and all you want. Religion, religion, my reader, will prove to be, if you try it, an engaging companion, a sympathizing comforter, an ever-present friend, and a sure guide to the fountain of happiness. Do not listen to the ignorant testimony of those who have never tried it, and who represent it as the enemy of human delight; but attend to the intelligent witness of those who speak from experience, and who declare it to be the very element of happiness. Who would take the evidence of a blind man about colour and form; or of a deaf one about sounds; or of one without the sense of taste about flavour? And equally irrational would it be to take the opinion of an ungodly man about religion.

It is a truth, which the experience of millions has proved, that " Wisdom's ways are ways of pleasantness, and all her paths are peace." Consider what religion is: not mere bodily exercise, a drudgery of forms and ceremonies: no, but an occupation of the mind and heart; an occupation, too, which engages the noblest contemplation of the former, and exercises the purest affections of the latter. It is the employment of the whole soul upon the sublimest object that mind can be conversant with. Mental occupation is essential to felicity, and here it is in perfection and permanence. Dwell upon the privileges of religion; the pardon of sin; the justification of our persons; the favour of the eternal

God,. together with the consciousness of that favour, and
communion with Him; peace of conscience, like the
sunshine of the breast; the renovation of our corrupt
nature; and the subjection of passion, appetite, and
animal propensity, to rules which revelation prescribes,
and reason approves : and all this united with the hope,
prospect, and foretaste of eternal glory.   I ask, can
the man whose mind is in this state be otherwise than
happy?   I wish to impress you with the idea that the
individual who is thus religious, whose piety is Scriptural, evangelical, experimental; and not superstitious,
nominal, and ignorant, must be happy; not, indeed, perfectly so, for perfect happiness is known only in the heavenly world; but he is contented and satisfied, as being
in a state of repose.   His mind is not anxiously and
ignorantly urging the question, "Who will show us any
good?"   He has a definite idea of what will make him
happy; he is not in quest of something to occupy his
mind and satisfy his heart, but has found it, and is at
rest.   He has become possessed of a supreme object
of interest, which his heart loves, and his conscience
approves, an object which has many and great advantages; it is always at hand, for it is with him, yea, in
him.   He proves the truth of the assertion, "The good
man shall be satisfied from himself;" because the spring
of his happiness is in his own bosom.   He is calm and
tranquil: his pleasures are not only pure, but peaceful;
they occasion no perturbation, no painful reflection, no
remorse; they are inexpensive; they do not unfit him
for, business, nor create in him a disgust with his trade
or profession, but brace and invigorate him to carry on
its labours, and endure its cares; they do not impair

his health or enervate his mind, but are all of a healthful nature, both as regards the body and the soul.

Religion, moreover, includes duties that are all agreeable. The love of God, the service of Christ, the practice of holiness, the destruction of sin, the cultivation of charity, all are pleasant. The Christian, in keeping holy the sabbath in the house of God, enjoys far more delight than he does who desecrates it by Sunday excursions. The reading of the Bible, although it does not fascinate the imagination, and kindle the passions, like a novel or licentious poem, soothes, softens, and sanctifies the heart. Prayer is one of the most elevating exercises in which the soul can be engaged, for it is man speaking to God; the poor frail, finite child of dust and ashes, admitted, through the mediation of Christ, to an audience with the King eternal, immortal, invisible, the only wise God. And as to the pleasures of friendship, where are they enjoyed in such perfection as in the communion of saints?

Nor is this all: for religion supplies an inexhaustible source of the deepest interest, in the various great and glorious institutions which are formed and in operation to promote the moral, spiritual, and eternal welfare of mankind; to many of these, young men are contributing, in different ways, their valuable assistance. I can with confidence ask, whether the polluted and polluting scenes of earthly pleasures, to which many resort, can yield half the satisfaction which is enjoyed at public meetings of religious institutions, where interesting facts unite to captivate the imagination and delight the heart: at the festive scenes of a tea-party, held by a company of Sunday-school teachers, or by the collectors of a juvenile missionary society, or the members of a society for mental improvement, there is more real enjoyment than in any of those sinful diversions in which men of corrupt taste find their amusement. The great moral enterprise for the conversion of the world, now carrying on its operations through all lands, supplies an object of unrivalled sublimity, splendour, and importance, and which, by firing the ambition, and employing the energies of youthful piety, never fails to be productive of pure delight, as often as the eye contemplates it, or the mind is conscious of promoting it.

Blessed with true piety, a youth may be happy any and every where. The apprentice, serving the most tyrannical master, or oppressed by the most unfeeling and hard-hearted mistress, will still find, if he possesses religion, a relief sufficient to lighten the yoke and soften the rigours of the service. And how it will cheer the solitude of the clerk or the shopman in his private lodgings, when neither friend nor companion is near! There he can commune with his God, and pray to his heavenly Father, though his earthly one be far from him. He is not now tempted to leave his cheerless dwelling in quest of comfort, for he can find enough in religious exercises : or if he wishes, as he lawfully may do, to relieve his solitude, he can be happy in hearing a sermon, or going to the meeting of some committee with which he is connected, or to the public meeting of some society which may be held in the neighbourhood. Solitude itself is not disagreeable, for he wishes to cultivate his mind by knowledge, and his heart by piety ; and when exchanged for social intercourse and pleasures, they are of a kind to do him not harm, but good. Religion thus makes him comfortable whether alone or in society. Young man, I want you to be happy, and I am sure there is only one thing that will make you so, and that is true piety. You may be amused and gratified, pleased and diverted, at least for a while, without this; but amusement and diversion are only substitutes for happiness, not the thing itself. Man was made for the service and enjoyment of God, and he cannot be truly happy till he is brought to answer the end of his creation.

Who can tell what sorrow awaits him in future life? Oh, could I lift up the veil of futurity, and disclose the scenes of your history, how would your heart sink to foresee the trials that are in reserve for you. Setting out upon the voyage of life, with a bright sky, a smooth sea, a fair wind, and every sail filled with the propitious breese, you may soon have to encounter the storm that will reduce you to a wreck on some inhospitable shore. Your trade may fail, your wife may die, and your constitution sink under the pressure of accumulated woes. What is there to comfort and support you amidst solitude, and the long, dark, wintry night of adversity? Religion, had you sought it in the season of youth and health, would have helped you to sustain the shock of misfortune by its consoling and strengthening influence: but you have neglected it, and in its absence there is nothing human or Divine to support you, and you fall, first into poverty, then to drinking, then to the grave, and then to the bottomless pit. How many who have died of a broken heart, or as martyrs to drunkenness, and have gone from the sorrows of time to the torments of eternity, would, if they had possessed religion, notwithstanding their misfortunes, have lived in peace, died in hope, and been blessed for ever! Religion, if it led only to misery upon earth, if it were really the gloomy and pleasure-destroying thing which many represent it, and others believe it to be, yet, as it leads from everlasting misery to eternal bliss hereafter, would be our highest as well as our incumbent duty; for who would not escape from hell and flee to heaven, if it could only be done by passing through Cimmerian shades, or a perpetual martyrdom? But instead of this, true piety is the most serene and delightsome thing on earth. It is the sweetener of our comforts, the softener of our cares, the solace of our sorrows. It deprives us of no enjoyment but what would injure us, and gives other and far better ones in place of those it takes. It is the spring flower of youth, and the summer sun of our manhood, the autumn fruits of our declining years, and the lunar brightness of the wintry night of our old age. It is a verdant, quiet, secluded path to the paradise of God; and, after giving us the light of his countenance in life, the support of his grace in death, will conduct us to his presence, where there is fulness of joy, and to his right hand, where there are pleasures for evermore.

CHAPTER X.

RELIGION A MEANS OF PROMOTING THE TEMPORAL INTEREST OF ITS POSSESSOR.

Did you ever consider the wise King's praise of Wisdom, and the beautiful personifications in which he conveys it? "Happy is the man that findeth wisdom, and the man that getteth understanding. For the merchandise of it is better than the merchandise of silver, and the gain thereof than fine gold. She is more precious than rubies, and all the things that thou canst desire are not to be compared unto her. Length of days is in her right hand; and in her left hand riches and honour. Her ways are ways of pleasantness, and all her paths are peace. She is a tree of life to them that lay hold upon her: and happy is everyone that retaineth her." This is one of the sparkling gems of composition which decorate and enliven the pages of Scripture. Go, young man, to this beautiful personification, this angel form; she has length of days in her right hand. Religion will not necessarily insure health and avert disease; but it will prevent the constitution from being destroyed or impaired by vice. Read the description which is given of the consequences of sin in the book of Job, as exhibited in an aged, worn-out sinner: "His bones are full of the sin of his youth, which shall lie down with him in the dust;" and then add the language of Solomon, where he says, "and thou mourn at the last, when thy flesh and thy bones are consumed, and say, 'How have I hated instruction, and my heart despised reproof; and have not obeyed the voice of my teachers, nor inclined mine ear to them that instructed me! I was almost in all evil in the midst of the congregation and assembly.'" Martyrs of concupiscence, victims of drunkenness, ye loathsome spectacles, ye living corpses, full of every thing that is tormenting to yourselves and disgusting to others, rise like spectres before the imagination of young men, to deter them from the crimes which have reduced you to corruption, even on this side of the grave. Religion would have guarded you from all this! Such men live out not half their days. But see what is in the left hand of wisdom; "riches and honour." Not that religion shields from poverty, and guides all her subjects to wealth : but still it prevents the crimes which lead to the one, and implants the virtues which tend to the other. Sin is an expensive thing, as I have already remarked; it is a constant drain upon the pocket, and keeps a man poor, or makes him dishonest : while piety is frugal, industrious, sober, and prudent; it makes a man trustworthy, confidential, and procures for him esteem, preference, and station. Do you wish to prosper, and get on in the world? (and it is quite lawful for you to wish it, you ought, indeed, to wish it,) go to wisdom, and take the blessing, even riches and honour, which she has in her left hand, and which she holds out to you. Go and pluck the fruit of this tree of life, or catch the precious produce as the boughs are shaken by the favouring gales of Providence.

How many young men have left their native village, and their father's house, with all the property they had on earth tied up in the bundle they carried in their hand, and have gone to London poor and almost friendless lads, who yet, because they became the disciples and admirers of this wisdom, have risen to opulence and respectability! What names could I record, dear to the church of God, and known to the friends of man throughout the country and the world, who, by the aid of religion, rose from obscurity to renown, and from poverty to wealth! Their history is a striking proof that "godliness is profitable unto all things, having promise of the life that now is, and of that which is to come." I could mention, were it proper, the name of one, who went into an extensive concern in London as a boy to sweep the shop and carry out goods, who became, at length, possessor of the whole concern, died rich, and his property, in part, became the foundation of a new charitable institution: of another, who, from a poor lad, became a leading man in one of our religious denominations, and the treasurer of one of our most useful societies: of a third, who, from being a shop-boy in the city, became the possessor of a large fortune, which at his decease enriched many of the noblest institutions of the present time. In these cases, religion, by rendering them steady, industrious, and confidential, was the means of their opulence and elevation. They shunned evil companions, evil places, evil habits, evil amusements, and, under the influence of piety, entered those paths which lead many from poverty to wealth, and from obscurity to renown. They sat down as young men at the feet of wisdom, learned her lessons, and received her rewards.

I do not mean to say that religion without application to business, or talents for it, will succeed ; but religion, by giving diligence and sharpening the faculties, will promote success. Piety exerts a favourable influence, not only on the morals, but on the secular habits of life : and one piece of advice which wisdom delivers, as she holds out her left hand blessings, is, " Be diligent in business, as well as fervent in spirit, serving the Lord." It is a lawful and proper ambition to try to excel in the profession or business to which you have devoted your life. You ought not to be satisfied with dull mediocrity, much less with creeping, grovelling inferiority. You happily live in a country where the summits of society are accessible to those who seem, by the circumstances of their birth, to be placed at the base ; but it is only talent, united with good conduct, that can expect to rise : while incompetence, which is more frequently the result of a want of application than of ability and indolence, will sink. Piety and a desire to excel in business are helpful to each other : the former will give the virtues necessary to the latter, while the latter will guard the former from being destroyed by many of those evils to which youth are exposed, and by which they are hindered from getting on in life.

The cultivation of the mind in all useful knowledge is also auxiliary to elevation in life. A religious dolt may rise, but it is not usual. Besides, admitting that religion does sometimes help ignorance up the steep ascent to wealth, it is knowledge alone that can fit a man for eminent usefulness. Employ your spare time in reading, and acquiring knowledge. Ignorance was never so inexcusable as it is now, when the fountains of science are opened all around us, and the streams of learning are flowing even into the cottages of the poor. Religion and knowledge agree well together, and are reciprocally helpful. Let your reading be select and useful. Squander not the little time you have to spare upon trash. Read history, natural philosophy, the evidences of revealed religion, and some of our best periodical publications.

How well is that young man defended from the dangers that surround him, and how likely to rise in life, who has religion to sanctify his heart, application to business to occupy his time, and a taste for reading to employ his leisure! It is he that receives from wisdom the blessings she holds forth in both of her hands; length of days in the right, and riches and honour in the left: and at the same time it is his to gather from the tree of life the fruit of glory and immortality.

CHAPTER XI.

To do good is God-like; to do evil is devil-like: and we are all imitating God or Satan, accordingly as we are leading a holy or a sinful life. It is said in Scripture, that "one sinner destroyeth much good;" he not only does not do good himself, but he destroys good in others. Instead of doing good, he does evil. He not only leaves unassisted all the great means and instruments for improving and blessing the world, and has no share in all that is being done for the spiritual and eternal welfare of mankind; but he opposes it, and seeks to perpetuate and extend the reign of sin, and the kingdom of Satan. He corrupts by his principles, seduces by his example, and leads others astray by his persuasions. Who can imagine, I again say, how many miserable ghosts await his arrival in hell, or follow him there to be his tormentors, in revenge for his having been their tempter. He is ever scattering the seeds of poison and death in his path. Religion happily saves from this mischief all who possess it: it makes a man an instrument of good, and not of evil, to his fellow creatures; it renders him a blessing, and not a curse; a saviour, and not a destroyer; a physician to heal, and not a murderer to destroy. He lives to do good, good of the noblest and most lasting kind ; good to the soul, good to distant nations, good to the world, good to unborn generations, good for eternity. He is a benefactor to his species, a philanthropist of the noblest order. By a pious example, he adorns religion, and recommends it to others, who, attracted by the beauties of holiness as they are reflected from his character, are led to imitate his conduct. He connects himself, while yet a youth, with a Sunday school, and trains up the minds of his scholars in the ways of virtue and religion.   He associates with a Tract Society, and visits the habitations of the poor with these admirable compends of Bible truth. As his life advances, his property increases, and his influence becomes more powerful, his sphere of usefulness widens, his energies strengthen, and his devotedness becomes more intense.   He consecrates a share of his gains to the funds of Bible, Missionary, and various other societies, and gives his time, wisdom, and labour to the committees that direct their affairs.   He thus lives not for himself alone, but for the glory of God, the spread of religion, and the salvation of souls.   To do good is his aim, his delight, his business. He catches the spirit of the times, and is a man of the age, and for the age.   In secret he swells the cloud of incense that rises from the church, and which no sooner touches the throne of grace than it descends in showers of blessings upon the world. He needs not the intoxicating cup of worldly amusement, as a relief and diversion from the toils of business, and the cares of life, but drinks a purer draught from the fountain of living waters which he is engaged in conveying to those who are sinking into eternal death. He is consulted on every new scheme of mercy, and called on to assist in working it for the

relief of human wretchedness. His name is enrolled
on the list of public benefactors, and pronounced with
respect by all who know him. The blessing of him that
was ready to perish comes upon him, and he has caused
the widow's heart to sing for joy. Thus he lives. A
happy death terminates a holy and useful life. " I heard
a voice from heaven saying unto me, Write, Blessed are
the dead which die in the Lord, from henceforth : Yea,
saith the Spirit, that they may rest from their labours ;
and their works do follow them." He is received into
glory by the Lord Jesus, who with a smile bids him
welcome, saying, " Well done, good and faithful servant,
enter thou into the joy of thy Lord." Transcendent
scene ! glorious spectacle ! His usefulness is seen in
living forms of glory everlasting. The good he did on
earth follows him to heaven, and is a part of it. He
will never cease to reap the rich reward of doing good,
as with adoring wonder and rapturous delight he hears
his name repeated with grateful praise in the golden
streets of the New Jerusalem, by those whom he was
the instrument of conducting to the celestial city.

Young man, have you ambition? Can your soul be
fired with the name of glory or the prospect of noble
deeds? Have you a pulse that beats to the sound
of immortality, that word which has raised and led to
action an army of heroic spirits panting for fame? Oh,
here, here, behold an object worthy to kindle this ardent
flame in the human breast. Here is the high road to
renown, and here alone. All else beside religion, and
that which religion produces, shall perish. The garlands
which are hung around the busts which have been
placed in the temple of fame shall perish, for the temple
itself shall perish in the great conflagration ; but here

is immortality. Souls are immortal; religion is immortal; salvation is immortal; and so is the renown of him "who converteth a sinner from the error of his ways, and saveth a soul from death." This renown is within your reach. It is not an object of only official and ministerial ambition; nor within the power of great wealth, or lofty genius, or commanding influence only; but always attainable by real piety, even piety in youth, and piety in humble life. The honour of being useful, the glory of being instrumental in saving souls, is placed within the reach of the youngest, poorest, and most illiterate aspirant after the mighty and truly sublime achievement.

Never, never, my young friend, were there such opportunities, or such means of holy usefulness, as there are now, and never were there such incentives to it. The world is in movement, and so is the church. The age of inactivity is past, the era of general action is come. The armies of good and evil are marching to the scene of conflict, and mustering in the valley of decision. The gospel trumpet is blowing, and calling the hosts of the Lord to the battle, which is to rescue the world from the slavery of sin and Satan, and restore it to God. Victory is certain, and the shout of it will one day be heard, ascending to heaven from this regenerated earth. Will you be idle? What! at such a time? Will you have no share in such a triumph? But this is not all. Will you be in the routed army, and belong to the discomfited foe, which you must be if you are not pious? The cause of religion is but one, and all the pious belong to it, and are identified with it; and the cause of sin is but one, and all the irreligious are identified with it. Religion is destined to victory all over the earth, and every true Christian does something to accelerate the triumph, and will share the honour of the glorious conquest. What, then, is a life of sin, of worldly pleasure, of gay dissipation, compared with a life of religion! What a contrast in their nature, and oh! what a contrast in their results! The former is the course of a demon, the latter of a ministering angel; and while the former shall eat the fruit of its doings for ever in the pit of destruction, the latter shall gather its everlasting reward from the tree of life in the paradise of God.

CHAPTER XII.

RELIGION AS A PREPARATION FOR BEING THE HEAD OF
A HOUSEHOLD UPON EARTH, AND FOR AN ETERNAL
HOME IN HEAVEN.

You are preparing, in your present situation, to act
the part to which Providence may have destined you
upon earth; and it is every way probable, according
to the natural course of events, that in a few years you
will be found at the head of a household of your own.
This opens to you not only an interesting scene, but
also an important and very responsible one. From the
nature and constitution of society, the destiny of one
generation is powerfully affected by the conduct of that
which precedes it. The husband influences the wife,
the father the child, and the master the servant;
consequently, of how much moment is the character
of the head of a family! How many households are
scenes of discord and wretchedness, and are at length
reduced to poverty and ruin, by a drunken pleasure-
loving or idle father! How many who enter life with
the fairest prospects of comfort and success, throw all
away by sin! They draw some lovely and virtuous
young woman into the companionship of life with them,
see a family rising around, and are bound by every tie
of justice and honour to provide for the comfort of their

wife, and the prosperity of their children; but they had acquired habits of indolence and extravagance in youth, and all goes wrong, till ruin drives them from that home, which industry and sobriety would have enabled them to maintain; at length the wife dies of a broken heart, and the children become vagrants in the world. Religion would have prevented all this, and preserved that home to be a scene of order, peace, plenty, and respectability.

But even where things do not reach this point, and there is neither vice nor want, but morality, and success, still think of a family without religion, an atheistic household, in which there is no worship, no instruction, no regard to eternity, a mere temporal confederation, though followed with eternal consequences. Every father and mother is answerable to God for the souls of their children and servants; and oh! what an account will those who are irreligious have to render to him at the day of judgment! What an eternity will such parents have to spend in the bottomless pit, with those children whose souls sank thither through their guilty neglect!

Religion will fit you to preside with dignity over your household: it will add the sanctity of the Christian to the authority of the parent and the master, and render obedience, on the part of your children and servants, more pleasant and easy, as given to one who has such high claims to it. How will your family prayers tend to keep up, in all other respects, family order! Piety will strengthen and soften every domestic tie, as well as consecrate every domestic occupation. It will lighten the cares of business, brighten the scenes of prosperity, and yield consolation in the dark season of family sorrow. If called to leave your wife and family, it will mitigate the pang of separation by the prospect of eternal union in a world where death has no power; or if required to surrender a pious wife or children, it will prevent the sting of that sorrow which has no hope. What a bliss then to a family, what a benign and heavenly inmate, is sincere, consistent, eminent religion, as it shines forth in the form and character of a godly father and master!

And now, young man, let me entreat you to consider what is the true character of your present life, viewed in relation to the life that is to come. Are you now at home, or are you away from home? Let the poet answer.

"Strangers into life we come,
And dying is but going home."

This world is not our home, and unhappy is the man who makes it such. Heaven is the home of immortal man. During the whole time we are upon earth, we are away from home; and away from it, that we may prepare, like a child at school, or a youth in his apprenticeship, to go at length finally and fully to possess and enjoy it. This is not your rest. How short and uncertain is your continuance upon earth! You cannot remain many years, you may not remain one; for what is your life but "a vapour, that appeareth for a little time, and then vanisheth away?" At a moment's notice you may depart. A flash of lightning, a stroke of apoplexy, a ruptured blood vessel, the overturn of a boat or a carriage, may plunge you suddenly into eternity. You are suspended over that vast gulf by the brittle thread of human life. Instead of living to old age, you may not live to be of age;

instead of living to be a master, you may die before
your apprenticeship is finished. Place your finger on
your pulse and say " If this stop but a second, and any
second it may stop, I am instantly in heaven or hell."
Can you call this home? Ought you to feel at home
here? Should you wish to consider this your home?
For what a home is it, but such a one as he had whose
dwelling was among the tombs? Home! What!
would you desire it to be such, where there is so much
to disturb, distress, and annoy? No. God has provided some better thing for us ; heaven, I repeat, is the
home of immortal man.

It is to this to which the hope of the pious in
every age has aspired; and the prospect of which has
cheered them amidst all the sorrows of life. " Two
more stiles," said the martyr, as he walked across the
fields to the place of execution, "and I shall be at
home, at my Father's house." " I am going home,"
is the common and joyful exclamation of many dying
Christians. And what a home ! The home of saints,
of martyrs, of angels, of Christ, of God !

What is the preparation for such a home? Religion : nothing but religion. That home is a holy one.
Heaven is in fact the home of religion itself : for here
it is only in a wayfaring pilgrimage state. Religion is
a heavenly visitant upon earth, travelling back to her
native skies, and will never be at rest till she finds
herself in the presence of God, her Divine Parent.
Nothing, therefore, but religion, can prepare a soul for
heaven. You may have a good knowledge of the arts ;
you may have a competent, or even profound acquaintance with learning and science; you may have talents

of a public order, that fit you for action and for influence among your fellow men; but what have these things to do with preparation for heaven? What reference have they to the eternal state? Nothing but holiness will prepare you for a holy heaven. Would a knowledge of trade, agriculture, or science, prepare any one, without the knowledge and manners of a courtier, to dwell at court? How much less in heaven! No, it is sincere, experimental piety alone, that can prepare you to enter into the presence of God. The heavenly character must be acquired on earth, or it can never be acquired at all. Begin then at once. It is a preparation for eternity, and who can commence such a work too early? You may have but little time allotted for this transcendently momentous affair. "Whatsoever thy hand findeth to do, do it with thy might; for there is no work, nor device, nor knowledge, nor wisdom, in the grave, whither thou goest." Live for eternity: live for heaven: and the only way to do this, is to live by faith. Once in heaven, you will never leave it. There will be no going out for ever. You will quit your Father's house no more. The celestial family will never break up. Once at home there, you will be at home for ever.

But neglect religion, and you can never be admitted to the regions of immortality. Your parents may be there, but you will be excluded, and shut up in outer darkness. I can imagine you in the day of judgment, pressing to lay hold upon the hand of your father, but he turns from you as from an object of disgust, exclaiming, "Your father no longer." You then direct an imploring eye to the mother that bore you, and laying hold on her robe, piteously exclaim, " My mother, do you not know me?" Gathering up her garment of light, she shakes you off, with the dreadful disownment, " I know not the enemies of my Lord." They pass to the right hand of the Judge, while you, by a power you cannot resist, are sent to the left; and what remains? You will present from that day the melancholy spectacle of an outcast from heaven, a homeless immortal, a vagrant in the universe, a wretched wanderer through eternity.

CHAPTER XIII.

SPECIAL ADDRESSES TO SEVERAL CLASSES OF YOUNG MEN.

I SELECT as the first whom I particularize, those who have left or are soon to leave their native country, whether for a permanent residence abroad, or only for a season. Numerous and very different are the causes which lead to this temporary or lasting expatriation. In some cases it is a mere curiosity to see the world ; in others a restless, dissatisfied, and indolent disposition ; in others a still worse cause ; while in some it is a step to which they are called by the plans of Providence, and which circumstances render, if not absolutely necessary, yet every way proper. Whatever may lead to it, however, it is always a course of danger, and sometimes of sorrow. That young man who can step from his native shores into the vessel which is to bear him to a distant part of the earth ; who can see the land of his nativity recede from his view, till its spires, hills, and its cliffs are lost amidst the mighty waste of its waters ; who can utter his adieu to the friends and scenes of his childhood, which he very probably may never revisit ; who can undertake the perils of the sea, and the danger of tropical climates, all without some degree of heart sickness, or, at least, evident sadness, must have a heart too cold and too hard to be at present the residence of piety and virtue, and affords little hope for the future. Insensibility under such circumstances proves a callous mind; while sadness and even sorrow are an honour, and not a weakness, to the youth who rather weeps than utters his last adieu.

If it be a bad cause that takes you to sea, you will have time for reflections upon the voyage. Use it well. As you pace the deck, with the moon and the stars speaking silently to you of God, think of your course, meditate upon your conduct; give conscience leave and time to speak, and listen to its voice. Imagine you see a mother's form lighting on the deck, pointing to heaven, and saying, as she smiles through her tears, " Repent my son, repent, and come back to us reclaimed : we wait to receive you to our arms, and to our hearts." Hear that gentle voice coming to your ears when nothing else is heard but the whistling of the wind, the dashing of the waves, and the creaking of the masts and rigging. Many a youth in those solemn moments has considered his evil ways, and turned from them to God. Cut off from many temptations and companions which beset him on shore, he has had wisdom given him to be sorry for the course he had run, has resolved to forsake it, and has returned home when the voyage was over, to heal by his good conduct the wounds which he had inflicted by his untoward behaviour on the hearts of his parents.

But if these scenes are not enough to awaken reflection, and to startle conscience from her slumber, may I hope that the roar of the tempest will do it ? Then, when the vessel, with her sails torn, her masts injured, or gone by the board, is driving before the

fury of the gale, on a rocky shore, and the horrors
of shipwreck and a grave among the monsters of the
deep are before you, then think of your ways, then look
back upon your wicked career, and cry to God for
mercy through Christ: if you perish at sea, perish
praying for pardon through the blood of the Lamb;
or if you survive the storm, let its perils never be
forgotten, nor the purposes and good resolutions which
in the hour of danger it led you to form. Do not
as some unhappy youths do, smile at your fears and
remorse, when you find that the vessel has outlived the
tempest and you are safe.

It is by no means uncommon for young men in
middle life, of unstable minds, and indolent roving
habits, when tired of the restraints of home, and the
remonstrances of parental authority, to disregard them·
all, and enlist into the army. It is often a dreadful
and desperate change. Some few, and but few instances have occurred, in which it has been followed by
reformation, and these youths have either risen in their
profession, or returned reclaimed to their father's house.
This book may perhaps be read by some who have thus
quitted the quiet scenes of home and trade, for the
wanderings, turbulence, and dangers of a soldier's life.
Oh what a contrast must you often draw, perhaps with
a sigh or a tear, between the moral and affectionate
inmates of the home you have left, and the low licentious
companions with whom you are compelled now to associate; between the comforts of your father's house, and
the tent, the barrack, or the public-house, where you
now lodge; between the kindness and indulgence of
your relatives, and the stern, unsoftened authority of a
military officer, whether subaltern or superior! Un-

happy youth! to have been reckless of all this, and to have exposed yourself to such annoyance, degradation, and wretchedness! Think of your ways. Look back upon the past with calmness, impartiality, and penitence. It is not yet too late to amend your conduct, and return to civil life. You have now much time for reflection. During those hours of the day which are spent upon some long and tiresome march; or of the night which you pass in solitude, pacing the sentinel's measured ground, when darkness shrouds you, or the storm is rolling its thunders over you, and darting its lightnings around, reflect, oh reflect upon your conduct! Think of the mother at home, whose rest is broken, or whose dreams are troubled at that moment by thoughts of her far-off soldier son. Or, when sailing in the crowded transport with your regiment to some distant, and perhaps unhealthy, colony, dwell upon the cause of your being there upon the troubled ocean, borne every moment farther and farther from the land of your birth. Or, when the evening order is given to prepare next morning to mount the breach and storm the besieged town, or to take the field of battle against the marshalled foe, let conscience, long asleep, awake and speak. Oh, in that dread hour, what voices cry, " Repent, repent!" Then think, how near you may be to death and eternity. When the roll shall be called over to the survivors, no exulting " Here," may follow the repetition of your name, but an awful silence seem to say, " Dead, slain." And if not slain, left to groan away a few days or weeks of miserable existence in a crowded hospital, amidst the most horrid sights and sounds of mortal woe. But without the battle or the storm, a soldier's life in tropical climates is fearfully perilous. Spectators have wept as they have seen the skeletons of regiments landed on the shores of their native country, and the thousand strong reduced to the fifty or the hundred wan and emaciated invalids. And where were the rest? Left amidst the sands of the East, or the charnel houses of the West Indies. Let those who in their petulant resistance of parental authority, or their sullen submission to the restraints of home, meditate such a change as this, think of the consequences of the rash act of enlisting before they commit it, and may those who in an unguarded moment have committed it, do the best, and all that is left them, to bring good out of evil. Let them avoid desertion: this will only expose them to greater evils. Their first business is, " Repentance towards God, and faith in our Lord Jesus Christ." Religion will soften the rigour of their situation, and prepare them for future danger and distress; or make way for their return to their father's house. Honourable dismission from the service is what they should seek; and in order to this, they should commend themselves to their friends as having learned wisdom by experience, and as being prepared to settle down to habits of application, and the pursuits of business. But if a discharge cannot be obtained, let them reconcile themselves to the disquietudes, dangers, and distress of their situation, by the recollection that they were the authors of their own misery; by a line of conduct that will conciliate the affections of those around them, and help their preferment; and especially by true penitence and piety, which will, when every other source of comfort is closed, open in any situation streams of consolation whose waters will never fail. Let them become good soldiers of Jesus Christ, and his service will soften the hardships of every other.

The moral dangers of foreign residence are most imminent. You are then not only more than ever, and farther than ever, removed from parental inspection and restraint, but you are removed also from the control of friends and of public opinion. You will have an opportunity, if you choose to embrace it, for gratifying to the greatest excess every youthful passion and every criminal appetite; and multitudes are swept into an early grave abroad in consequence of their enormous lusts, or else become confirmed for ever in habits of immorality.

The motives which lead young men to sea are rarely laudable, and often criminal, as the following impressive fact will prove. Read it with attention.

Two young men, the children of pious and wealthy parents, felt themselves exceedingly displeased at being constantly refused the family carriage on the Lord's day. It was the father's settled rule, that the authority which commanded him to rest included also his servants and horses; he therefore turned a deaf ear to their entreaties and remonstrances. In their madness, or in their folly, they determined to resent this refusal, by leaving their situations and going to sea. Intelligence of this step was transmitted to the Rev. John Griffin, of Portsea, and he was requested to make diligent inquiry, and on finding them to use every possible means to induce them to return home. After some search, he found them in a rendezvous house. He addressed them by their real name, and, on their exhibiting signs of undoubted though reluctant recognition of it, he succeeded, after much persuasion, in inducing them to leave the house, with the intention of accompanying him home; one of them, on the way, looked in Mr Griffin's face, somewhat amusingly, but with much obstinacy said, "I have seen your face in the print-shops, you are a minister, I will not go with you;" but Mr Griffin now interposed with much firmness, and at length succeeded in bringing both of them to his house. He now pleaded with them, with tears of affection; he besought them with the feelings of a parent; he warned them with the disinterested and dignified air of a Christian minister. One of them was overcome with the meekness and force of his subduing and fatherly eloquence. The occasion, though secret and unobserved, and of a domestic nature, was worthy of the exertion of such a quality. The youth who promised to return, went back, and it is believed became a respectable and pious character. The other obstinately refused to return, and on his finally, after much patient persuasion, persisting in the expression of his determination to go to sea, Mr Griffin said, "Well, young man, if you go, remember it is in disregard of the persuasive tears of your family, the advice and remonstrance of your friends; I can now do no more for you, than remind you solemnly in the words of Scripture, 'Be sure your sin will find you out.'" They stopped that night at Mr Griffin's house; and the next morning, notwithstanding the determination not to return expressed by the one, Mr Griffin so far disregarded it as that he would and did see both of them on the coach for London; but, on stopping at the first stage, the obstinate young man acted on his expressed determination, and his younger brother returned to town alone.

Some time after, a letter was delivered to Mr Griffin one morning by a waterman, who stated that it had come from a man in a ship then lying at Spithead, who had been sentenced to death. Mr Griffin immediately determined to go off to the ship. On his arrival at the ship, he was conducted to the prisoner, who was found confined, and heavily ironed. He said, " Well, young man, I have come at your request, and I hope to do you good; but why did you send for me? I have no knowledge of you." "Oh, sir, then you don't recollect me? Do you remember, some time ago, saying to a young man in your own parlour, who refused to return home with his brother, ' Be sure your sin will find you out?' " Mr Griffin's feelings may be more easily conceived than described. The youth had not disclosed his real name; and, as he had been led to expect no pardon or remission of his sentence, he seemed to show, even in the depth of his despair, some remaining feeling and sense of his former respectability, by intimating that it would be some little satisfaction that he was not condemned, and would not be executed, under the name of his injured family. The offence was that of having violently struck his captain while on duty, which, especially in a time of war, was considered a crime so dangerous, from its tendency to traitorous mutiny, that it was generally supposed the sentence would be executed. But no life had been taken; no serious personal injury on the individual officer had been inflicted; and considering the youth of the offender, mercy might be prayed for, not only without fair objection, but with propriety. At least, such was the opinion of Mr Griffin, as a man and a Christian minister. Without having excited any hopes in the mind of the condemned, or having even informed him at all of his intention, he at once resolved to use his utmost exertions to procure the pardon of the unfortunate young man, or at least the mitigation of his punishment. On his return from the ship he wrote immediately to Lord Melville, who was then the first lord of the Admiralty, with a statement of the case, and of the circumstances which had brought him acquainted with it. He also used his exertions with some of the government and other authorities to aid his prayer. To the honour of the humanity of his Majesty's advisers, in kind consideration of these applications, and of simultaneous ones on the part of the family, the fatal sentence was remitted, and not only the life of the youth spared, but a free pardon generously granted. The intelligence of this did not, it is understood, arrive till early on the morning appointed for the execution. This, however, was kindly communicated, it is believed, from the Admiralty at Portsmouth, to Mr Griffin, so early, and in such a manner, that he was permitted to be the person first to disclose this happy intelligence to this hitherto hopeless youth. It would be in vain for any one not present to attempt to portray the intensely interesting character of this blessed scene. It is more likely to be productive of a true effect on the mind of the reader, to leave the matter for his own imagination. The mother and a brother of the youth were present, and saw, it is believed, their unfortunate relative at Portsea after the condemnation; but returning to London, it was only on their arrival there that they heard the intelligence of the free pardon.

The fact just given is replete with salutary warning to all young men, not to neglect the advice of pious parents, nor to violate the commands of God; while, at the same time, it admonishes them, if unhappily they have done so, to repent of their sins, and to alter their course, instead of fleeing from restraint to the dangers of a sea-faring life. Wherever they go, their sins follow after them, and sooner or later will find them out. In some few cases, the fugitive who has, like Jonah, fled from duty to sea, has been overtaken by the fearful visitations of the Almighty, and brought to repentance by a mixture of judgment and mercy; but in by far the greater number of instances, those who betake themselves to the sea, under the influence of indolence, unsettledness, or sin, become abandoned in character and miserable in circumstances.

There are some who are gone, or about to go abroad, at the call of duty. Their course of life lies that way, and they are yet happily free from vice, and even from unsteadiness of temper. To such I would say, Leave not your native land without real and decided religion as your companion in travel, or if you have left it without this friend, protector, and guide, instantly seek its possession. Religion will soften the pang of separation from your relatives, will open a source of happiness on the voyage, and will cover you with a protecting shield, amidst the dangers of a foreign land. As you travel, or as you dwell among a strange people, often alone and without a friend with whom to converse, you will feel, and sadly feel, your forlorn and desolate condition : and when the hour of sickness comes, and you are laid up with a fever or consumption in a land of strangers, oh, think of the long nights and weary days of restlessness and pain, with no mother, no sister near to nurse and comfort you, no, none but strangers, and they perhaps, speaking a language you do not understand! will not religion be needed then? Would not religion soothe you then? Yes, it would be your nurse, your friend, your comforter, your support.

What an exquisite illustration of the power of religion to comfort, support, and animate the mind in the most forlorn and distressing circumstances, is to be found in the journal of that most interesting traveller, Mungo Park.*

What can more beautifully or affectingly prove and illustrate the power of religion in the most trying circumstances and apalling danger, than this touching fact. Let me therefore entreat you to seek the same source of consolation. Not only take the Bible in your trunk, but its influence in your heart. Cut off from the means of grace, surrounded by Pagan, Mohammedan, or Popish rites, all of them superstitious, and some of them polluting, you will be in danger of losing all sense of piety when you need it most. Fear God, and you will be safe and happy, wander or rest wherever you may; for He is there: reverence his presence, obey his authority, enjoy his favour, and you are blessed. You may die, and leave your bones in a foreign land; but, as one of the sages of antiquity said, "Every place is equally near to heaven."

Orphans. For you my tenderest sympathies are awakened, and my most affectionate anxieties engaged. You are, indeed, away from home; for you have no home but that which you occupy as an apprentice, shopman, or clerk. The grave has closed over your father and mother; and that habitation once the scene of your childhood, and which you then never entered but with delight, is now the residence of strangers.

* The quotation will be found at p. 272 of this volume.

That threshold you will never cross again. A father's hand, a mother's smile, will welcome you no more to that abode; bnt you can never pass it even now, without looking up to the chamber window, within which the quiet nights of childhood were slept away in comparative innocence and peace, and saying with a sigh, "My mother,

> 'Life has passed
> With me but roughly, since I saw thee last.'"

Oh! this is a cold and selfish world. Those who should have loved and befriended you, if not for your own, yet for your parents' sakes, have forgotten you; and perhaps, even in the circle of your relatives, you find scarcely any one who interests himself in your behalf. There was an orphan of old, who cheered himself thus, "When my father and my mother forsake me, then the Lord will take me up." He found it so, and left his experience upon record for your encouragement and hope. Go to the same God by faith, by trust, and prayer, and seek his favour, his guardianship, and guidance. He will be your Friend, and never forsake you. He will be a Father to you, and will never be removed by death. He styles himself, and it is one of his tenderest titles, "The father of the fatherless." His friendship will be more than a compensation for all you have lost, and he will raise you up other friends on earth. What have you lost in earthly parents, which cannot be more than made up in God? "What have I lost," say you, "what have I not lost? They were my dearest, my kindest, my most valuable friends: their counsels guided me, their care protected me, their daily converse was the joy of my life, their sympathy revived me, and their bounty supplied my wants. And now they are gone how justly may I say, that my dearest comforts and hopes lie buried with their precious remains!" Well, but cannot God counsel you, protect you, converse with you, sympathize with you, supply you, far more effectually than they did? Your father and mother are dead, but God, your heavenly Father, can never die. If you commit your way to him, by holy fear and earnest prayer, he will guide you through all the intricacies of life, protect you amidst its dangers, comfort you under its sorrows, and conduct you safely, notwithstanding your gloomy prospects, through this mortal life, till you come at last to your Father's house in peace. Seek to have God for your Father, and you will never want a friend. Choose religion, and you will never want a portion. Unite yourself with the church of Christ, and you will never want a home.

But, at the same time, you should be told that you can expect no safety but from piety. Left at an early age without the guides and guardians of your youth, without the check and restraint that even a distant father, while he lived, imposed by his correspondence, you will be an object for Satan's wiles, and for the arts of those who lie in wait to deceive. There are many who date their ruin from the day of their parents' death, and consider that event as the commencement of their downward career. Some have plunged into dissipation to hush their sorrows, increased by the selfishness and unkindness of friends: while others, who had hitherto felt a parent's admonitions an impediment to a life of sin, have rushed into vice, as soon as this obstacle was removed by death. If either of these dangers be yours, may your parent's venerable shade appear to your imagination, as troubled by your misconduct, and warn you from a course of sin, which, if persisted in, will lead to destruction. You have lost them for a season, and will you by sin lose them for ever?

Pious young men. You form a happy and an important class, if not a numerous one. Receive my congratulations on the rich and sovereign mercy which has called you out of darkness, and made you the children of light. Bless God, that while so many are walking according to the course of this world, and fulfilling the desires of the flesh and of the mind, you are walking in the ways of godliness and peace. And while you are thankful, be humble, be circumspect, and prayerful. You are, and will be exposed to great and sore trials of your stedfastness. Perhaps you are placed in a situation, where you find not one like-minded with yourself. You alone are " faithful found among the faithless," and will need great grace to stand your ground against the annoyance ridicule and opposition, with which your religion will be assailed, by a set of gay dissipated and irreligious youths. It is of vast importance, that you should at once, and without hesitation, let it be seen and known that you fear God. Let there be no attempt to conceal your principles or your practices. Let those with whom you are to associate, know at your first entrance among them, that you profess to regard the claims of religion. If you begin by concealing your principles, it will be extremely difficult to exhibit them afterwards, and thus your life will be wretched under the stings of conscience reproaching you for cowardice, and the dread of open avowal. Moreover, you will often be obliged, or tempted at any rate, in order to keep up the delusion, to do things which you know to be wrong, and thus bring much remorse into your bosom. Remember who has said, " Whosoever shall be ashamed of me and of my words, in this adulterous and sinful generation, of him also shall the Son of man be ashamed, when he cometh in the glory of his Father with the holy angels." Pray much, and pray earnestly and believingly, for moral courage. Entreat of God to be with you. Beseech him to stand by you, and uphold you with a strength greater than your own. You will be in imminent peril without great watchfulness. Every ingenious art and device will be tried to shake your constancy. The licentious or sceptical work will often be placed in your way. You will be besieged, and if the smallest breach be made, in even the outworks of your character, the advantage will be plied against you till the whole is carried by storm or capitulation. The first temptation presented by your companions will be to small offences, to matters of doubtful or debateable propriety, and if these succeed, they will become more bold. Steel your heart against ridicule. Betray no irritability. Bear all with dignified meekness. Petulance will only provoke to greater annoyance. Forbearance on your part will be most likely to induce them to desist. They will soon feel, that it is useless to laugh at a man, who accounts their scorn his praise, and who glories in their reproach as his honour; and they will at length respect the firmness of mind, strength of principle, and heroism of character, which their assaults can neither break nor bend. It will tend much to your defence and stability, by inspiring them with respect, if you are skilful in your business, and possess a well-cultivated mind. Strive to be superior in all that constitutes the clever tradesman or professional man, and the well informed man. Convince them, that although religion is the enemy of sin, it is the friend of all that can benefit and adorn humanity. Study well and deeply the evidences of revealed religion, and make yourself intimately acquainted with the method of meeting all the objections of the popular infidelity of the day. But especially be consistent. Let your piety be unvarying and universal, and interwoven with the whole texture of your character. It should produce, not only the fear of God, but the love of man : it should blend the amiable and the devout, the cheerful and the serious, the useful and the happy. You should seek, by the steady consistent influence of example, as well as by the occasional and well-timed persuasion of direct address, to reclaim those who are gone astray. You should judiciously and affectionately warn your associates, who are seeking the pleasures of sin, of their danger. You may be honoured to convert them from the error of their ways, and save their souls from death. It is astonishing what small means may sometimes do much good, even when nothing is said, and where it is only the power of example that operates. As a proof of this, I will mention a fact which I know to have occurred in the history of a well-known and successful minister of the gospel. At the time of leaving home, he was strictly moral, and had some veneration for godliness; but soon became careless and indifferent. He could not, however, give up all attention to the welfare of his soul. It was his custom to retire to his room for prayer on Sundays between the public services of religion; neglecting it at all other times, and being ashamed to pray in the presence of his fellow apprentice. Aware of the sinfulness of his conduct, and wanting the courage and resolution to change, he earnestly and sincerely besought God to raise up some one in the house to help and guide him in this momentous concern. After a time, a third apprentice was taken into the business. The first night he slept in the house, on retiring to bed, he fell on his knees, and continued some time in prayer. The effect of this upon the mind of the youth, whose history I am relating, was instantaneous and powerful. It seemed to him as if a voice, in impressive accents, said, " Behold the answer of your prayer: there is the individual sent to guide you into the way of true religion." Serious reflection followed; his conscience was awakened; his heart was interested; and decided piety was at length the result. He was introduced by his companion to a circle of pious friends, and after a year or two exchanged secular for sacred pursuits, went to college, became a minister of the gospel, and has been greatly honoured by the usefulness both of his preaching and his publications. And I have heard him say, that he traces up all his usefulness to the prayer of that youth, who had the moral courage to bend his knee and acknowledge God before his new companions, from whom he plainly saw he should receive no countenance in the habits of piety. This fact should be a motive and an encouragement to those who have any sense of religion never to conceal it, but to let their light shine before others, that they, seeing their good works, may glorify God their heavenly Father.

Prodigals. By this term, I mean those young men who find their picture drawn by the pencil of inspiration in that most touching and beautiful of all our Lord's parables, usually denominated the " Prodigal Son." Oh,

could I hope that some of this class will read these
pages, I should entertain the further expectation that
what I now address to them would be the means, under
the blessing of God, of conducting them from the paths
of sin to those of wisdom, piety, and peace. You have
left your father's house, because, perhaps, you could not
endure its rules and restraints, and have well-nigh
broken your father's heart, after having considerably
impoverished his circumstances by your idleness extravagance and dissipation : and you are still going on in
the career of vice and destruction. Permit me to plead
with you, first on your own account. I need not ask
if you are happy; for it is impossible you should be,
unless folly sin and shame can make you so. Oh no,
there are moments when you are awakened by reflection
to the horrors of your situation, and, under the united
influence of remorse and despair, are ready to put an
end, by suicide, to your miserable existence. You have
proved the deceitfulness of sin, which promised you
pleasure, and has inflicted unutterable misery. You
have found the yoke of Satan to be galling iron to
your neck, instead of the happy freedom under which
his service was set forth to captivate your youthful imagination. Rise, deluded, degraded, and half-destroyed
youth, against these murderous tyrants, who have
brought you to the brink of the pit, but have not yet,
with all their artifice and cruelty, thrust you into
it. You are not yet irrecoverably ruined for earth, nor
enclosed in the prison of hell. Bad as you are, there
is hope for you; yes, even for you. Turn, oh turn,
from the road that leads to destruction. Think, I
beseech you, upon your parents, not quite but almost

crushed into the grave by your evil ways. It is not yet too late to restore their peace of mind, so long broken by your misconduct; nor the elasticity of their frame, so heavily pressed down by years of trouble, brought on by your guilty wanderings. "None but a parent's heart can know the anguish of parting with a sweet babe." But there is an agony deeper and more inconsolable than that. It is occasioned by a vicious son. I have seen one of the tenderest and best of mothers console her mind on the death of a darling child by the hope that it was with Christ in a better world. On the same day I have seen another mother pour forth, from a heart which no consolations could reach, tears of bitterness over a perverse and wicked son, and have heard her say, "The death of an infant is nothing to this: would that my son had died in his infancy!" Hasten, hasten, young man, that by your reformation you may spare your mother the anguish of saying with her last breath, "I am dying of a broken heart; my son, my wicked and unhappy son, has killed me." Unless you soon repent and arise and go to your father, and say, "Father, I have sinned against Heaven, and in thy sight," you will lie down in the grave of a parricide, and have inscribed, by the finger of public infamy, upon your tomb, if a tomb shall be given you, "Here lies the murderer of his father and his mother." The last stab, however, is not yet given to them; the dagger of your unkindness, and your profligacy, has not yet reached a vital part, and all their other wounds may be alleviated if not perfectly healed, by your reformation. Yes, that venerable pair may yet say, if you will permit them to do so, by your conversion to God, and consequent holiness, "It is meet that we should make merry: for this our son was dead, and is alive again; was lost, and is found." Brothers, who had long since disowned you, as far as they could do it, may yet restore you to their fraternal love. Sisters, who once regarded you as their joy and boast, when they saw you leave your father's home, a fair and promising youth, but who, in your fallen condition, could never hear your name pronounced without blushes and tears, shall again, if you repent, exclaim with throbbing hearts, "My brother." O prodigal, return; return by true repentance and faith to God, your Father in heaven, and in the same state of mind to your father on earth. Both are looking out for you; both will receive you; both will rejoice over you.

Numerous instances might be mentioned to awaken hope, and encourage this return. Do not despair of amendment. Do not say, there is no hope. None, not even you, are too bad to be reclaimed. Read the beautiful parable to which I have already referred. What prodigal can wander further, sink lower, or seem more out of the way of recovery, or more remote from the region of hope, than he was; yet he was restored. And why was the parable spoken, and why was it written, but to encourage hope, in cases seemingly the most deplorable and abandoned?

I knew a case, which is both a salutary warning against sin, and an encouragement to those who have gone far and long astray, to consider that it is never too late to repent. One winter evening as I was sitting by my fire, I heard a knock at the door, and a servant announced that a person wished to speak to me. I went out, and found a shabby-looking, dirty, squalid creature, who, after some apology for the intrusion, introduced himself as the son of ——. I had heard for many years of his career, and lamented it, for his father's sake, who was an eminent minister of the gospel, as well as for his own. Although I had known him in his better days I did not recognize him in his prodigal appearance. As soon as he was seated in the dining-room, and I had the opportunity more clearly to see his degradation and wretchedness, I burst into tears, and he too was affected to see that the knowledge of his career had not extinguished all my sympathy for his misery. I relieved him, and he departed. This youth, after being spoiled by his mother, whose only child he was, and who, though she erred in this instance, was in most others, an admirable woman, became wayward at home, and unsettled abroad. He served his time with a professional gentleman, and at this period formed some bad associations, and contracted some bad habits, among which was a fatal propensity to drinking. By various plans formed and broken, about settling in business, he wasted all his patrimony, and became dependent on his friends, still retaining his habits of idleness and drinking. One situation after another was found for him by those whose kindness he defeated in all their attempts to serve him; till, at length, wearied in endeavouring to serve a man who would not serve himself, they were obliged to give him up. His ruin now was complete. He became a perfect vagabond, and roamed through the country, herding with the lowest wretches, sometimes begging, and resorting to all kinds of methods to procure a meagre

sustenance and drag on his miserable life. On one
occasion, he called upon a friend of his father's in
London, in such a beggarly, filthy condition, that
before he could be admitted into the house a tub
of water was placed in an out-building that he might
cleanse himself, a suit of old clothes was given him,
and his rags instantly consumed. Thus clothed and
relieved, it was hoped he might now do better, according
to his promise : but in a few days, all was pawned, and
he was again clothed in rags, that he might drink with
the few shillings obtained as the balance in this barter
of decent apparel for that which merely covered his
limbs. Thus he went on, till he had become a frequent
inmate of workhouses, lock-up houses, and prisons. He
had associated with the offscouring of society, had become
hardened in vice, and almost stupified by want and woe ;
and, one should suppose, had been long lost to every
sense of decency, and every hope or desire of reformation. Yet, did this prodigal of prodigals at last find
his way back to his heavenly Father's house. In his
wanderings, he rambled into a town, where he made
himself known to a minister of the gospel, who felt an
interest in him for his reverend father's sake. This
gentleman, not discouraged or disheartened by the
numerous disappointments which had already occurred,
took him under his care, clothed him, and procured him
support. The prodigal's heart melted under this distinguished kindness ; his mind opened to religious
instruction ; and repentance toward God and faith
in our Lord Jesus Christ followed. He lived long
enough to make a consistent profession of true religion,
and died in the peaceful hope of that blessed world

into which "nothing entereth that defileth, or worketh abomination, or maketh a lie." His repentance, however, came too late to gladden the spirit of his mother; (his father died before his vicious course commenced;) her constitution was impaired by grief, and she sank broken-hearted to the grave. What a meeting in the heavenly world, who can imagine it? of this hopeless, disappointed, and sorrow-stricken mother, and this returned prodigal, the source of her deepest grief, and the hastener of her death!

Prodigal son, was there ever a seemingly more hopeless case than this? Is yours more hopeless? Turn, then, from your evil ways. God's mercy, through Christ, is great enough to pardon even your sins, if you truly repent and unfeignedly believe in the promise of salvation. The Holy Spirit can change even your hard heart, if you wish to be changed, and if you pray in faith for the grace that is necessary to effect it.

If your parents yet live, return to your father's house reformed, and do all that can be done to heal the wounds of his bleeding heart, and to wipe away the tears from your mother's eyes. Make them yet rejoice that you are their son. In the evening-tide of their existence, let there be light. Let their grey hairs go down to the grave, not in sorrow, but in joy; and let it be a consolation to them on their death-bed, that they have received you, penitent and reformed, to their earthly home, and hope to meet you and dwell with you for ever in their heavenly mansion. Or, if your repentance comes too late to stay their progress to the tomb, or cheer their hearts, sickened and saddened with the foreboding that they are parting from you for ever, go sorrowfully all your days, at the thought of having shortened their existence by your sins, but still comforted and sustained by the hope that they were among the spirits in heaven that rejoiced over your repentance, and that they gave utterance to their joys among the angels of God, saying, " Rejoice with us, for this our son was dead, and is alive; was lost, and is found." There is a home for all truly penitent prodigals, in heaven ; and there is a home for all impenitent ones, but it is, in hell.

END OF THE FIFTH VOLUME.

HUDSON AND SON, PRINTERS, BULL STREET, BIRMINGHAM.